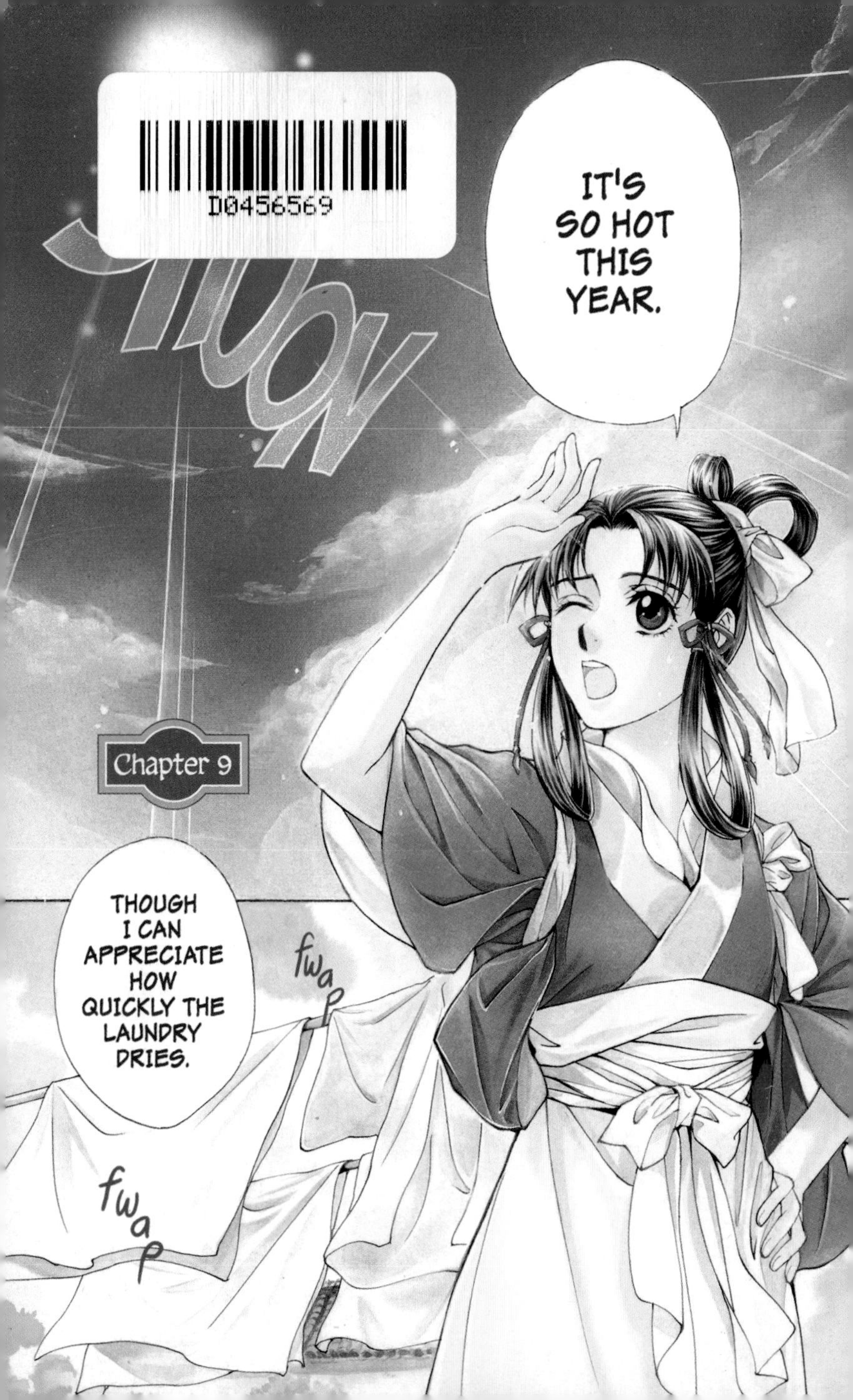
IT'S SO HOT THIS YEAR.
Chapter 9
THOUGH I CAN APPRECIATE HOW QUICKLY THE LAUNDRY DRIES.
fwap
fwap

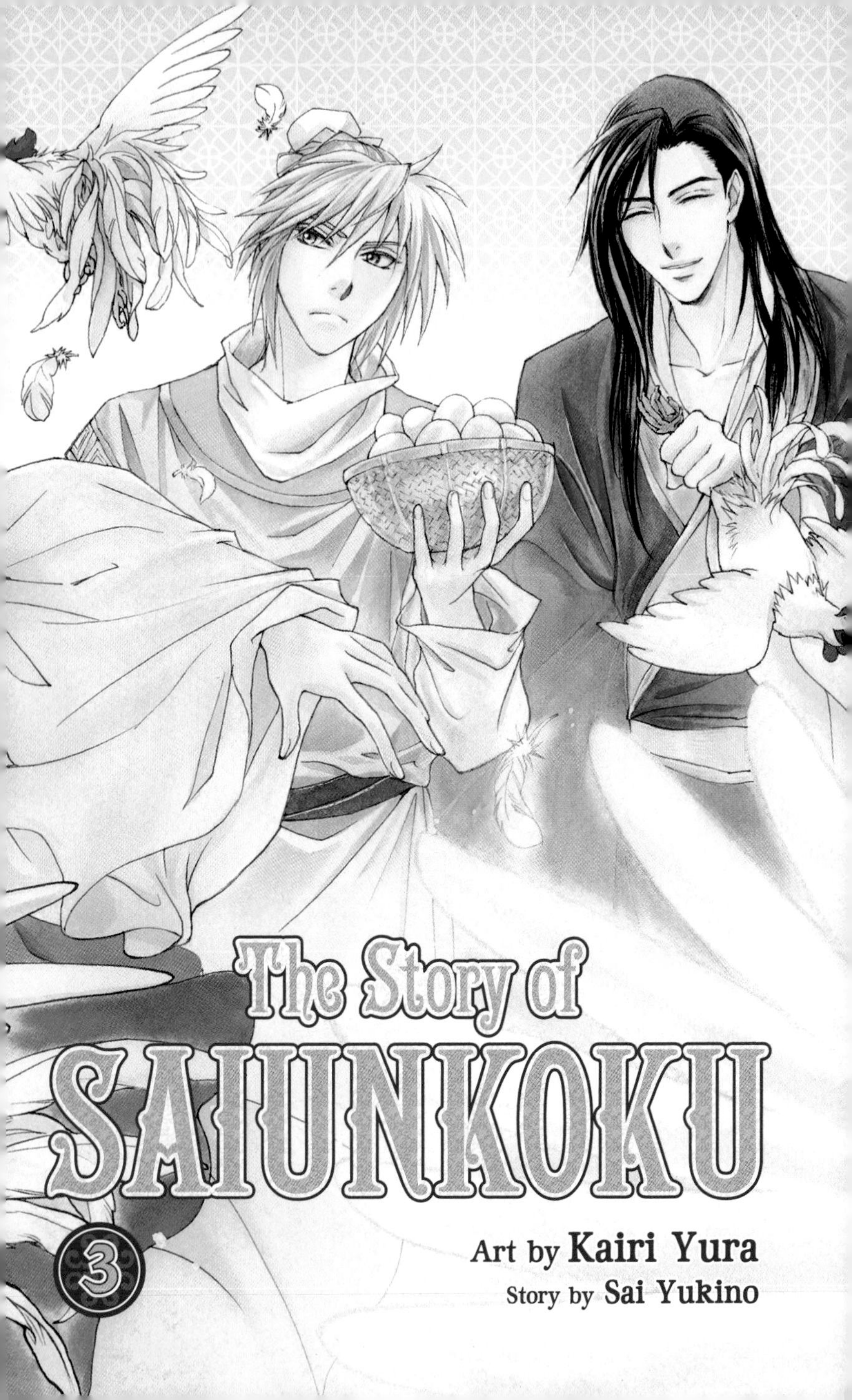
The Story of
SAIUNKOKU
3
Art by Kairi Yura
Story by Sai Yukino

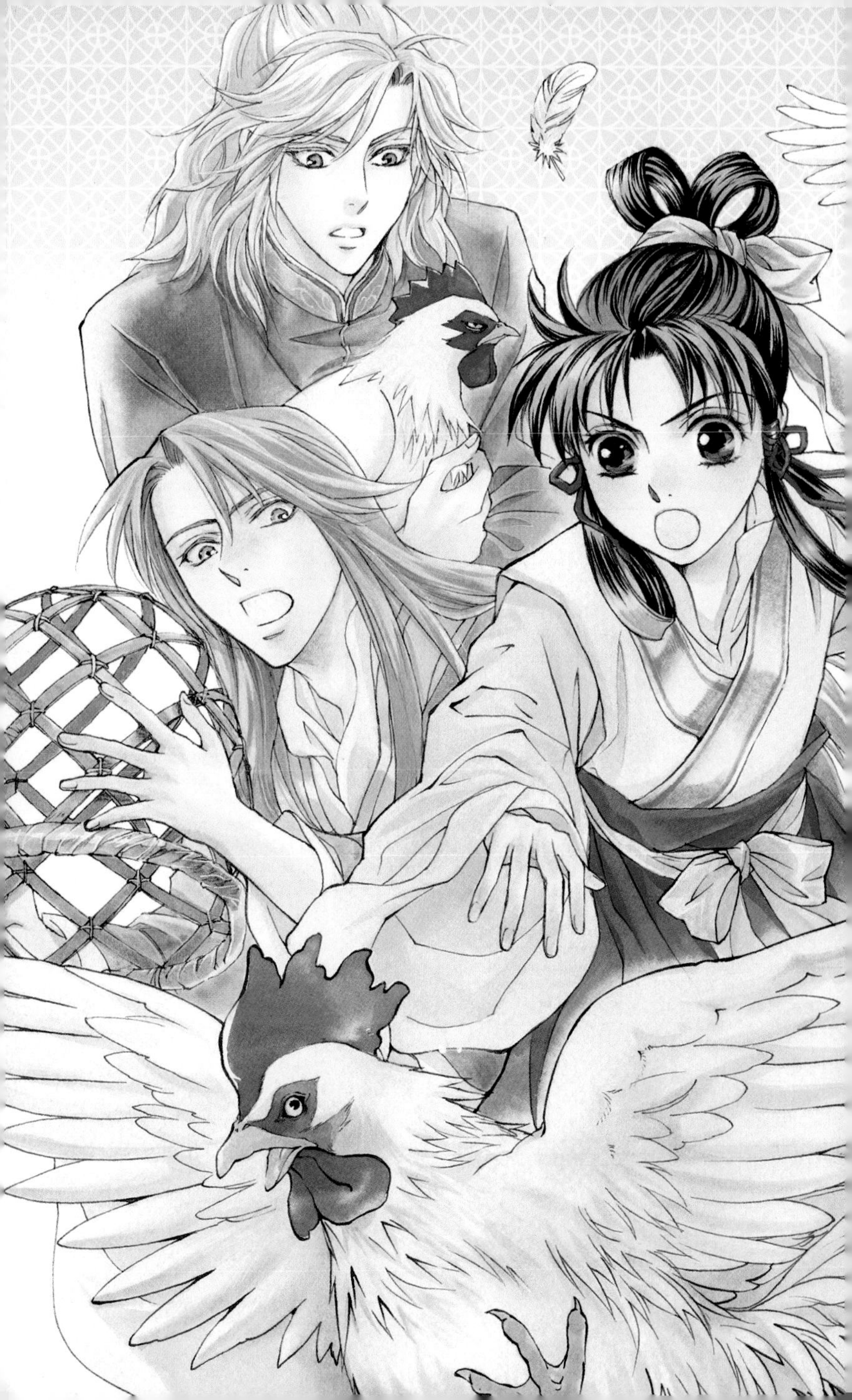

Volume 3
Contents

Story Thus Far

Lured by the promise of 500 gold ryo, the impoverished Lady Shurei of the noble Hong clan agreed to enter the Inner Court to serve as Noble Consort and private tutor to Ryuki, the young emperor of Saiunkoku. There, she encountered many new faces and experiences—both friendly and hostile—and after much toil, succeeded in instilling Ryuki with the will to govern his country properly. Her mission accomplished, Shurei departed the palace to return to her humble former life. It has been two months since that time. Saiunkoku's capital city looks toward the onset of summer, and Shurei is busy with the restoration of her dilapidated family home. However, another ill-boding but irresistibly enticing offer comes her way...

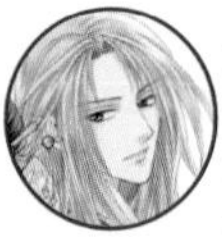

Ryuki Shi
The young emperor of Saiunkoku. He is widely known as an "idiot ruler," but it seems he has his reasons for appearing so.

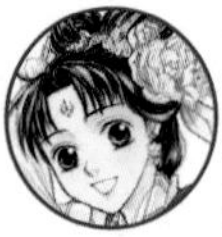

Shurei Hong
A young noblewoman of the prestigious but impoverished Hong clan. She recently entered the Inner Court as Ryuki's tutor and erstwhile Noble Consort.

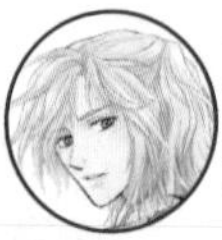

Seiran Shi
After being taken in by Shurei's father Shoka, Seiran has served the Hong household as its faithful retainer ever since. He is Shurei's protector.

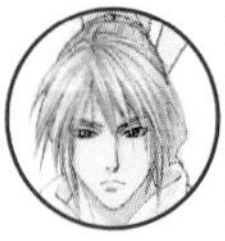

Koyu Ri
A civil servant renowned throughout the court as a genius, currently stuck in a frivolous position (perhaps?) serving Ryuki. He has a hopelessly bad sense of direction.

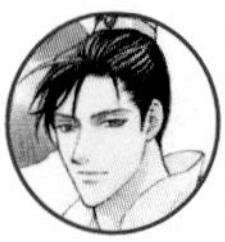

Shuei Ran
A military officer. He is a general of the Yulin Guard, a squad of soldiers charged with protecting the emperor. He is inseparable from Koyu (much to his friend's ire).

The Three Great Excellencies
Since the time of the previous emperor, three elderly advisors have served the throne: Lord Advisor Sho, Lord Advisor Sou and Lord Advisor Sa. They are scheming to advance Ryuki's education.

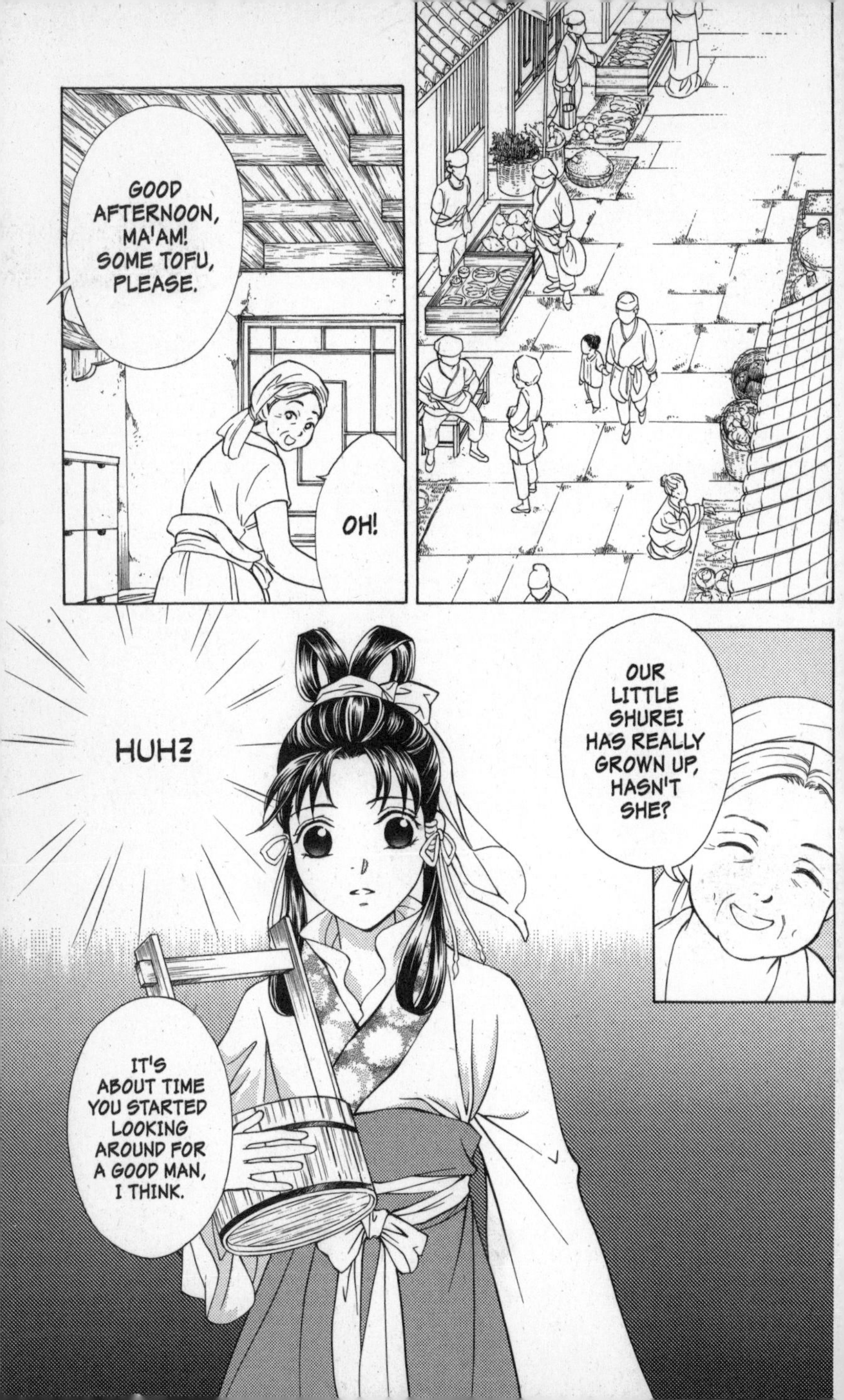
GOOD AFTERNOON, MA'AM! SOME TOFU, PLEASE.
OH!
OUR LITTLE SHUREI HAS REALLY GROWN UP, HASN'T SHE?
HUH?
IT'S ABOUT TIME YOU STARTED LOOKING AROUND FOR A GOOD MAN, I THINK.

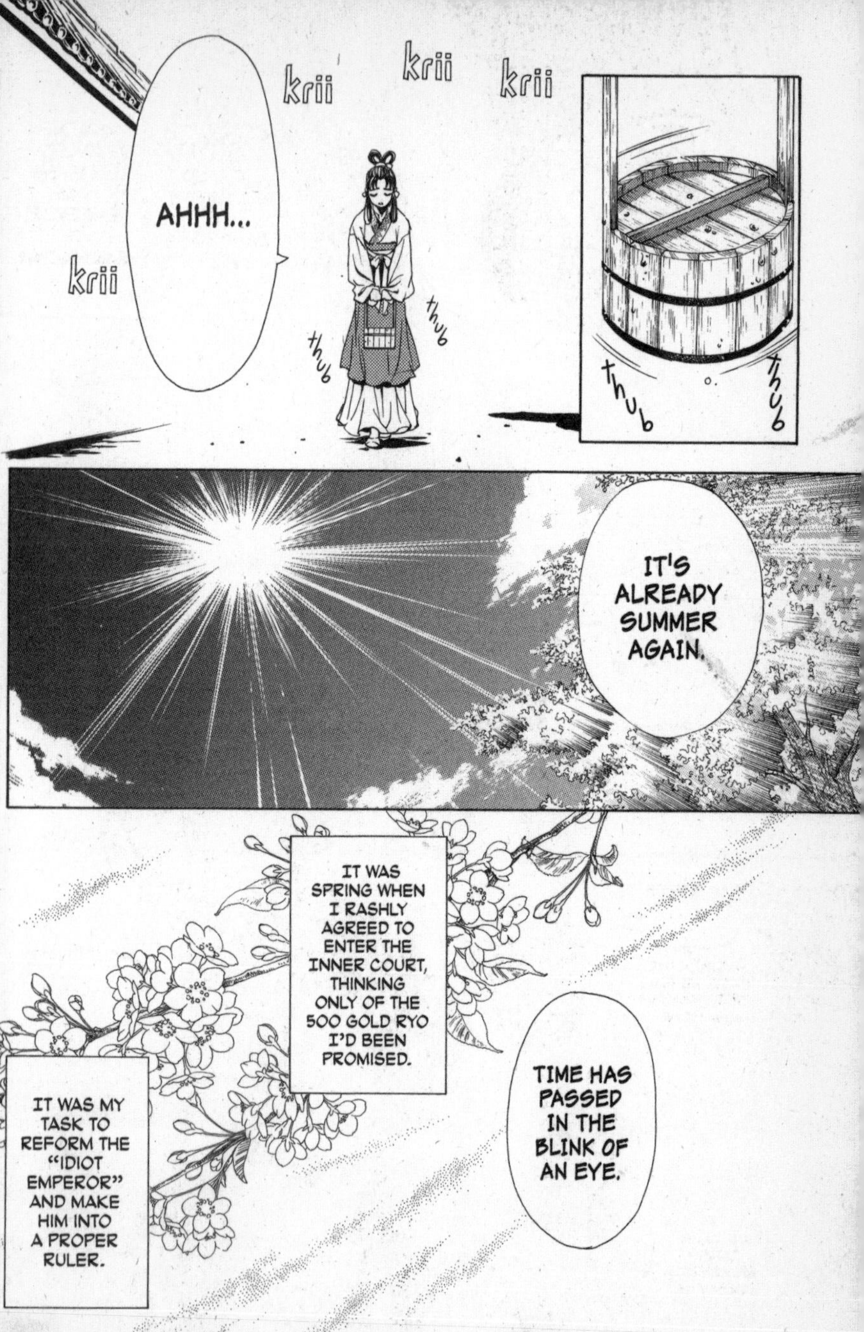
thub
thub
krii
krii
krii
AHHH...
thub
thub
krii
IT'S ALREADY SUMMER AGAIN.
IT WAS SPRING WHEN I RASHLY AGREED TO ENTER THE INNER COURT, THINKING ONLY OF THE 500 GOLD RYO I'D BEEN PROMISED.
TIME HAS PASSED IN THE BLINK OF AN EYE.
IT WAS MY TASK TO REFORM THE "IDIOT EMPEROR" AND MAKE HIM INTO A PROPER RULER.

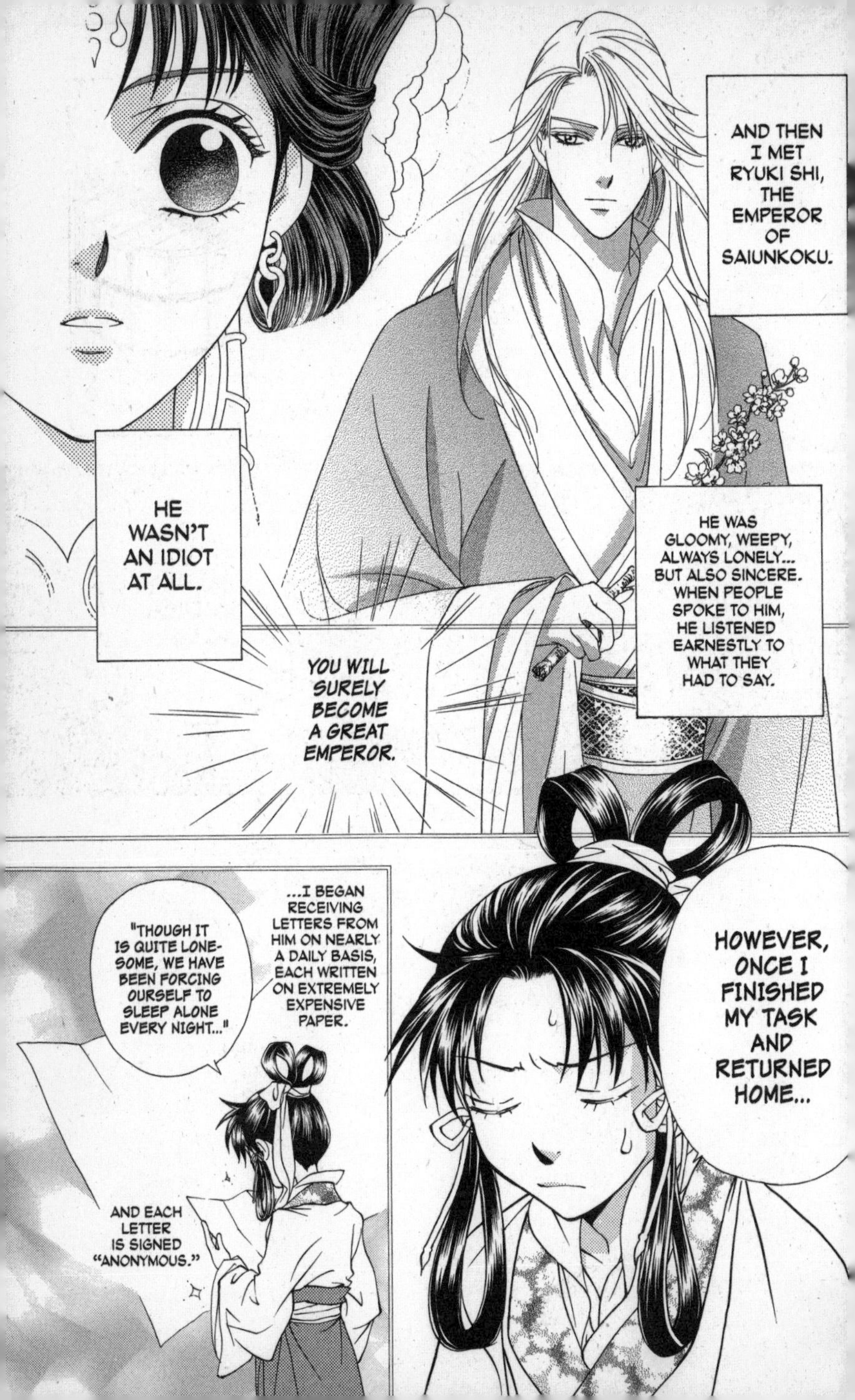
AND THEN I MET RYUKI SHI, THE EMPEROR OF SAIUNKOKU.
HE WAS GLOOMY, WEEPY, ALWAYS LONELY... BUT ALSO SINCERE. WHEN PEOPLE SPOKE TO HIM, HE LISTENED EARNESTLY TO WHAT THEY HAD TO SAY.
HE WASN'T AN IDIOT AT ALL.
YOU WILL SURELY BECOME A GREAT EMPEROR.
HOWEVER, ONCE I FINISHED MY TASK AND RETURNED HOME...
...I BEGAN RECEIVING LETTERS FROM HIM ON NEARLY A DAILY BASIS, EACH WRITTEN ON EXTREMELY EXPENSIVE PAPER.
"THOUGH IT IS QUITE LONE-SOME, WE HAVE BEEN FORCING OURSELF TO SLEEP ALONE EVERY NIGHT..."
AND EACH LETTER IS SIGNED "ANONYMOUS."

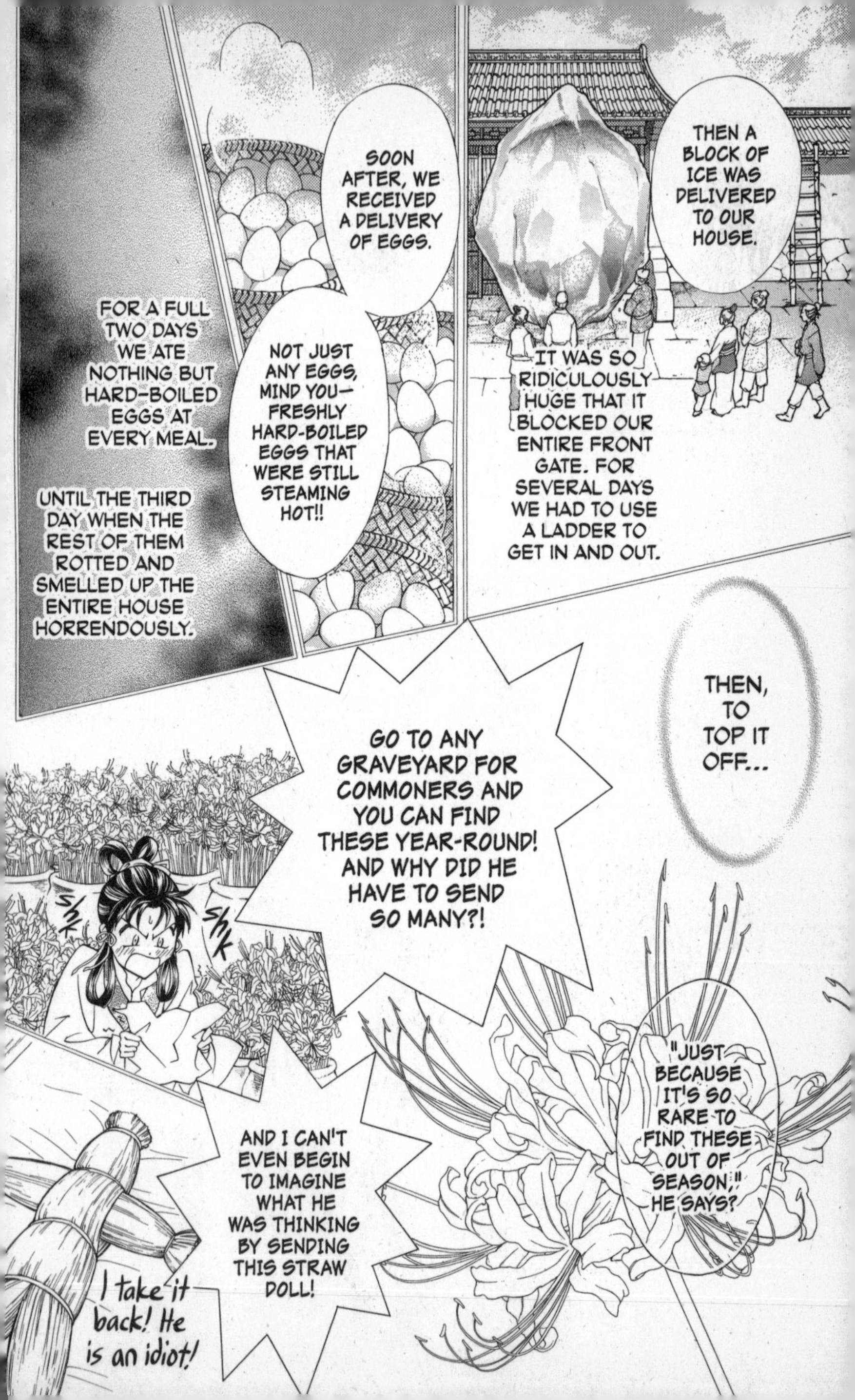
THEN A BLOCK OF ICE WAS DELIVERED TO OUR HOUSE.
IT WAS SO RIDICULOUSLY HUGE THAT IT BLOCKED OUR ENTIRE FRONT GATE. FOR SEVERAL DAYS WE HAD TO USE A LADDER TO GET IN AND OUT.
SOON AFTER, WE RECEIVED A DELIVERY OF EGGS.
NOT JUST ANY EGGS, MIND YOU—FRESHLY HARD-BOILED EGGS THAT WERE STILL STEAMING HOT!!
FOR A FULL TWO DAYS WE ATE NOTHING BUT HARD-BOILED EGGS AT EVERY MEAL.
UNTIL THE THIRD DAY WHEN THE REST OF THEM ROTTED AND SMELLED UP THE ENTIRE HOUSE HORRENDOUSLY.
THEN, TO TOP IT OFF...
"JUST BECAUSE IT'S SO RARE TO FIND THESE OUT OF SEASON," HE SAYS?
GO TO ANY GRAVEYARD FOR COMMONERS AND YOU CAN FIND THESE YEAR-ROUND! AND WHY DID HE HAVE TO SEND SO MANY?!
SHK
SHK
AND I CAN'T EVEN BEGIN TO IMAGINE WHAT HE WAS THINKING BY SENDING THIS STRAW DOLL!
I take it back! He is an idiot!

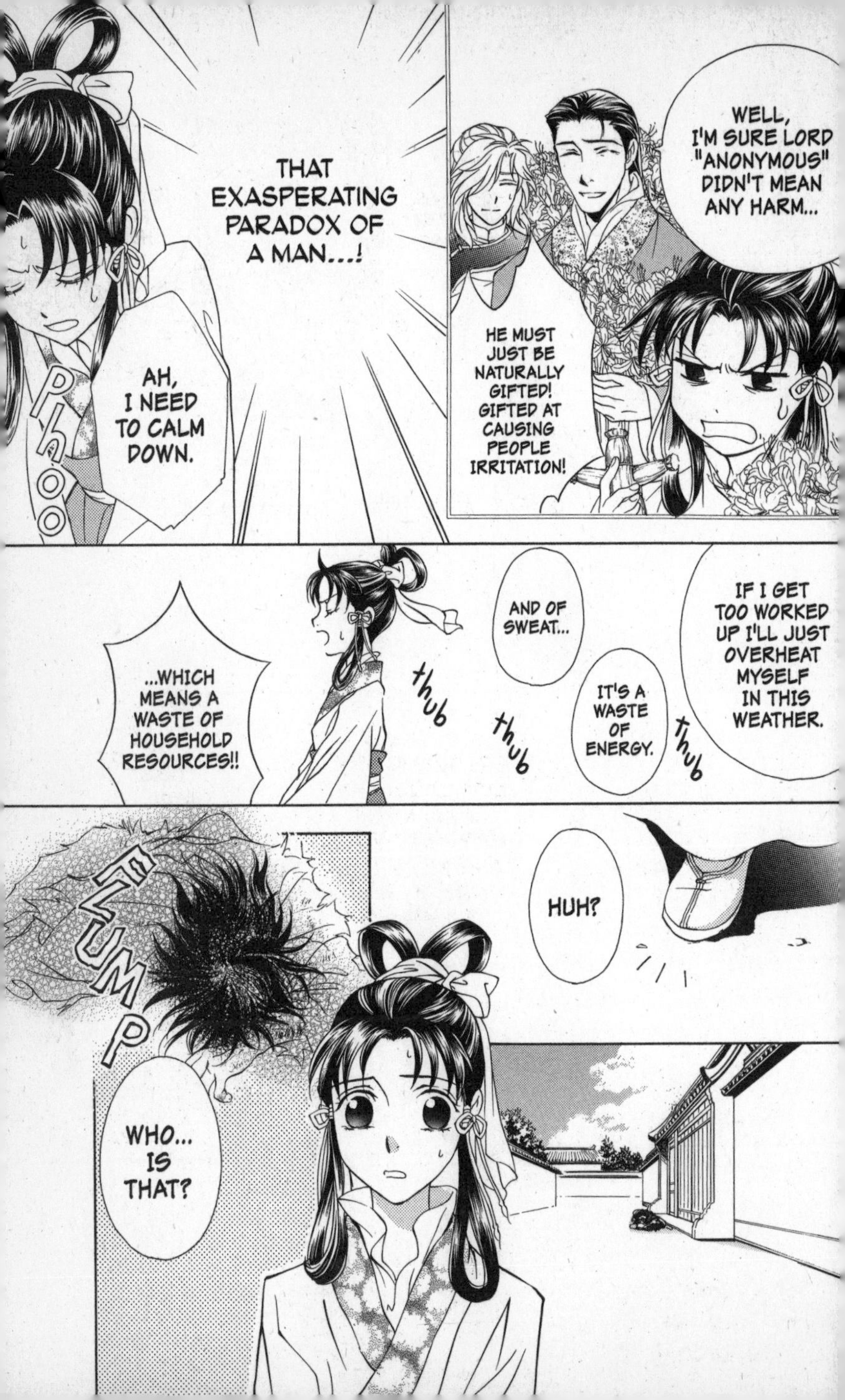
WELL, I'M SURE LORD "ANONYMOUS" DIDN'T MEAN ANY HARM...
HE MUST JUST BE NATURALLY GIFTED! GIFTED AT CAUSING PEOPLE IRRITATION!
THAT EXASPERATING PARADOX OF A MAN...!
AH, I NEED TO CALM DOWN.
PHOOO
IF I GET TOO WORKED UP I'LL JUST OVERHEAT MYSELF IN THIS WEATHER.
thub
IT'S A WASTE OF ENERGY.
thub
AND OF SWEAT...
thub
...WHICH MEANS A WASTE OF HOUSEHOLD RESOURCES!!
HUH?
FLUMP
WHO... IS THAT?

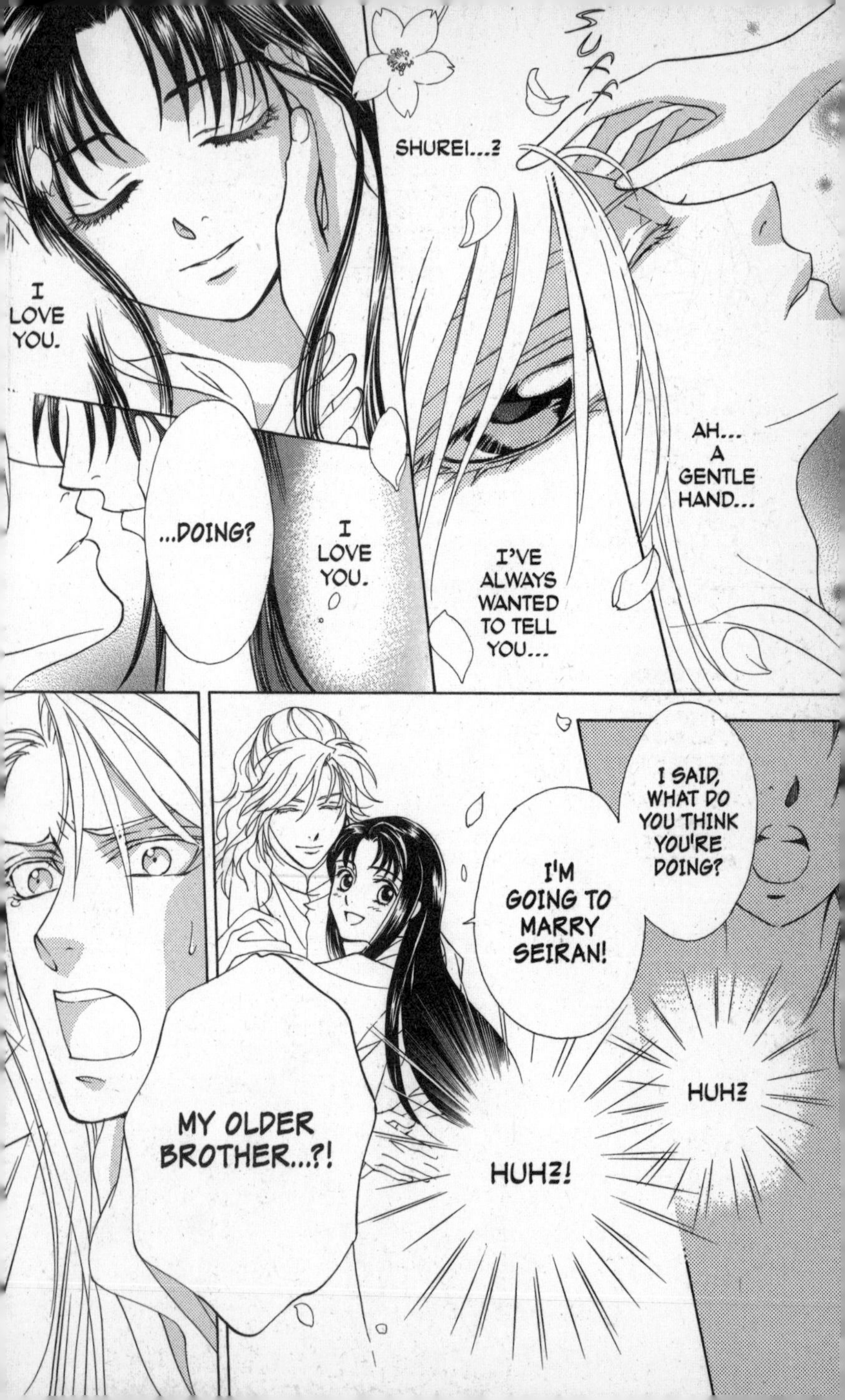
SUFF
SHUREI...?
AH... A GENTLE HAND...
I'VE ALWAYS WANTED TO TELL YOU...
I LOVE YOU.
I LOVE YOU.
...DOING?
I SAID, WHAT DO YOU THINK YOU'RE DOING?
I'M GOING TO MARRY SEIRAN!
HUH?
HUH?!
MY OLDER BROTHER...?!

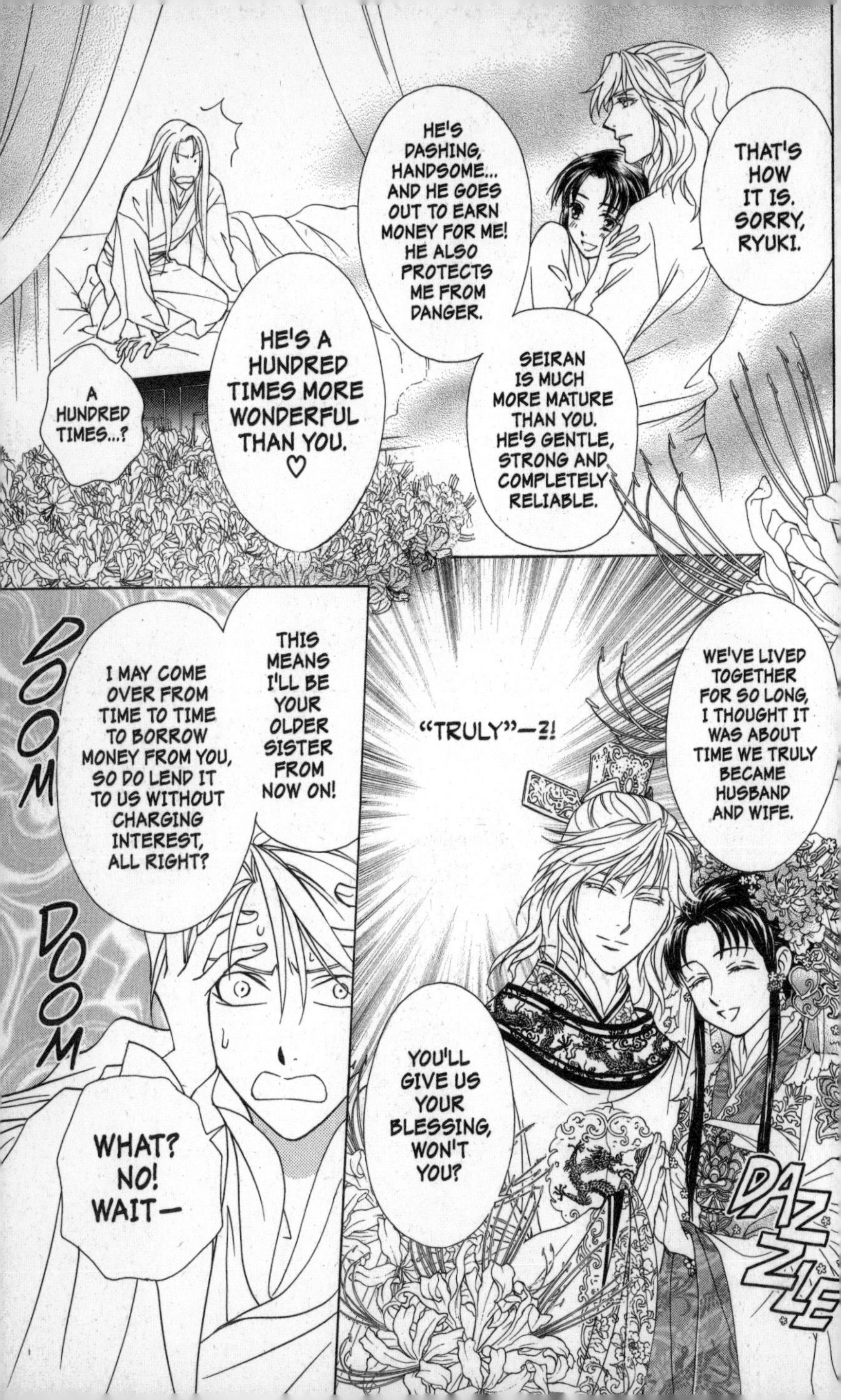
THAT'S HOW IT IS. SORRY, RYUKI.
HE'S DASHING, HANDSOME... AND HE GOES OUT TO EARN MONEY FOR ME! HE ALSO PROTECTS ME FROM DANGER.
SEIRAN IS MUCH MORE MATURE THAN YOU. HE'S GENTLE, STRONG AND COMPLETELY RELIABLE.
HE'S A HUNDRED TIMES MORE WONDERFUL THAN YOU. ♡
A HUNDRED TIMES...?
WE'VE LIVED TOGETHER FOR SO LONG, I THOUGHT IT WAS ABOUT TIME WE TRULY BECAME HUSBAND AND WIFE.
"TRULY"—?!
YOU'LL GIVE US YOUR BLESSING, WON'T YOU?
DAZZLE
THIS MEANS I'LL BE YOUR OLDER SISTER FROM NOW ON!
I MAY COME OVER FROM TIME TO TIME TO BORROW MONEY FROM YOU, SO DO LEND IT TO US WITHOUT CHARGING INTEREST, ALL RIGHT?
DOOM
DOOM
DOOM
WHAT? NO! WAIT—

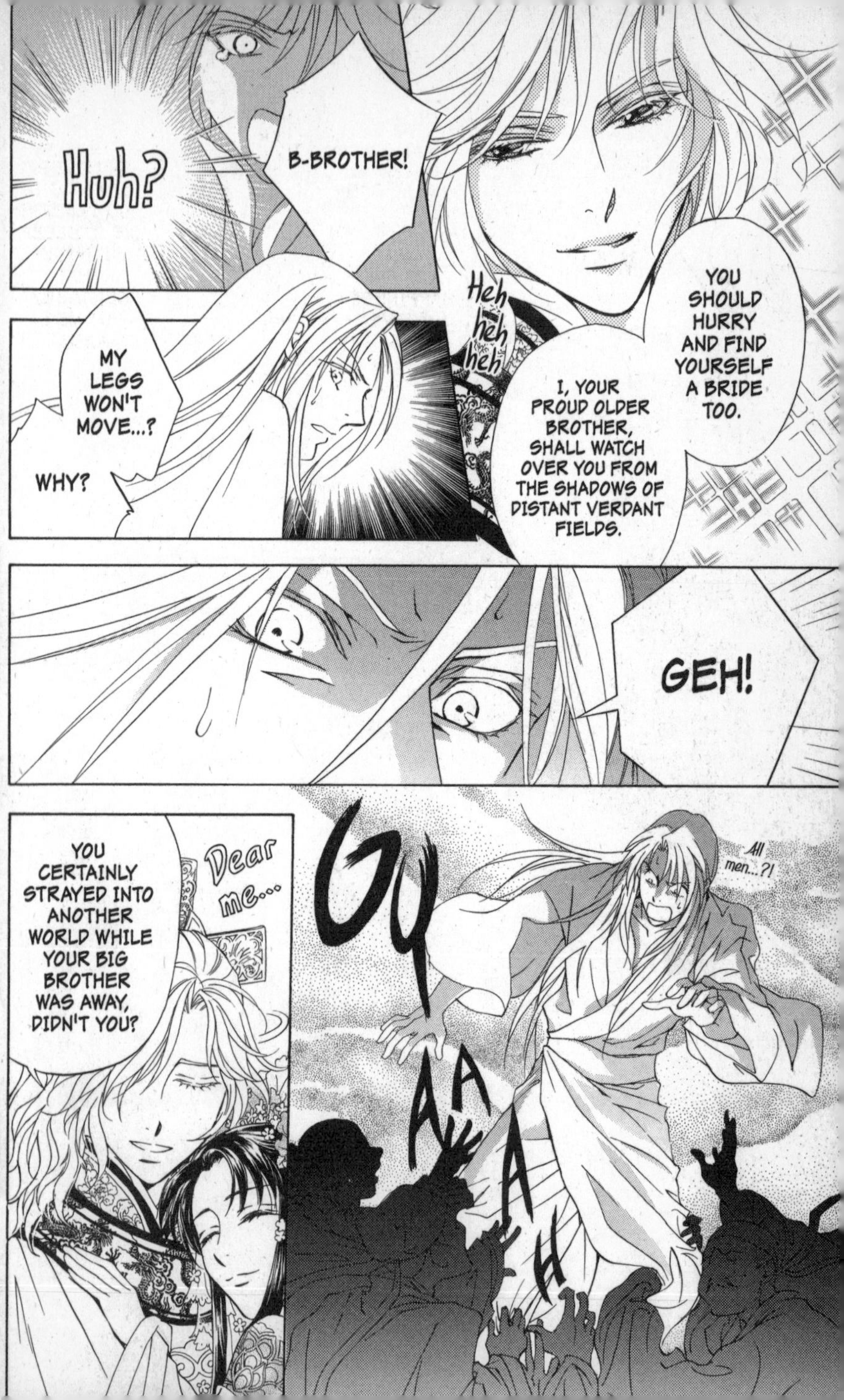

B-BROTHER!
Huh?
Heh heh heh
YOU SHOULD HURRY AND FIND YOURSELF A BRIDE TOO.
I, YOUR PROUD OLDER BROTHER, SHALL WATCH OVER YOU FROM THE SHADOWS OF DISTANT VERDANT FIELDS.
MY LEGS WON'T MOVE...?
WHY?
GEH!
All men...?!
GYAAAAH
Dear me...
YOU CERTAINLY STRAYED INTO ANOTHER WORLD WHILE YOUR BIG BROTHER WAS AWAY, DIDN'T YOU?

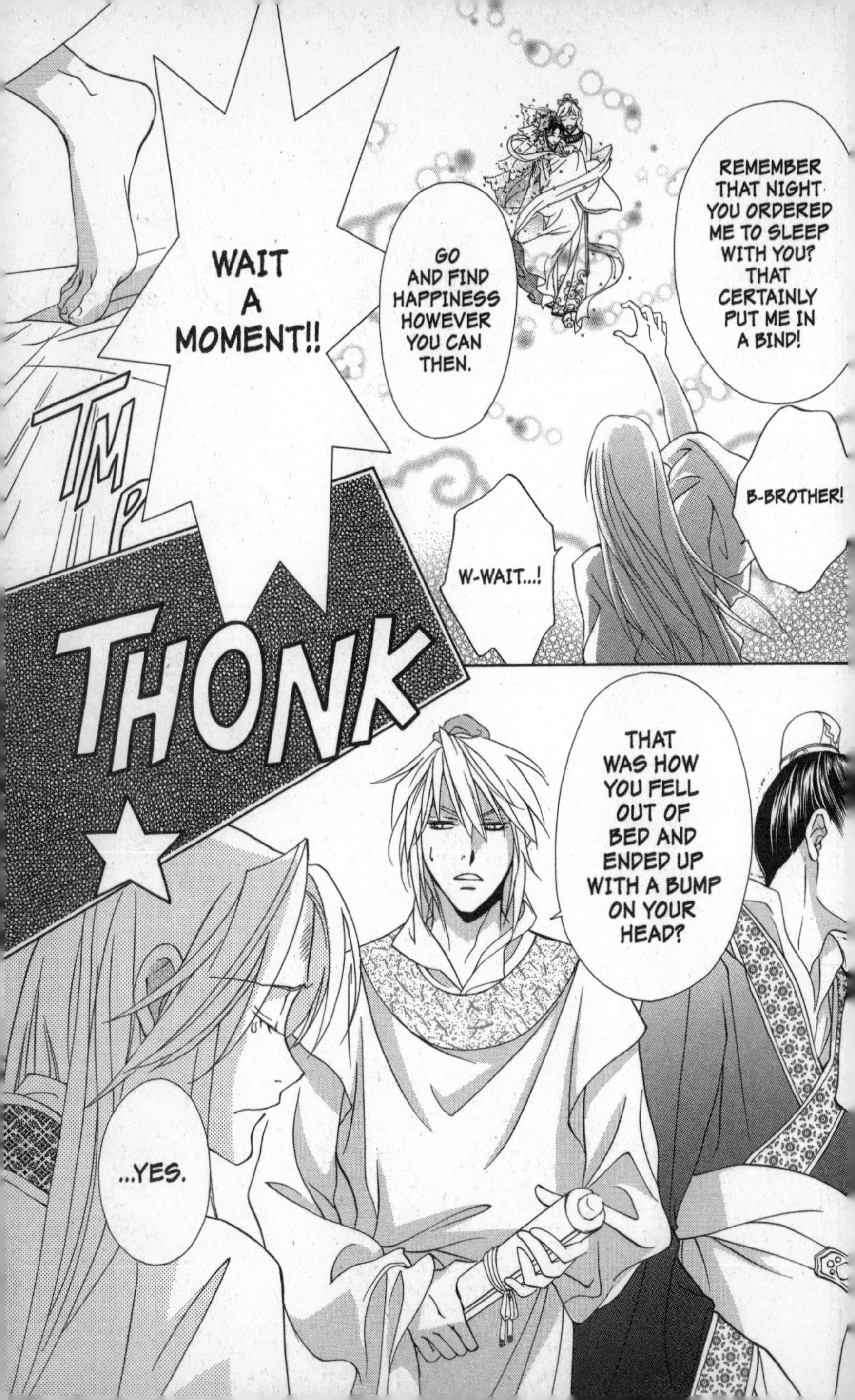
REMEMBER THAT NIGHT YOU ORDERED ME TO SLEEP WITH YOU? THAT CERTAINLY PUT ME IN A BIND!
GO AND FIND HAPPINESS HOWEVER YOU CAN THEN.
B-BROTHER!
W-WAIT...!
WAIT A MOMENT!!
TMP
THONK
THAT WAS HOW YOU FELL OUT OF BED AND ENDED UP WITH A BUMP ON YOUR HEAD?
...YES.

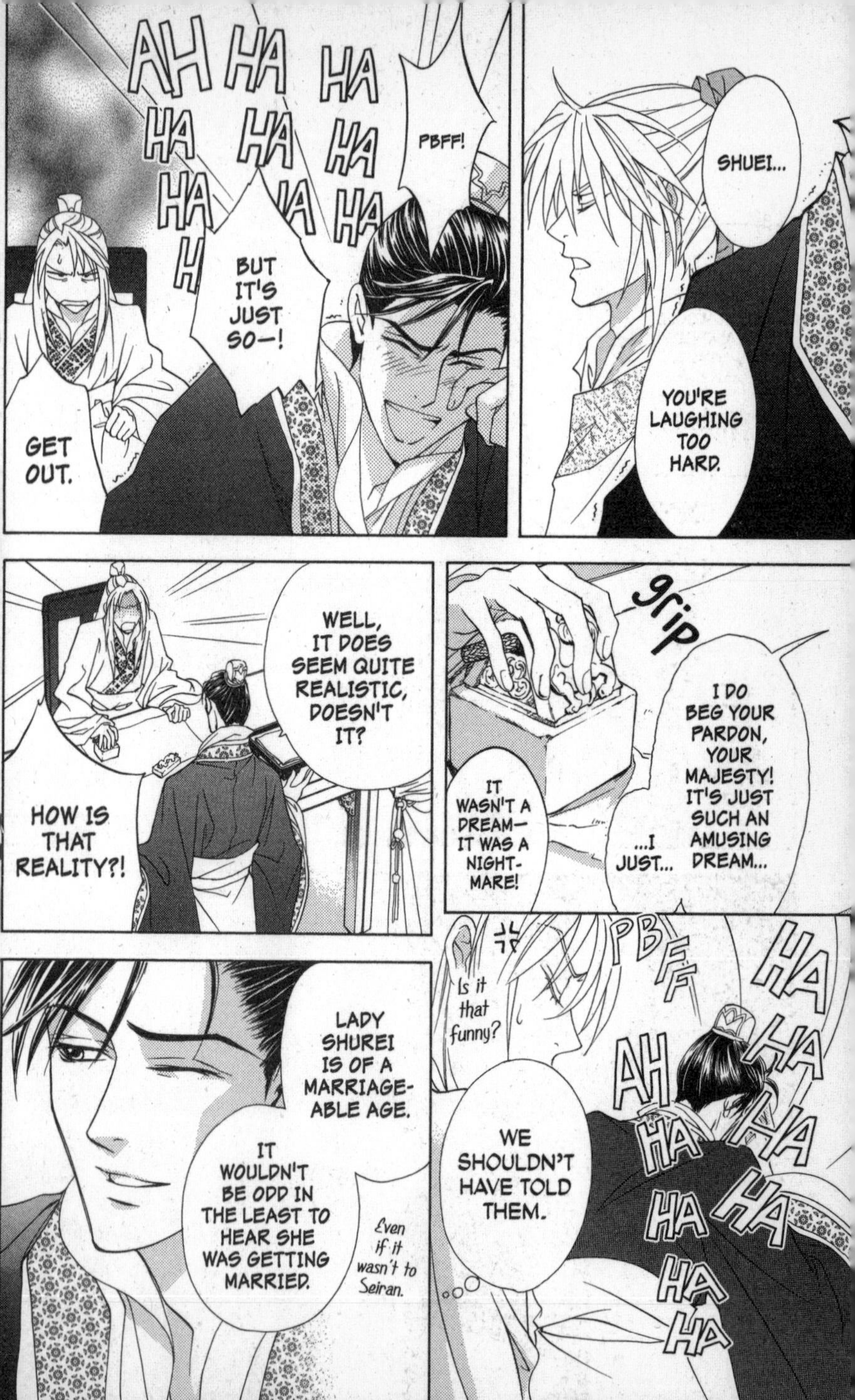
SHUEI...
YOU'RE LAUGHING TOO HARD.
PBFF!
AH HA HA HA HA HA HA HA HA H
BUT IT'S JUST SO—!
GET OUT.
grip
I DO BEG YOUR PARDON, YOUR MAJESTY! IT'S JUST SUCH AN AMUSING DREAM...
...I JUST...
IT WASN'T A DREAM— IT WAS A NIGHT-MARE!
WELL, IT DOES SEEM QUITE REALISTIC, DOESN'T IT?
HOW IS THAT REALITY?!
HA HA PBFF AH HA HA HA HA HA HA HA HA
Is it that funny?
WE SHOULDN'T HAVE TOLD THEM.
LADY SHUREI IS OF A MARRIAGE-ABLE AGE.
IT WOULDN'T BE ODD IN THE LEAST TO HEAR SHE WAS GETTING MARRIED.
Even if it wasn't to Seiran.

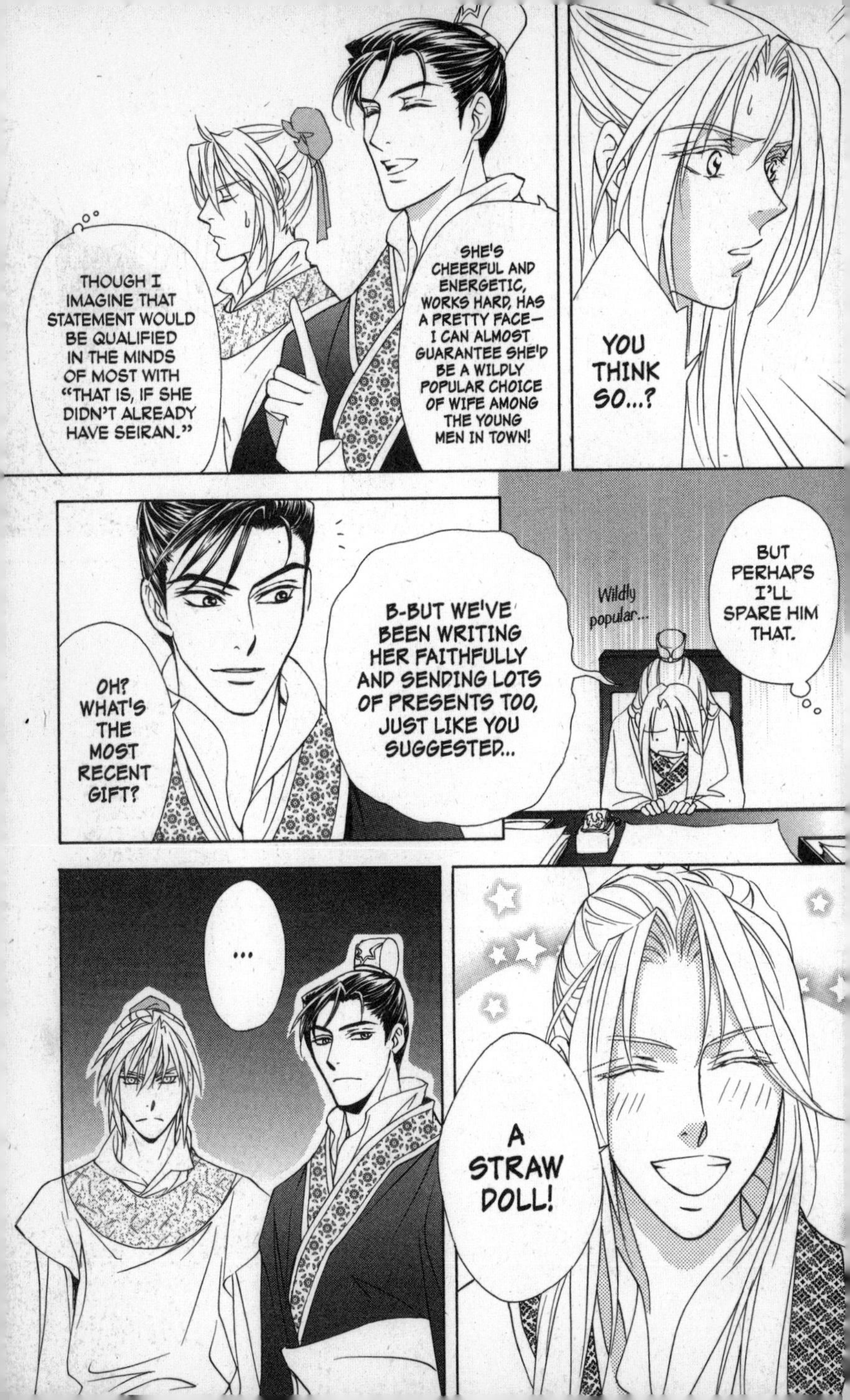
YOU THINK SO...?
SHE'S CHEERFUL AND ENERGETIC, WORKS HARD, HAS A PRETTY FACE—I CAN ALMOST GUARANTEE SHE'D BE A WILDLY POPULAR CHOICE OF WIFE AMONG THE YOUNG MEN IN TOWN!
THOUGH I IMAGINE THAT STATEMENT WOULD BE QUALIFIED IN THE MINDS OF MOST WITH "THAT IS, IF SHE DIDN'T ALREADY HAVE SEIRAN."
BUT PERHAPS I'LL SPARE HIM THAT.
Wildly popular...
B-BUT WE'VE BEEN WRITING HER FAITHFULLY AND SENDING LOTS OF PRESENTS TOO, JUST LIKE YOU SUGGESTED...
OH? WHAT'S THE MOST RECENT GIFT?
A STRAW DOLL!
...

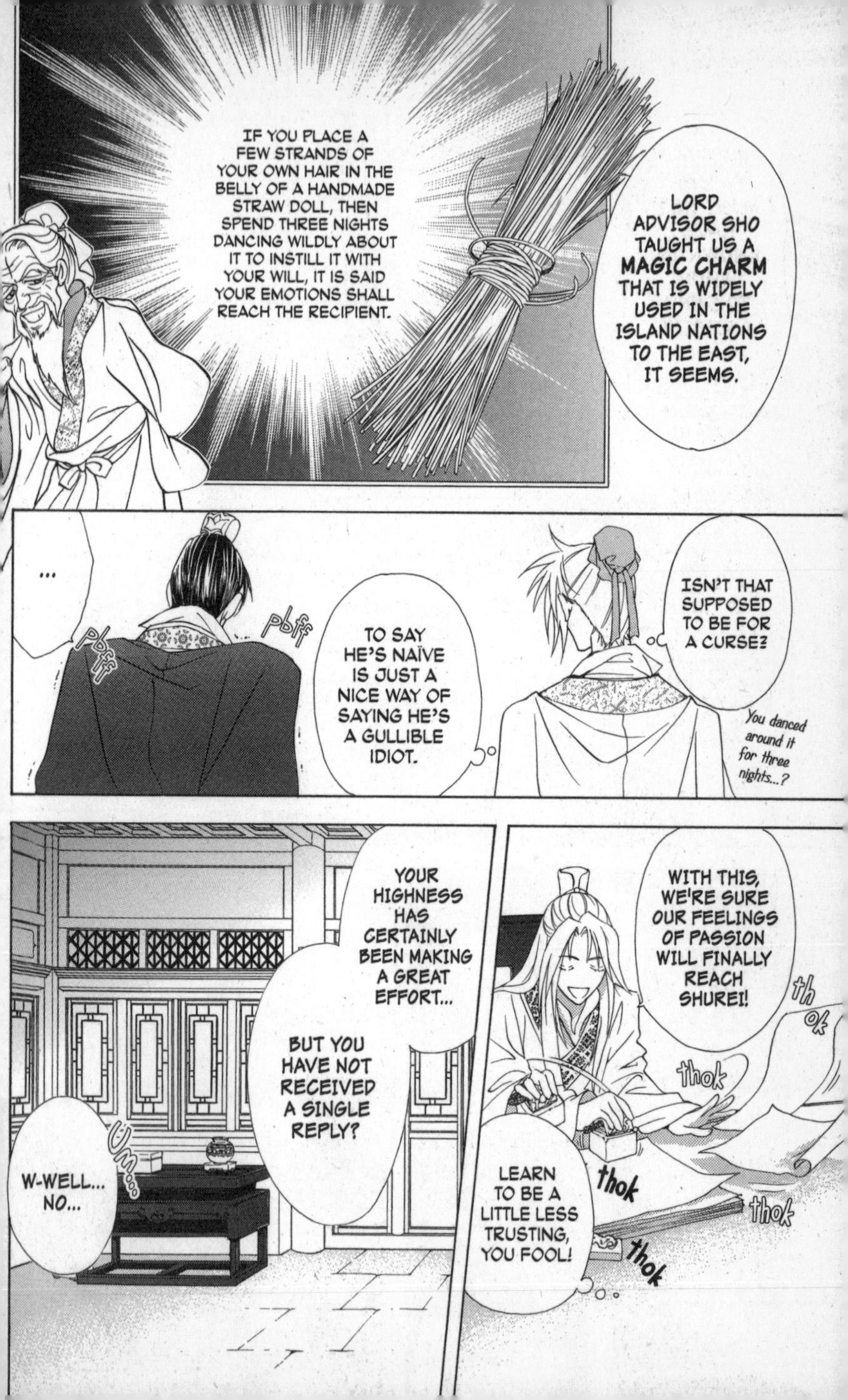
LORD ADVISOR SHO TAUGHT US A MAGIC CHARM THAT IS WIDELY USED IN THE ISLAND NATIONS TO THE EAST, IT SEEMS.
IF YOU PLACE A FEW STRANDS OF YOUR OWN HAIR IN THE BELLY OF A HANDMADE STRAW DOLL, THEN SPEND THREE NIGHTS DANCING WILDLY ABOUT IT TO INSTILL IT WITH YOUR WILL, IT IS SAID YOUR EMOTIONS SHALL REACH THE RECIPIENT.
ISN'T THAT SUPPOSED TO BE FOR A CURSE?
You danced around it for three nights...?
TO SAY HE'S NAÏVE IS JUST A NICE WAY OF SAYING HE'S A GULLIBLE IDIOT.
pbff
pbff
...
WITH THIS, WE'RE SURE OUR FEELINGS OF PASSION WILL FINALLY REACH SHUREI!
thok
thok
thok
thok
thok
LEARN TO BE A LITTLE LESS TRUSTING, YOU FOOL!
YOUR HIGHNESS HAS CERTAINLY BEEN MAKING A GREAT EFFORT...
BUT YOU HAVE NOT RECEIVED A SINGLE REPLY?
Um...
W-WELL... NO...

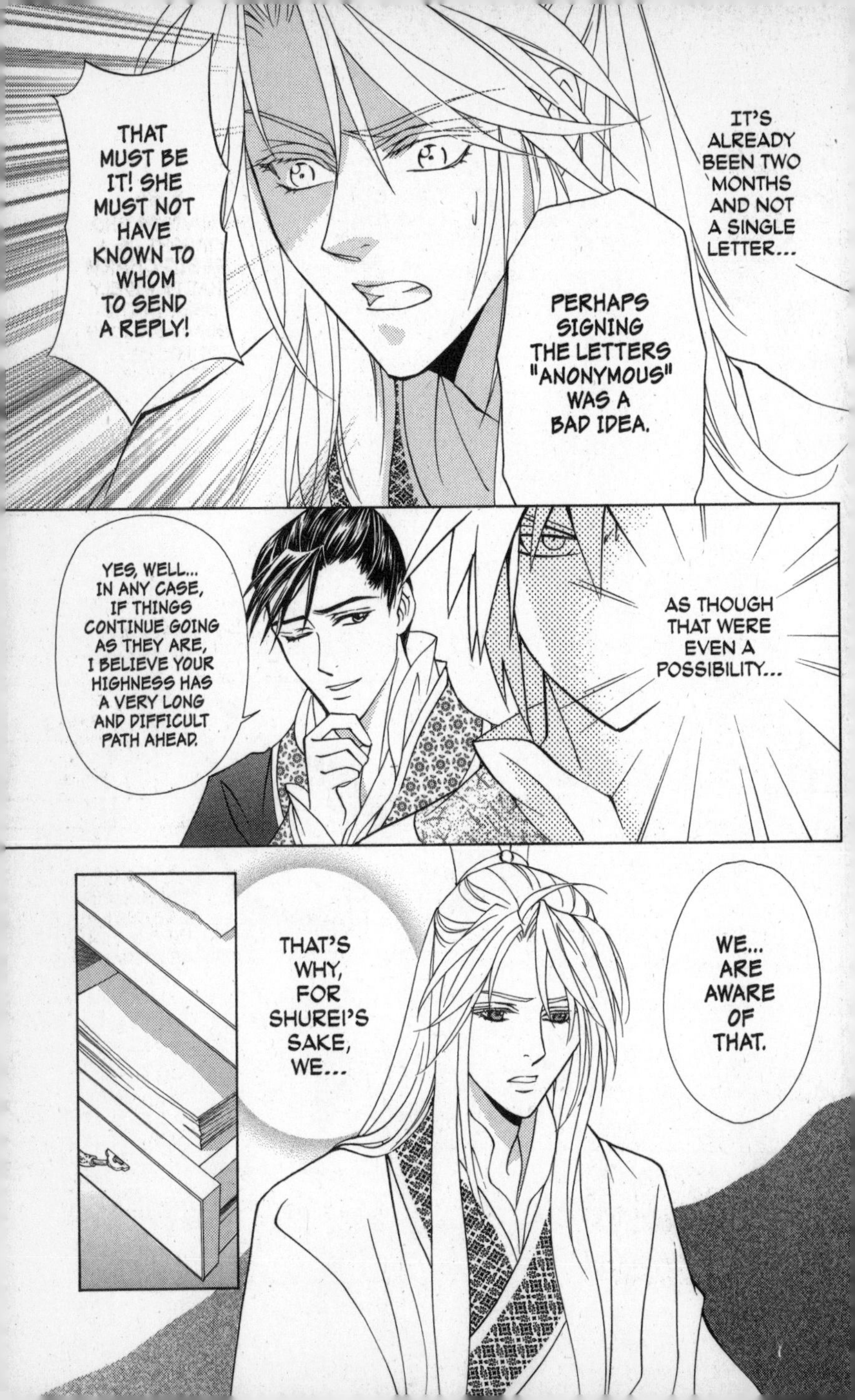
IT'S ALREADY BEEN TWO MONTHS AND NOT A SINGLE LETTER...
PERHAPS SIGNING THE LETTERS "ANONYMOUS" WAS A BAD IDEA.
THAT MUST BE IT! SHE MUST NOT HAVE KNOWN TO WHOM TO SEND A REPLY!
AS THOUGH THAT WERE EVEN A POSSIBILITY...
YES, WELL... IN ANY CASE, IF THINGS CONTINUE GOING AS THEY ARE, I BELIEVE YOUR HIGHNESS HAS A VERY LONG AND DIFFICULT PATH AHEAD.
WE... ARE AWARE OF THAT.
THAT'S WHY, FOR SHUREI'S SAKE, WE...

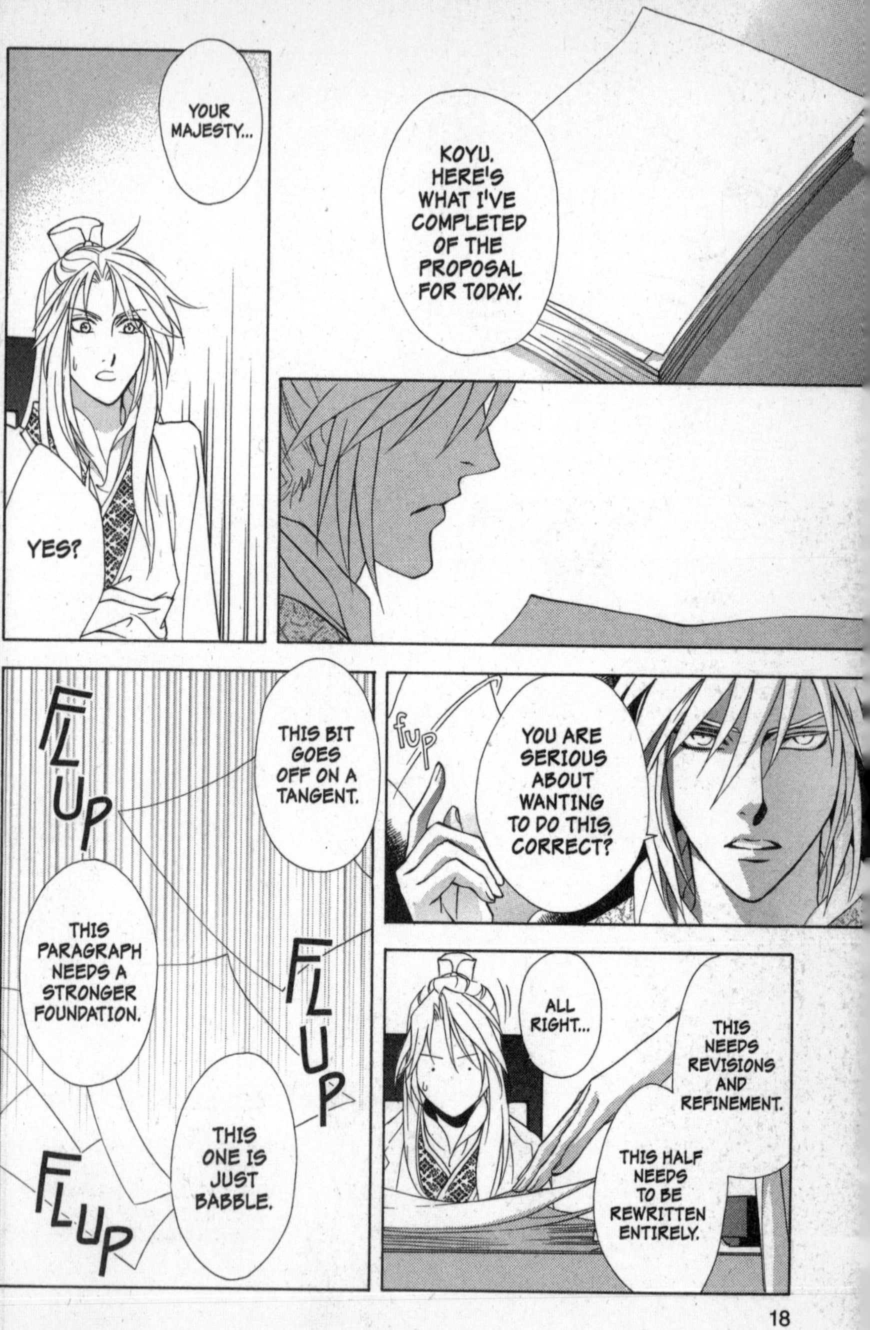
KOYU. HERE'S WHAT I'VE COMPLETED OF THE PROPOSAL FOR TODAY.
YOUR MAJESTY...
YES?
fup
YOU ARE SERIOUS ABOUT WANTING TO DO THIS, CORRECT?
THIS NEEDS REVISIONS AND REFINEMENT.
ALL RIGHT...
THIS HALF NEEDS TO BE REWRITTEN ENTIRELY.
FLUP
THIS BIT GOES OFF ON A TANGENT.
THIS PARAGRAPH NEEDS A STRONGER FOUNDATION.
FLUP
THIS ONE IS JUST BABBLE.
FLUP

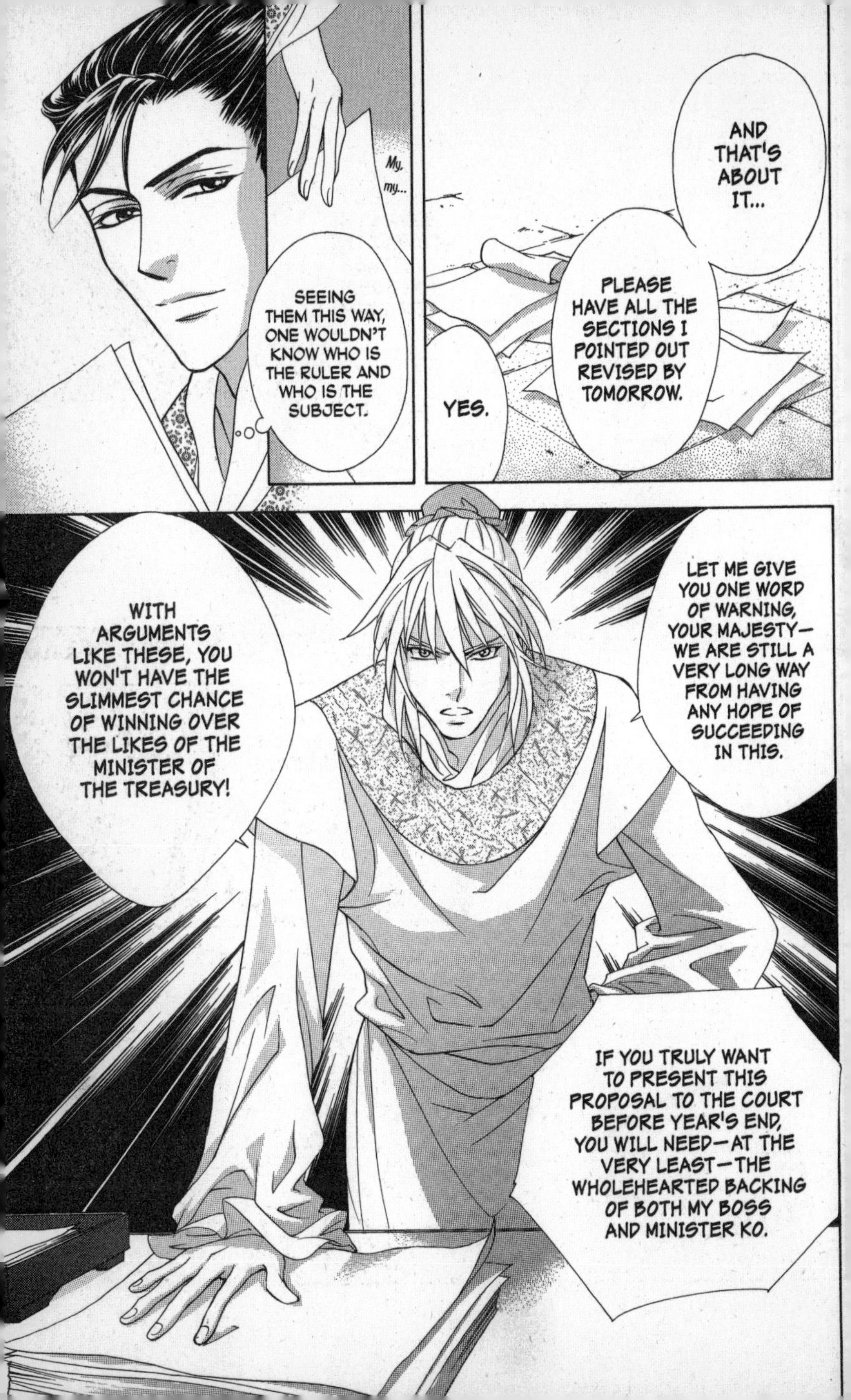
AND THAT'S ABOUT IT...
PLEASE HAVE ALL THE SECTIONS I POINTED OUT REVISED BY TOMORROW.
YES.
My, my...
SEEING THEM THIS WAY, ONE WOULDN'T KNOW WHO IS THE RULER AND WHO IS THE SUBJECT.
LET ME GIVE YOU ONE WORD OF WARNING, YOUR MAJESTY—WE ARE STILL A VERY LONG WAY FROM HAVING ANY HOPE OF SUCCEEDING IN THIS.
WITH ARGUMENTS LIKE THESE, YOU WON'T HAVE THE SLIMMEST CHANCE OF WINNING OVER THE LIKES OF THE MINISTER OF THE TREASURY!
IF YOU TRULY WANT TO PRESENT THIS PROPOSAL TO THE COURT BEFORE YEAR'S END, YOU WILL NEED—AT THE VERY LEAST—THE WHOLEHEARTED BACKING OF BOTH MY BOSS AND MINISTER KO.

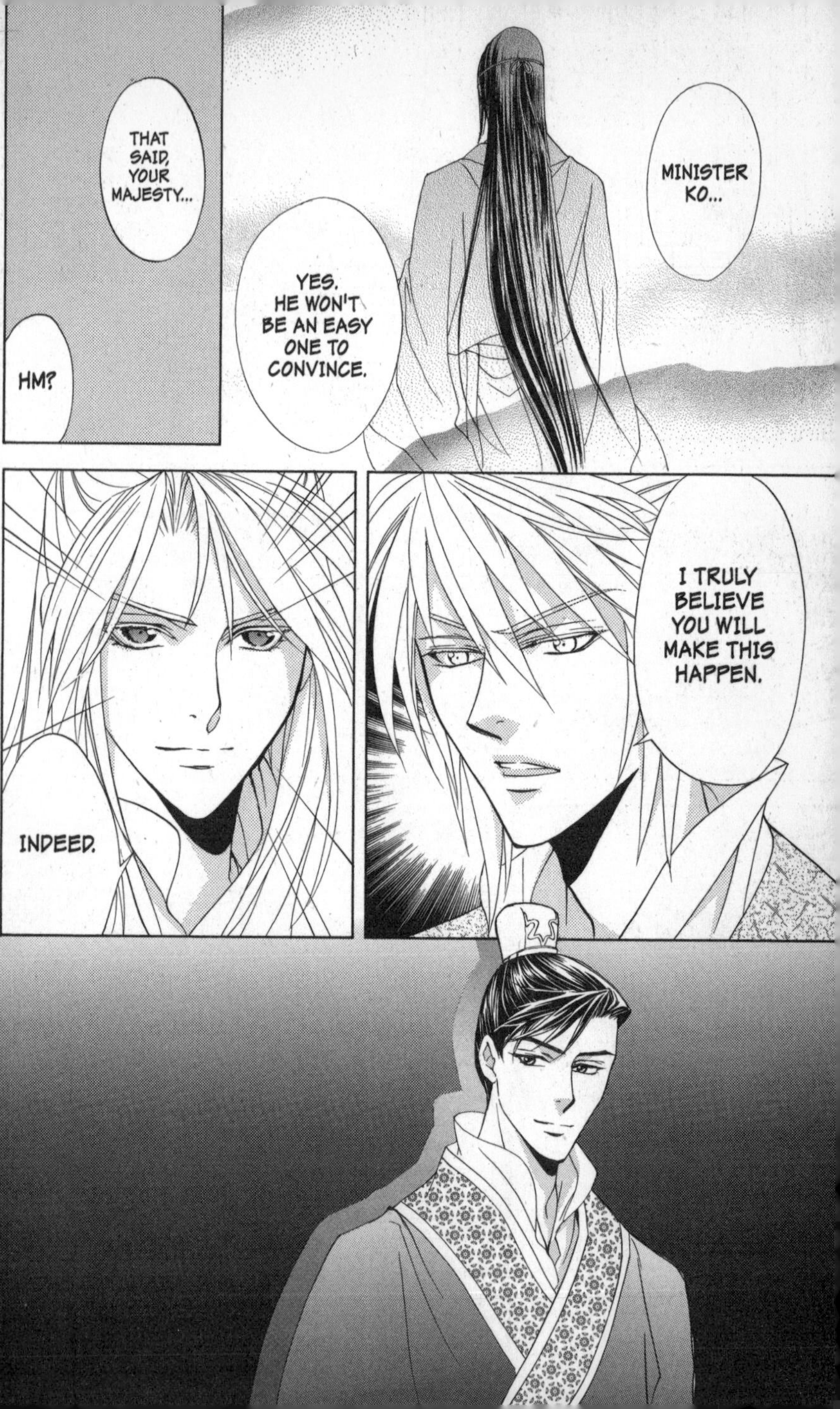
MINISTER KO...
YES. HE WON'T BE AN EASY ONE TO CONVINCE.
THAT SAID, YOUR MAJESTY...
HM?
I TRULY BELIEVE YOU WILL MAKE THIS HAPPEN.
INDEED.

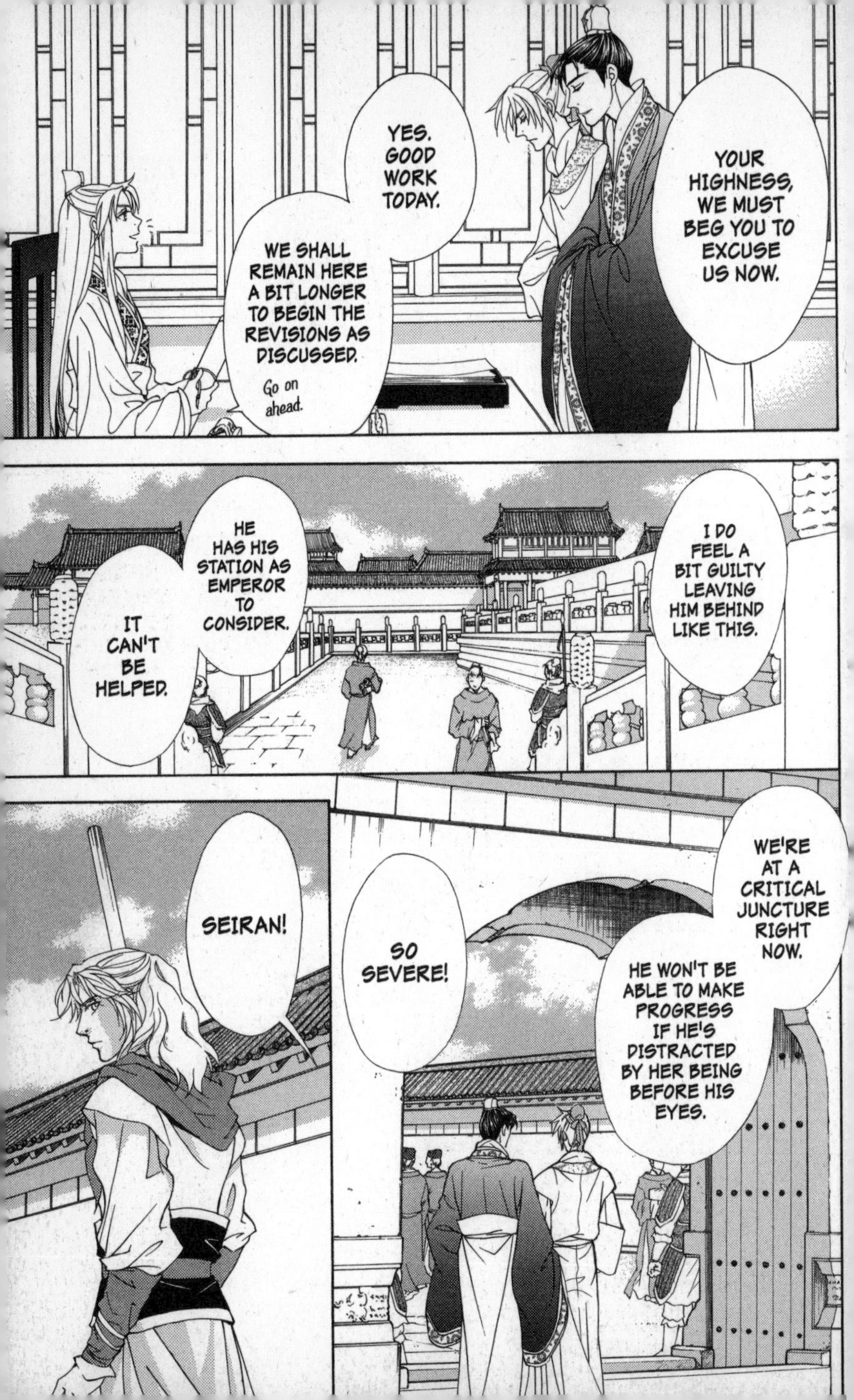
YOUR HIGHNESS, WE MUST BEG YOU TO EXCUSE US NOW.
YES. GOOD WORK TODAY.
WE SHALL REMAIN HERE A BIT LONGER TO BEGIN THE REVISIONS AS DISCUSSED.
Go on ahead.
I DO FEEL A BIT GUILTY LEAVING HIM BEHIND LIKE THIS.
HE HAS HIS STATION AS EMPEROR TO CONSIDER.
IT CAN'T BE HELPED.
WE'RE AT A CRITICAL JUNCTURE RIGHT NOW.
HE WON'T BE ABLE TO MAKE PROGRESS IF HE'S DISTRACTED BY HER BEING BEFORE HIS EYES.
SO SEVERE!
SEIRAN!

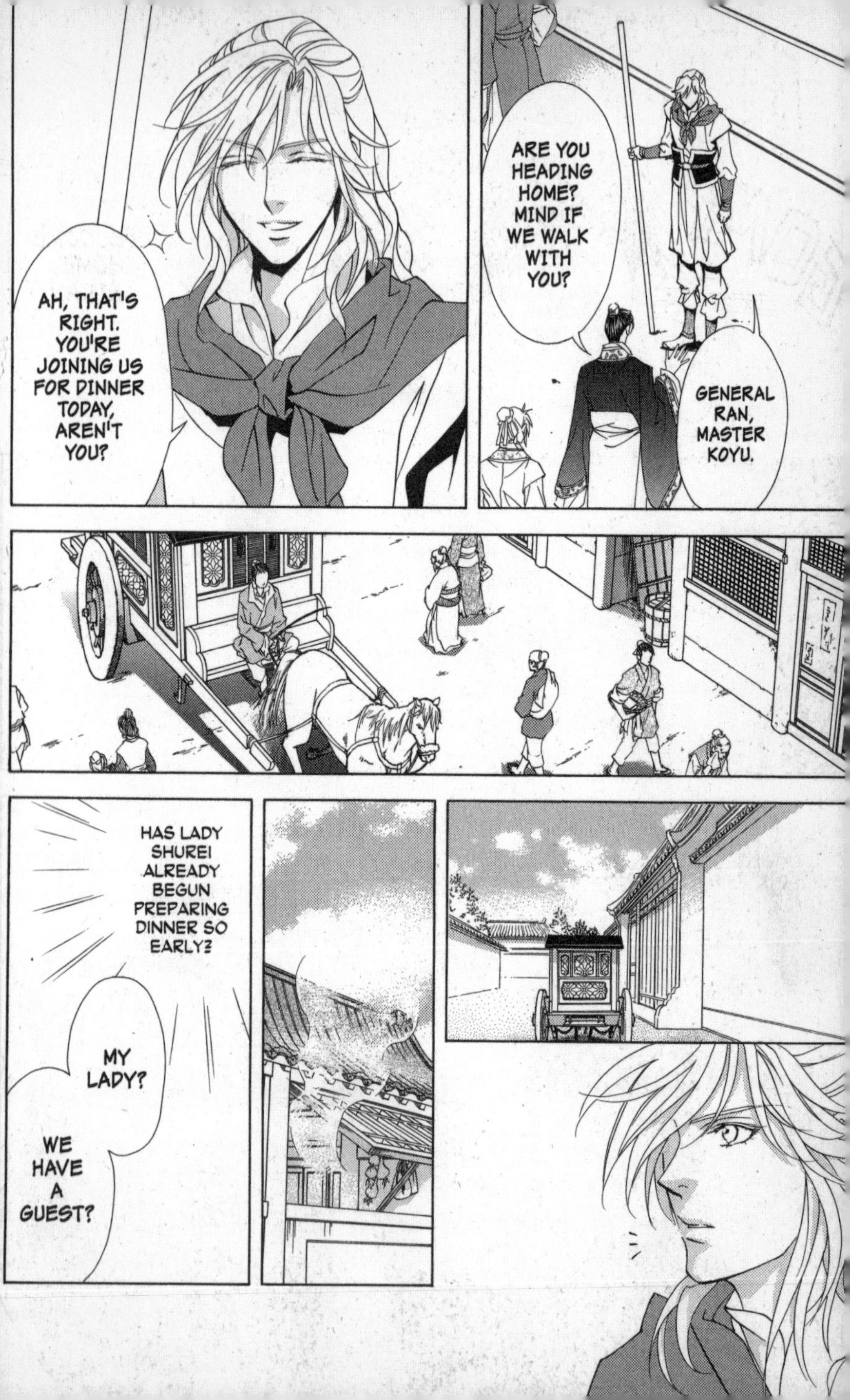
ARE YOU HEADING HOME? MIND IF WE WALK WITH YOU?
GENERAL RAN, MASTER KOYU.
AH, THAT'S RIGHT. YOU'RE JOINING US FOR DINNER TODAY, AREN'T YOU?
HAS LADY SHUREI ALREADY BEGUN PREPARING DINNER SO EARLY?
MY LADY?
WE HAVE A GUEST?

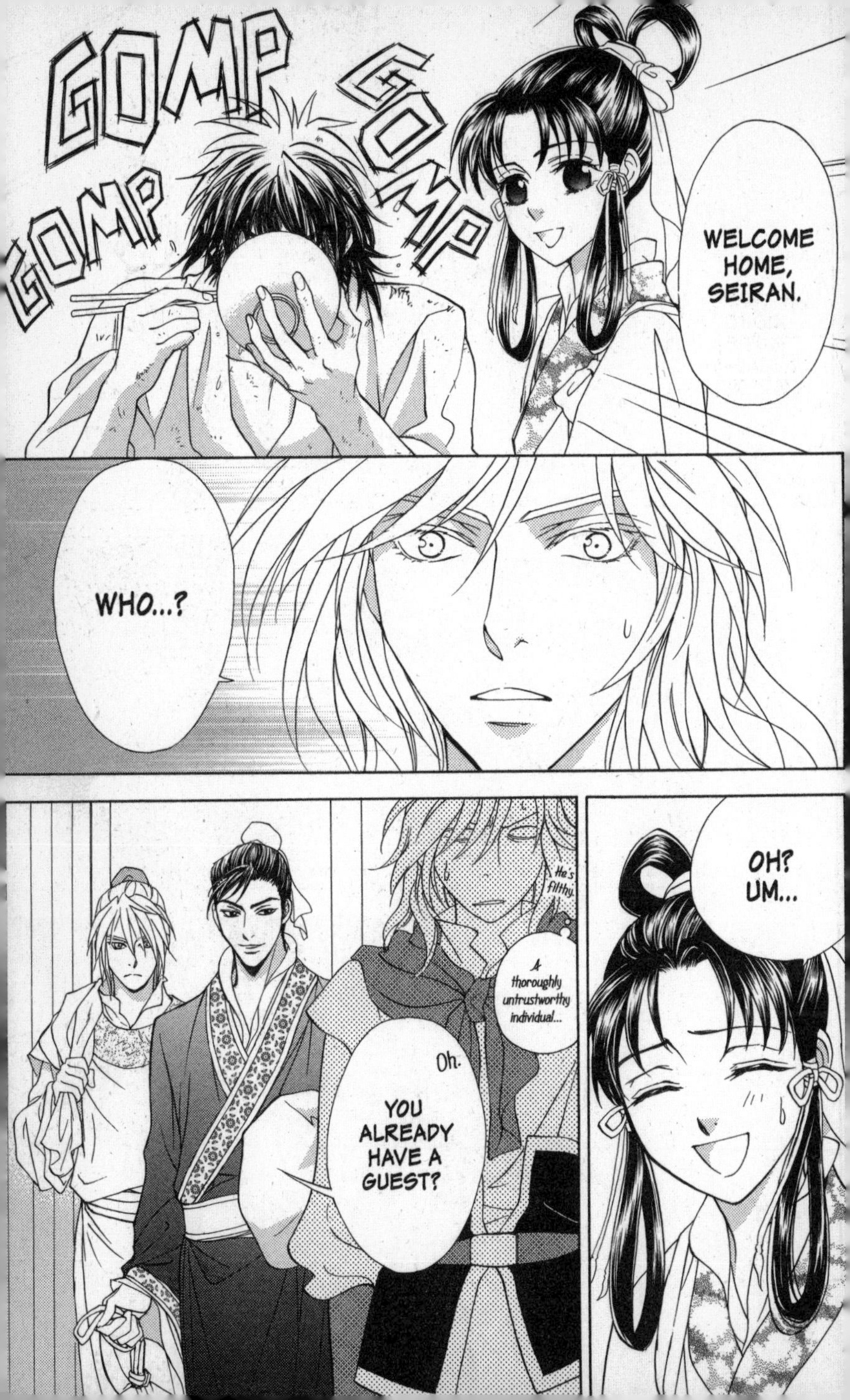
WELCOME HOME, SEIRAN.
GOMP
GOMP
GOMP
WHO...?
OH? UM...
He's filthy.
A thoroughly untrustworthy individual...
Oh.
YOU ALREADY HAVE A GUEST?

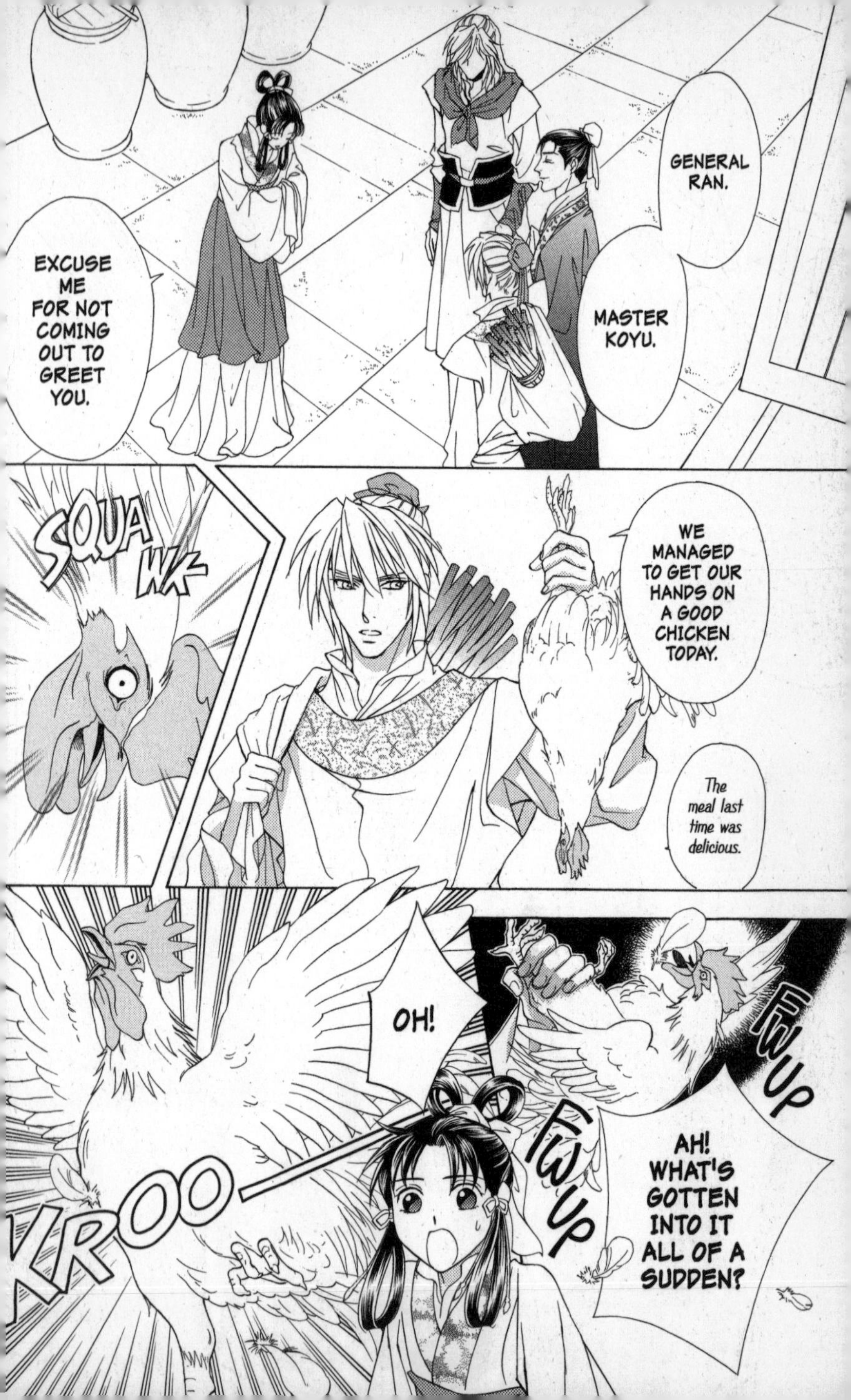
GENERAL RAN.
MASTER KOYU.
EXCUSE ME FOR NOT COMING OUT TO GREET YOU.
WE MANAGED TO GET OUR HANDS ON A GOOD CHICKEN TODAY.
The meal last time was delicious.
SQUAWK
FWUP
AH! WHAT'S GOTTEN INTO IT ALL OF A SUDDEN?
FWUP
OH!

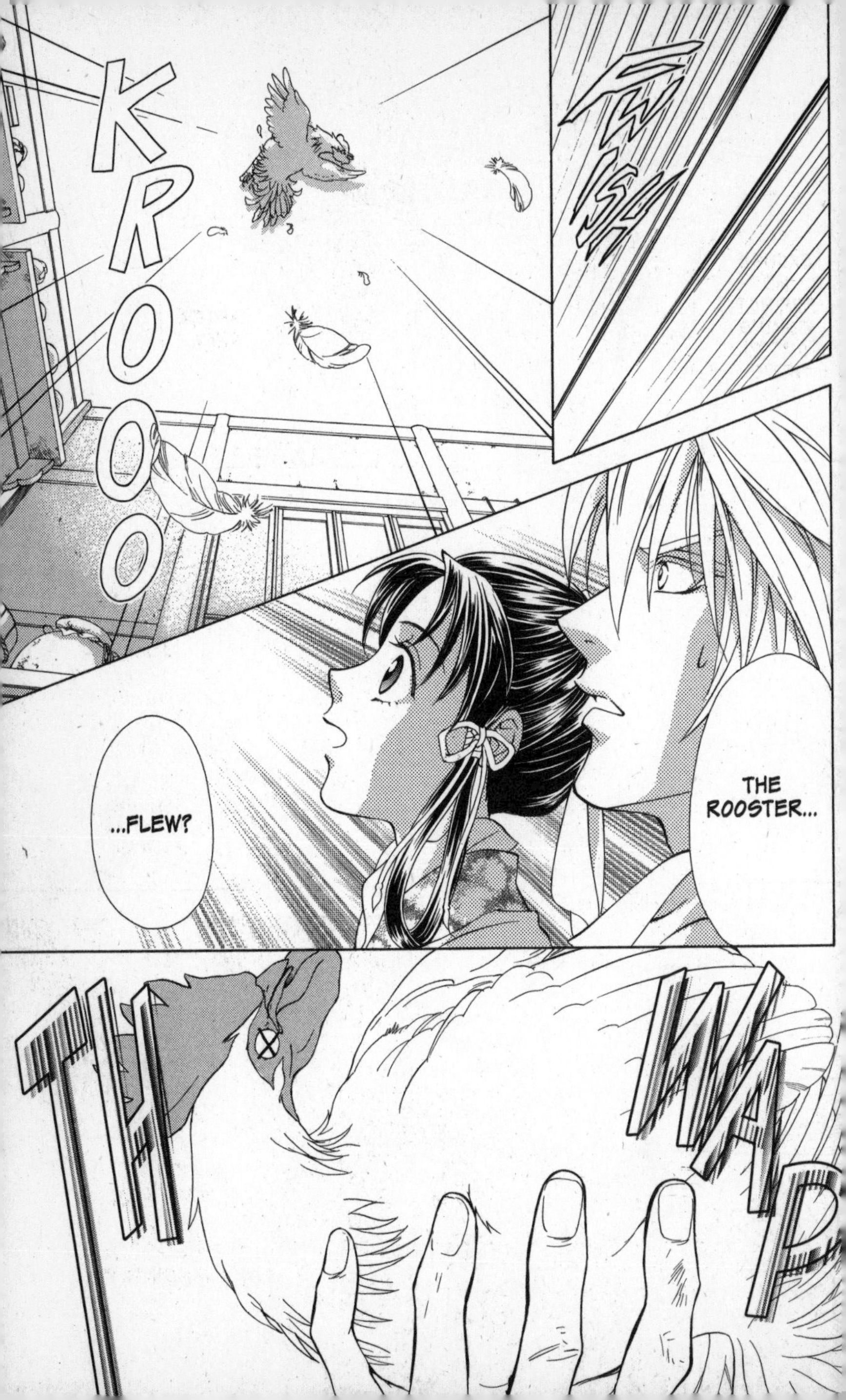
FWISH
KROOOO
THE ROOSTER...
...FLEW?
THWAP

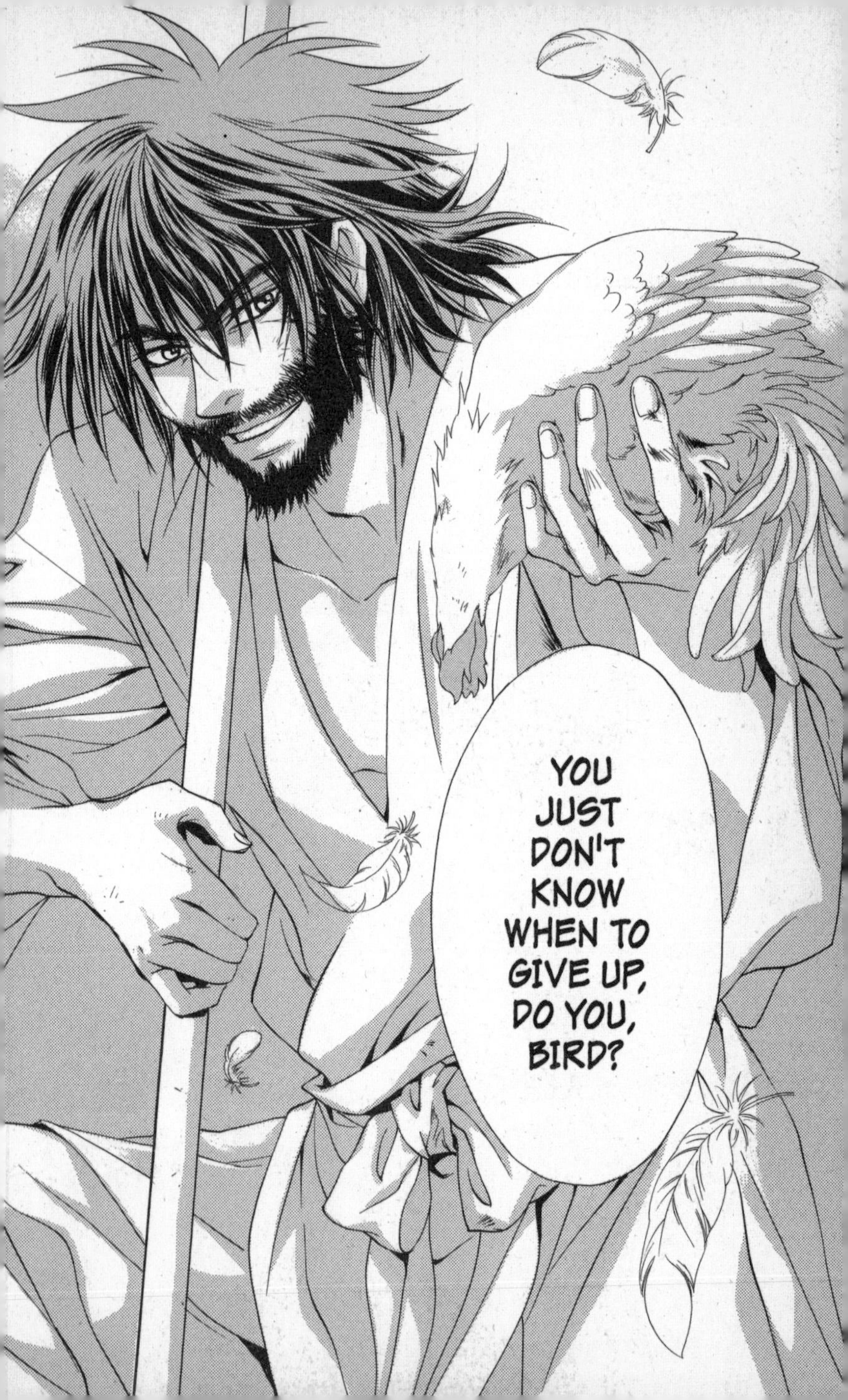
YOU JUST DON'T KNOW WHEN TO GIVE UP, DO YOU, BIRD?

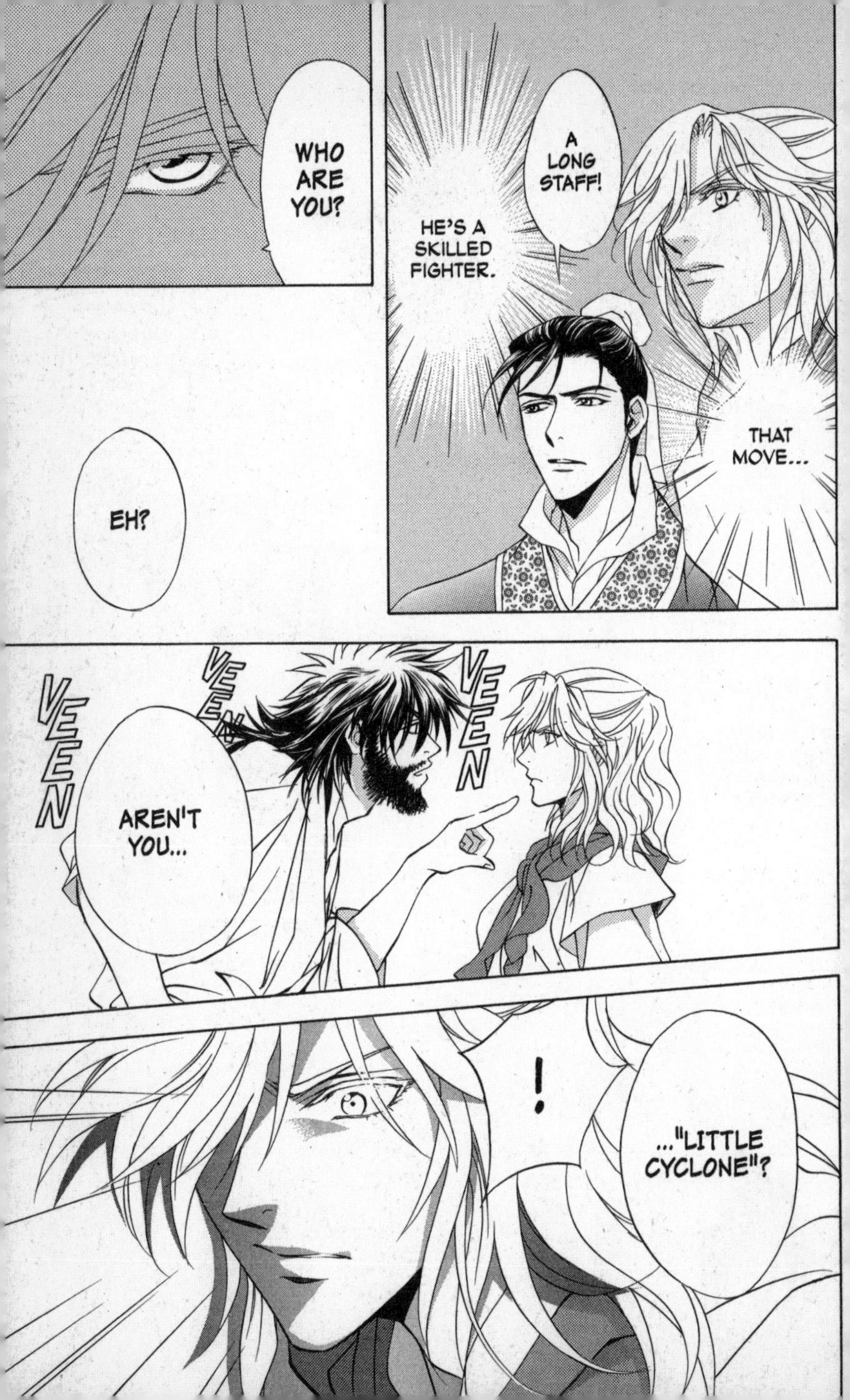
A LONG STAFF!
HE'S A SKILLED FIGHTER.
THAT MOVE...
WHO ARE YOU?
EH?
VEEN
VEEN
VEEN
AREN'T YOU...
..."LITTLE CYCLONE"?
!

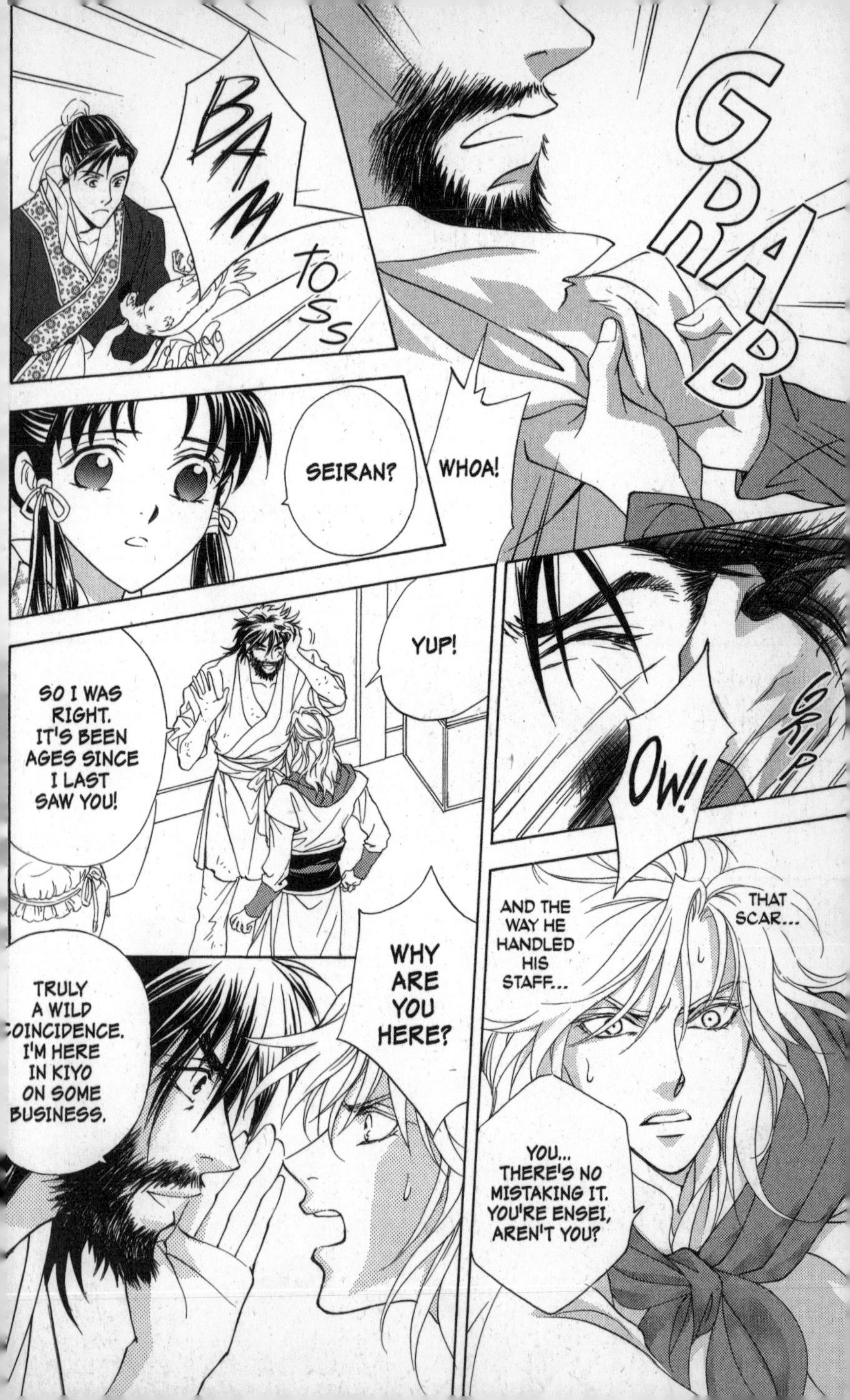
GRABB
WHOA!
BAM
TOSS
SEIRAN?
OW!
GRIP
YUP!
SO I WAS RIGHT. IT'S BEEN AGES SINCE I LAST SAW YOU!
THAT SCAR...
AND THE WAY HE HANDLED HIS STAFF...
YOU... THERE'S NO MISTAKING IT. YOU'RE ENSEI, AREN'T YOU?
WHY ARE YOU HERE?
TRULY A WILD COINCIDENCE. I'M HERE IN KIYO ON SOME BUSINESS.

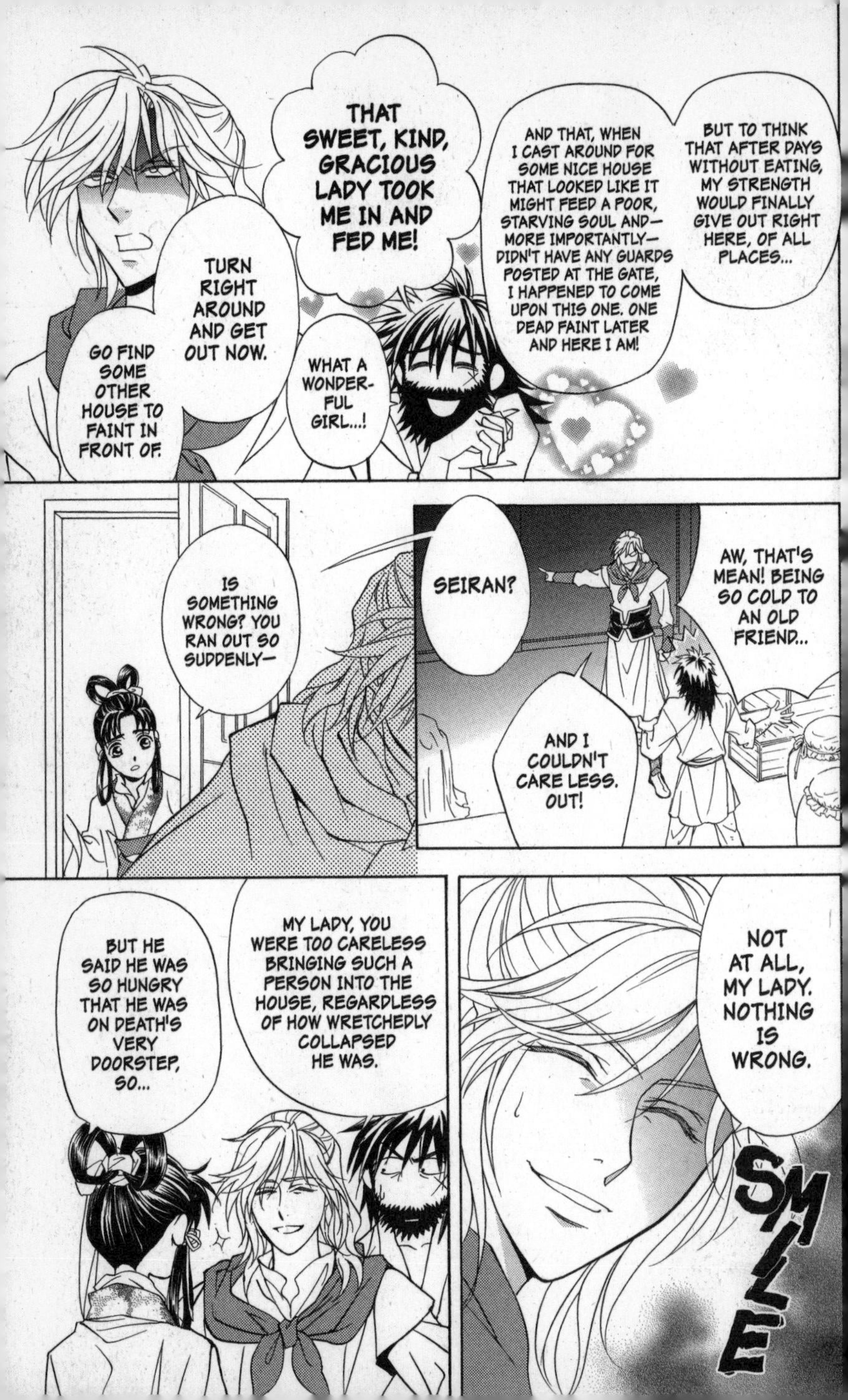
BUT TO THINK THAT AFTER DAYS WITHOUT EATING, MY STRENGTH WOULD FINALLY GIVE OUT RIGHT HERE, OF ALL PLACES...
AND THAT, WHEN I CAST AROUND FOR SOME NICE HOUSE THAT LOOKED LIKE IT MIGHT FEED A POOR, STARVING SOUL AND—MORE IMPORTANTLY—DIDN'T HAVE ANY GUARDS POSTED AT THE GATE, I HAPPENED TO COME UPON THIS ONE. ONE DEAD FAINT LATER AND HERE I AM!
THAT SWEET, KIND, GRACIOUS LADY TOOK ME IN AND FED ME!
WHAT A WONDERFUL GIRL...!
TURN RIGHT AROUND AND GET OUT NOW.
GO FIND SOME OTHER HOUSE TO FAINT IN FRONT OF.
AW, THAT'S MEAN! BEING SO COLD TO AN OLD FRIEND...
AND I COULDN'T CARE LESS. OUT!
SEIRAN?
IS SOMETHING WRONG? YOU RAN OUT SO SUDDENLY—
NOT AT ALL, MY LADY. NOTHING IS WRONG.
SMILE
MY LADY, YOU WERE TOO CARELESS BRINGING SUCH A PERSON INTO THE HOUSE, REGARDLESS OF HOW WRETCHEDLY COLLAPSED HE WAS.
BUT HE SAID HE WAS SO HUNGRY THAT HE WAS ON DEATH'S VERY DOORSTEP, SO...

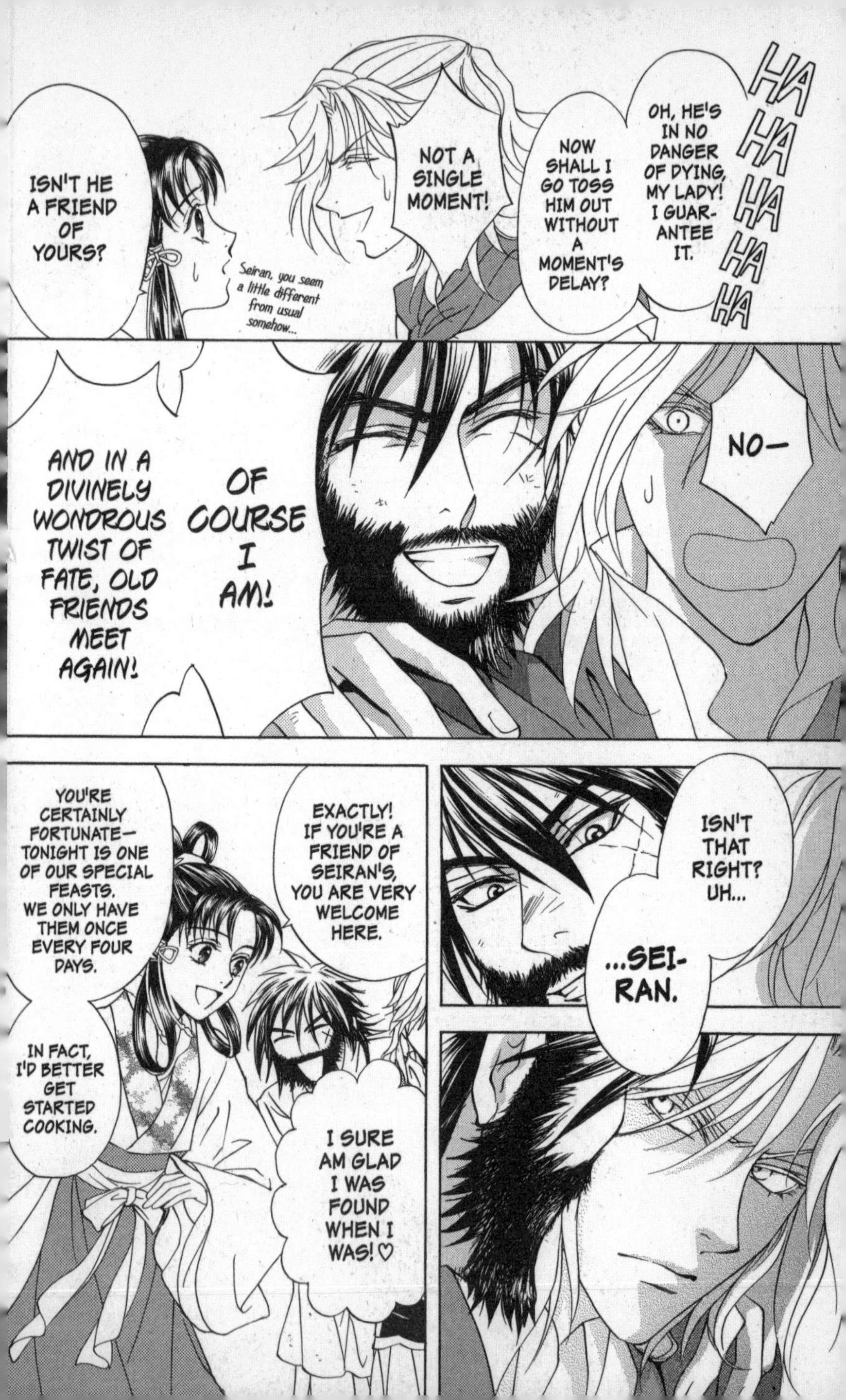
HA HA HA HA HA HA
OH, HE'S IN NO DANGER OF DYING, MY LADY! I GUARANTEE IT.
NOW SHALL I GO TOSS HIM OUT WITHOUT A MOMENT'S DELAY?
NOT A SINGLE MOMENT!
Seiran, you seem a little different from usual somehow...
ISN'T HE A FRIEND OF YOURS?
NO—
OF COURSE I AM!
AND IN A DIVINELY WONDROUS TWIST OF FATE, OLD FRIENDS MEET AGAIN!
ISN'T THAT RIGHT? UH...
...SEIRAN.
EXACTLY! IF YOU'RE A FRIEND OF SEIRAN'S, YOU ARE VERY WELCOME HERE.
YOU'RE CERTAINLY FORTUNATE—TONIGHT IS ONE OF OUR SPECIAL FEASTS. WE ONLY HAVE THEM ONCE EVERY FOUR DAYS.
I SURE AM GLAD I WAS FOUND WHEN I WAS! ♡
IN FACT, I'D BETTER GET STARTED COOKING.

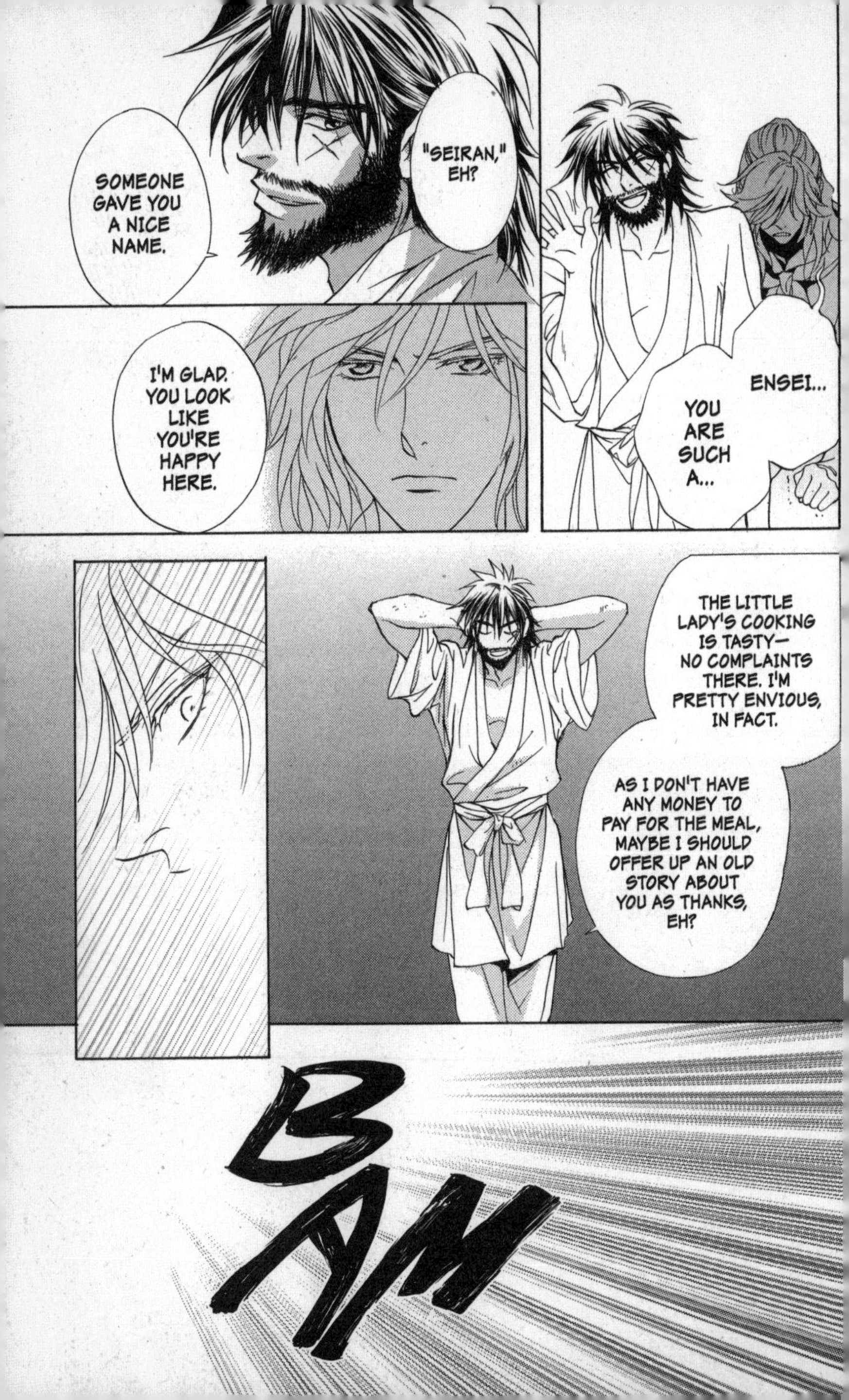
ENSEI...
YOU ARE SUCH A...
"SEIRAN," EH?
SOMEONE GAVE YOU A NICE NAME.
I'M GLAD. YOU LOOK LIKE YOU'RE HAPPY HERE.
THE LITTLE LADY'S COOKING IS TASTY— NO COMPLAINTS THERE. I'M PRETTY ENVIOUS, IN FACT.
AS I DON'T HAVE ANY MONEY TO PAY FOR THE MEAL, MAYBE I SHOULD OFFER UP AN OLD STORY ABOUT YOU AS THANKS, EH?
BAM

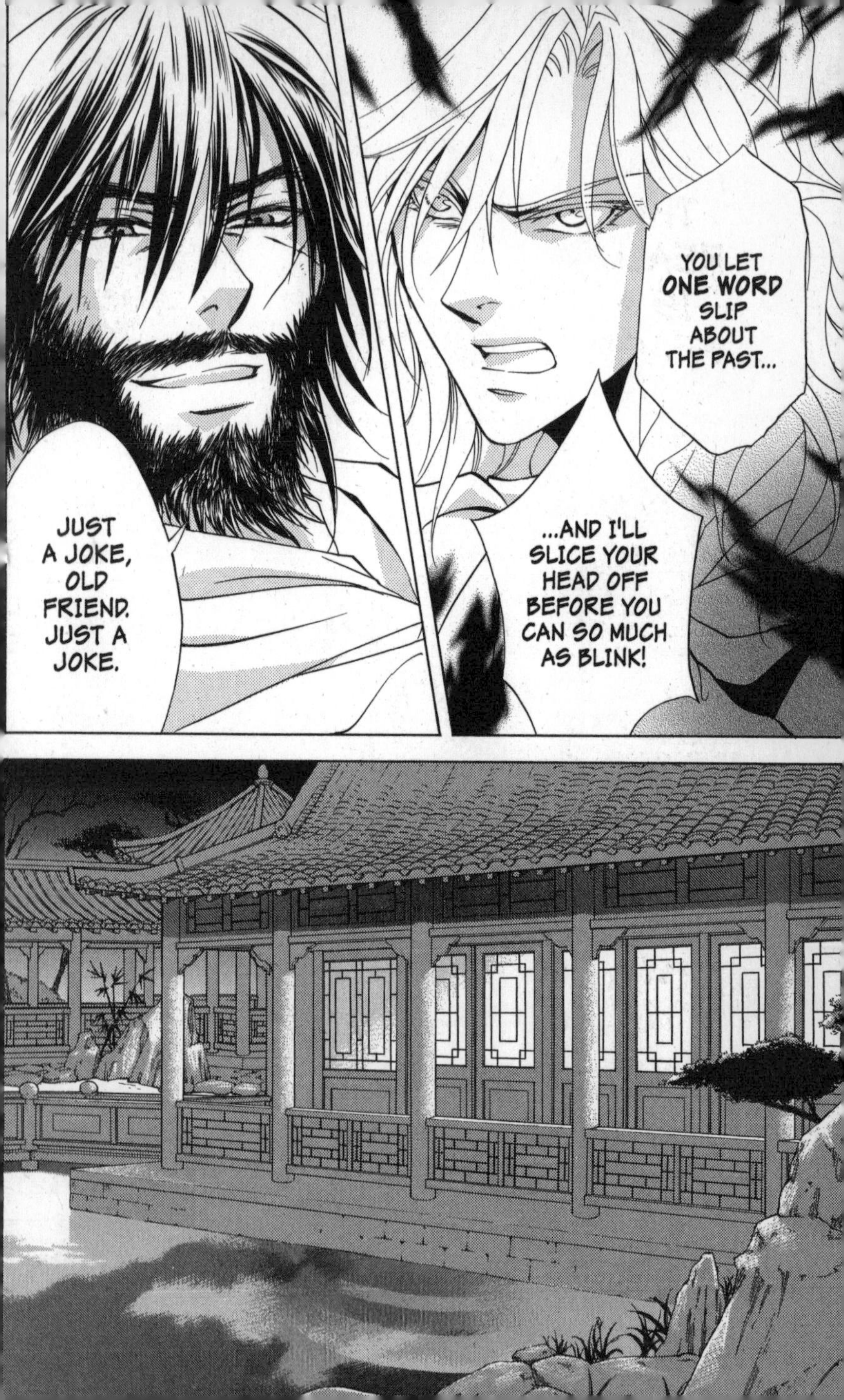
YOU LET ONE WORD SLIP ABOUT THE PAST...
...AND I'LL SLICE YOUR HEAD OFF BEFORE YOU CAN SO MUCH AS BLINK!
JUST A JOKE, OLD FRIEND. JUST A JOKE.

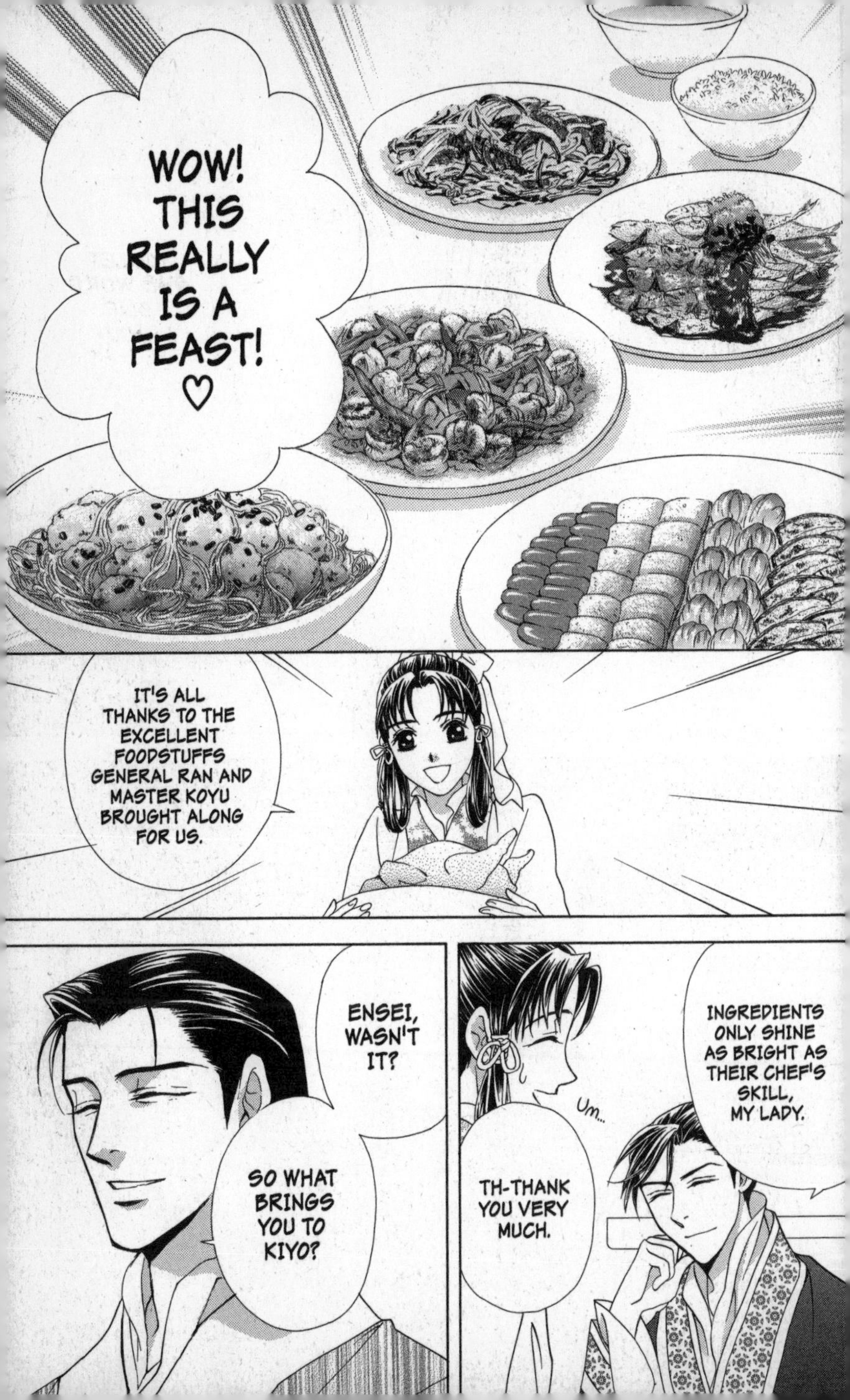
WOW! THIS REALLY IS A FEAST! ♡
IT'S ALL THANKS TO THE EXCELLENT FOODSTUFFS GENERAL RAN AND MASTER KOYU BROUGHT ALONG FOR US.
INGREDIENTS ONLY SHINE AS BRIGHT AS THEIR CHEF'S SKILL, MY LADY.
Um...
TH-THANK YOU VERY MUCH.
ENSEI, WASN'T IT?
SO WHAT BRINGS YOU TO KIYO?

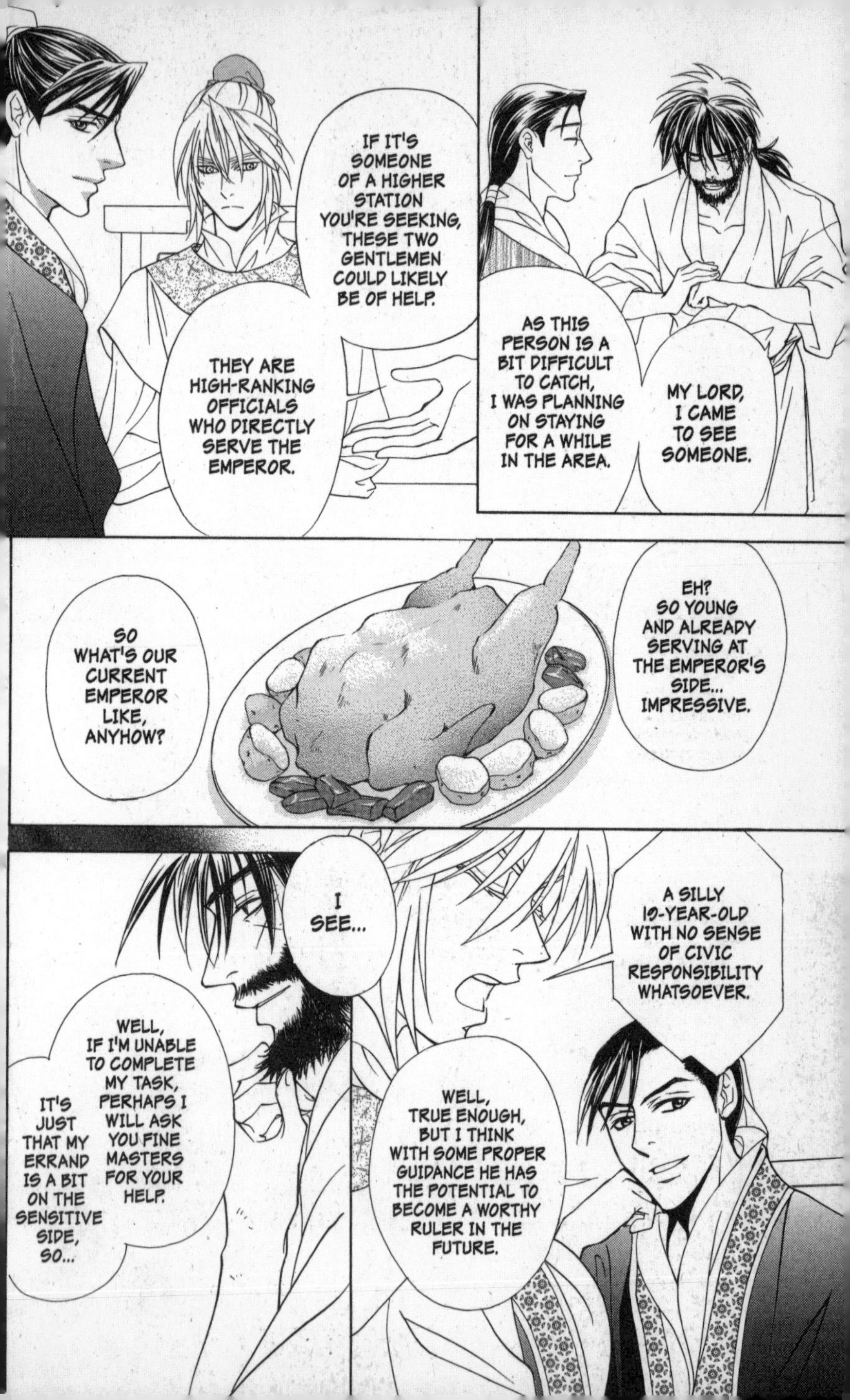
MY LORD, I CAME TO SEE SOMEONE.
AS THIS PERSON IS A BIT DIFFICULT TO CATCH, I WAS PLANNING ON STAYING FOR A WHILE IN THE AREA.
IF IT'S SOMEONE OF A HIGHER STATION YOU'RE SEEKING, THESE TWO GENTLEMEN COULD LIKELY BE OF HELP.
THEY ARE HIGH-RANKING OFFICIALS WHO DIRECTLY SERVE THE EMPEROR.
EH? SO YOUNG AND ALREADY SERVING AT THE EMPEROR'S SIDE... IMPRESSIVE.
SO WHAT'S OUR CURRENT EMPEROR LIKE, ANYHOW?
A SILLY 19-YEAR-OLD WITH NO SENSE OF CIVIC RESPONSIBILITY WHATSOEVER.
I SEE...
WELL, TRUE ENOUGH, BUT I THINK WITH SOME PROPER GUIDANCE HE HAS THE POTENTIAL TO BECOME A WORTHY RULER IN THE FUTURE.
WELL, IF I'M UNABLE TO COMPLETE MY TASK, PERHAPS I WILL ASK YOU FINE MASTERS FOR YOUR HELP.
IT'S JUST THAT MY ERRAND IS A BIT ON THE SENSITIVE SIDE, SO...

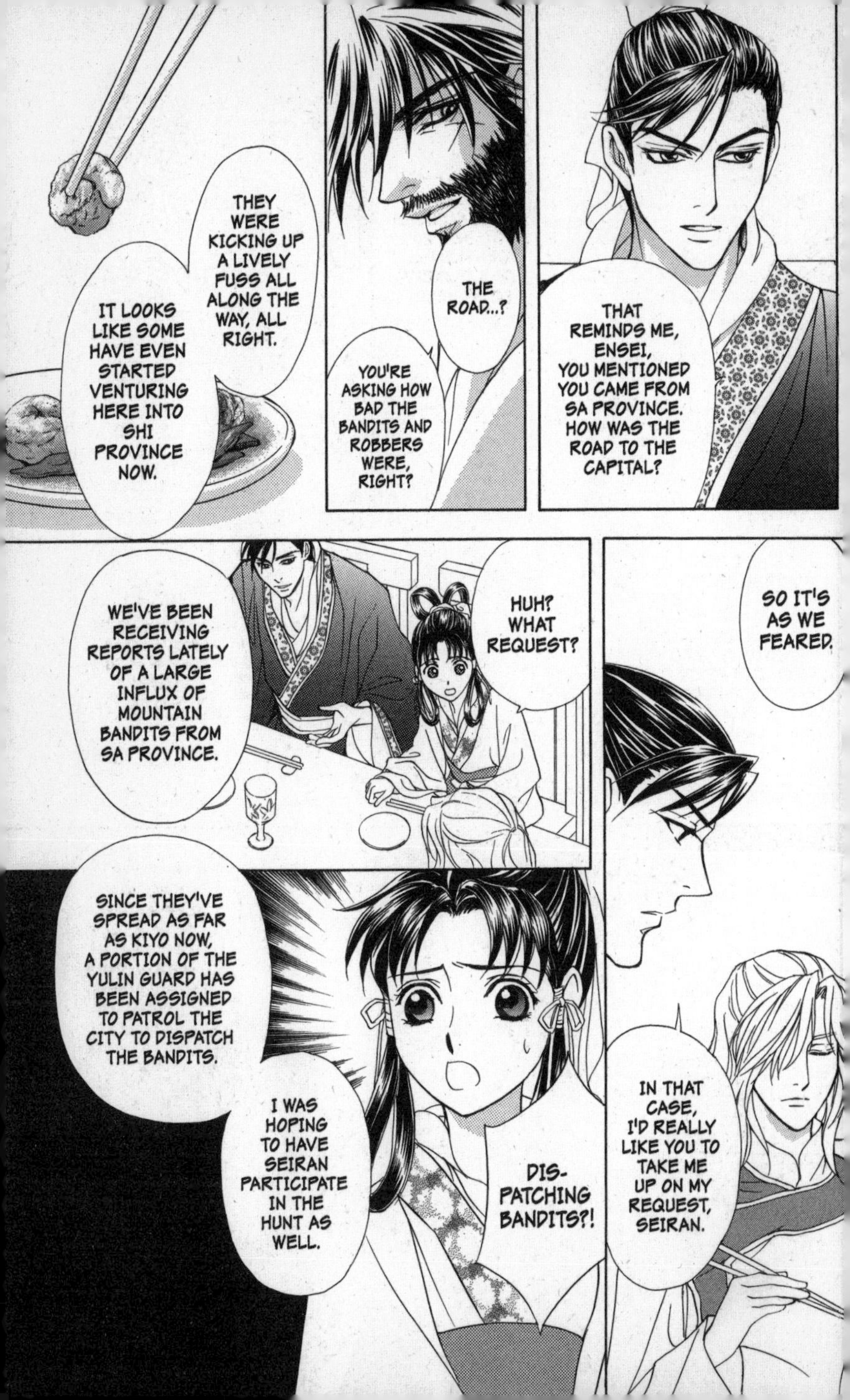
THAT REMINDS ME, ENSEI, YOU MENTIONED YOU CAME FROM SA PROVINCE. HOW WAS THE ROAD TO THE CAPITAL?
THE ROAD...?
YOU'RE ASKING HOW BAD THE BANDITS AND ROBBERS WERE, RIGHT?
THEY WERE KICKING UP A LIVELY FUSS ALL ALONG THE WAY, ALL RIGHT.
IT LOOKS LIKE SOME HAVE EVEN STARTED VENTURING HERE INTO SHI PROVINCE NOW.
SO IT'S AS WE FEARED.
IN THAT CASE, I'D REALLY LIKE YOU TO TAKE ME UP ON MY REQUEST, SEIRAN.
HUH? WHAT REQUEST?
WE'VE BEEN RECEIVING REPORTS LATELY OF A LARGE INFLUX OF MOUNTAIN BANDITS FROM SA PROVINCE.
SINCE THEY'VE SPREAD AS FAR AS KIYO NOW, A PORTION OF THE YULIN GUARD HAS BEEN ASSIGNED TO PATROL THE CITY TO DISPATCH THE BANDITS.
I WAS HOPING TO HAVE SEIRAN PARTICIPATE IN THE HUNT AS WELL.
DIS-PATCHING BANDITS?!

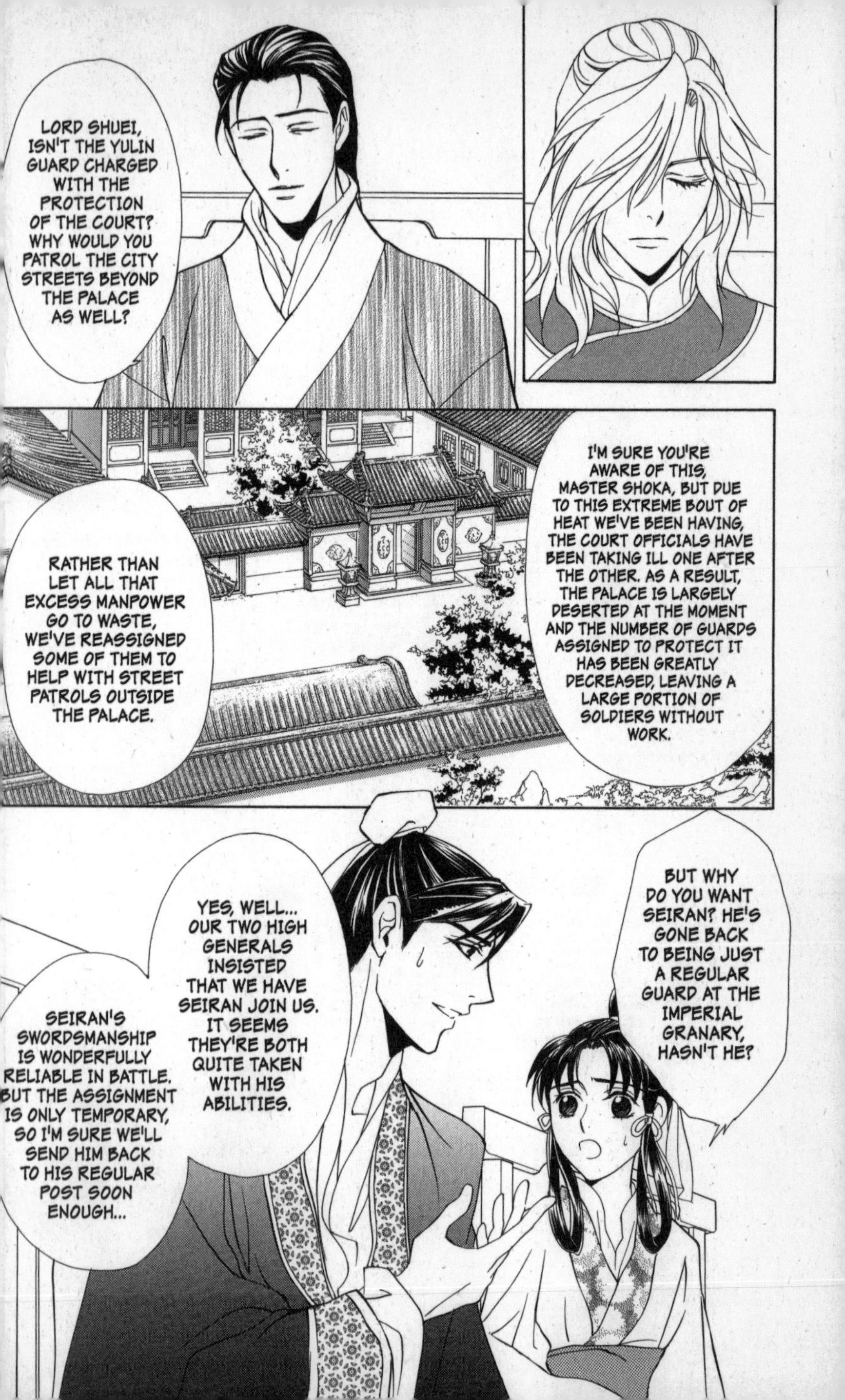
LORD SHUEI, ISN'T THE YULIN GUARD CHARGED WITH THE PROTECTION OF THE COURT? WHY WOULD YOU PATROL THE CITY STREETS BEYOND THE PALACE AS WELL?
I'M SURE YOU'RE AWARE OF THIS, MASTER SHOKA, BUT DUE TO THIS EXTREME BOUT OF HEAT WE'VE BEEN HAVING, THE COURT OFFICIALS HAVE BEEN TAKING ILL ONE AFTER THE OTHER. AS A RESULT, THE PALACE IS LARGELY DESERTED AT THE MOMENT AND THE NUMBER OF GUARDS ASSIGNED TO PROTECT IT HAS BEEN GREATLY DECREASED, LEAVING A LARGE PORTION OF SOLDIERS WITHOUT WORK.
RATHER THAN LET ALL THAT EXCESS MANPOWER GO TO WASTE, WE'VE REASSIGNED SOME OF THEM TO HELP WITH STREET PATROLS OUTSIDE THE PALACE.
BUT WHY DO YOU WANT SEIRAN? HE'S GONE BACK TO BEING JUST A REGULAR GUARD AT THE IMPERIAL GRANARY, HASN'T HE?
YES, WELL... OUR TWO HIGH GENERALS INSISTED THAT WE HAVE SEIRAN JOIN US. IT SEEMS THEY'RE BOTH QUITE TAKEN WITH HIS ABILITIES.
SEIRAN'S SWORDSMANSHIP IS WONDERFULLY RELIABLE IN BATTLE. BUT THE ASSIGNMENT IS ONLY TEMPORARY, SO I'M SURE WE'LL SEND HIM BACK TO HIS REGULAR POST SOON ENOUGH...

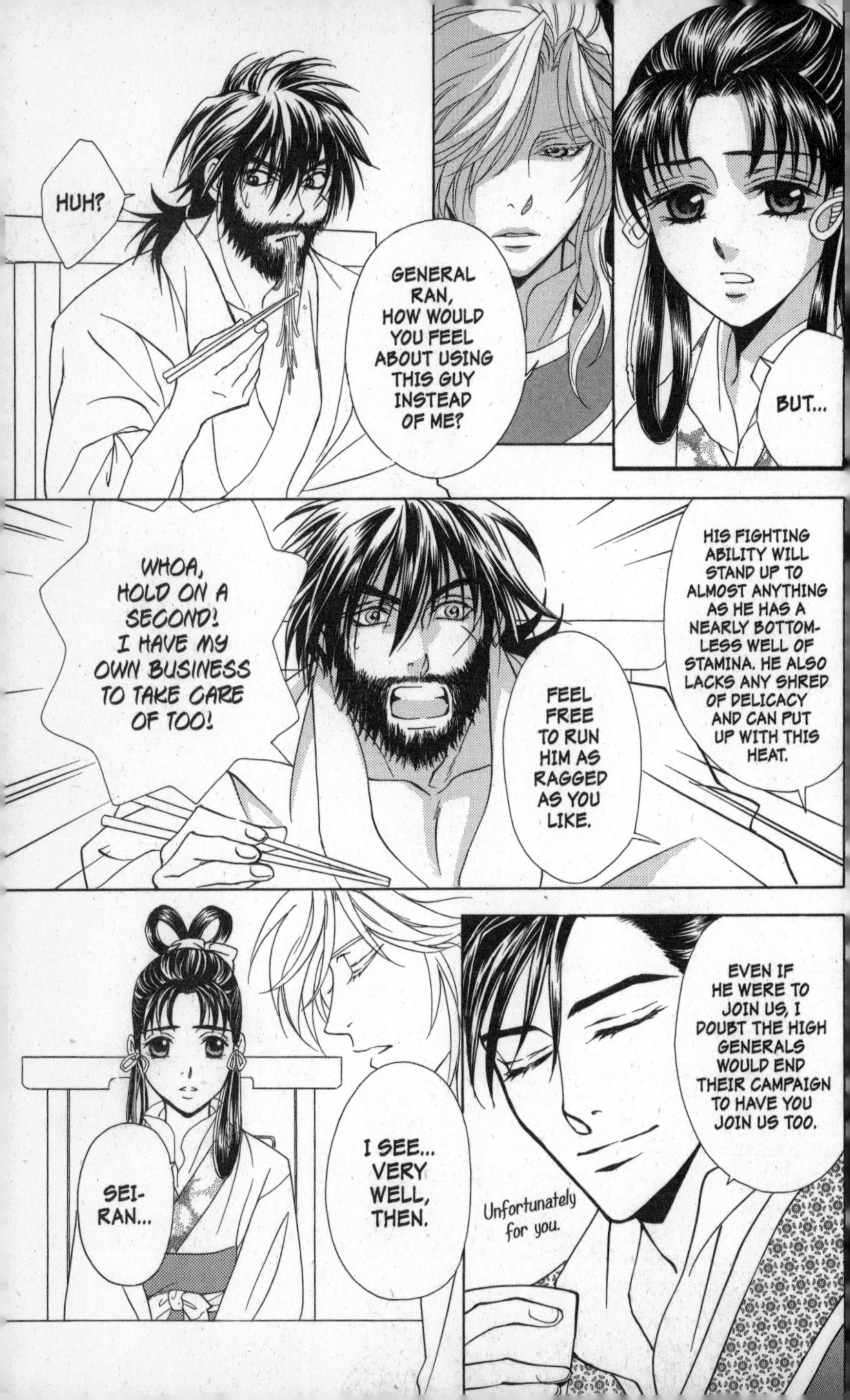
BUT...
GENERAL RAN, HOW WOULD YOU FEEL ABOUT USING THIS GUY INSTEAD OF ME?
HUH?
HIS FIGHTING ABILITY WILL STAND UP TO ALMOST ANYTHING AS HE HAS A NEARLY BOTTOM-LESS WELL OF STAMINA. HE ALSO LACKS ANY SHRED OF DELICACY AND CAN PUT UP WITH THIS HEAT.
FEEL FREE TO RUN HIM AS RAGGED AS YOU LIKE.
WHOA, HOLD ON A SECOND! I HAVE MY OWN BUSINESS TO TAKE CARE OF TOO!
EVEN IF HE WERE TO JOIN US, I DOUBT THE HIGH GENERALS WOULD END THEIR CAMPAIGN TO HAVE YOU JOIN US TOO.
Unfortunately for you.
I SEE... VERY WELL, THEN.
SEI-RAN...

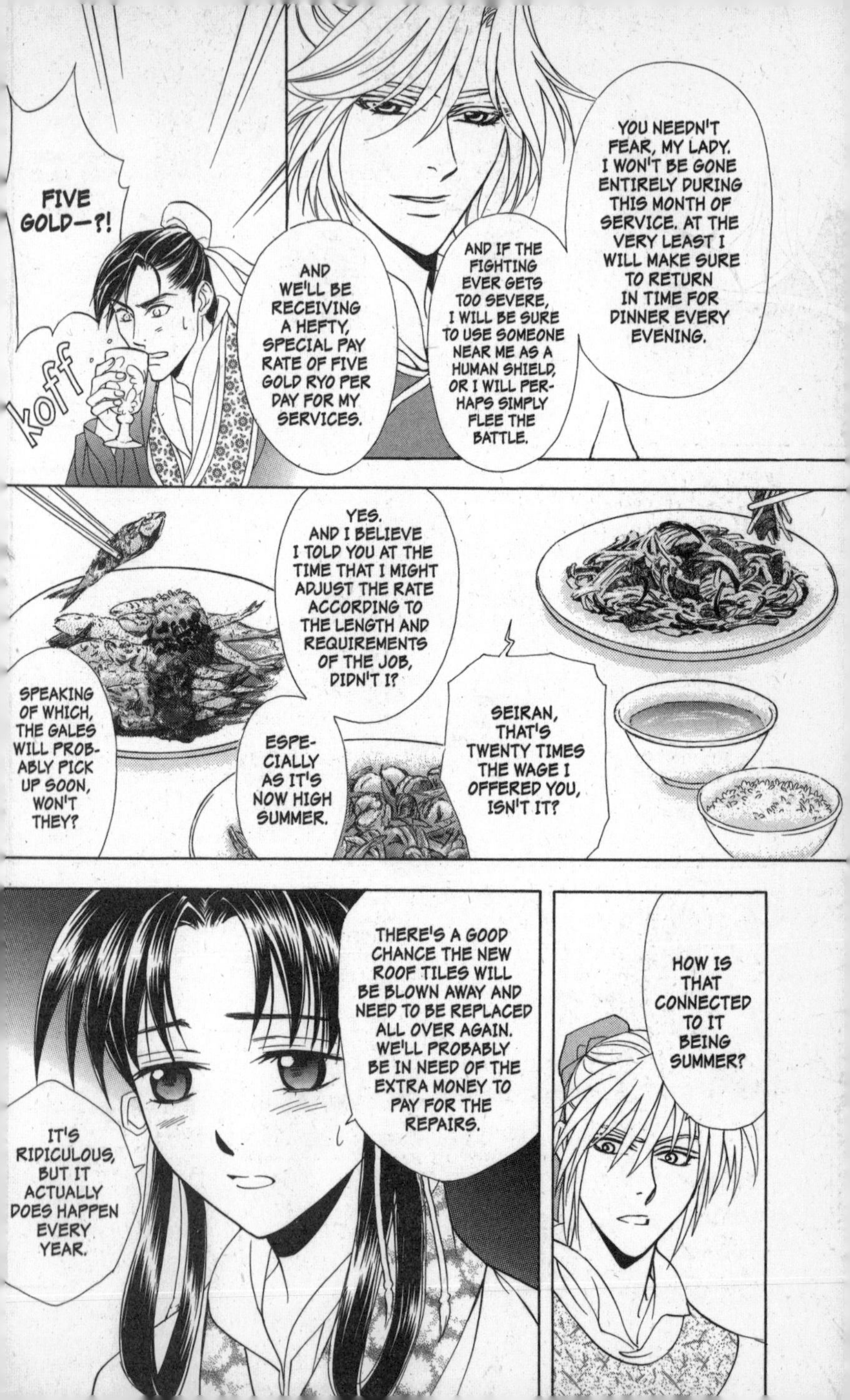
YOU NEEDN'T FEAR, MY LADY. I WON'T BE GONE ENTIRELY DURING THIS MONTH OF SERVICE. AT THE VERY LEAST I WILL MAKE SURE TO RETURN IN TIME FOR DINNER EVERY EVENING.
AND IF THE FIGHTING EVER GETS TOO SEVERE, I WILL BE SURE TO USE SOMEONE NEAR ME AS A HUMAN SHIELD, OR I WILL PERHAPS SIMPLY FLEE THE BATTLE.
AND WE'LL BE RECEIVING A HEFTY, SPECIAL PAY RATE OF FIVE GOLD RYO PER DAY FOR MY SERVICES.
FIVE GOLD—?!
koff
SEIRAN, THAT'S TWENTY TIMES THE WAGE I OFFERED YOU, ISN'T IT?
YES. AND I BELIEVE I TOLD YOU AT THE TIME THAT I MIGHT ADJUST THE RATE ACCORDING TO THE LENGTH AND REQUIREMENTS OF THE JOB, DIDN'T I?
ESPECIALLY AS IT'S NOW HIGH SUMMER.
SPEAKING OF WHICH, THE GALES WILL PROBABLY PICK UP SOON, WON'T THEY?
HOW IS THAT CONNECTED TO IT BEING SUMMER?
THERE'S A GOOD CHANCE THE NEW ROOF TILES WILL BE BLOWN AWAY AND NEED TO BE REPLACED ALL OVER AGAIN. WE'LL PROBABLY BE IN NEED OF THE EXTRA MONEY TO PAY FOR THE REPAIRS.
IT'S RIDICULOUS, BUT IT ACTUALLY DOES HAPPEN EVERY YEAR.

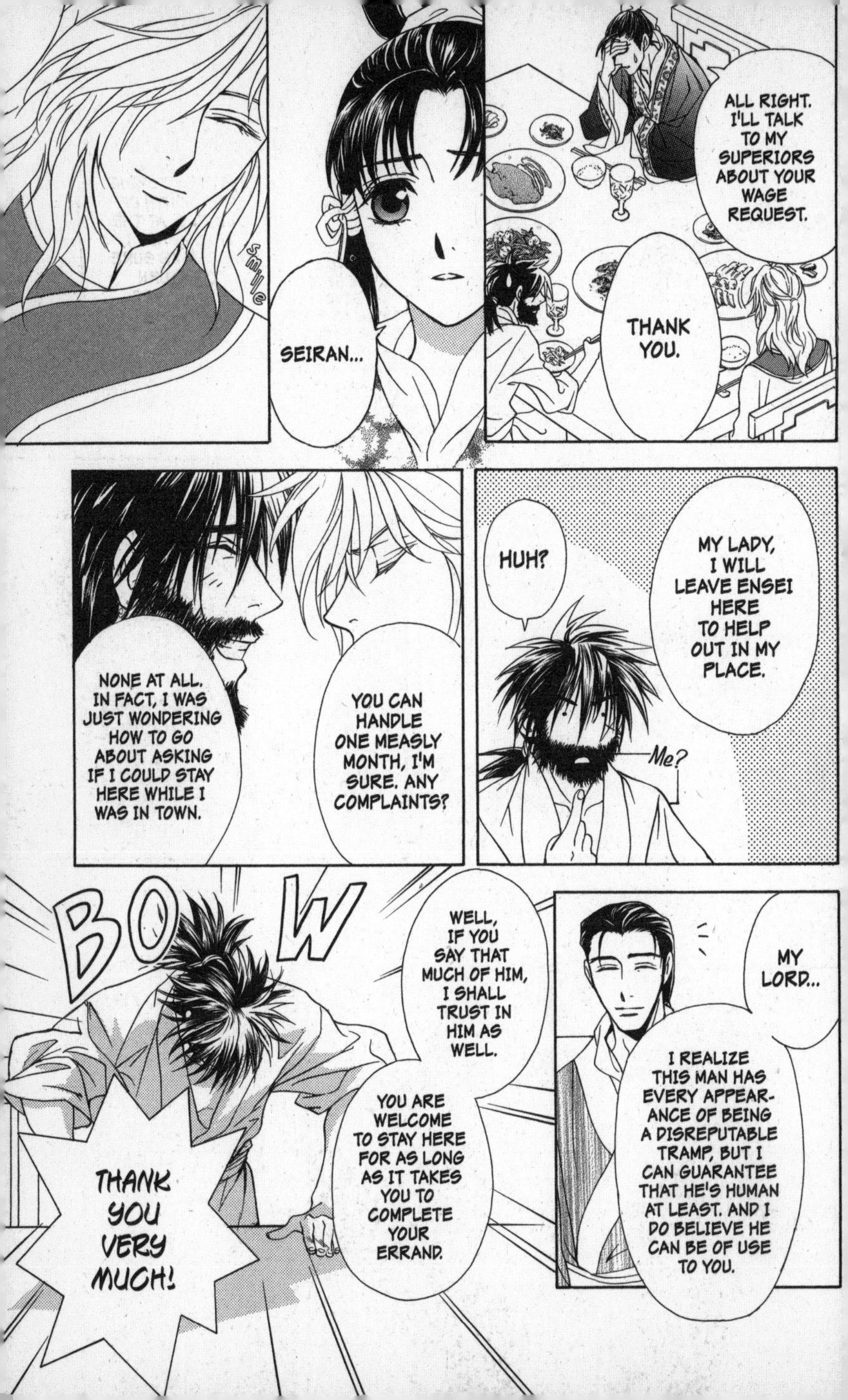
ALL RIGHT. I'LL TALK TO MY SUPERIORS ABOUT YOUR WAGE REQUEST.
THANK YOU.
SEIRAN...
smile
MY LADY, I WILL LEAVE ENSEI HERE TO HELP OUT IN MY PLACE.
HUH?
Me?
YOU CAN HANDLE ONE MEASLY MONTH, I'M SURE. ANY COMPLAINTS?
NONE AT ALL. IN FACT, I WAS JUST WONDERING HOW TO GO ABOUT ASKING IF I COULD STAY HERE WHILE I WAS IN TOWN.
MY LORD...
I REALIZE THIS MAN HAS EVERY APPEAR-ANCE OF BEING A DISREPUTABLE TRAMP, BUT I CAN GUARANTEE THAT HE'S HUMAN AT LEAST. AND I DO BELIEVE HE CAN BE OF USE TO YOU.
WELL, IF YOU SAY THAT MUCH OF HIM, I SHALL TRUST IN HIM AS WELL.
YOU ARE WELCOME TO STAY HERE FOR AS LONG AS IT TAKES YOU TO COMPLETE YOUR ERRAND.
BOW
THANK YOU VERY MUCH!

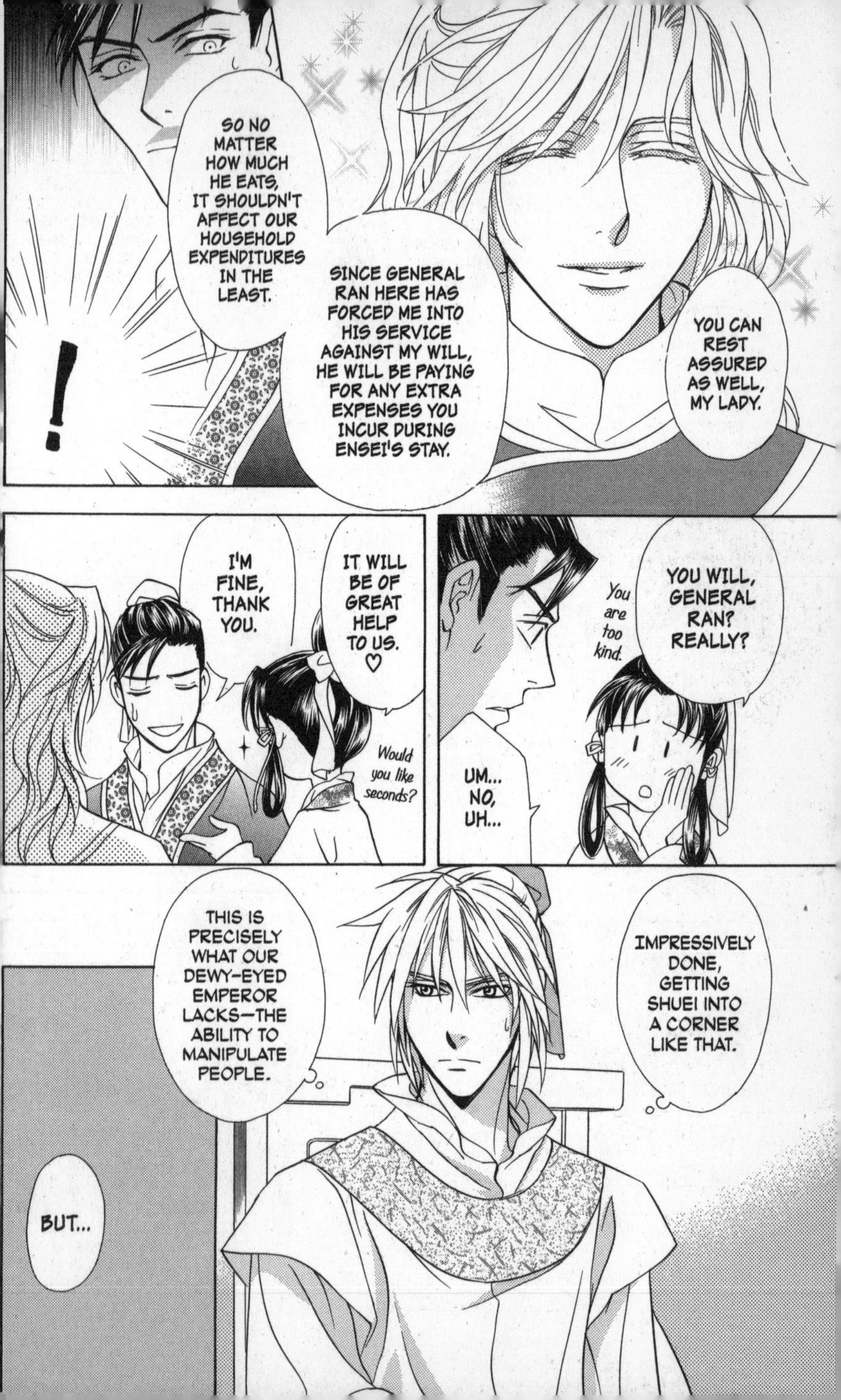

YOU CAN REST ASSURED AS WELL, MY LADY.
SINCE GENERAL RAN HERE HAS FORCED ME INTO HIS SERVICE AGAINST MY WILL, HE WILL BE PAYING FOR ANY EXTRA EXPENSES YOU INCUR DURING ENSEI'S STAY.
SO NO MATTER HOW MUCH HE EATS, IT SHOULDN'T AFFECT OUR HOUSEHOLD EXPENDITURES IN THE LEAST.
!
YOU WILL, GENERAL RAN? REALLY?
You are too kind.
UM... NO, UH...
IT WILL BE OF GREAT HELP TO US. ♡
Would you like seconds?
I'M FINE, THANK YOU.
IMPRESSIVELY DONE, GETTING SHUEI INTO A CORNER LIKE THAT.
THIS IS PRECISELY WHAT OUR DEWY-EYED EMPEROR LACKS—THE ABILITY TO MANIPULATE PEOPLE.
BUT...

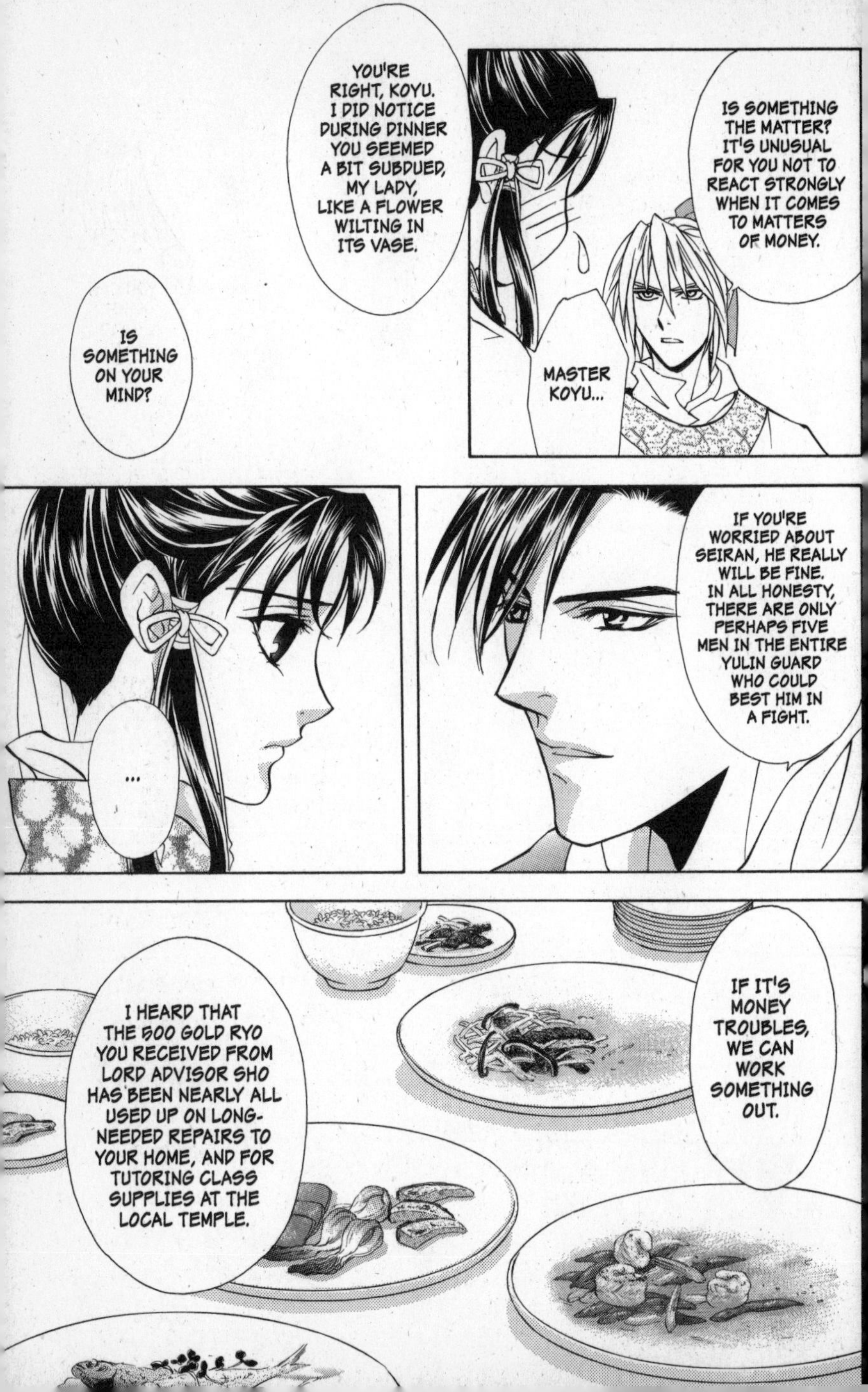
IS SOMETHING THE MATTER? IT'S UNUSUAL FOR YOU NOT TO REACT STRONGLY WHEN IT COMES TO MATTERS OF MONEY.
MASTER KOYU...
YOU'RE RIGHT, KOYU. I DID NOTICE DURING DINNER YOU SEEMED A BIT SUBDUED, MY LADY, LIKE A FLOWER WILTING IN ITS VASE.
IS SOMETHING ON YOUR MIND?
IF YOU'RE WORRIED ABOUT SEIRAN, HE REALLY WILL BE FINE. IN ALL HONESTY, THERE ARE ONLY PERHAPS FIVE MEN IN THE ENTIRE YULIN GUARD WHO COULD BEST HIM IN A FIGHT.
...
IF IT'S MONEY TROUBLES, WE CAN WORK SOMETHING OUT.
I HEARD THAT THE 500 GOLD RYO YOU RECEIVED FROM LORD ADVISOR SHO HAS BEEN NEARLY ALL USED UP ON LONG-NEEDED REPAIRS TO YOUR HOME, AND FOR TUTORING CLASS SUPPLIES AT THE LOCAL TEMPLE.

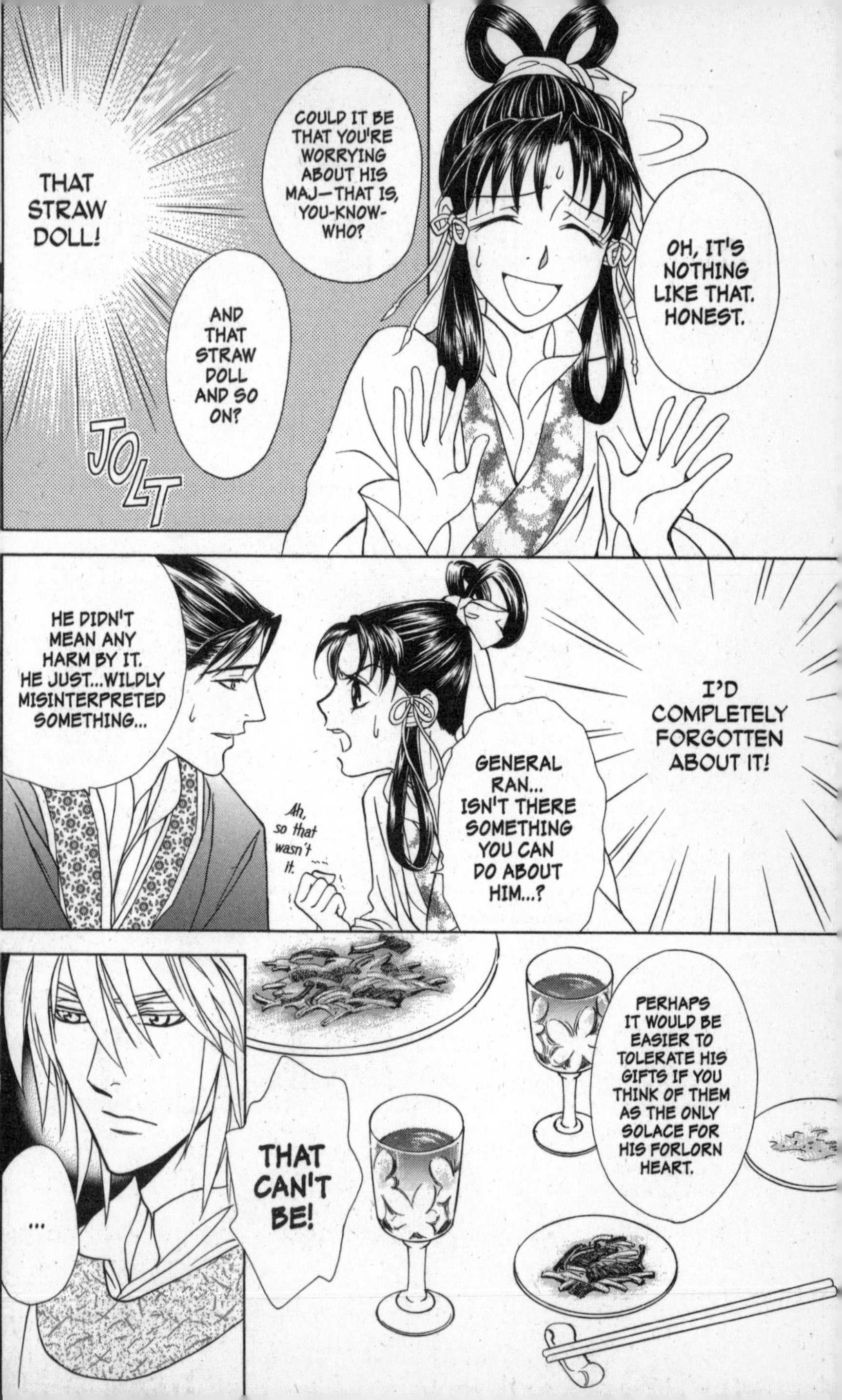
OH, IT'S NOTHING LIKE THAT. HONEST.
COULD IT BE THAT YOU'RE WORRYING ABOUT HIS MAJ—THAT IS, YOU-KNOW-WHO?
AND THAT STRAW DOLL AND SO ON?
JOLT
THAT STRAW DOLL!
I'D COMPLETELY FORGOTTEN ABOUT IT!
GENERAL RAN... ISN'T THERE SOMETHING YOU CAN DO ABOUT HIM...?
Ah, so that wasn't it.
HE DIDN'T MEAN ANY HARM BY IT. HE JUST...WILDLY MISINTERPRETED SOMETHING...
PERHAPS IT WOULD BE EASIER TO TOLERATE HIS GIFTS IF YOU THINK OF THEM AS THE ONLY SOLACE FOR HIS FORLORN HEART.
THAT CAN'T BE!
...

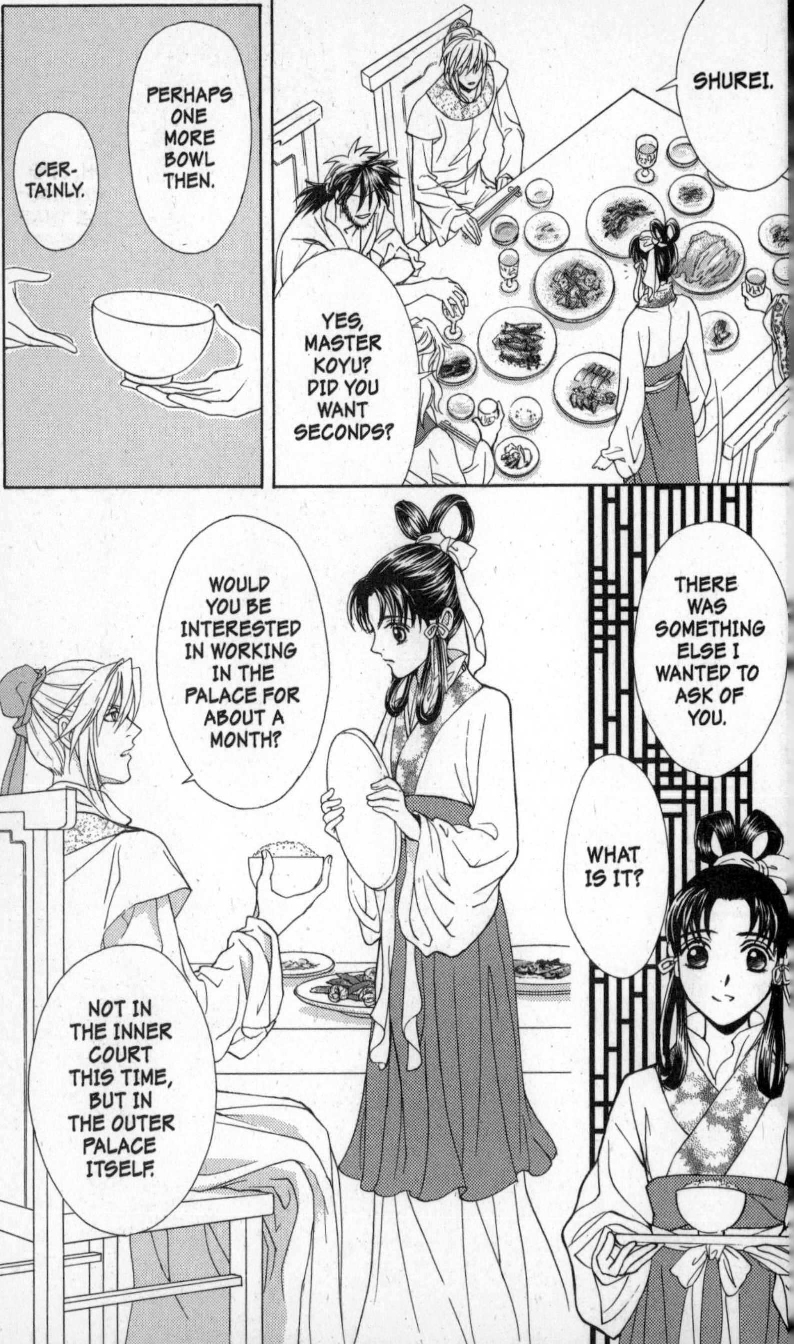
SHUREI.
YES, MASTER KOYU? DID YOU WANT SECONDS?
PERHAPS ONE MORE BOWL THEN.
CER-TAINLY.
THERE WAS SOMETHING ELSE I WANTED TO ASK OF YOU.
WHAT IS IT?
WOULD YOU BE INTERESTED IN WORKING IN THE PALACE FOR ABOUT A MONTH?
NOT IN THE INNER COURT THIS TIME, BUT IN THE OUTER PALACE ITSELF.

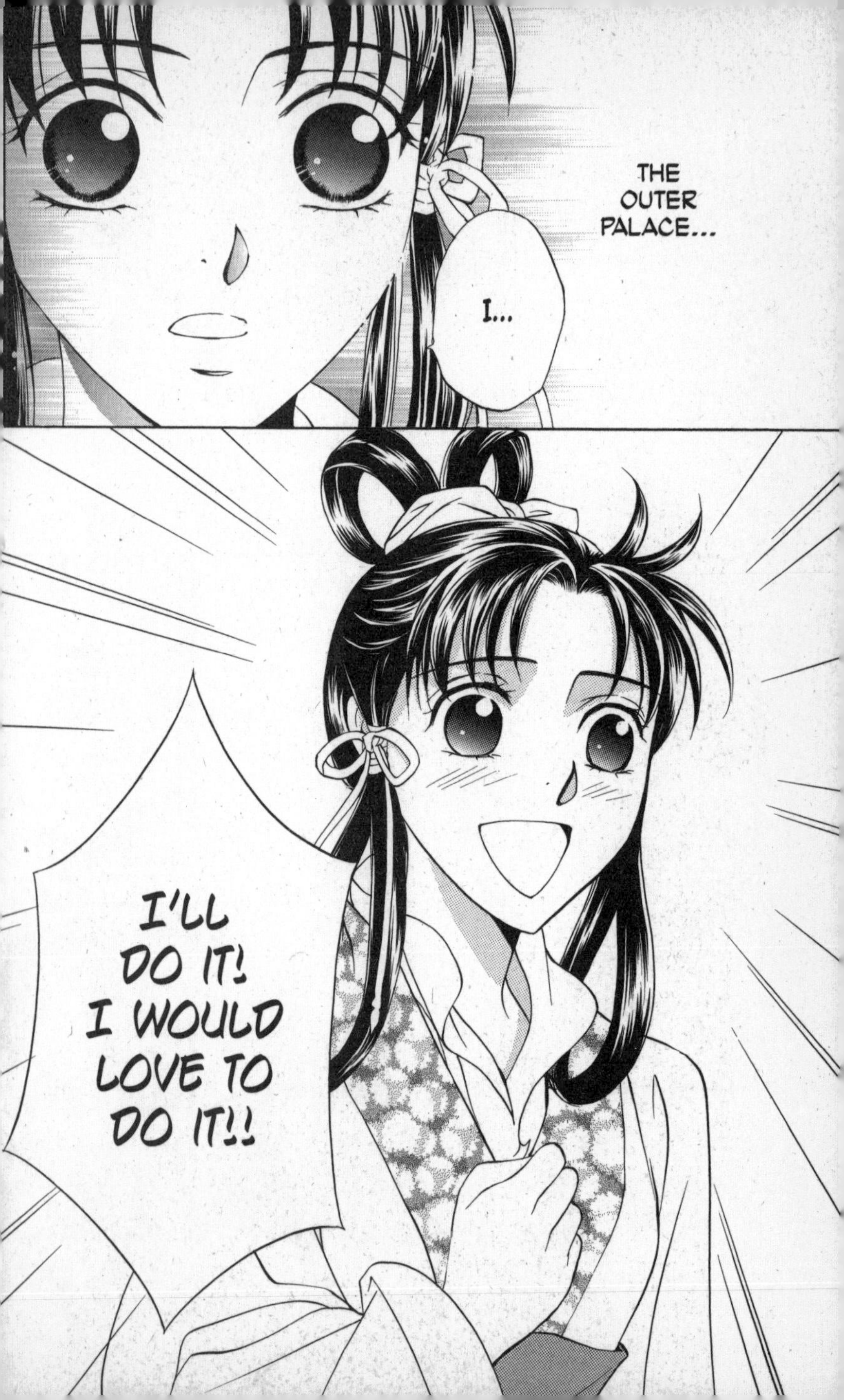
THE OUTER PALACE...
I...
I'LL DO IT! I WOULD LOVE TO DO IT!!

Chapter 10

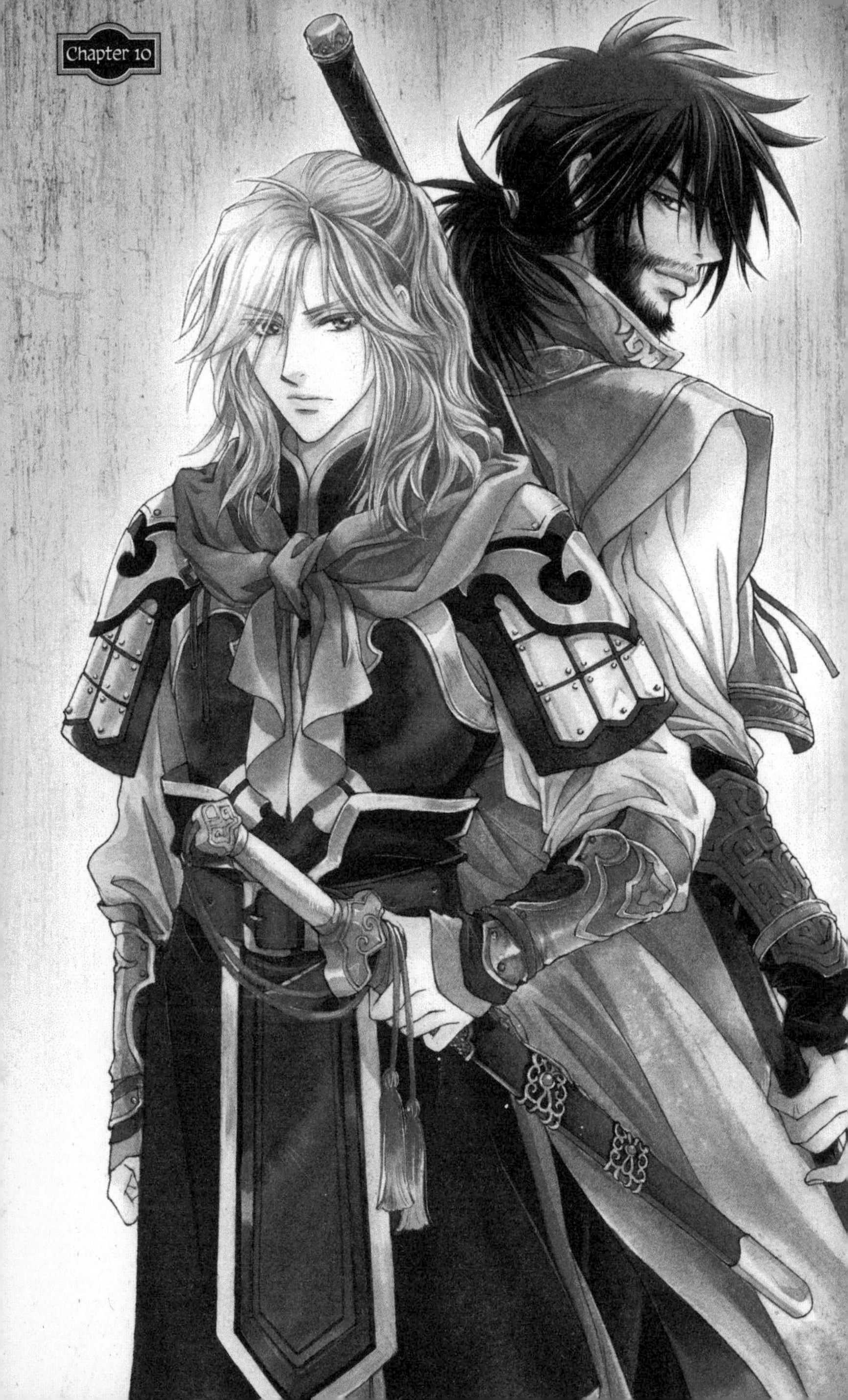

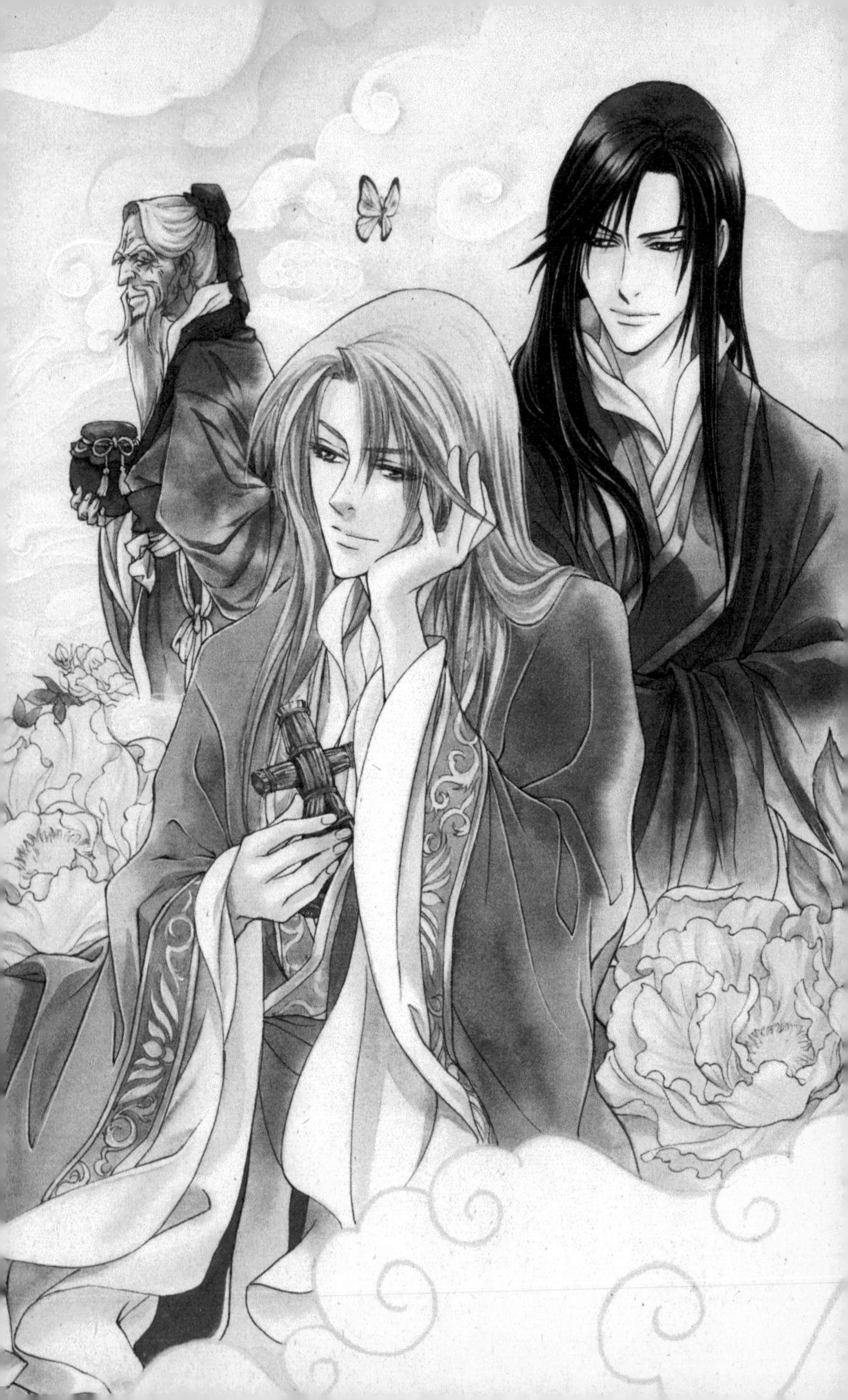

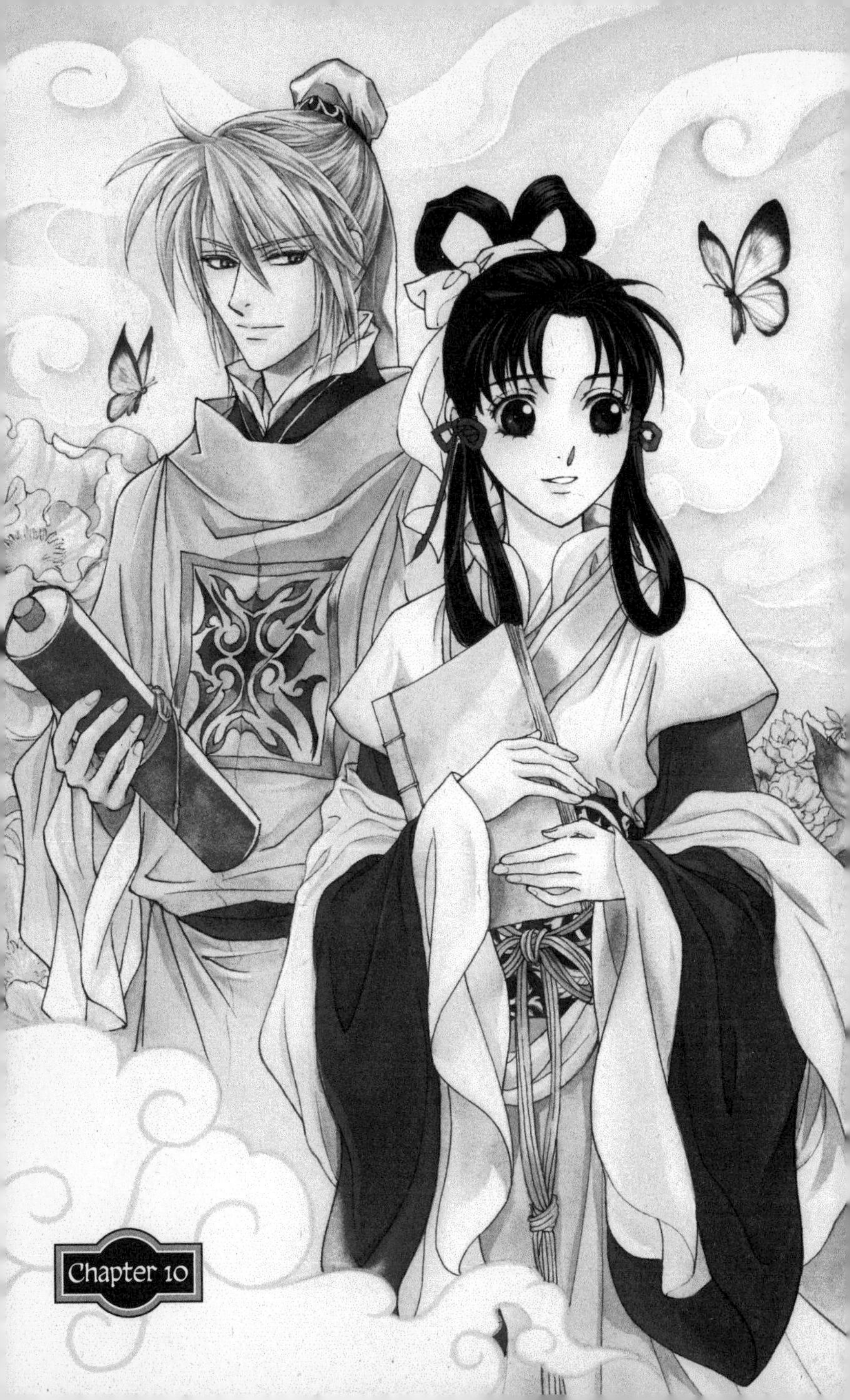
Chapter 10

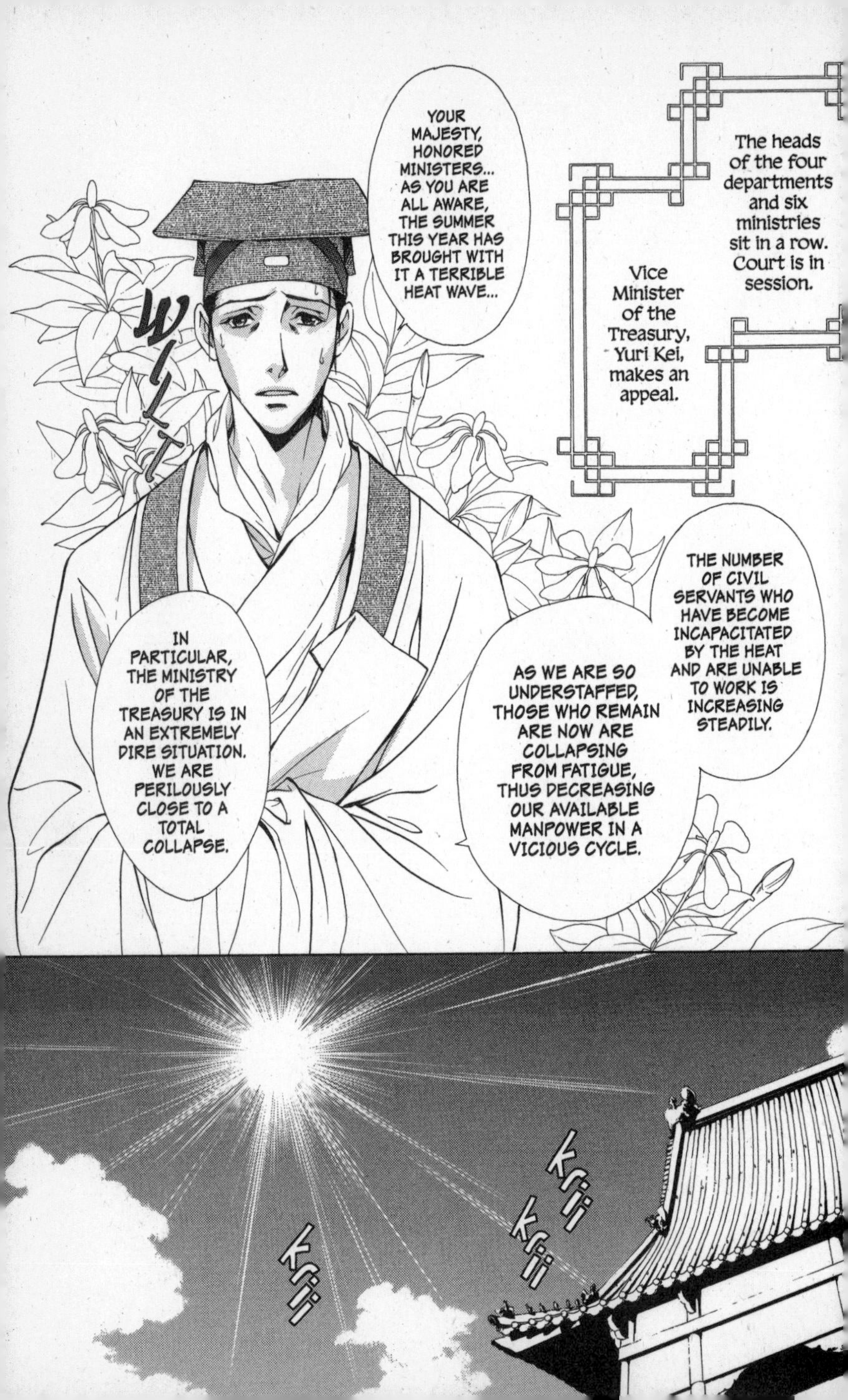
The heads of the four departments and six ministries sit in a row. Court is in session.
Vice Minister of the Treasury, Yuri Kei, makes an appeal.
YOUR MAJESTY, HONORED MINISTERS... AS YOU ARE ALL AWARE, THE SUMMER THIS YEAR HAS BROUGHT WITH IT A TERRIBLE HEAT WAVE...
WILT
THE NUMBER OF CIVIL SERVANTS WHO HAVE BECOME INCAPACITATED BY THE HEAT AND ARE UNABLE TO WORK IS INCREASING STEADILY.
AS WE ARE SO UNDERSTAFFED, THOSE WHO REMAIN ARE NOW ARE COLLAPSING FROM FATIGUE, THUS DECREASING OUR AVAILABLE MANPOWER IN A VICIOUS CYCLE.
IN PARTICULAR, THE MINISTRY OF THE TREASURY IS IN AN EXTREMELY DIRE SITUATION. WE ARE PERILOUSLY CLOSE TO A TOTAL COLLAPSE.
kriii
kriii
kriii

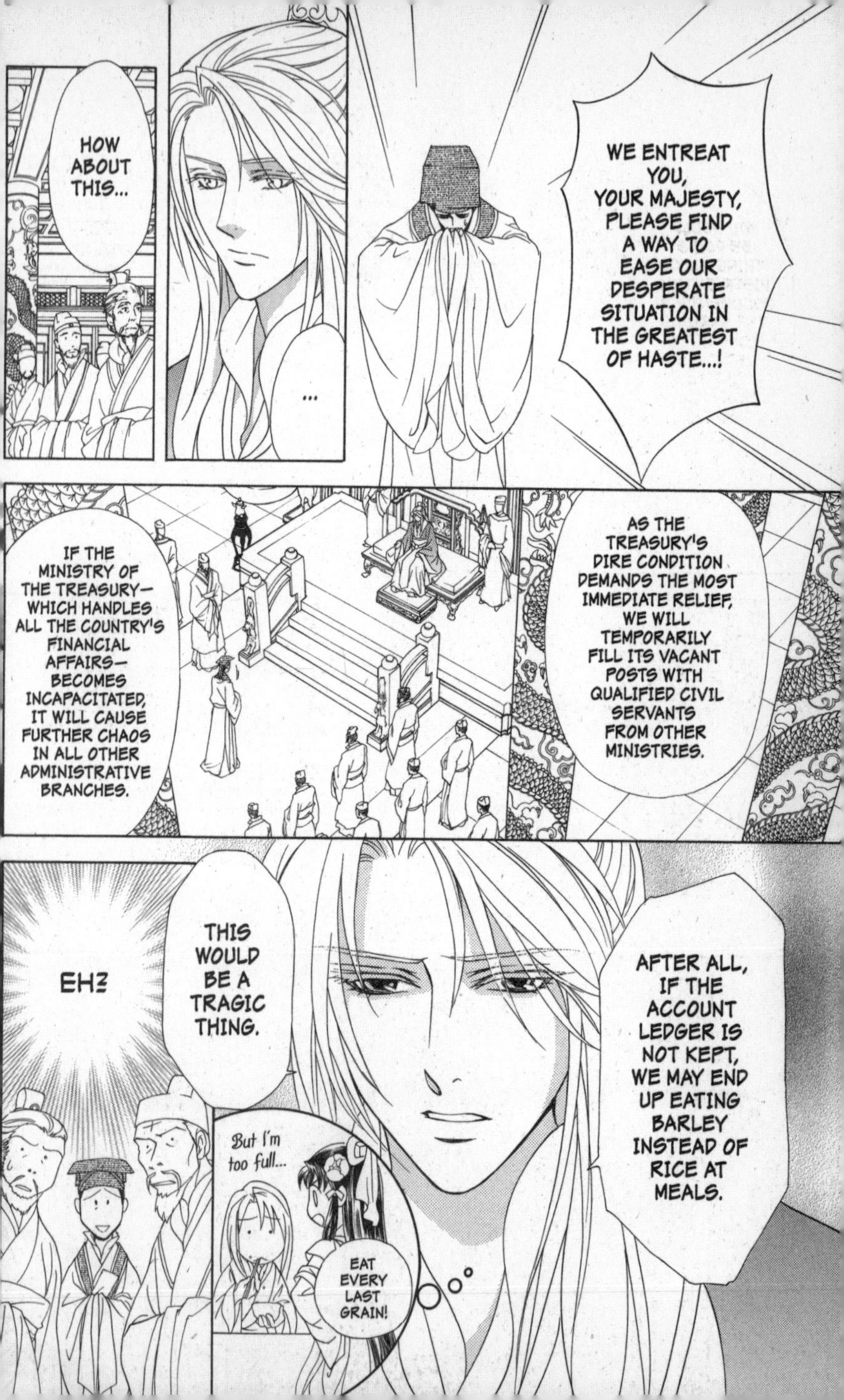
WE ENTREAT YOU, YOUR MAJESTY, PLEASE FIND A WAY TO EASE OUR DESPERATE SITUATION IN THE GREATEST OF HASTE...!
...
HOW ABOUT THIS...
AS THE TREASURY'S DIRE CONDITION DEMANDS THE MOST IMMEDIATE RELIEF, WE WILL TEMPORARILY FILL ITS VACANT POSTS WITH QUALIFIED CIVIL SERVANTS FROM OTHER MINISTRIES.
IF THE MINISTRY OF THE TREASURY—WHICH HANDLES ALL THE COUNTRY'S FINANCIAL AFFAIRS—BECOMES INCAPACITATED, IT WILL CAUSE FURTHER CHAOS IN ALL OTHER ADMINISTRATIVE BRANCHES.
AFTER ALL, IF THE ACCOUNT LEDGER IS NOT KEPT, WE MAY END UP EATING BARLEY INSTEAD OF RICE AT MEALS.
THIS WOULD BE A TRAGIC THING.
EH?
EAT EVERY LAST GRAIN!
But I'm too full...

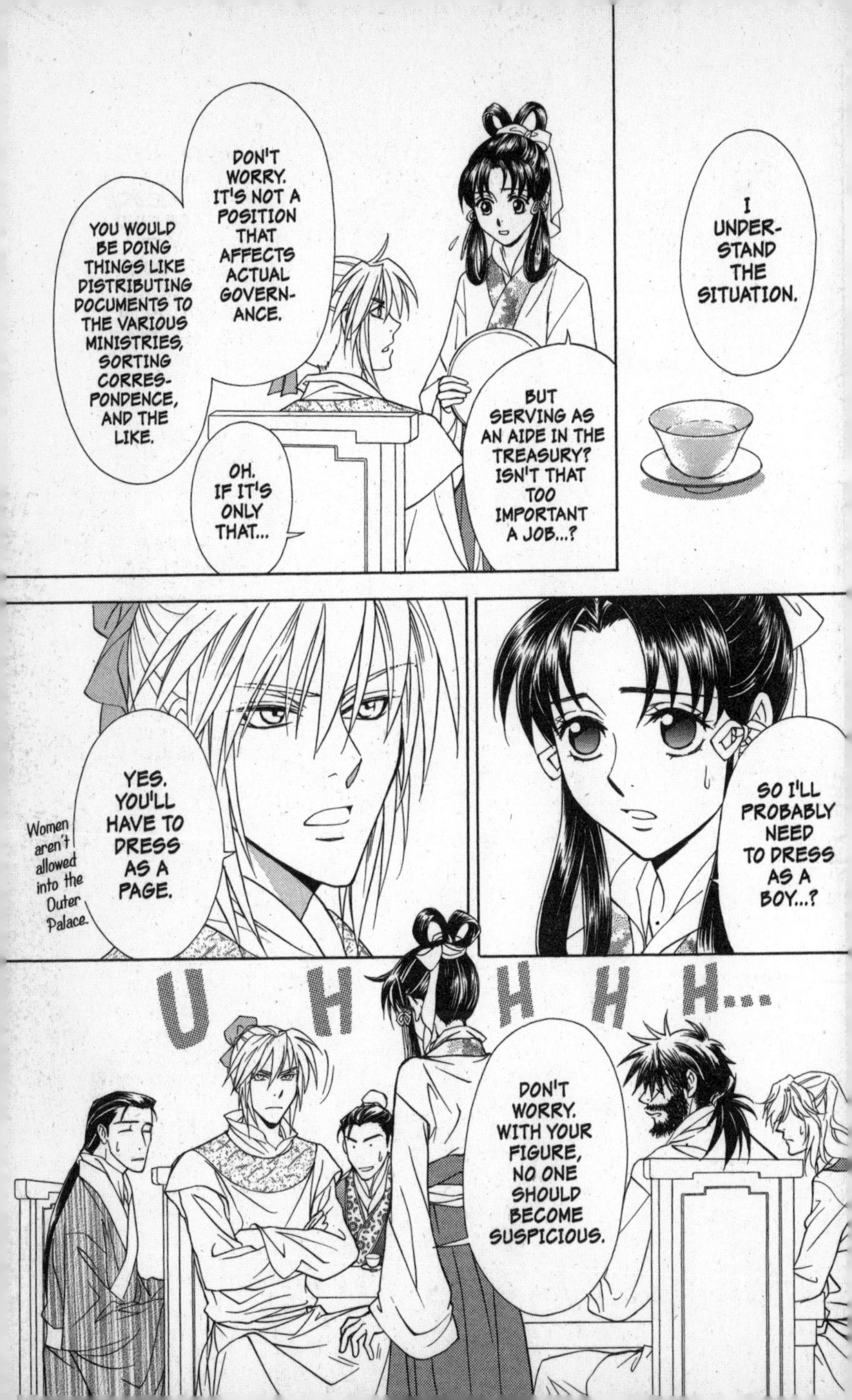
I UNDERSTAND THE SITUATION.
BUT SERVING AS AN AIDE IN THE TREASURY? ISN'T THAT TOO IMPORTANT A JOB...?
DON'T WORRY. IT'S NOT A POSITION THAT AFFECTS ACTUAL GOVERNANCE.
YOU WOULD BE DOING THINGS LIKE DISTRIBUTING DOCUMENTS TO THE VARIOUS MINISTRIES, SORTING CORRESPONDENCE, AND THE LIKE.
OH. IF IT'S ONLY THAT...
SO I'LL PROBABLY NEED TO DRESS AS A BOY...?
YES. YOU'LL HAVE TO DRESS AS A PAGE.
Women aren't allowed into the Outer Palace.
UHHHH...
DON'T WORRY. WITH YOUR FIGURE, NO ONE SHOULD BECOME SUSPICIOUS.

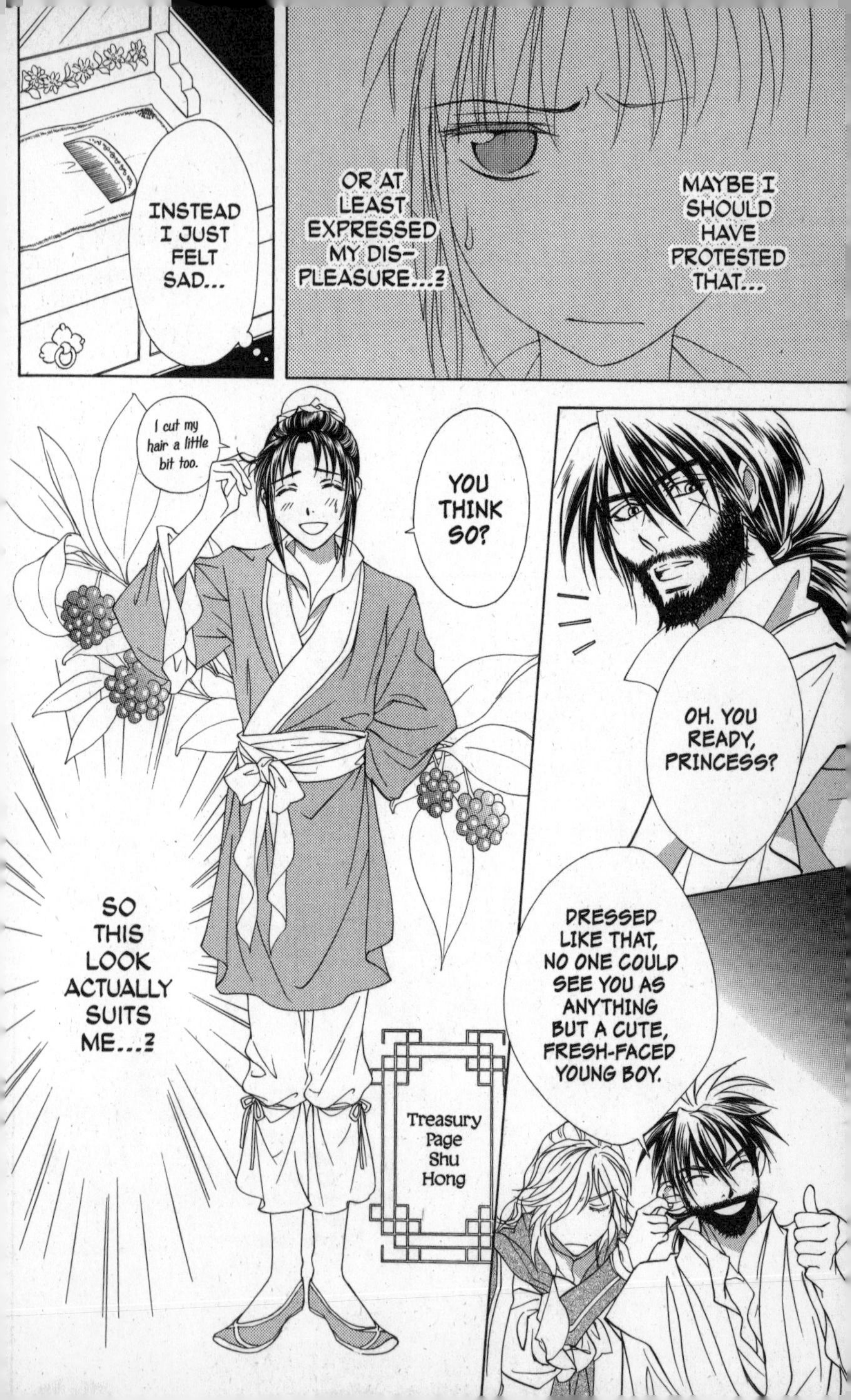
MAYBE I SHOULD HAVE PROTESTED THAT...
OR AT LEAST EXPRESSED MY DIS-PLEASURE...?
INSTEAD I JUST FELT SAD...
OH. YOU READY, PRINCESS?
DRESSED LIKE THAT, NO ONE COULD SEE YOU AS ANYTHING BUT A CUTE, FRESH-FACED YOUNG BOY.
YOU THINK SO?
I cut my hair a little bit too.
SO THIS LOOK ACTUALLY SUITS ME...?
Treasury Page Shu Hong

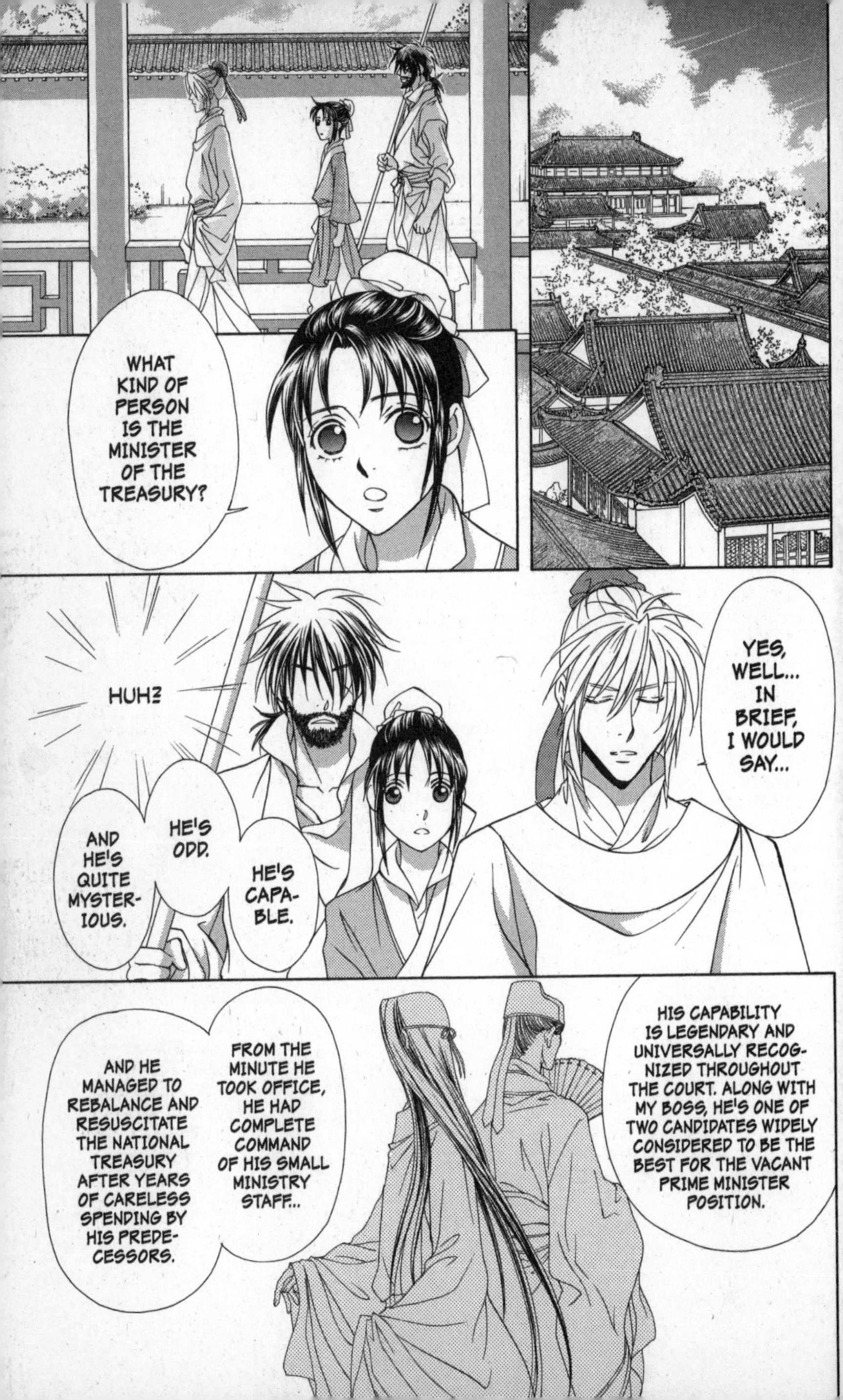
WHAT KIND OF PERSON IS THE MINISTER OF THE TREASURY?
YES, WELL... IN BRIEF, I WOULD SAY...
HE'S CAPABLE.
HE'S ODD.
AND HE'S QUITE MYSTERIOUS.
HUH?
HIS CAPABILITY IS LEGENDARY AND UNIVERSALLY RECOGNIZED THROUGHOUT THE COURT. ALONG WITH MY BOSS, HE'S ONE OF TWO CANDIDATES WIDELY CONSIDERED TO BE THE BEST FOR THE VACANT PRIME MINISTER POSITION.
FROM THE MINUTE HE TOOK OFFICE, HE HAD COMPLETE COMMAND OF HIS SMALL MINISTRY STAFF...
AND HE MANAGED TO REBALANCE AND RESUSCITATE THE NATIONAL TREASURY AFTER YEARS OF CARELESS SPENDING BY HIS PREDECESSORS.

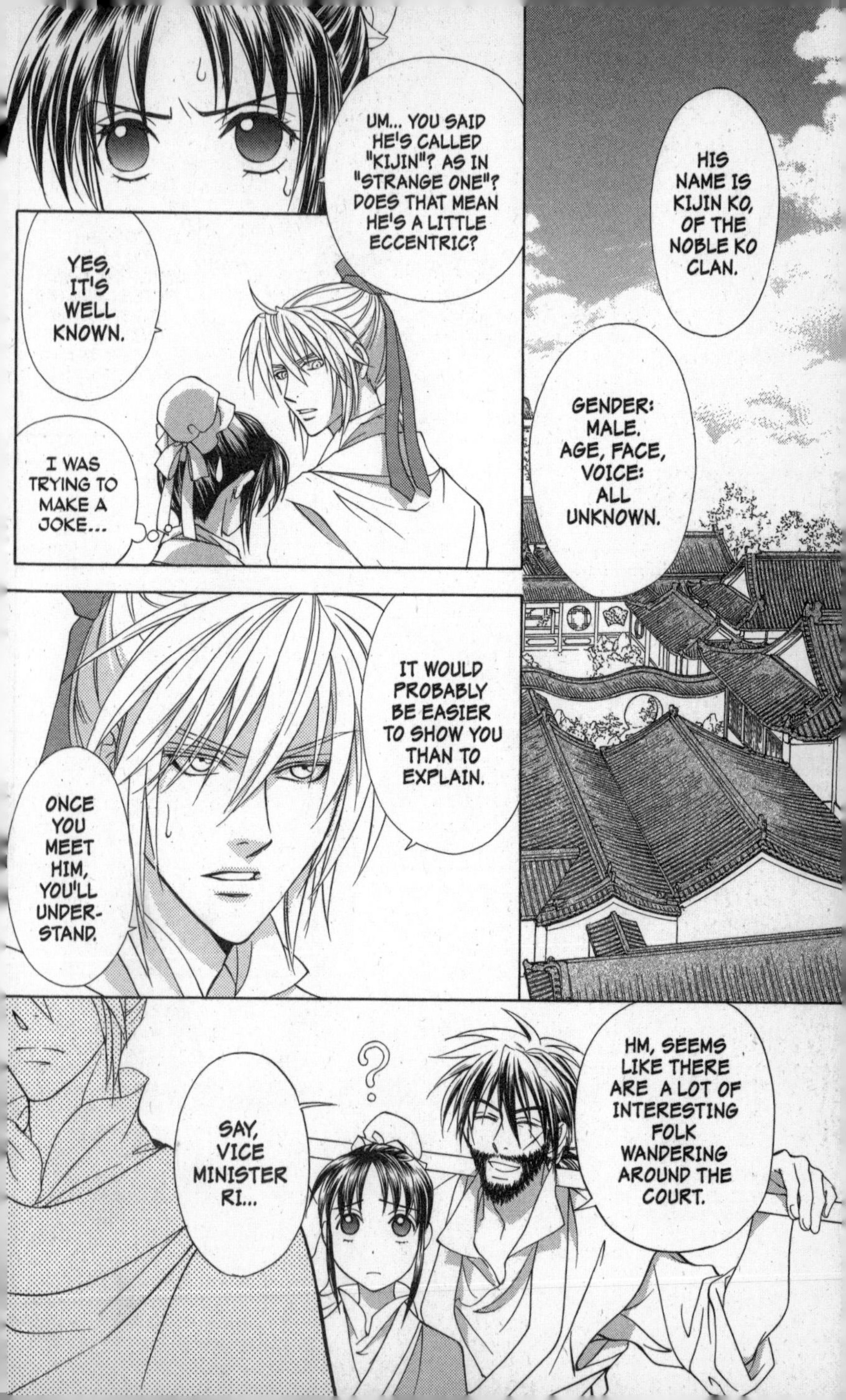
HIS NAME IS KIJIN KO, OF THE NOBLE KO CLAN.
GENDER: MALE. AGE, FACE, VOICE: ALL UNKNOWN.
UM... YOU SAID HE'S CALLED "KIJIN"? AS IN "STRANGE ONE"? DOES THAT MEAN HE'S A LITTLE ECCENTRIC?
YES, IT'S WELL KNOWN.
I WAS TRYING TO MAKE A JOKE...
IT WOULD PROBABLY BE EASIER TO SHOW YOU THAN TO EXPLAIN.
ONCE YOU MEET HIM, YOU'LL UNDER-STAND.
HM, SEEMS LIKE THERE ARE A LOT OF INTERESTING FOLK WANDERING AROUND THE COURT.
?
SAY, VICE MINISTER RI...

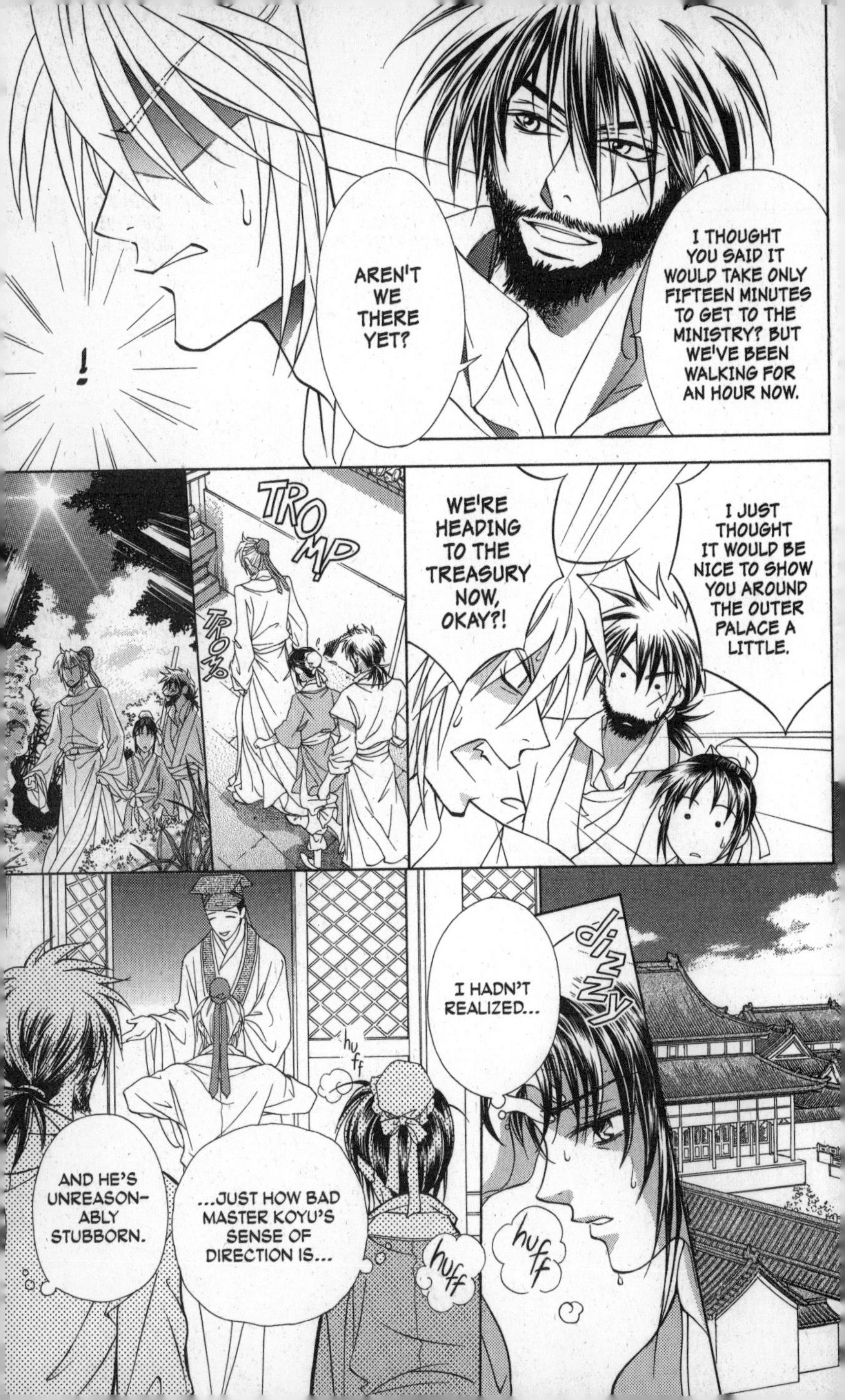
I THOUGHT YOU SAID IT WOULD TAKE ONLY FIFTEEN MINUTES TO GET TO THE MINISTRY? BUT WE'VE BEEN WALKING FOR AN HOUR NOW.
AREN'T WE THERE YET?
!
I JUST THOUGHT IT WOULD BE NICE TO SHOW YOU AROUND THE OUTER PALACE A LITTLE.
WE'RE HEADING TO THE TREASURY NOW, OKAY?!
TROMP
TROMP
dizzy
I HADN'T REALIZED...
huff
huff
huff
...JUST HOW BAD MASTER KOYU'S SENSE OF DIRECTION IS...
AND HE'S UNREASON-ABLY STUBBORN.

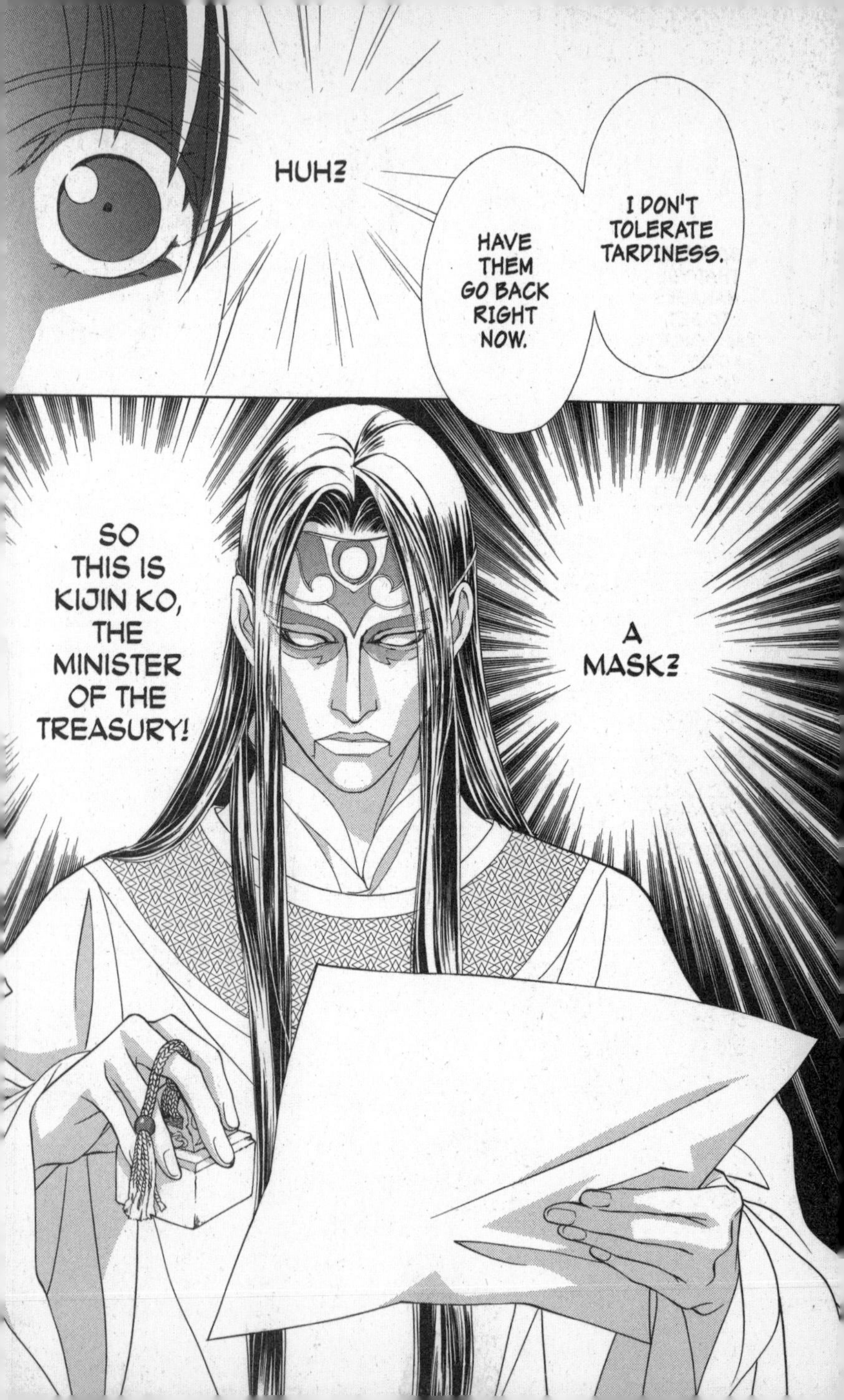
I DON'T TOLERATE TARDINESS.
HAVE THEM GO BACK RIGHT NOW.
HUH?
A MASK?
SO THIS IS KIJIN KO, THE MINISTER OF THE TREASURY!

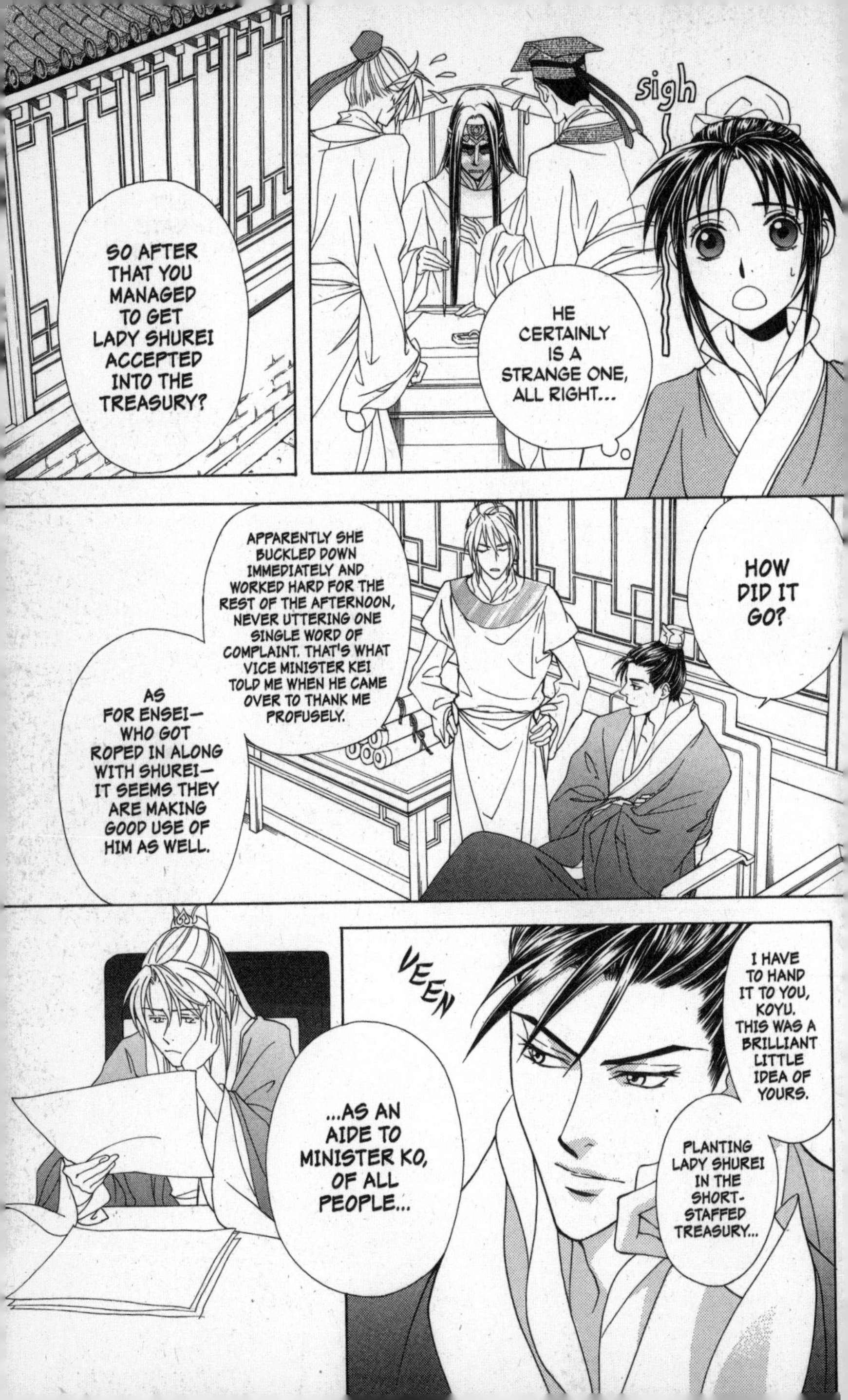
sigh
HE CERTAINLY IS A STRANGE ONE, ALL RIGHT...
SO AFTER THAT YOU MANAGED TO GET LADY SHUREI ACCEPTED INTO THE TREASURY?
HOW DID IT GO?
APPARENTLY SHE BUCKLED DOWN IMMEDIATELY AND WORKED HARD FOR THE REST OF THE AFTERNOON, NEVER UTTERING ONE SINGLE WORD OF COMPLAINT. THAT'S WHAT VICE MINISTER KEI TOLD ME WHEN HE CAME OVER TO THANK ME PROFUSELY.
AS FOR ENSEI—WHO GOT ROPED IN ALONG WITH SHUREI—IT SEEMS THEY ARE MAKING GOOD USE OF HIM AS WELL.
I HAVE TO HAND IT TO YOU, KOYU. THIS WAS A BRILLIANT LITTLE IDEA OF YOURS.
PLANTING LADY SHUREI IN THE SHORT-STAFFED TREASURY...
...AS AN AIDE TO MINISTER KO, OF ALL PEOPLE...
VEEN

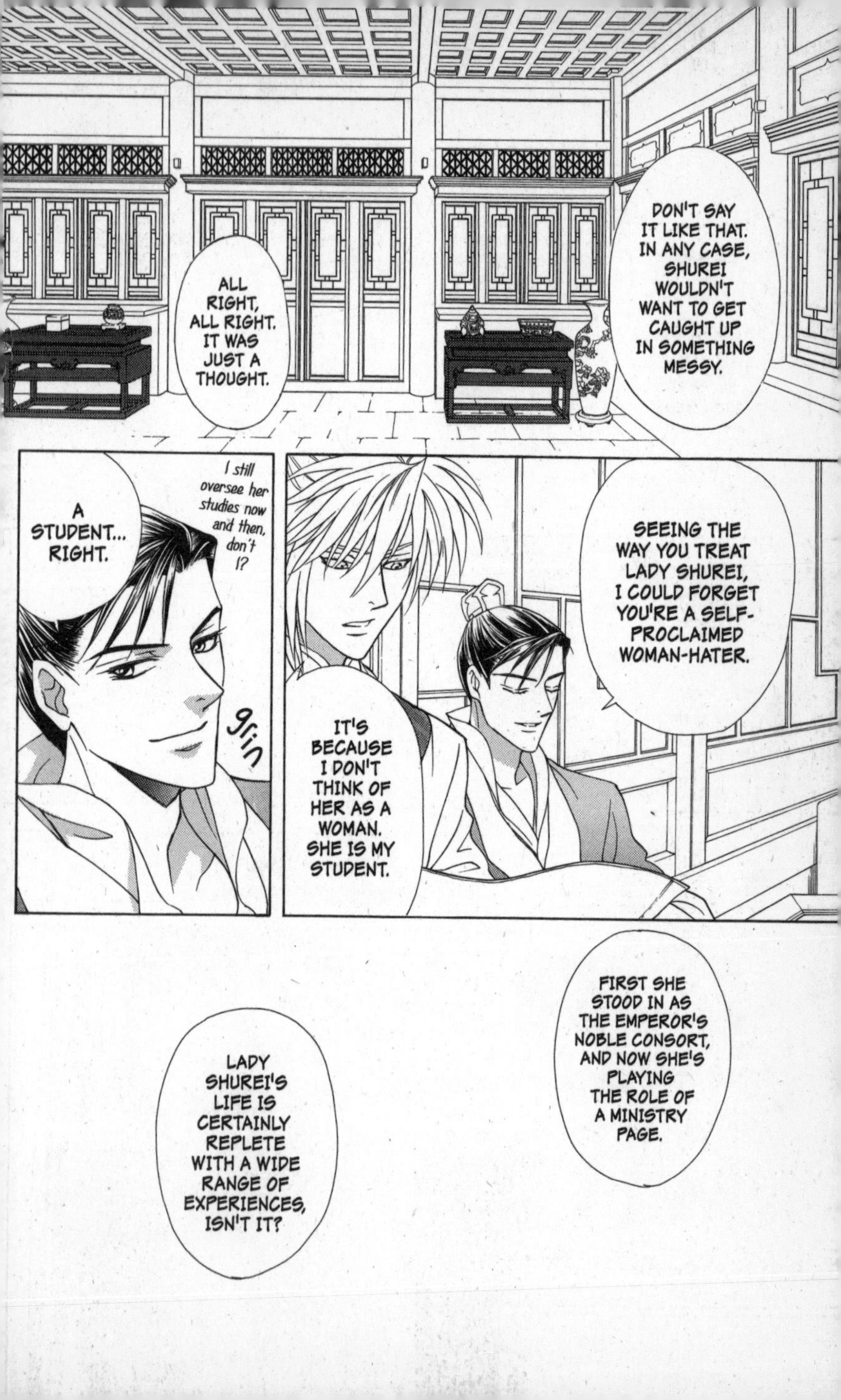
DON'T SAY IT LIKE THAT. IN ANY CASE, SHUREI WOULDN'T WANT TO GET CAUGHT UP IN SOMETHING MESSY.
ALL RIGHT, ALL RIGHT. IT WAS JUST A THOUGHT.
SEEING THE WAY YOU TREAT LADY SHUREI, I COULD FORGET YOU'RE A SELF-PROCLAIMED WOMAN-HATER.
IT'S BECAUSE I DON'T THINK OF HER AS A WOMAN. SHE IS MY STUDENT.
A STUDENT... RIGHT.
I still oversee her studies now and then, don't I?
grin
FIRST SHE STOOD IN AS THE EMPEROR'S NOBLE CONSORT, AND NOW SHE'S PLAYING THE ROLE OF A MINISTRY PAGE.
LADY SHUREI'S LIFE IS CERTAINLY REPLETE WITH A WIDE RANGE OF EXPERIENCES, ISN'T IT?

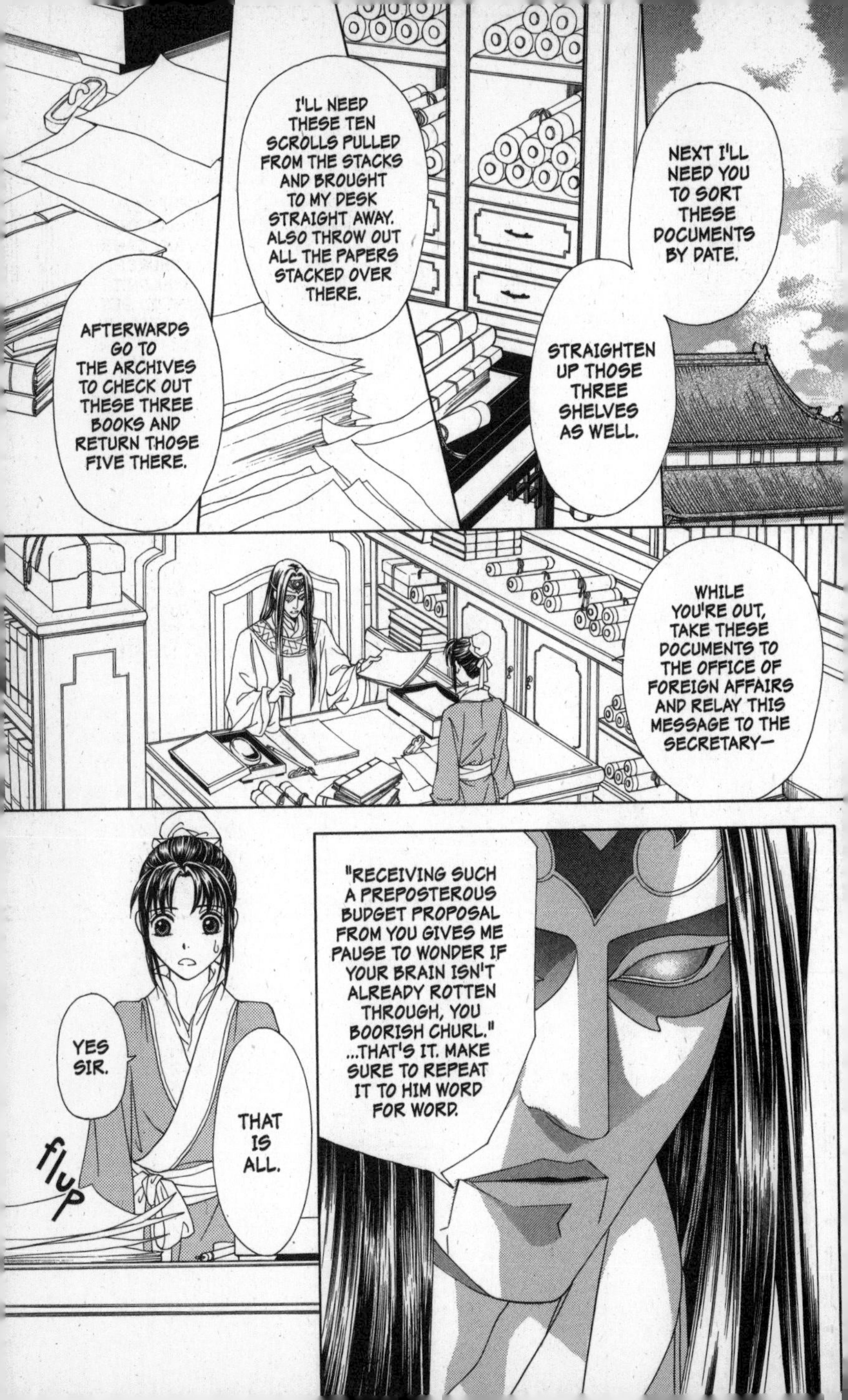
NEXT I'LL NEED YOU TO SORT THESE DOCUMENTS BY DATE.
STRAIGHTEN UP THOSE THREE SHELVES AS WELL.
I'LL NEED THESE TEN SCROLLS PULLED FROM THE STACKS AND BROUGHT TO MY DESK STRAIGHT AWAY. ALSO THROW OUT ALL THE PAPERS STACKED OVER THERE.
AFTERWARDS GO TO THE ARCHIVES TO CHECK OUT THESE THREE BOOKS AND RETURN THOSE FIVE THERE.
WHILE YOU'RE OUT, TAKE THESE DOCUMENTS TO THE OFFICE OF FOREIGN AFFAIRS AND RELAY THIS MESSAGE TO THE SECRETARY—
"RECEIVING SUCH A PREPOSTEROUS BUDGET PROPOSAL FROM YOU GIVES ME PAUSE TO WONDER IF YOUR BRAIN ISN'T ALREADY ROTTEN THROUGH, YOU BOORISH CHURL." ...THAT'S IT. MAKE SURE TO REPEAT IT TO HIM WORD FOR WORD.
THAT IS ALL.
YES SIR.
flup

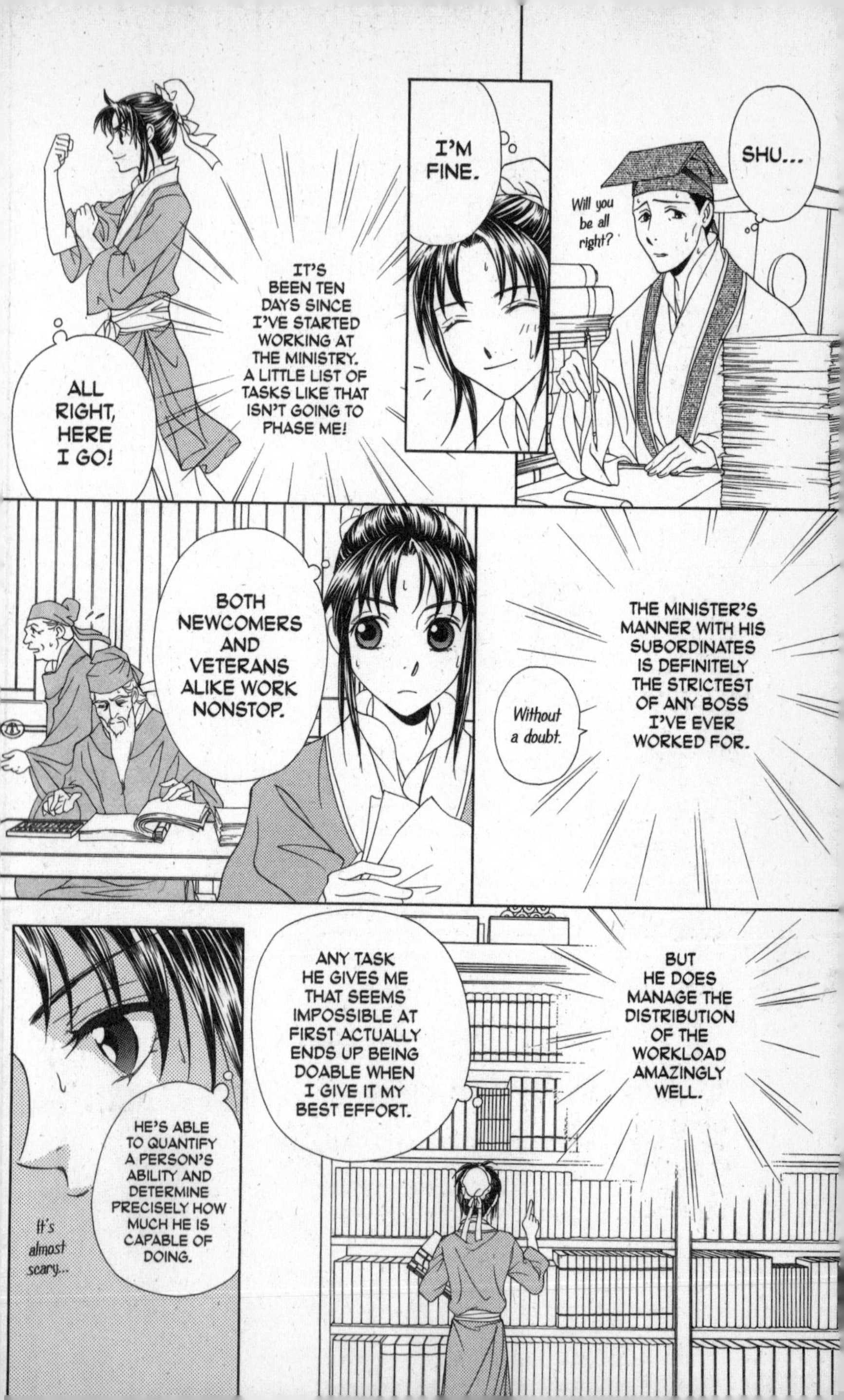
SHU...
Will you be all right?
I'M FINE.
IT'S BEEN TEN DAYS SINCE I'VE STARTED WORKING AT THE MINISTRY. A LITTLE LIST OF TASKS LIKE THAT ISN'T GOING TO PHASE ME!
ALL RIGHT, HERE I GO!
THE MINISTER'S MANNER WITH HIS SUBORDINATES IS DEFINITELY THE STRICTEST OF ANY BOSS I'VE EVER WORKED FOR.
Without a doubt.
BOTH NEWCOMERS AND VETERANS ALIKE WORK NONSTOP.
BUT HE DOES MANAGE THE DISTRIBUTION OF THE WORKLOAD AMAZINGLY WELL.
ANY TASK HE GIVES ME THAT SEEMS IMPOSSIBLE AT FIRST ACTUALLY ENDS UP BEING DOABLE WHEN I GIVE IT MY BEST EFFORT.
HE'S ABLE TO QUANTIFY A PERSON'S ABILITY AND DETERMINE PRECISELY HOW MUCH HE IS CAPABLE OF DOING.
It's almost scary...

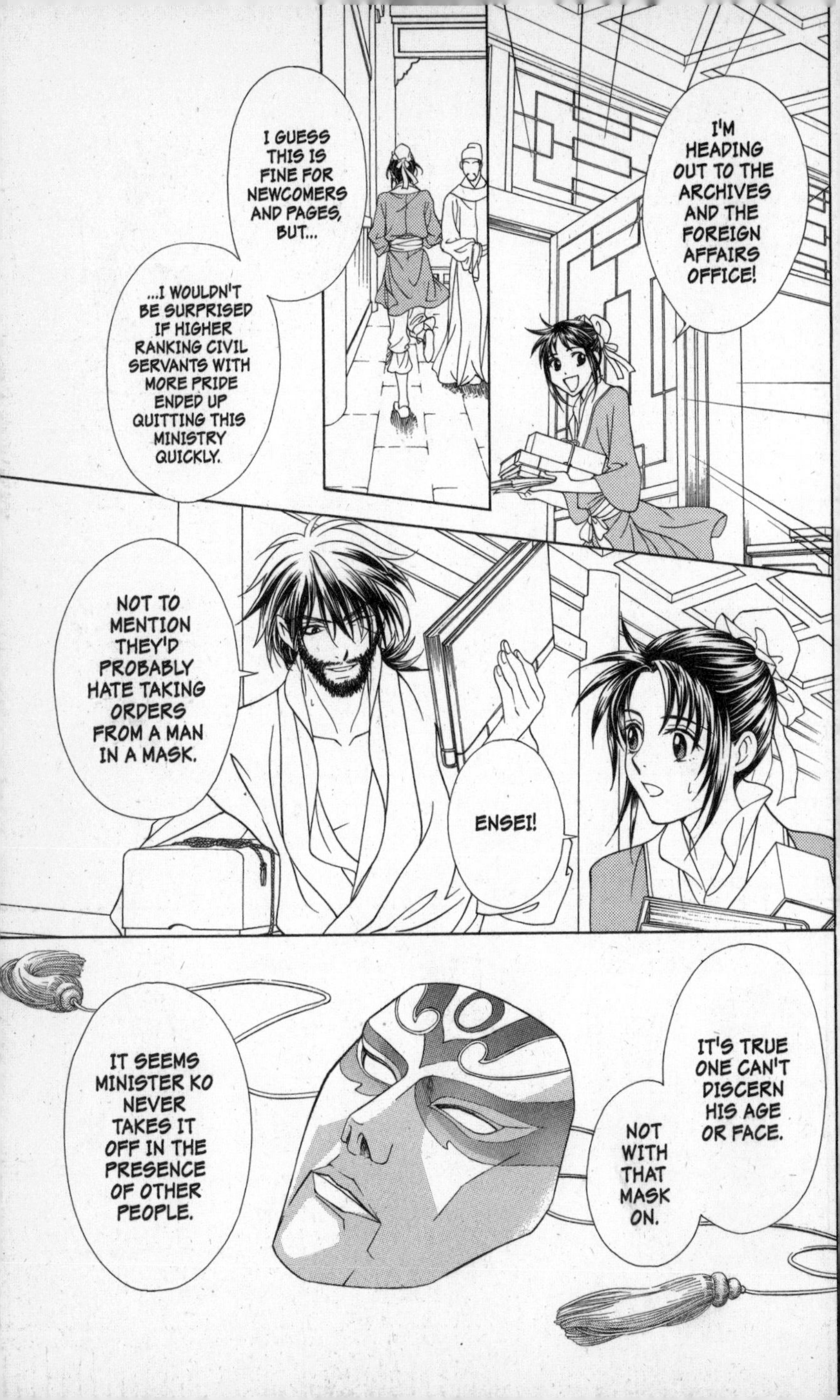
I'M HEADING OUT TO THE ARCHIVES AND THE FOREIGN AFFAIRS OFFICE!
I GUESS THIS IS FINE FOR NEWCOMERS AND PAGES, BUT...
...I WOULDN'T BE SURPRISED IF HIGHER RANKING CIVIL SERVANTS WITH MORE PRIDE ENDED UP QUITTING THIS MINISTRY QUICKLY.
NOT TO MENTION THEY'D PROBABLY HATE TAKING ORDERS FROM A MAN IN A MASK.
ENSEI!
IT'S TRUE ONE CAN'T DISCERN HIS AGE OR FACE.
NOT WITH THAT MASK ON.
IT SEEMS MINISTER KO NEVER TAKES IT OFF IN THE PRESENCE OF OTHER PEOPLE.

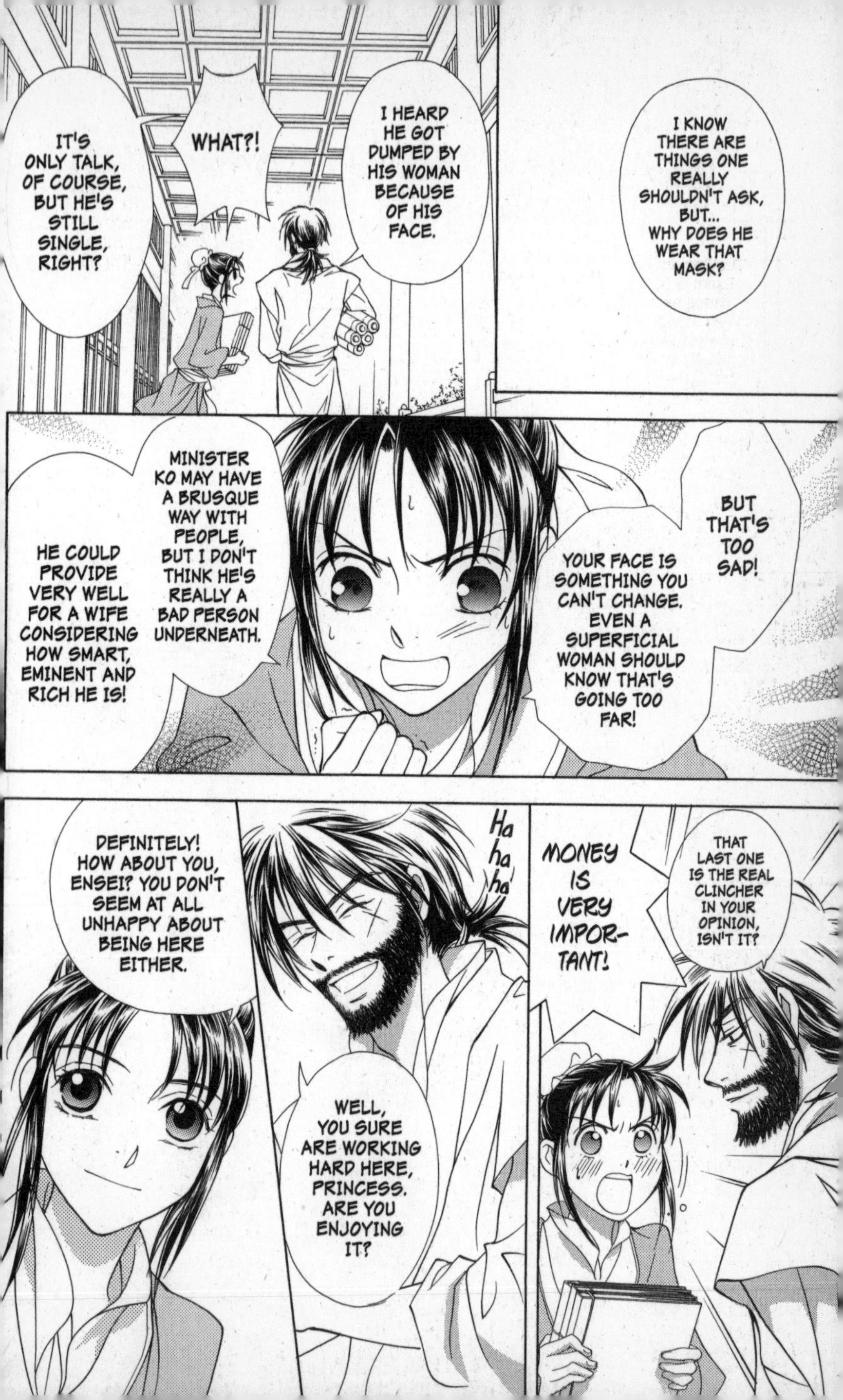
I KNOW THERE ARE THINGS ONE REALLY SHOULDN'T ASK, BUT... WHY DOES HE WEAR THAT MASK?
I HEARD HE GOT DUMPED BY HIS WOMAN BECAUSE OF HIS FACE.
WHAT?!
IT'S ONLY TALK, OF COURSE, BUT HE'S STILL SINGLE, RIGHT?
BUT THAT'S TOO SAD!
YOUR FACE IS SOMETHING YOU CAN'T CHANGE. EVEN A SUPERFICIAL WOMAN SHOULD KNOW THAT'S GOING TOO FAR!
MINISTER KO MAY HAVE A BRUSQUE WAY WITH PEOPLE, BUT I DON'T THINK HE'S REALLY A BAD PERSON UNDERNEATH.
HE COULD PROVIDE VERY WELL FOR A WIFE CONSIDERING HOW SMART, EMINENT AND RICH HE IS!
THAT LAST ONE IS THE REAL CLINCHER IN YOUR OPINION, ISN'T IT?
MONEY IS VERY IMPORTANT!
Ha ha ha
WELL, YOU SURE ARE WORKING HARD HERE, PRINCESS. ARE YOU ENJOYING IT?
DEFINITELY! HOW ABOUT YOU, ENSEI? YOU DON'T SEEM AT ALL UNHAPPY ABOUT BEING HERE EITHER.

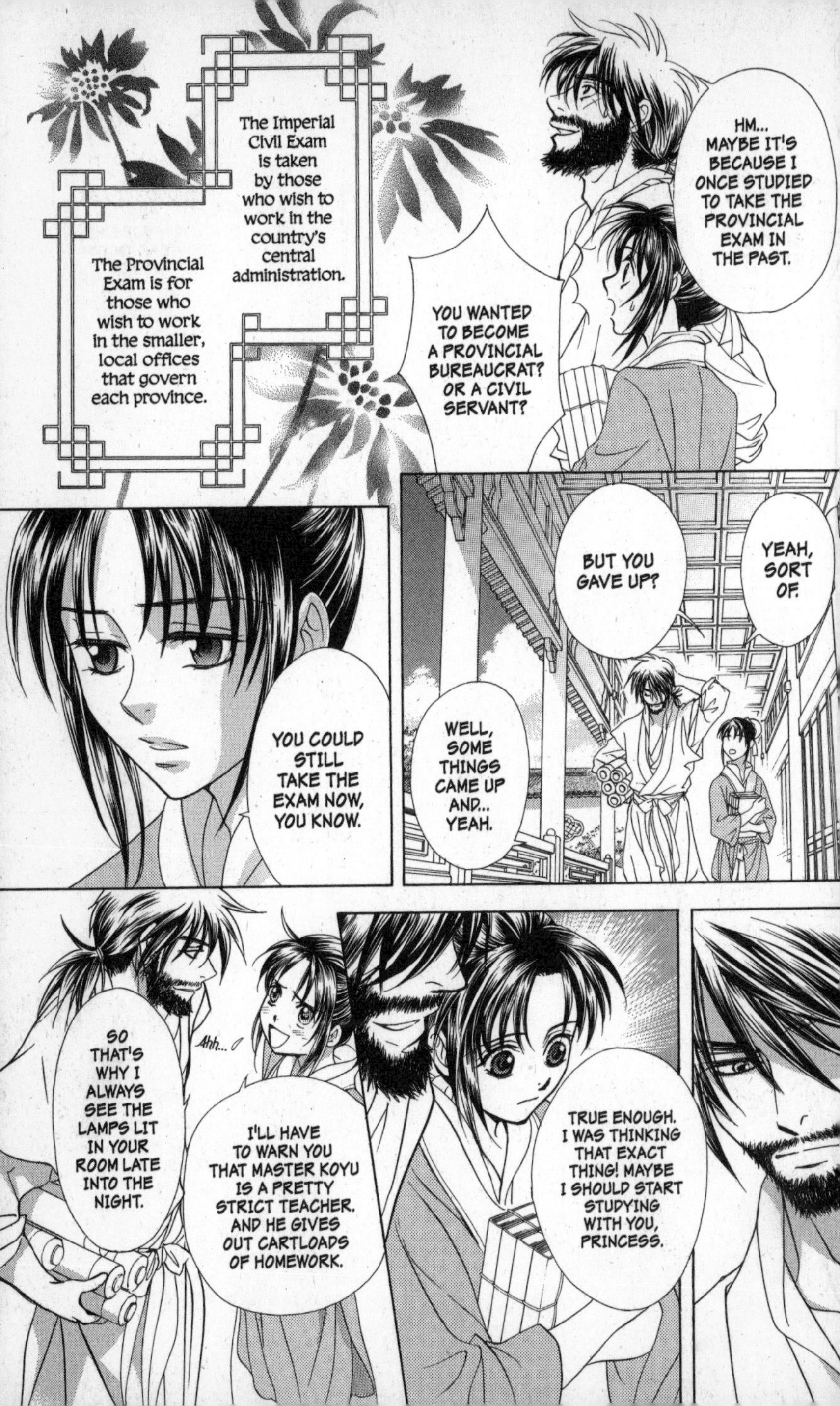
HM... MAYBE IT'S BECAUSE I ONCE STUDIED TO TAKE THE PROVINCIAL EXAM IN THE PAST.
YOU WANTED TO BECOME A PROVINCIAL BUREAUCRAT? OR A CIVIL SERVANT?
The Imperial Civil Exam is taken by those who wish to work in the country's central administration.
The Provincial Exam is for those who wish to work in the smaller, local offices that govern each province.
BUT YOU GAVE UP?
YEAH, SORT OF.
WELL, SOME THINGS CAME UP AND... YEAH.
YOU COULD STILL TAKE THE EXAM NOW, YOU KNOW.
TRUE ENOUGH. I WAS THINKING THAT EXACT THING! MAYBE I SHOULD START STUDYING WITH YOU, PRINCESS.
Ahh...
SO THAT'S WHY I ALWAYS SEE THE LAMPS LIT IN YOUR ROOM LATE INTO THE NIGHT.
I'LL HAVE TO WARN YOU THAT MASTER KOYU IS A PRETTY STRICT TEACHER. AND HE GIVES OUT CARTLOADS OF HOMEWORK.

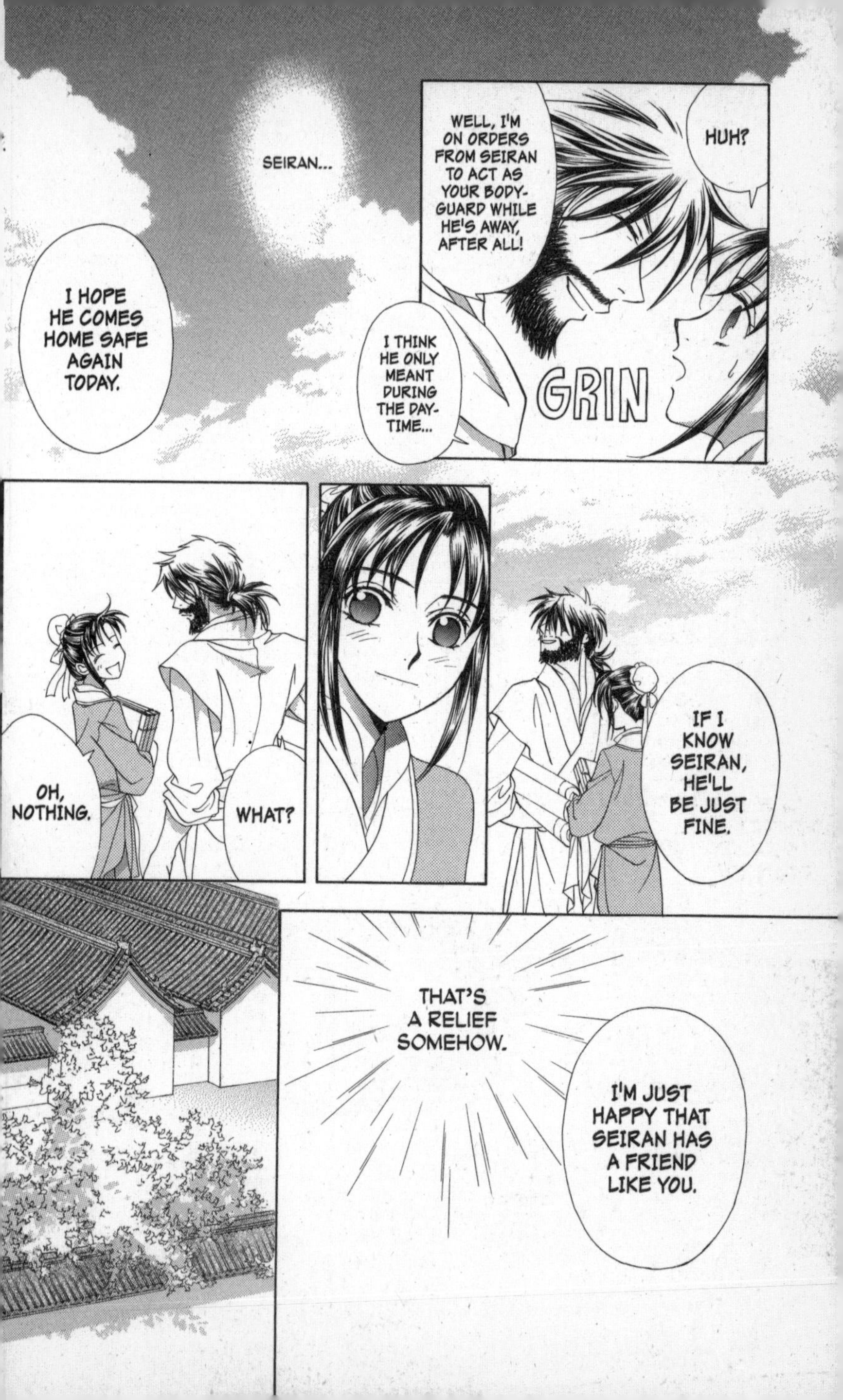
HUH?
WELL, I'M ON ORDERS FROM SEIRAN TO ACT AS YOUR BODY-GUARD WHILE HE'S AWAY, AFTER ALL!
GRIN
I THINK HE ONLY MEANT DURING THE DAY-TIME...
SEIRAN...
I HOPE HE COMES HOME SAFE AGAIN TODAY.
IF I KNOW SEIRAN, HE'LL BE JUST FINE.
WHAT?
OH, NOTHING.
I'M JUST HAPPY THAT SEIRAN HAS A FRIEND LIKE YOU.
THAT'S A RELIEF SOMEHOW.

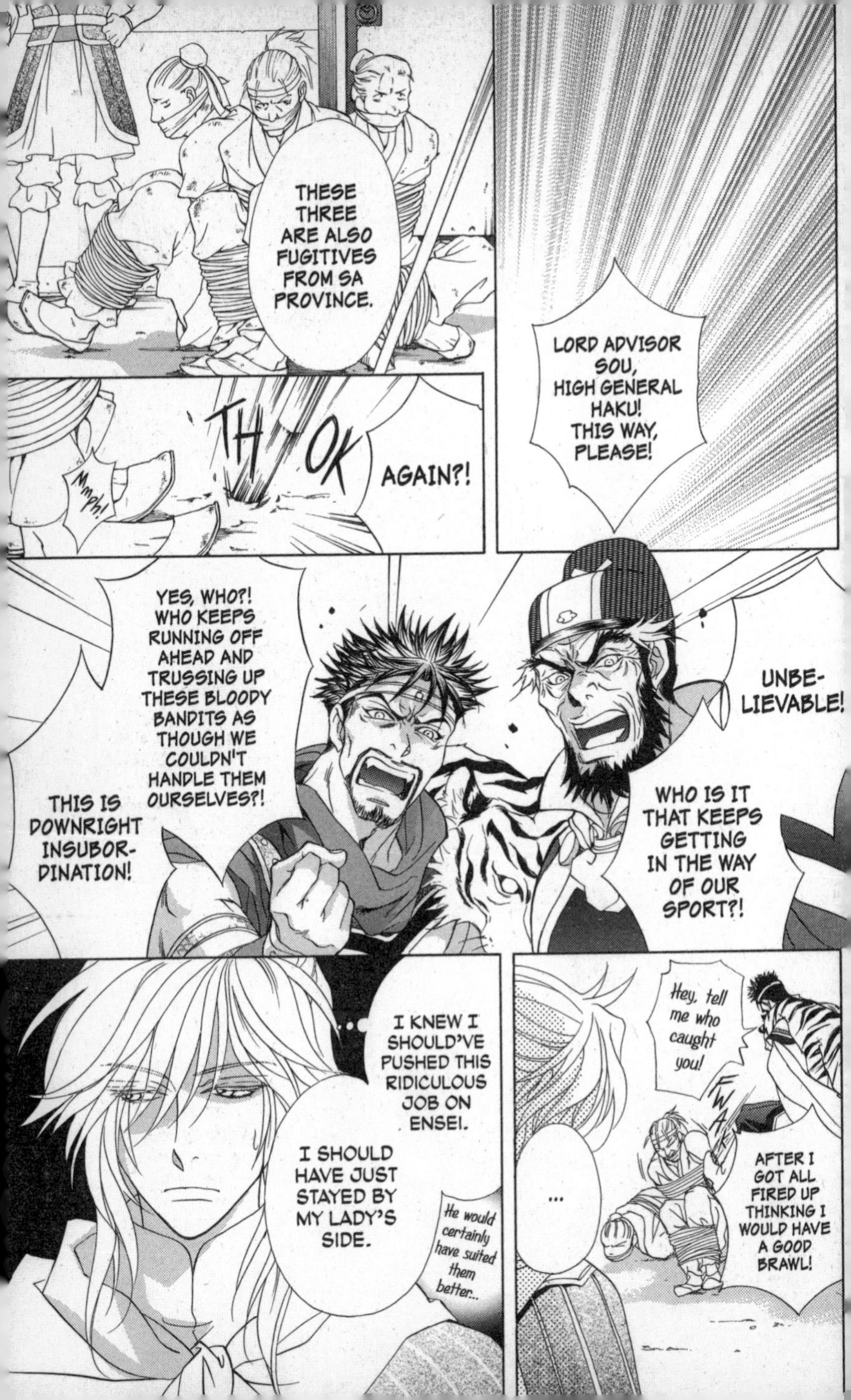
LORD ADVISOR SOU, HIGH GENERAL HAKU! THIS WAY, PLEASE!
THESE THREE ARE ALSO FUGITIVES FROM SA PROVINCE.
AGAIN?!
THTOK
Mmph!
UNBE-LIEVABLE!
WHO IS IT THAT KEEPS GETTING IN THE WAY OF OUR SPORT?!
YES, WHO?! WHO KEEPS RUNNING OFF AHEAD AND TRUSSING UP THESE BLOODY BANDITS AS THOUGH WE COULDN'T HANDLE THEM OURSELVES?!
THIS IS DOWNRIGHT INSUBORDINATION!
Hey, tell me who caught you!
FWAK
AFTER I GOT ALL FIRED UP THINKING I WOULD HAVE A GOOD BRAWL!
...
...
I KNEW I SHOULD'VE PUSHED THIS RIDICULOUS JOB ON ENSEI.
I SHOULD HAVE JUST STAYED BY MY LADY'S SIDE.
He would certainly have suited them better...

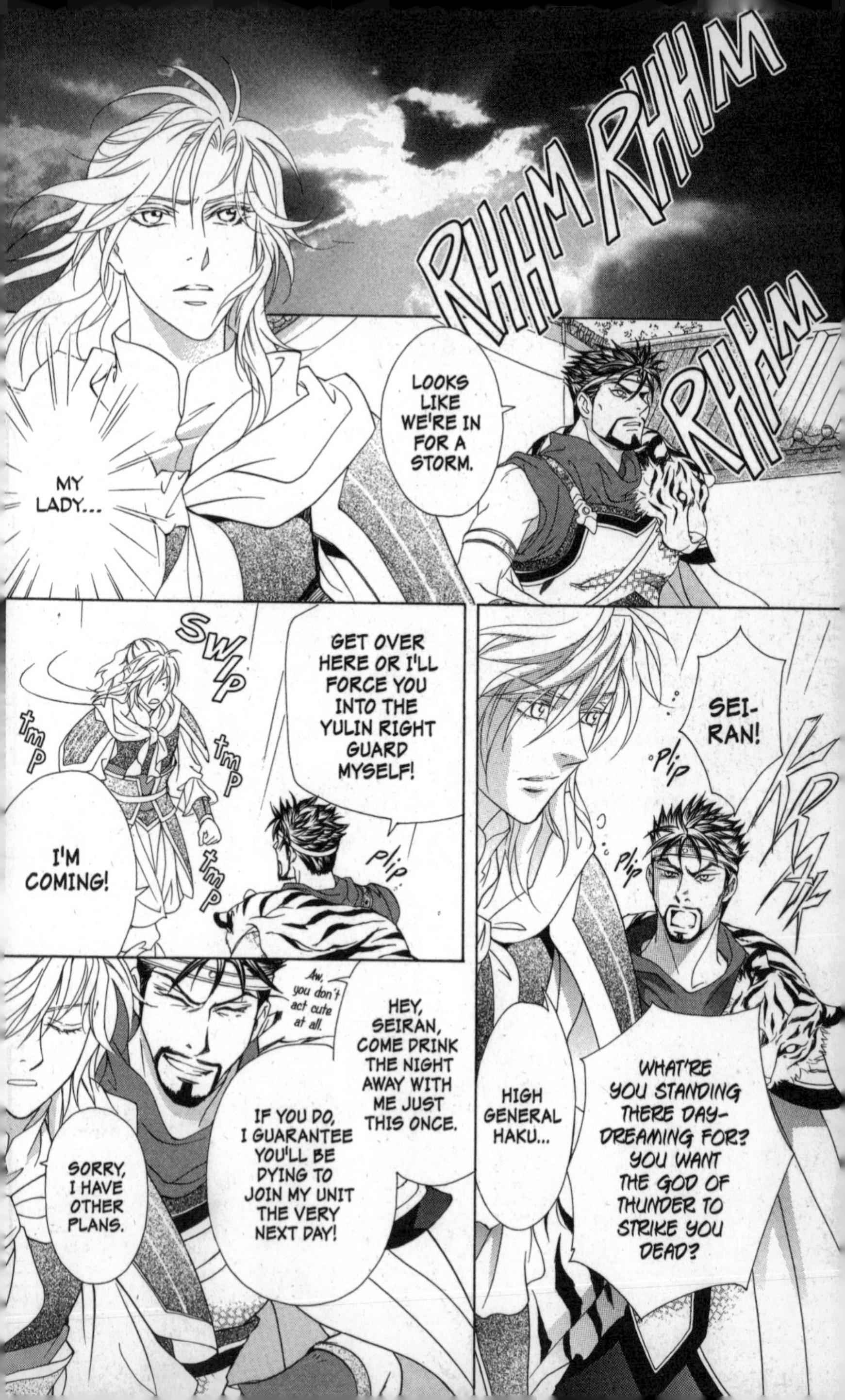
RHHM RHHM
RHHM
RHHM
LOOKS LIKE WE'RE IN FOR A STORM.
MY LADY...
SEI-RAN!
KRAK
plip
plip
WHAT'RE YOU STANDING THERE DAY-DREAMING FOR? YOU WANT THE GOD OF THUNDER TO STRIKE YOU DEAD?
HIGH GENERAL HAKU...
GET OVER HERE OR I'LL FORCE YOU INTO THE YULIN RIGHT GUARD MYSELF!
SWIP
plip
tmp
tmp
tmp
I'M COMING!
HEY, SEIRAN, COME DRINK THE NIGHT AWAY WITH ME JUST THIS ONCE.
Aw, you don't act cute at all.
IF YOU DO, I GUARANTEE YOU'LL BE DYING TO JOIN MY UNIT THE VERY NEXT DAY!
SORRY, I HAVE OTHER PLANS.

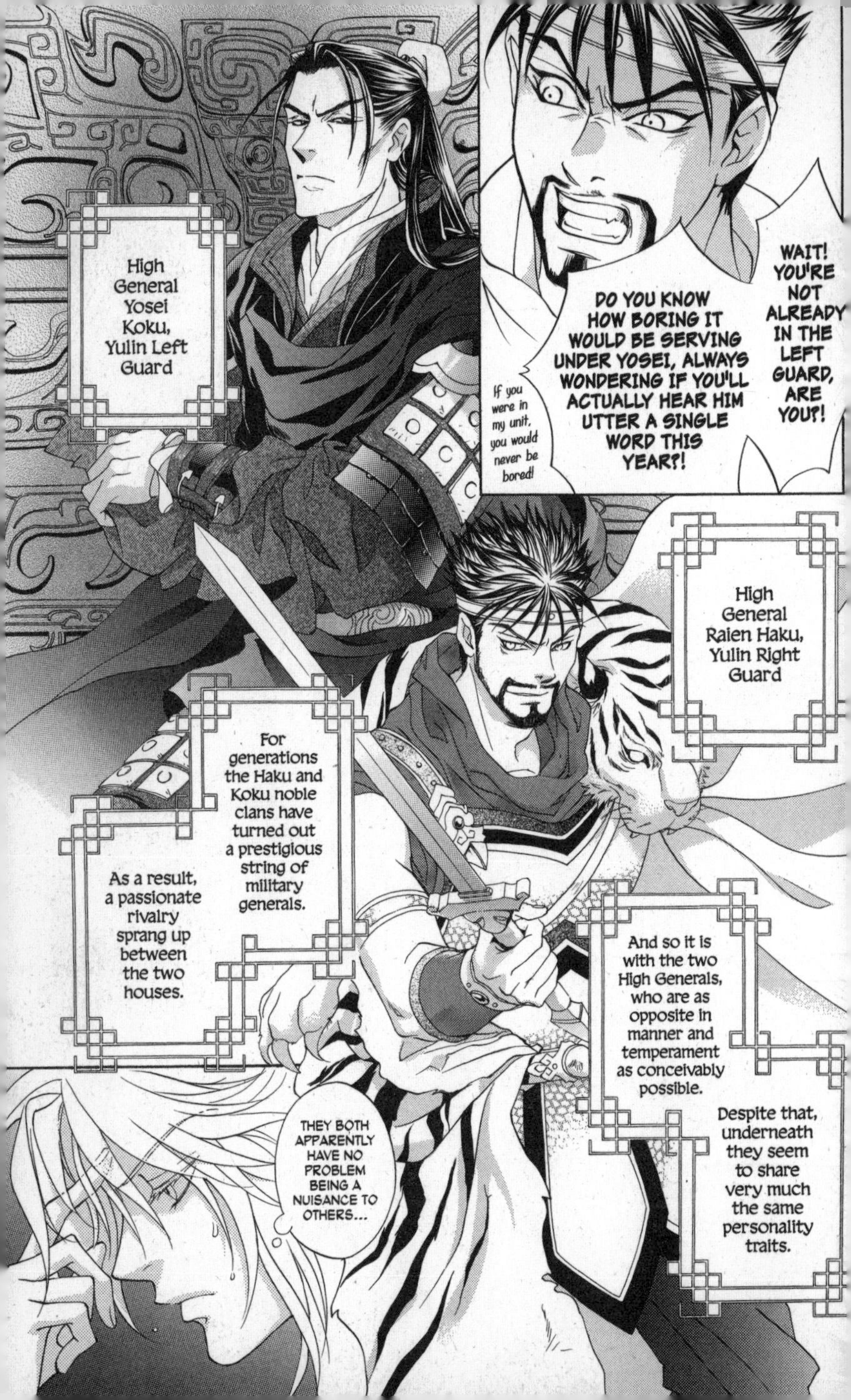
WAIT! YOU'RE NOT ALREADY IN THE LEFT GUARD, ARE YOU?!
DO YOU KNOW HOW BORING IT WOULD BE SERVING UNDER YOSEI, ALWAYS WONDERING IF YOU'LL ACTUALLY HEAR HIM UTTER A SINGLE WORD THIS YEAR?!
If you were in my unit, you would never be bored!
High General Yosei Koku, Yulin Left Guard
High General Raien Haku, Yulin Right Guard
For generations the Haku and Koku noble clans have turned out a prestigious string of military generals.
As a result, a passionate rivalry sprang up between the two houses.
And so it is with the two High Generals, who are as opposite in manner and temperament as conceivably possible.
Despite that, underneath they seem to share very much the same personality traits.
THEY BOTH APPARENTLY HAVE NO PROBLEM BEING A NUISANCE TO OTHERS...

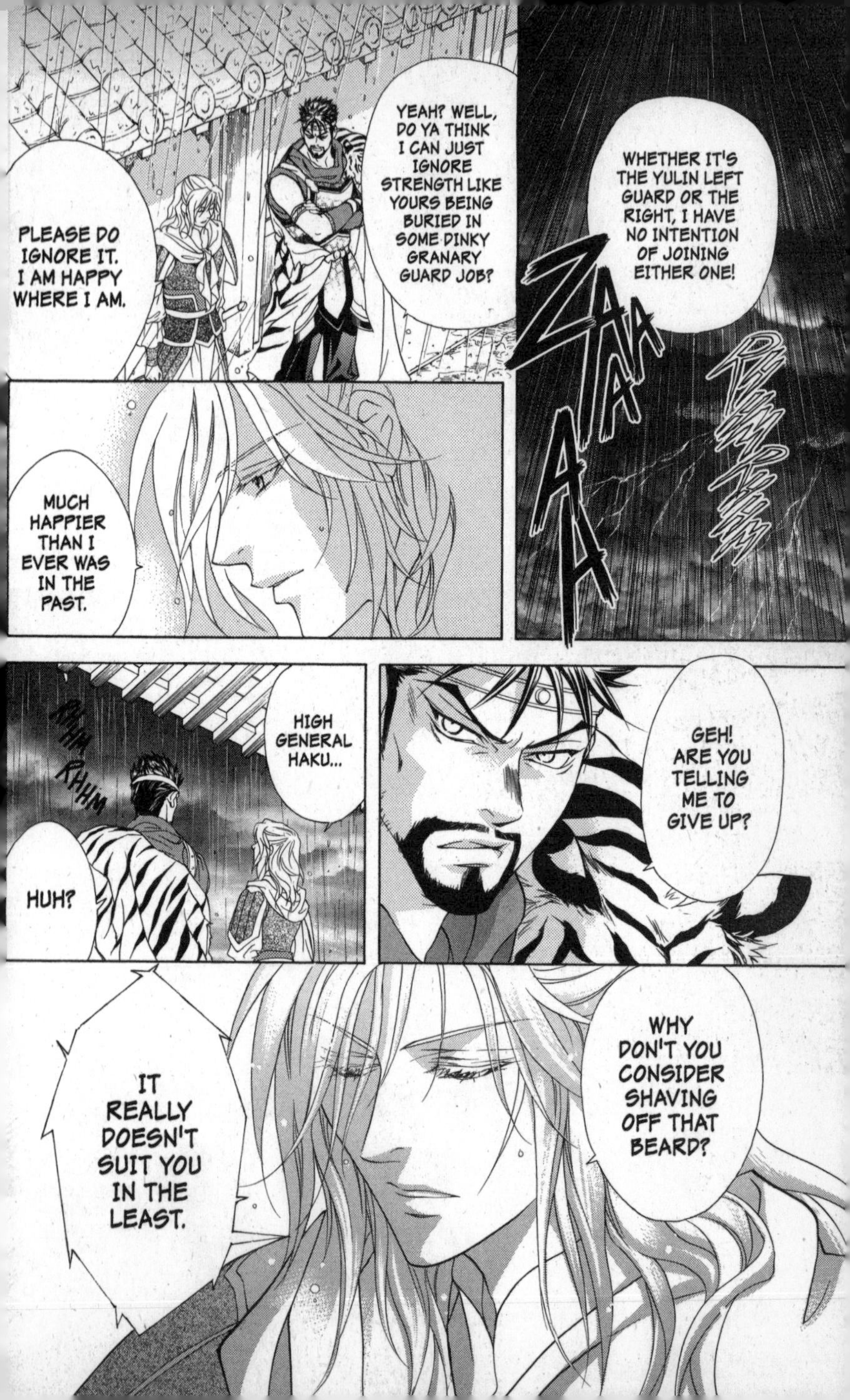
WHETHER IT'S THE YULIN LEFT GUARD OR THE RIGHT, I HAVE NO INTENTION OF JOINING EITHER ONE!
ZAAAAA
RHMMRHMM
YEAH? WELL, DO YA THINK I CAN JUST IGNORE STRENGTH LIKE YOURS BEING BURIED IN SOME DINKY GRANARY GUARD JOB?
PLEASE DO IGNORE IT. I AM HAPPY WHERE I AM.
MUCH HAPPIER THAN I EVER WAS IN THE PAST.
GEH! ARE YOU TELLING ME TO GIVE UP?
HIGH GENERAL HAKU...
RHMM RHMM
HUH?
WHY DON'T YOU CONSIDER SHAVING OFF THAT BEARD?
IT REALLY DOESN'T SUIT YOU IN THE LEAST.

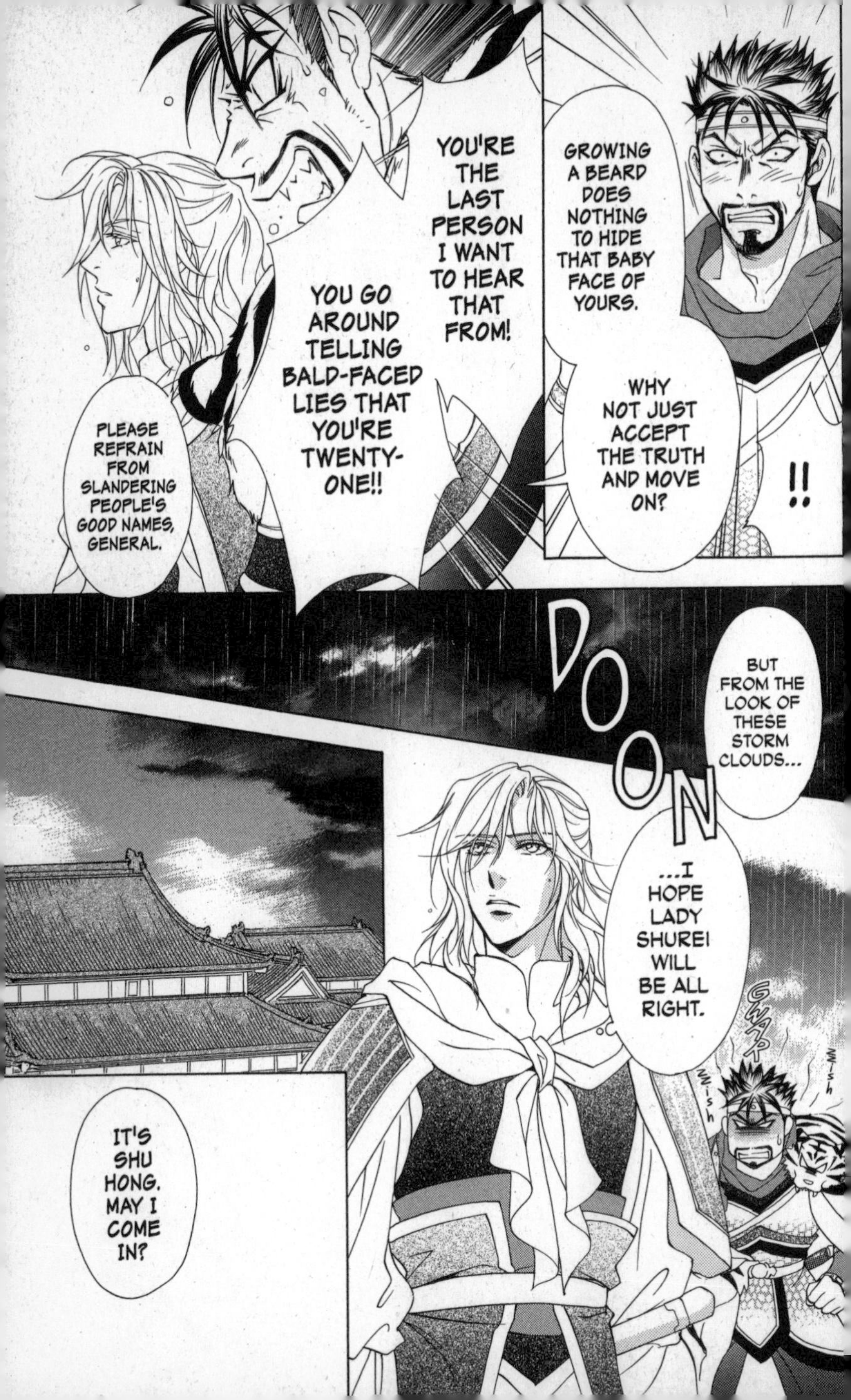
GROWING A BEARD DOES NOTHING TO HIDE THAT BABY FACE OF YOURS.
WHY NOT JUST ACCEPT THE TRUTH AND MOVE ON?
!!
YOU'RE THE LAST PERSON I WANT TO HEAR THAT FROM!
YOU GO AROUND TELLING BALD-FACED LIES THAT YOU'RE TWENTY-ONE!!
PLEASE REFRAIN FROM SLANDERING PEOPLE'S GOOD NAMES, GENERAL.
DOOON
BUT FROM THE LOOK OF THESE STORM CLOUDS...
...I HOPE LADY SHUREI WILL BE ALL RIGHT.
GWAR
Zish
Zish
IT'S SHU HONG. MAY I COME IN?

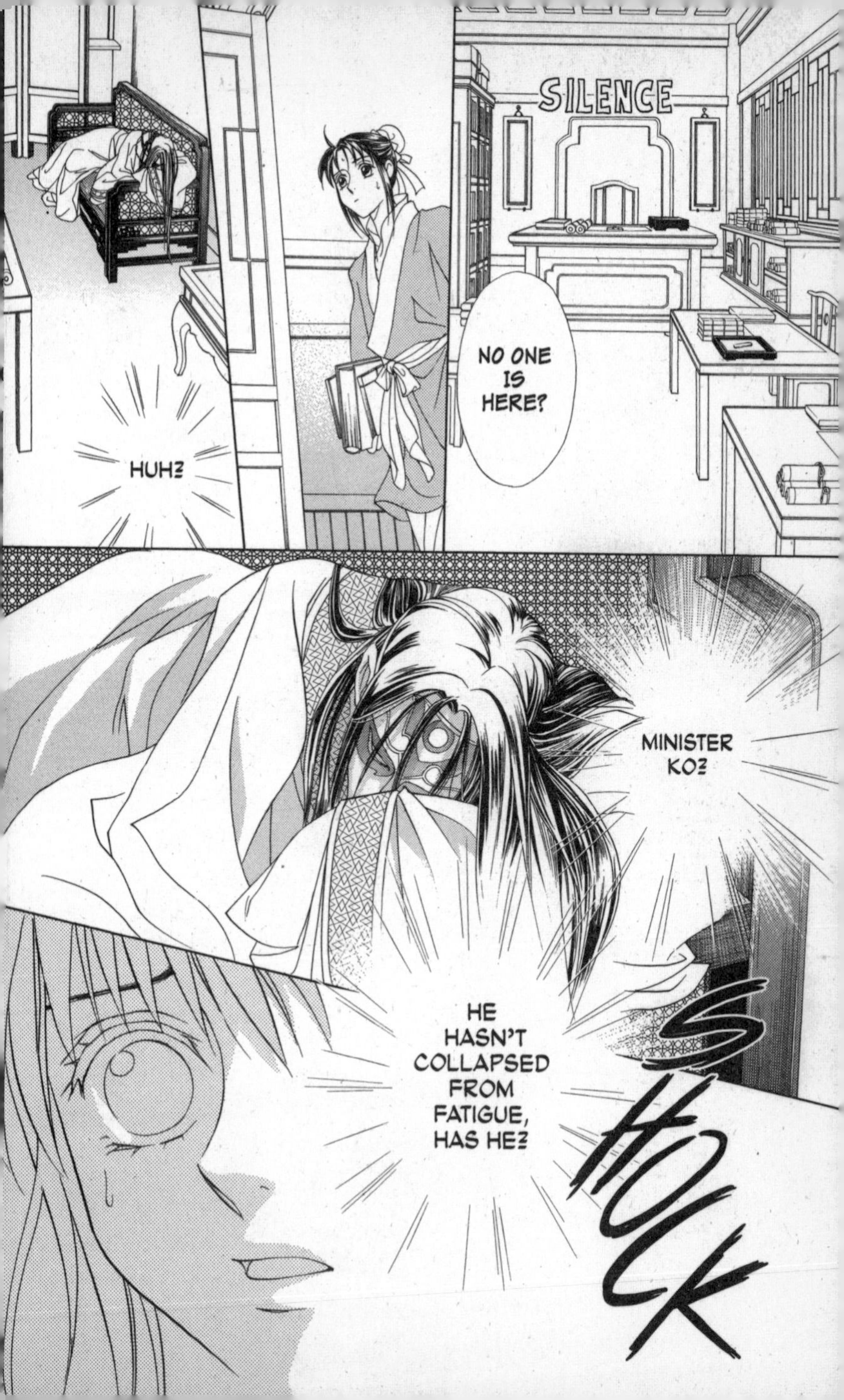
SILENCE
NO ONE IS HERE?
HUH?
MINISTER KO?
HE HASN'T COLLAPSED FROM FATIGUE, HAS HE?
SHOCK

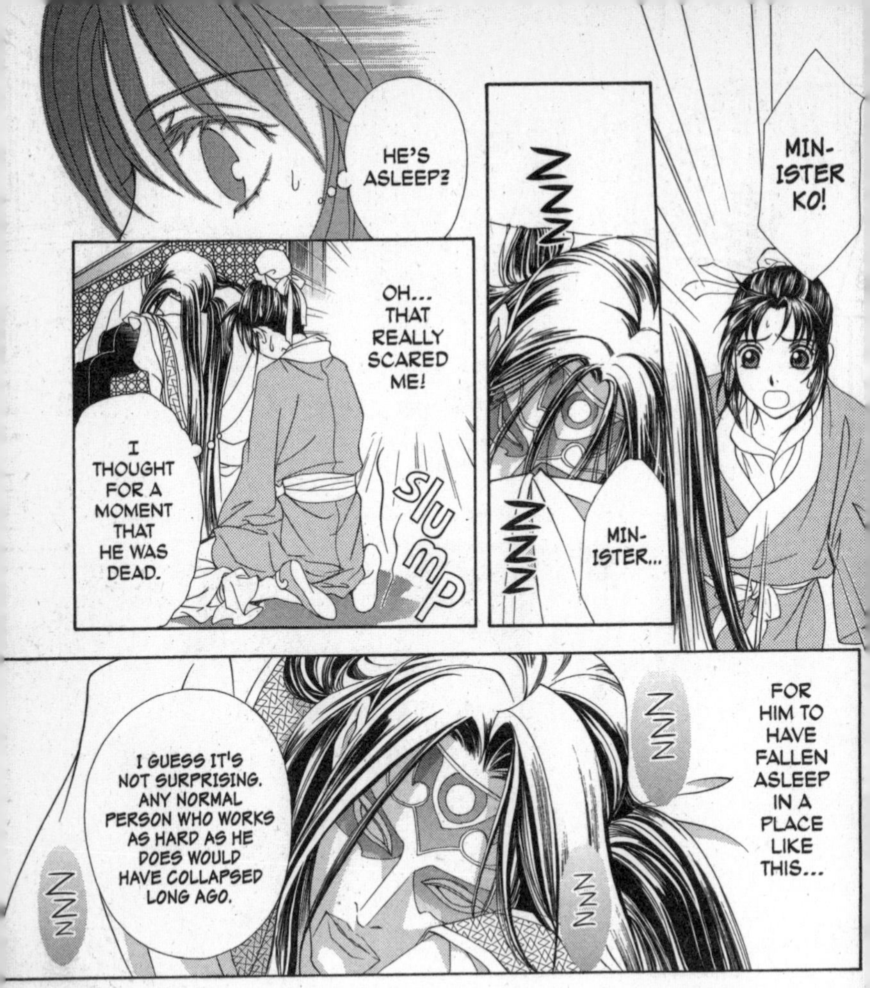
MINISTER KO!
ZZZ
MINISTER...
ZZZ
HE'S ASLEEP?
OH... THAT REALLY SCARED ME!
SLUMP
I THOUGHT FOR A MOMENT THAT HE WAS DEAD.
FOR HIM TO HAVE FALLEN ASLEEP IN A PLACE LIKE THIS...
ZZZ
ZZZ
I GUESS IT'S NOT SURPRISING. ANY NORMAL PERSON WHO WORKS AS HARD AS HE DOES WOULD HAVE COLLAPSED LONG AGO.
ZZZ

MINISTER KO DOES SEVERAL TIMES THE WORK HE ASSIGNS ANY OF HIS SUBORDINATES.

ALL OF THEM KNOW IT TOO, WHICH IS WHY NO ONE EVER COMPLAINS, EVEN WHEN HE GIVES OUT A HUGE PILE OF ASSIGNMENTS.

THOSE WHO REMAIN WORKING FOR HIM ALL COMPLETELY UNDERSTAND THE WAY HE WORKS AND HAVE DECIDED TO FOLLOW HIM LOYALLY.

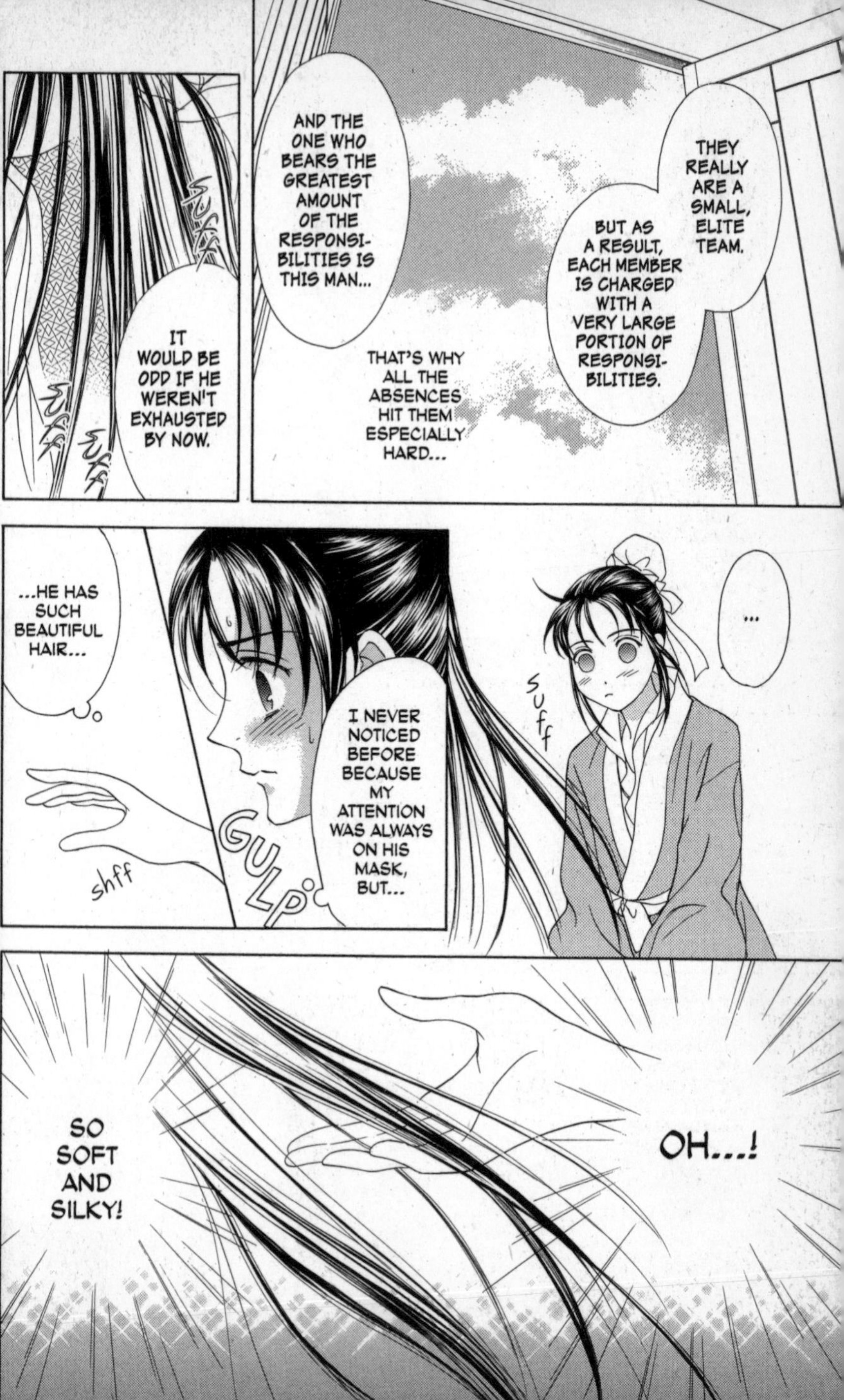
THEY REALLY ARE A SMALL, ELITE TEAM.
BUT AS A RESULT, EACH MEMBER IS CHARGED WITH A VERY LARGE PORTION OF RESPONSI-BILITIES.
THAT'S WHY ALL THE ABSENCES HIT THEM ESPECIALLY HARD...
AND THE ONE WHO BEARS THE GREATEST AMOUNT OF THE RESPONSI-BILITIES IS THIS MAN...
SUFF
IT WOULD BE ODD IF HE WEREN'T EXHAUSTED BY NOW.
SUFF
SUFF
...
SUFF
I NEVER NOTICED BEFORE BECAUSE MY ATTENTION WAS ALWAYS ON HIS MASK, BUT...
...HE HAS SUCH BEAUTIFUL HAIR...
GULP
shff
OH...!
SO SOFT AND SILKY!

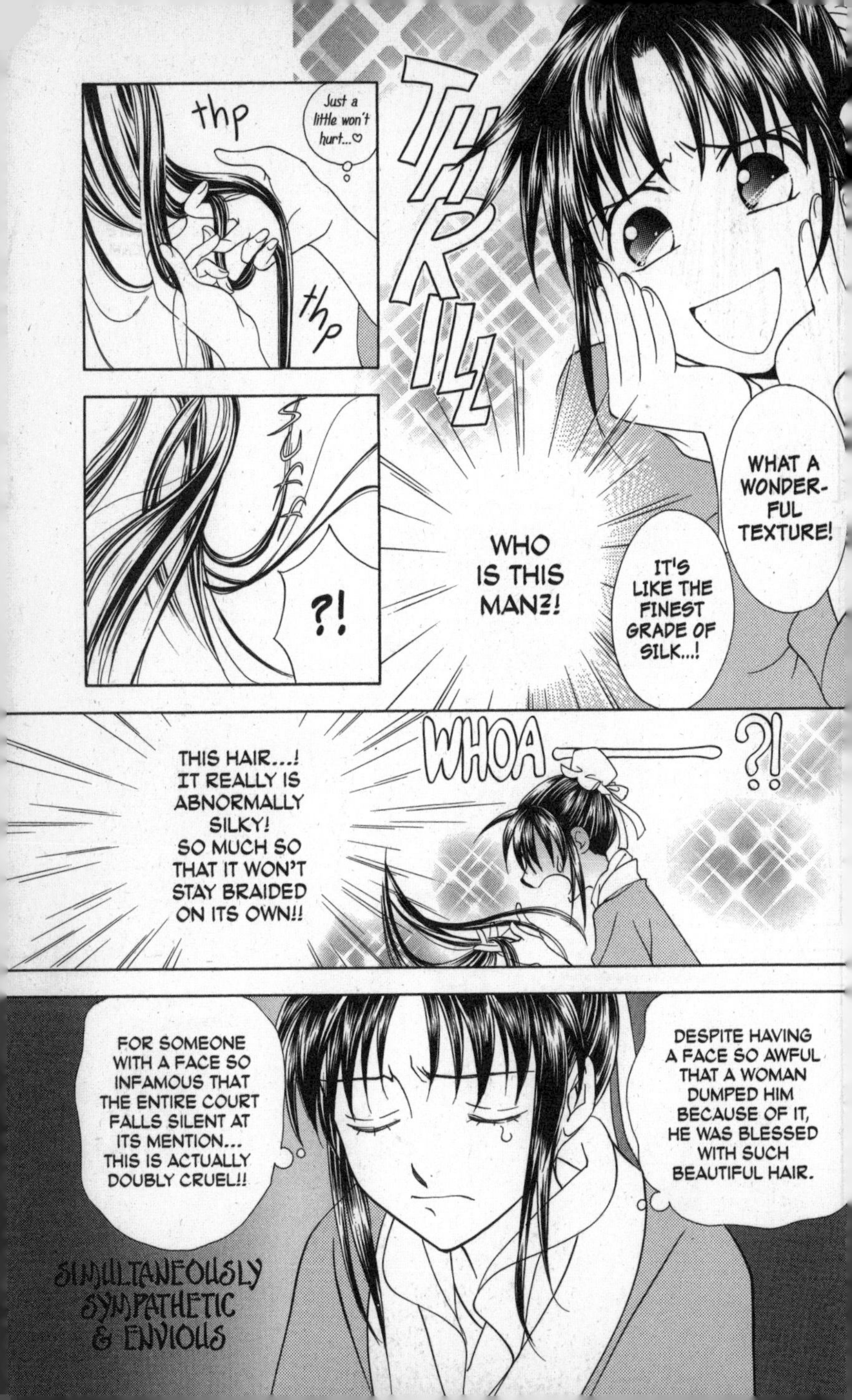
THRILL
WHAT A WONDERFUL TEXTURE!
IT'S LIKE THE FINEST GRADE OF SILK...!
WHO IS THIS MAN?!
thp
Just a little won't hurt...♡
thp
suff
?!
WHOA——?!
THIS HAIR...! IT REALLY IS ABNORMALLY SILKY! SO MUCH SO THAT IT WON'T STAY BRAIDED ON ITS OWN!!
DESPITE HAVING A FACE SO AWFUL THAT A WOMAN DUMPED HIM BECAUSE OF IT, HE WAS BLESSED WITH SUCH BEAUTIFUL HAIR.
FOR SOMEONE WITH A FACE SO INFAMOUS THAT THE ENTIRE COURT FALLS SILENT AT ITS MENTION... THIS IS ACTUALLY DOUBLY CRUEL!!
SIMULTANEOUSLY SYMPATHETIC & ENVIOUS

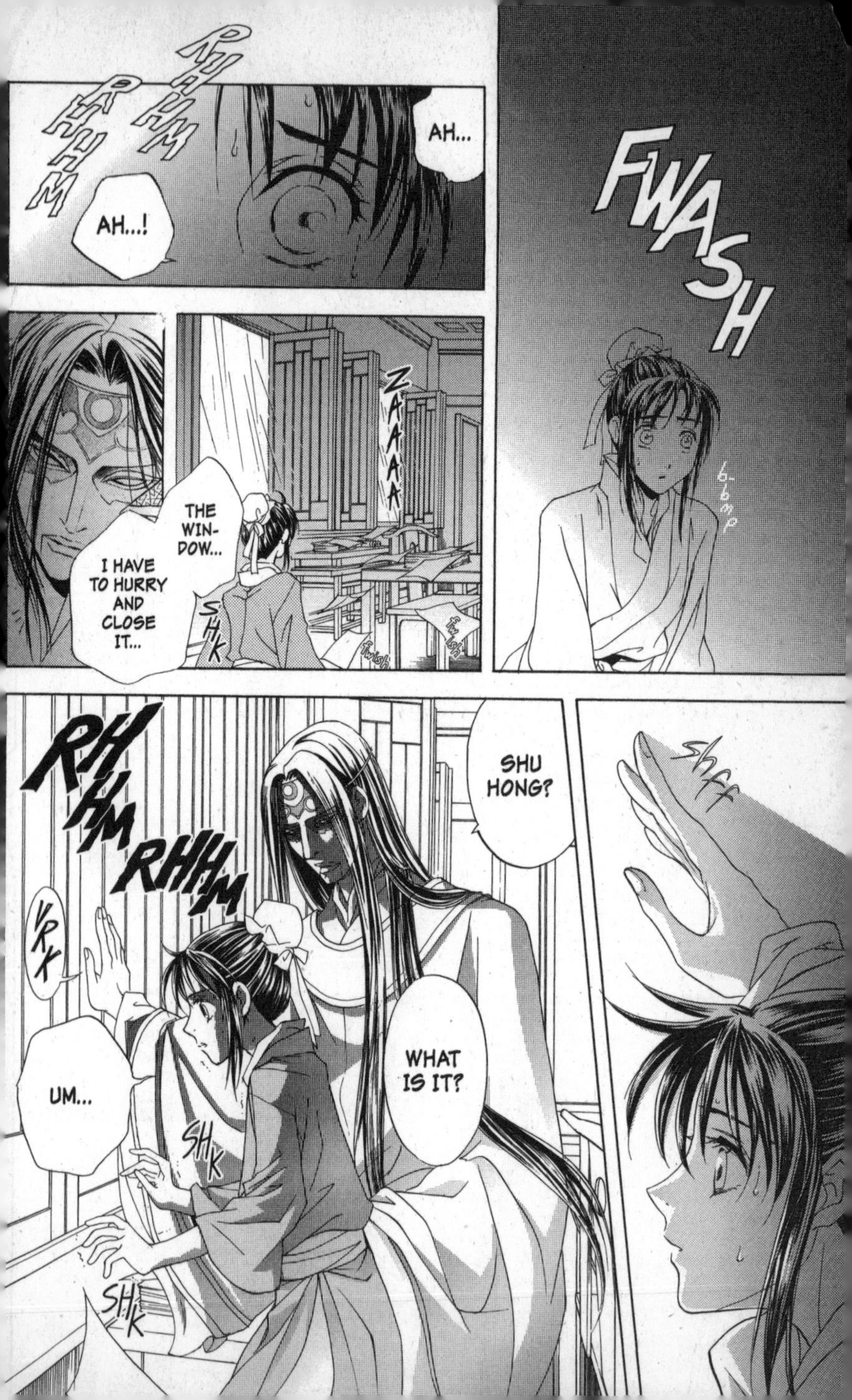
FWASH
b-bmp
AH...
RHHM
RHHM
AH...!
ZAAAAA
THE WIN-DOW...
I HAVE TO HURRY AND CLOSE IT...
SHK
fwish
fwish
shff
SHU HONG?
WHAT IS IT?
RHHM RHHM
VRK
UM...
SHK
SHK

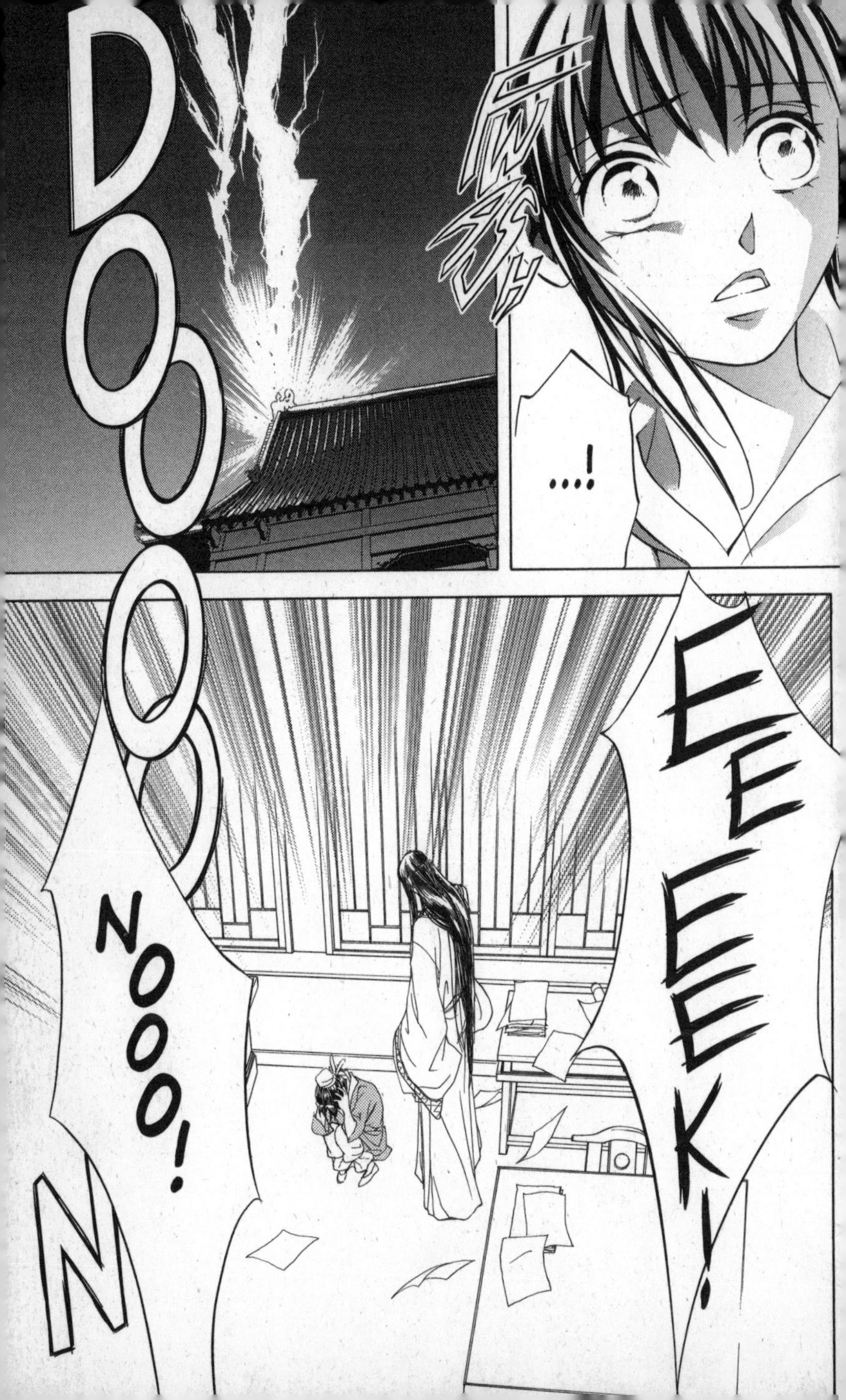
DOOOOOON
FWASSH
...!
EEEEEEK!
NOOO!

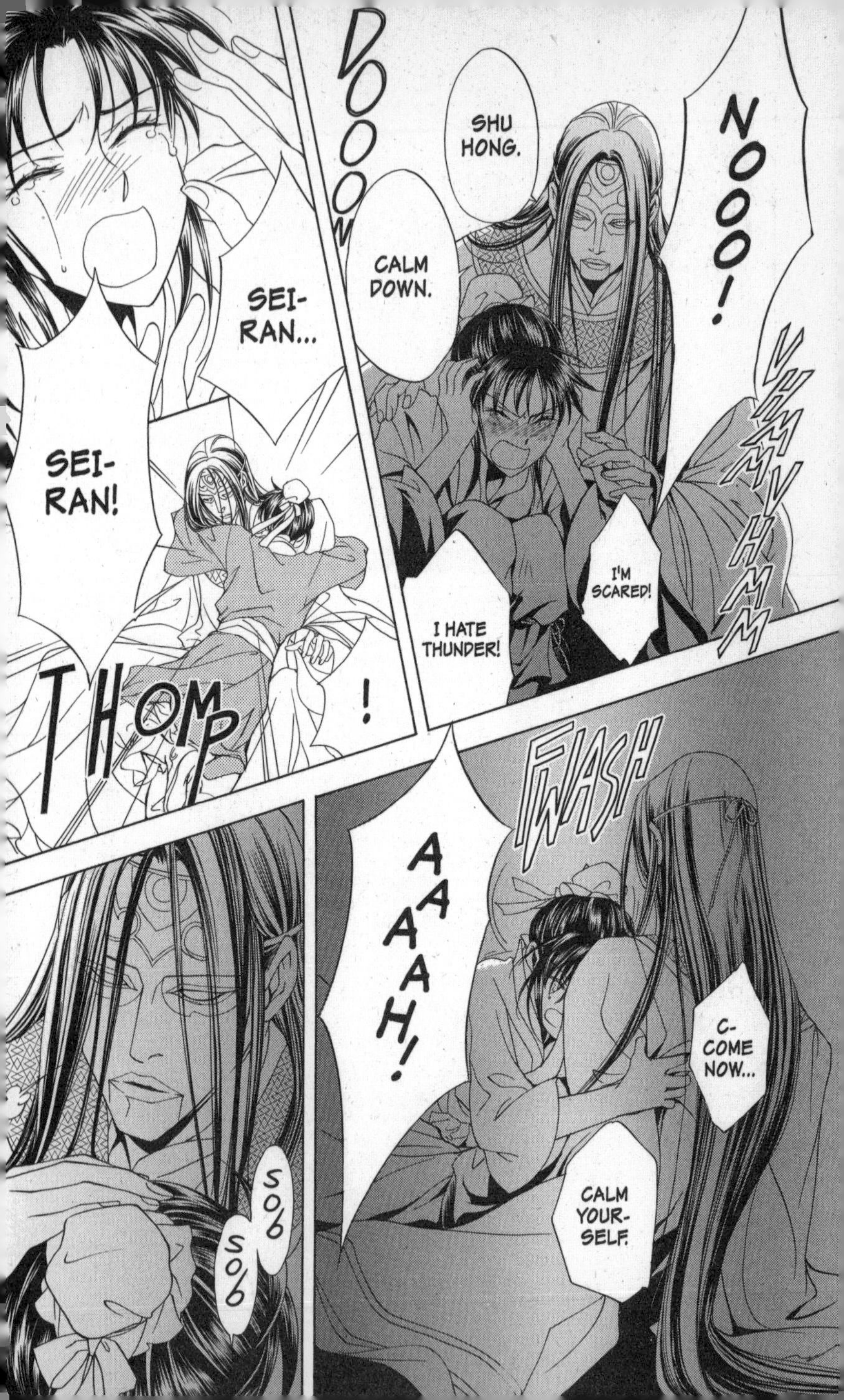
NOOOO!
SHU HONG.
DOOOON
CALM DOWN.
VHMMVHMMM
I'M SCARED!
I HATE THUNDER!
SEI-RAN...
SEI-RAN!
THOMP
!
FWASH
AAAAH!
C-COME NOW...
CALM YOURSELF.
SOB
SOB

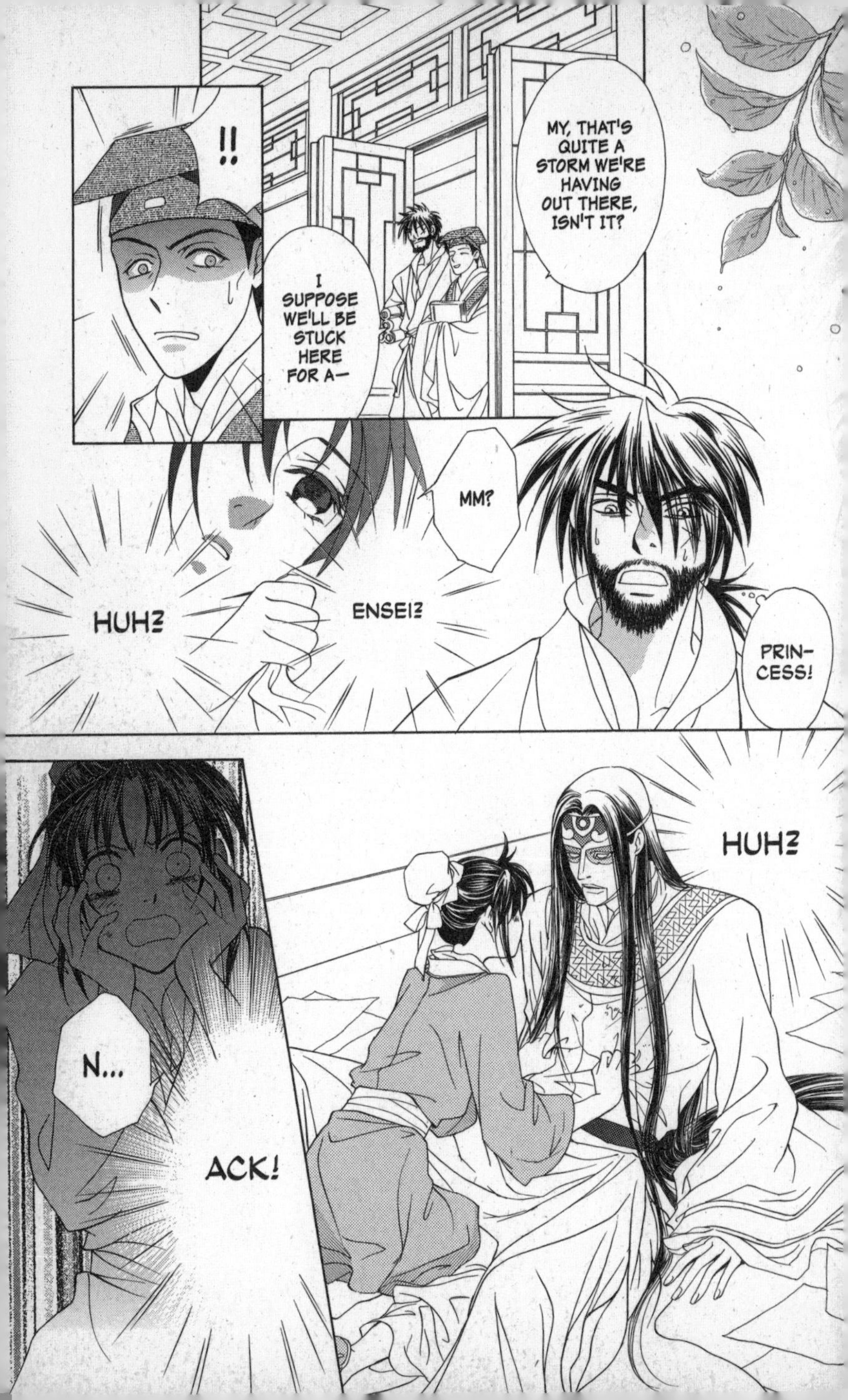
MY, THAT'S QUITE A STORM WE'RE HAVING OUT THERE, ISN'T IT?
I SUPPOSE WE'LL BE STUCK HERE FOR A—
!!
PRIN-CESS!
MM?
ENSEI!?
HUH!?
HUH!?
N...
ACK!

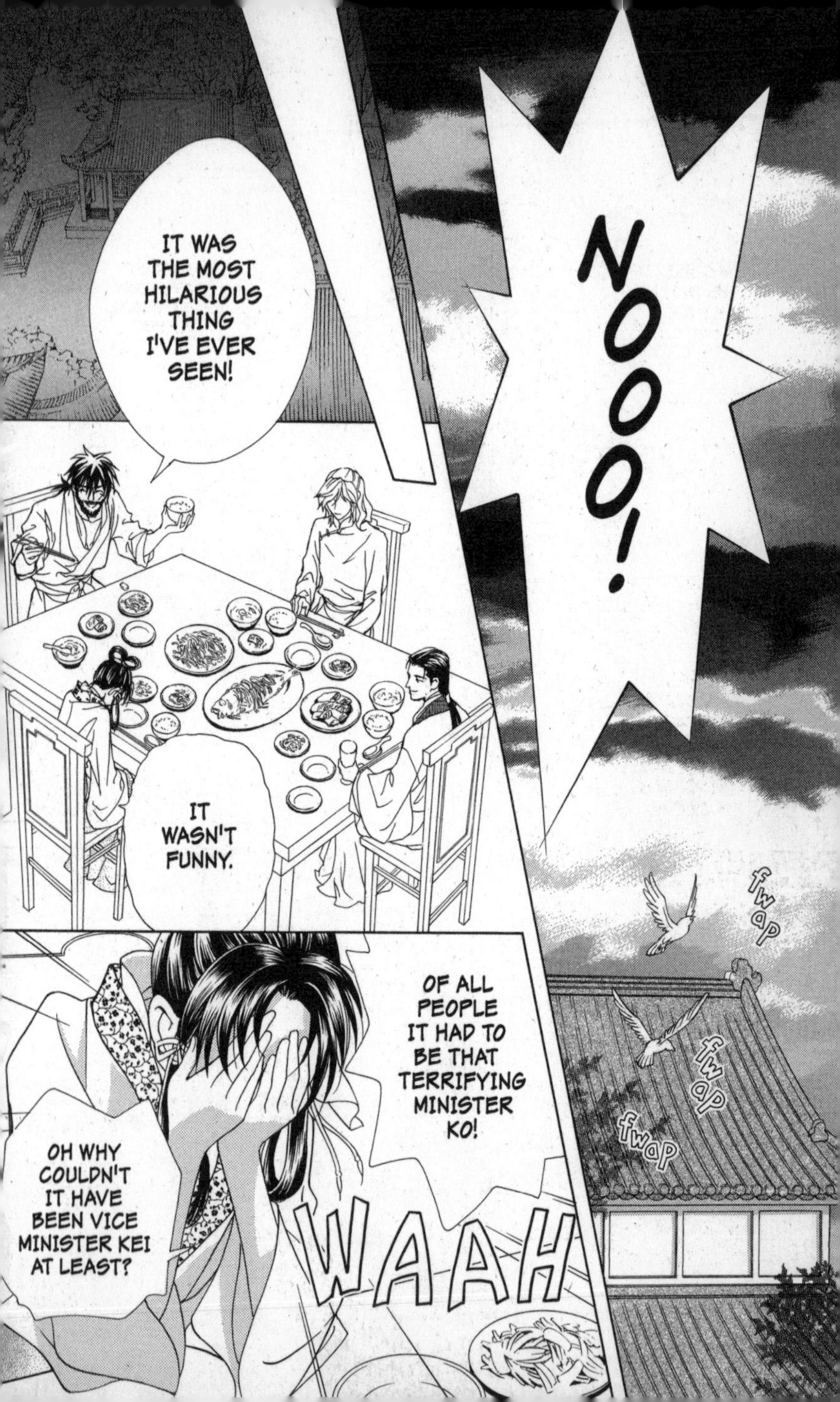
NOOOO!
fwap
fwap
fwap
IT WAS THE MOST HILARIOUS THING I'VE EVER SEEN!
IT WASN'T FUNNY.
OF ALL PEOPLE IT HAD TO BE THAT TERRIFYING MINISTER KO!
OH WHY COULDN'T IT HAVE BEEN VICE MINISTER KEI AT LEAST?
WAAH

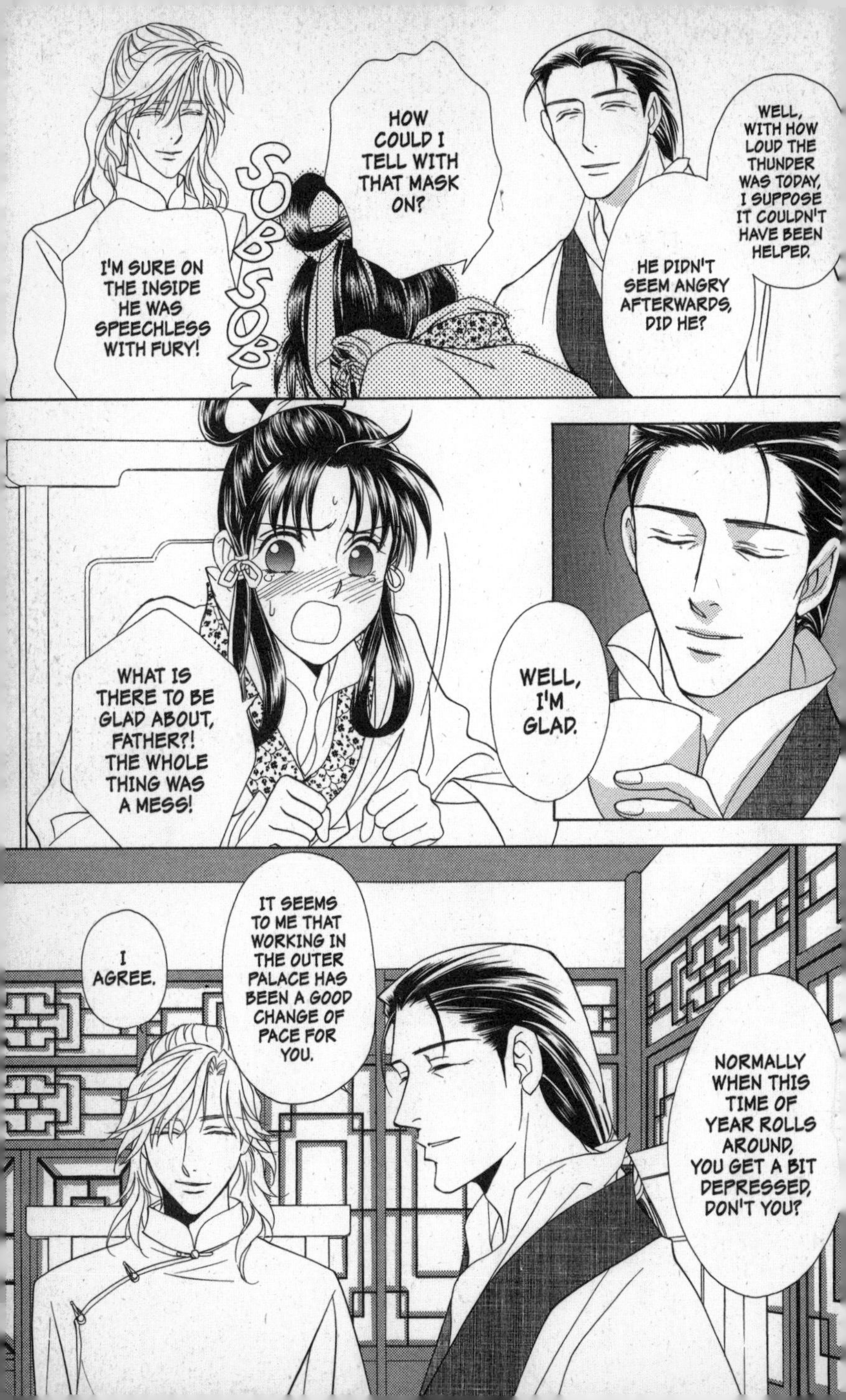
WELL, WITH HOW LOUD THE THUNDER WAS TODAY, I SUPPOSE IT COULDN'T HAVE BEEN HELPED.
HE DIDN'T SEEM ANGRY AFTERWARDS, DID HE?
HOW COULD I TELL WITH THAT MASK ON?
SOB SOB
I'M SURE ON THE INSIDE HE WAS SPEECHLESS WITH FURY!
WELL, I'M GLAD.
WHAT IS THERE TO BE GLAD ABOUT, FATHER?! THE WHOLE THING WAS A MESS!
NORMALLY WHEN THIS TIME OF YEAR ROLLS AROUND, YOU GET A BIT DEPRESSED, DON'T YOU?
IT SEEMS TO ME THAT WORKING IN THE OUTER PALACE HAS BEEN A GOOD CHANGE OF PACE FOR YOU.
I AGREE.

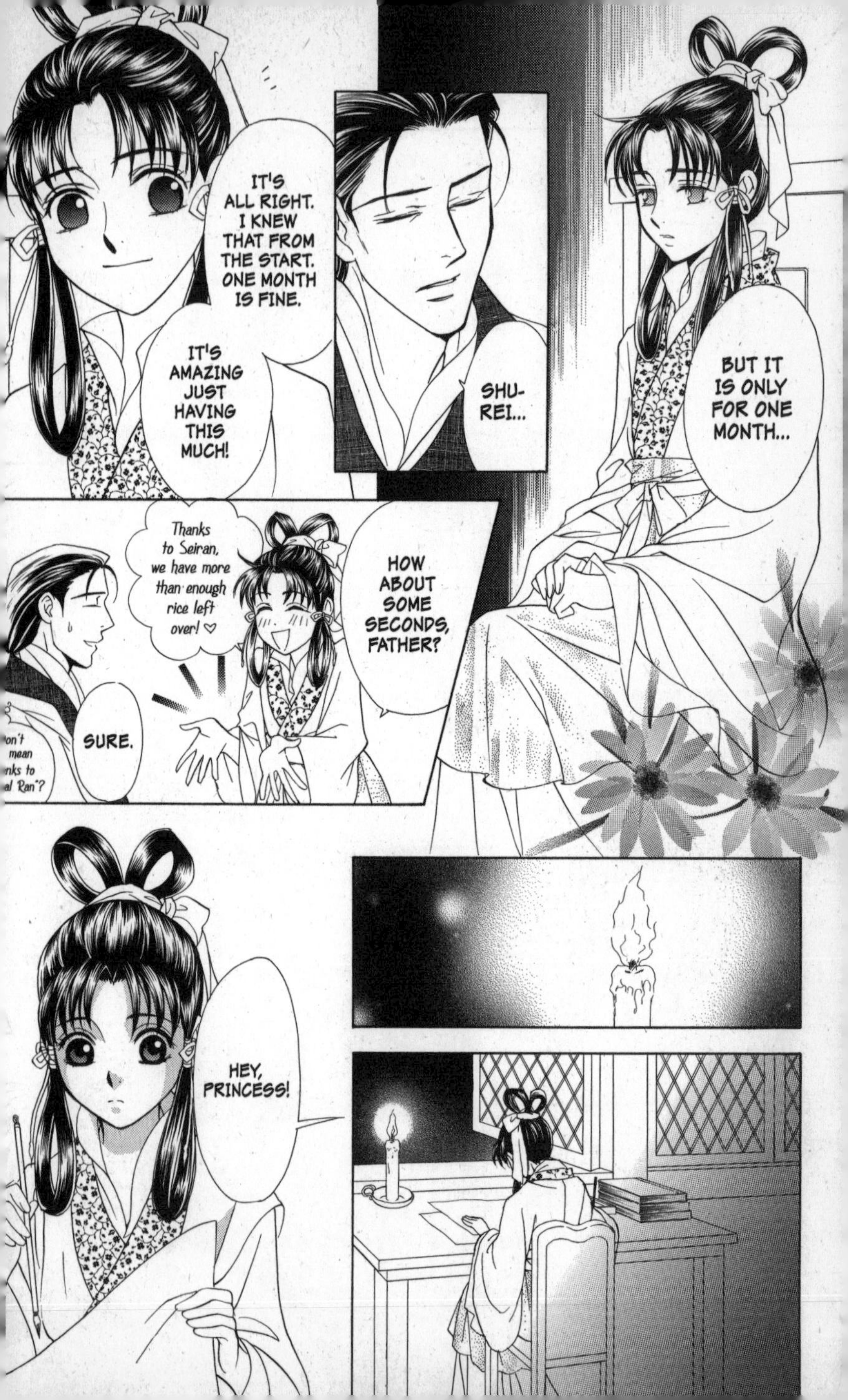
BUT IT IS ONLY FOR ONE MONTH...
SHU-REI...
IT'S ALL RIGHT. I KNEW THAT FROM THE START. ONE MONTH IS FINE.
IT'S AMAZING JUST HAVING THIS MUCH!
HOW ABOUT SOME SECONDS, FATHER?
Thanks to Seiran, we have more than enough rice left over! ♡
SURE.
HEY, PRINCESS!

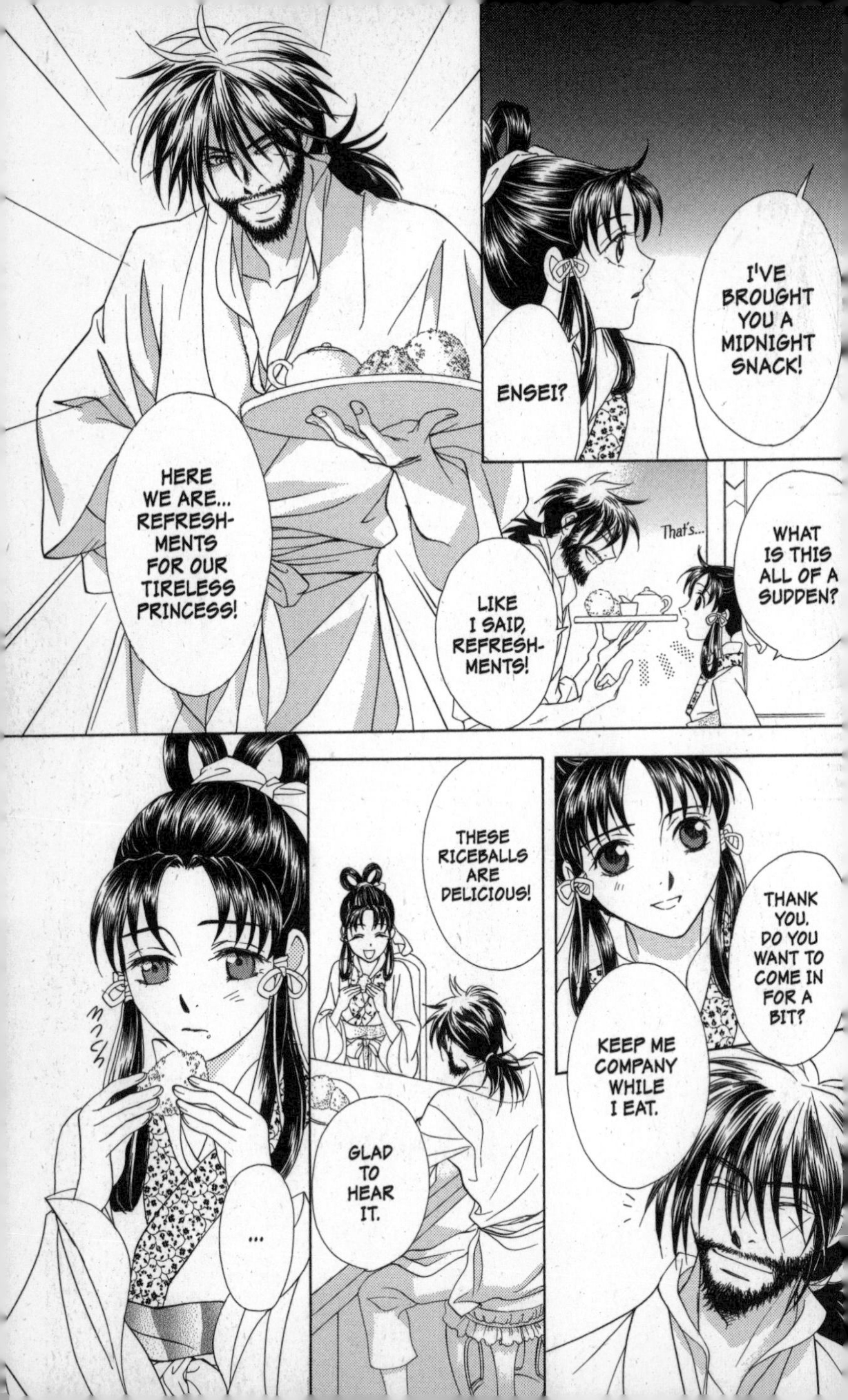
I'VE BROUGHT YOU A MIDNIGHT SNACK!
ENSEI?
WHAT IS THIS ALL OF A SUDDEN?
That's...
LIKE I SAID, REFRESHMENTS!
HERE WE ARE... REFRESHMENTS FOR OUR TIRELESS PRINCESS!
THANK YOU. DO YOU WANT TO COME IN FOR A BIT?
KEEP ME COMPANY WHILE I EAT.
THESE RICEBALLS ARE DELICIOUS!
GLAD TO HEAR IT.
...

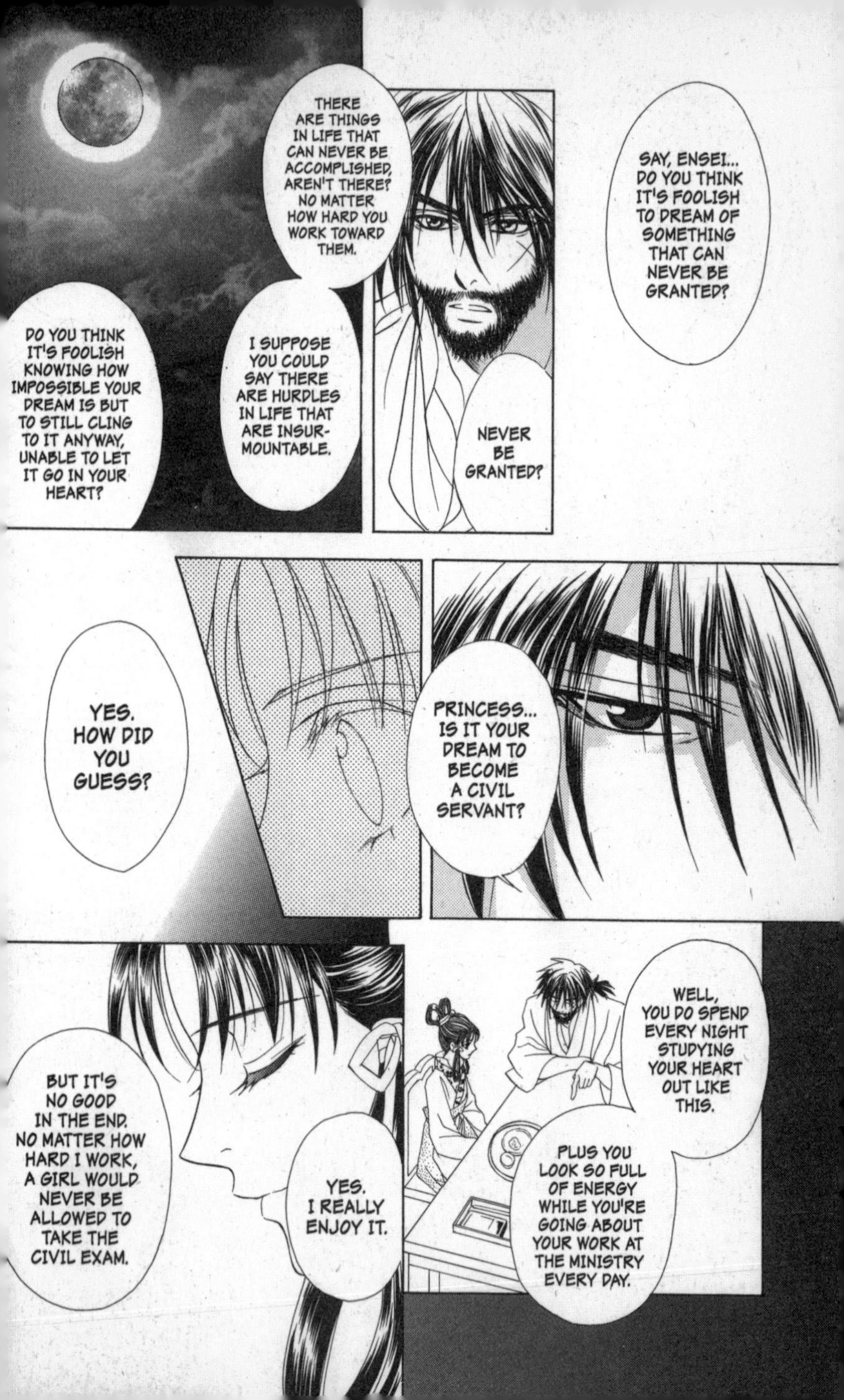
SAY, ENSEI... DO YOU THINK IT'S FOOLISH TO DREAM OF SOMETHING THAT CAN NEVER BE GRANTED?
NEVER BE GRANTED?
THERE ARE THINGS IN LIFE THAT CAN NEVER BE ACCOMPLISHED, AREN'T THERE? NO MATTER HOW HARD YOU WORK TOWARD THEM.
I SUPPOSE YOU COULD SAY THERE ARE HURDLES IN LIFE THAT ARE INSUR-MOUNTABLE.
DO YOU THINK IT'S FOOLISH KNOWING HOW IMPOSSIBLE YOUR DREAM IS BUT TO STILL CLING TO IT ANYWAY, UNABLE TO LET IT GO IN YOUR HEART?
PRINCESS... IS IT YOUR DREAM TO BECOME A CIVIL SERVANT?
YES. HOW DID YOU GUESS?
WELL, YOU DO SPEND EVERY NIGHT STUDYING YOUR HEART OUT LIKE THIS.
PLUS YOU LOOK SO FULL OF ENERGY WHILE YOU'RE GOING ABOUT YOUR WORK AT THE MINISTRY EVERY DAY.
YES. I REALLY ENJOY IT.
BUT IT'S NO GOOD IN THE END. NO MATTER HOW HARD I WORK, A GIRL WOULD NEVER BE ALLOWED TO TAKE THE CIVIL EXAM.

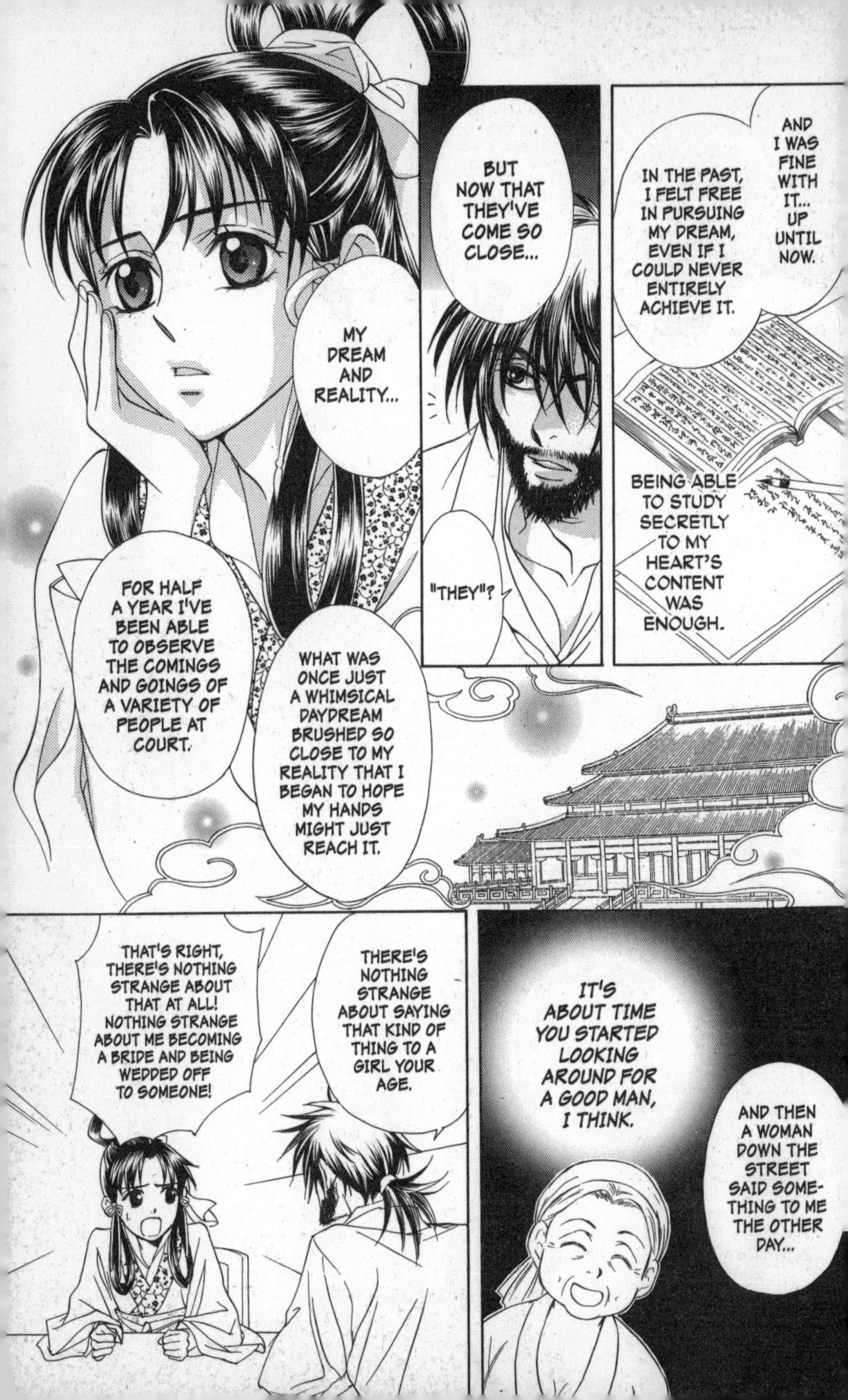
IN THE PAST, I FELT FREE IN PURSUING MY DREAM, EVEN IF I COULD NEVER ENTIRELY ACHIEVE IT.
AND I WAS FINE WITH IT... UP UNTIL NOW.
BEING ABLE TO STUDY SECRETLY TO MY HEART'S CONTENT WAS ENOUGH.
BUT NOW THAT THEY'VE COME SO CLOSE...
"THEY"?
MY DREAM AND REALITY...
FOR HALF A YEAR I'VE BEEN ABLE TO OBSERVE THE COMINGS AND GOINGS OF A VARIETY OF PEOPLE AT COURT.
WHAT WAS ONCE JUST A WHIMSICAL DAYDREAM BRUSHED SO CLOSE TO MY REALITY THAT I BEGAN TO HOPE MY HANDS MIGHT JUST REACH IT.
AND THEN A WOMAN DOWN THE STREET SAID SOME-THING TO ME THE OTHER DAY...
IT'S ABOUT TIME YOU STARTED LOOKING AROUND FOR A GOOD MAN, I THINK.
THERE'S NOTHING STRANGE ABOUT SAYING THAT KIND OF THING TO A GIRL YOUR AGE.
THAT'S RIGHT, THERE'S NOTHING STRANGE ABOUT THAT AT ALL! NOTHING STRANGE ABOUT ME BECOMING A BRIDE AND BEING WEDDED OFF TO SOMEONE!

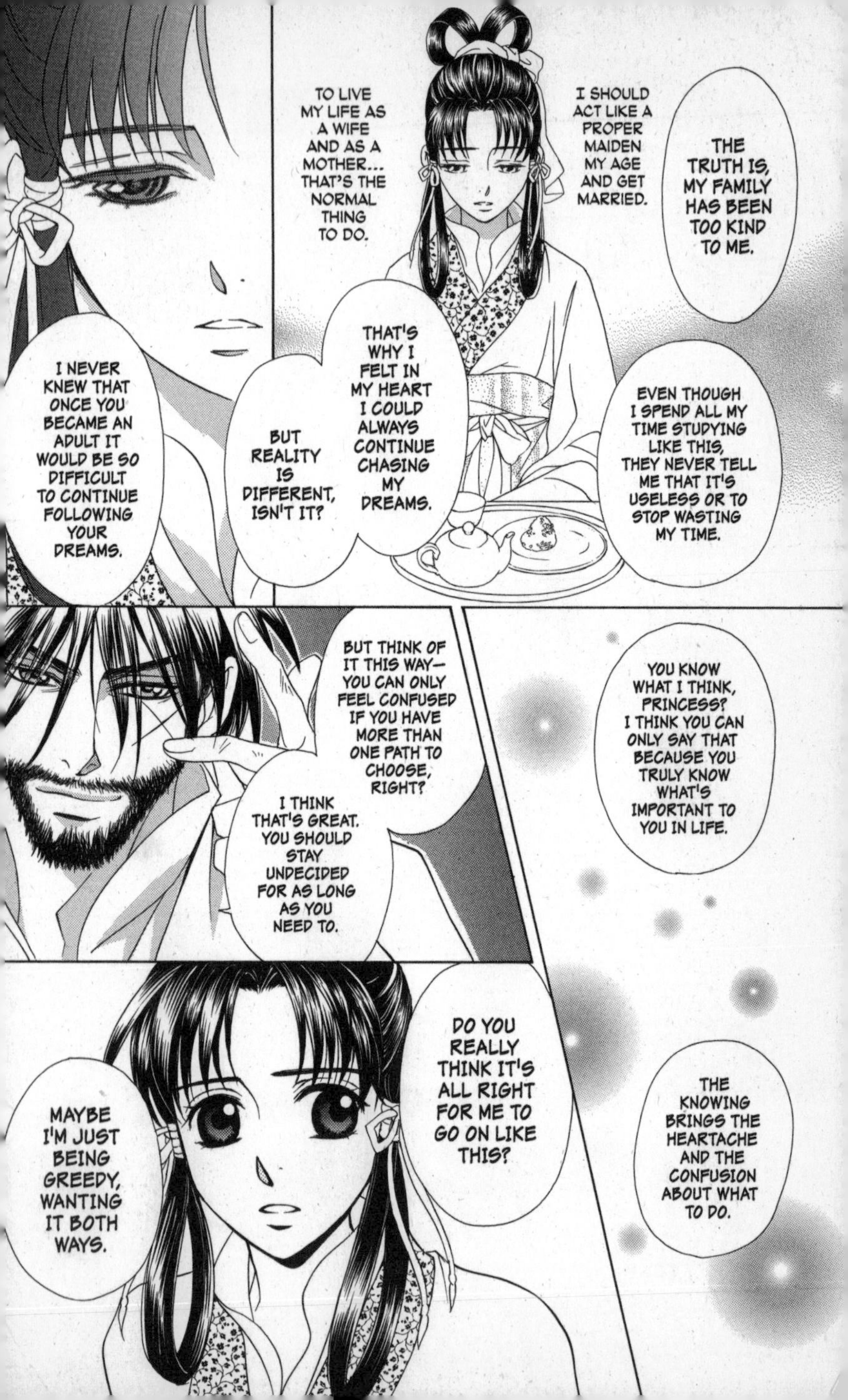
THE TRUTH IS, MY FAMILY HAS BEEN TOO KIND TO ME.
EVEN THOUGH I SPEND ALL MY TIME STUDYING LIKE THIS, THEY NEVER TELL ME THAT IT'S USELESS OR TO STOP WASTING MY TIME.
THAT'S WHY I FELT IN MY HEART I COULD ALWAYS CONTINUE CHASING MY DREAMS.
BUT REALITY IS DIFFERENT, ISN'T IT?
I SHOULD ACT LIKE A PROPER MAIDEN MY AGE AND GET MARRIED.
TO LIVE MY LIFE AS A WIFE AND AS A MOTHER... THAT'S THE NORMAL THING TO DO.
I NEVER KNEW THAT ONCE YOU BECAME AN ADULT IT WOULD BE SO DIFFICULT TO CONTINUE FOLLOWING YOUR DREAMS.
YOU KNOW WHAT I THINK, PRINCESS? I THINK YOU CAN ONLY SAY THAT BECAUSE YOU TRULY KNOW WHAT'S IMPORTANT TO YOU IN LIFE.
BUT THINK OF IT THIS WAY— YOU CAN ONLY FEEL CONFUSED IF YOU HAVE MORE THAN ONE PATH TO CHOOSE, RIGHT?
I THINK THAT'S GREAT. YOU SHOULD STAY UNDECIDED FOR AS LONG AS YOU NEED TO.
THE KNOWING BRINGS THE HEARTACHE AND THE CONFUSION ABOUT WHAT TO DO.
DO YOU REALLY THINK IT'S ALL RIGHT FOR ME TO GO ON LIKE THIS?
MAYBE I'M JUST BEING GREEDY, WANTING IT BOTH WAYS.

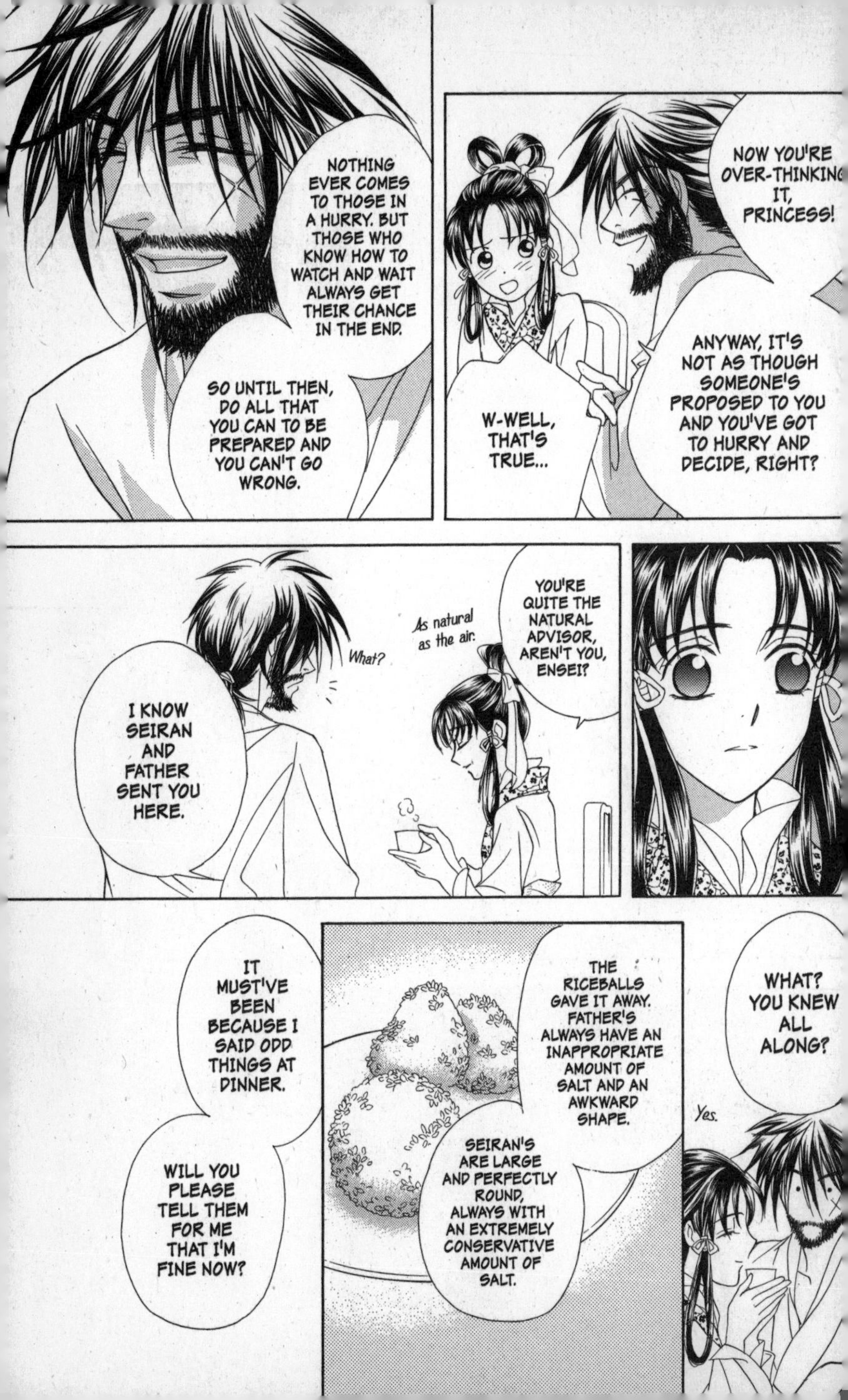
NOW YOU'RE OVER-THINKING IT, PRINCESS!
ANYWAY, IT'S NOT AS THOUGH SOMEONE'S PROPOSED TO YOU AND YOU'VE GOT TO HURRY AND DECIDE, RIGHT?
W-WELL, THAT'S TRUE...
NOTHING EVER COMES TO THOSE IN A HURRY. BUT THOSE WHO KNOW HOW TO WATCH AND WAIT ALWAYS GET THEIR CHANCE IN THE END.
SO UNTIL THEN, DO ALL THAT YOU CAN TO BE PREPARED AND YOU CAN'T GO WRONG.
YOU'RE QUITE THE NATURAL ADVISOR, AREN'T YOU, ENSEI?
As natural as the air.
What?
I KNOW SEIRAN AND FATHER SENT YOU HERE.
WHAT? YOU KNEW ALL ALONG?
Yes.
THE RICEBALLS GAVE IT AWAY. FATHER'S ALWAYS HAVE AN INAPPROPRIATE AMOUNT OF SALT AND AN AWKWARD SHAPE.
SEIRAN'S ARE LARGE AND PERFECTLY ROUND, ALWAYS WITH AN EXTREMELY CONSERVATIVE AMOUNT OF SALT.
IT MUST'VE BEEN BECAUSE I SAID ODD THINGS AT DINNER.
WILL YOU PLEASE TELL THEM FOR ME THAT I'M FINE NOW?

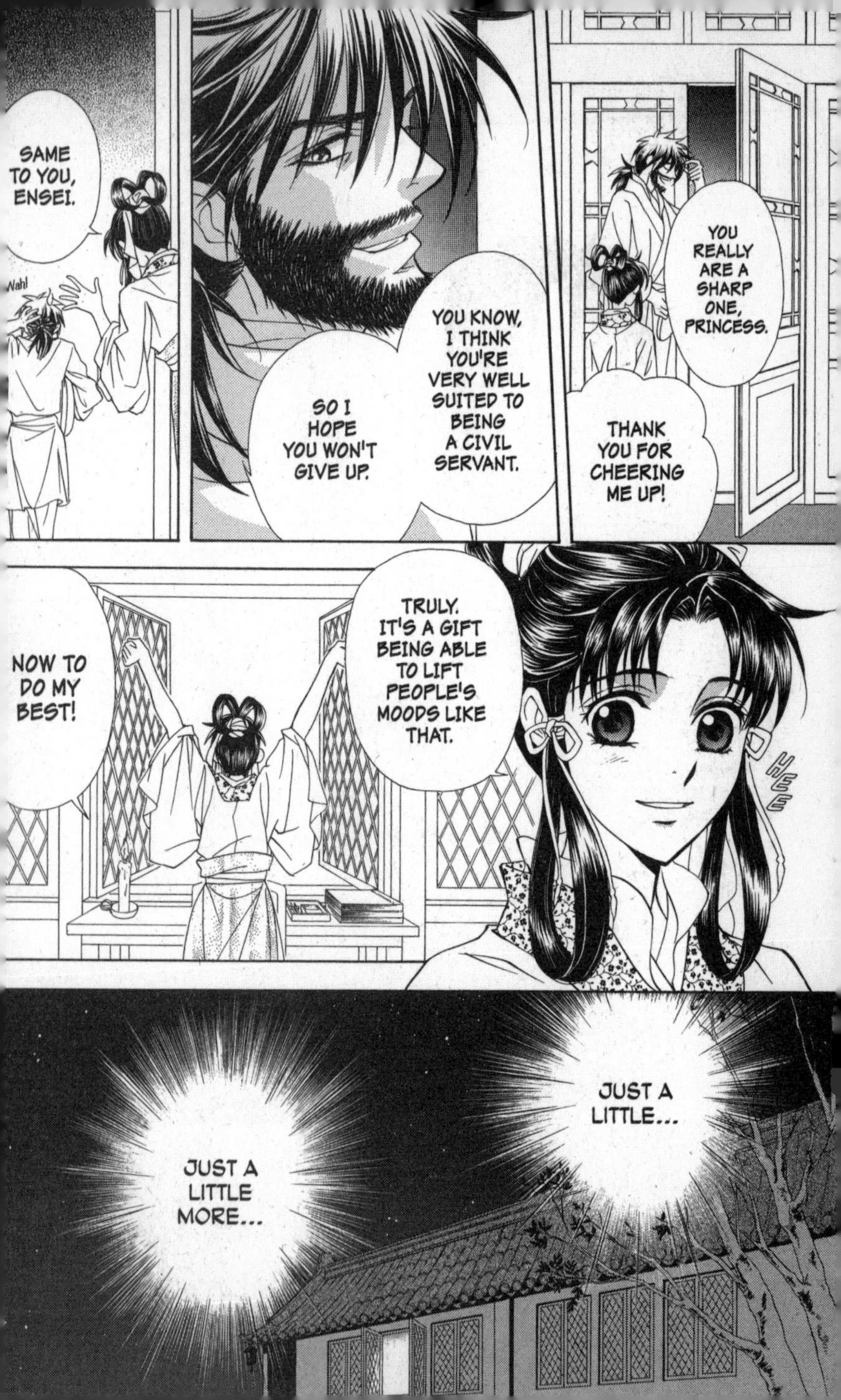

YOU REALLY ARE A SHARP ONE, PRINCESS.
THANK YOU FOR CHEERING ME UP!
YOU KNOW, I THINK YOU'RE VERY WELL SUITED TO BEING A CIVIL SERVANT.
SO I HOPE YOU WON'T GIVE UP.
SAME TO YOU, ENSEI.
Wah!
TRULY. IT'S A GIFT BEING ABLE TO LIFT PEOPLE'S MOODS LIKE THAT.
HEE
NOW TO DO MY BEST!
JUST A LITTLE...
JUST A LITTLE MORE...

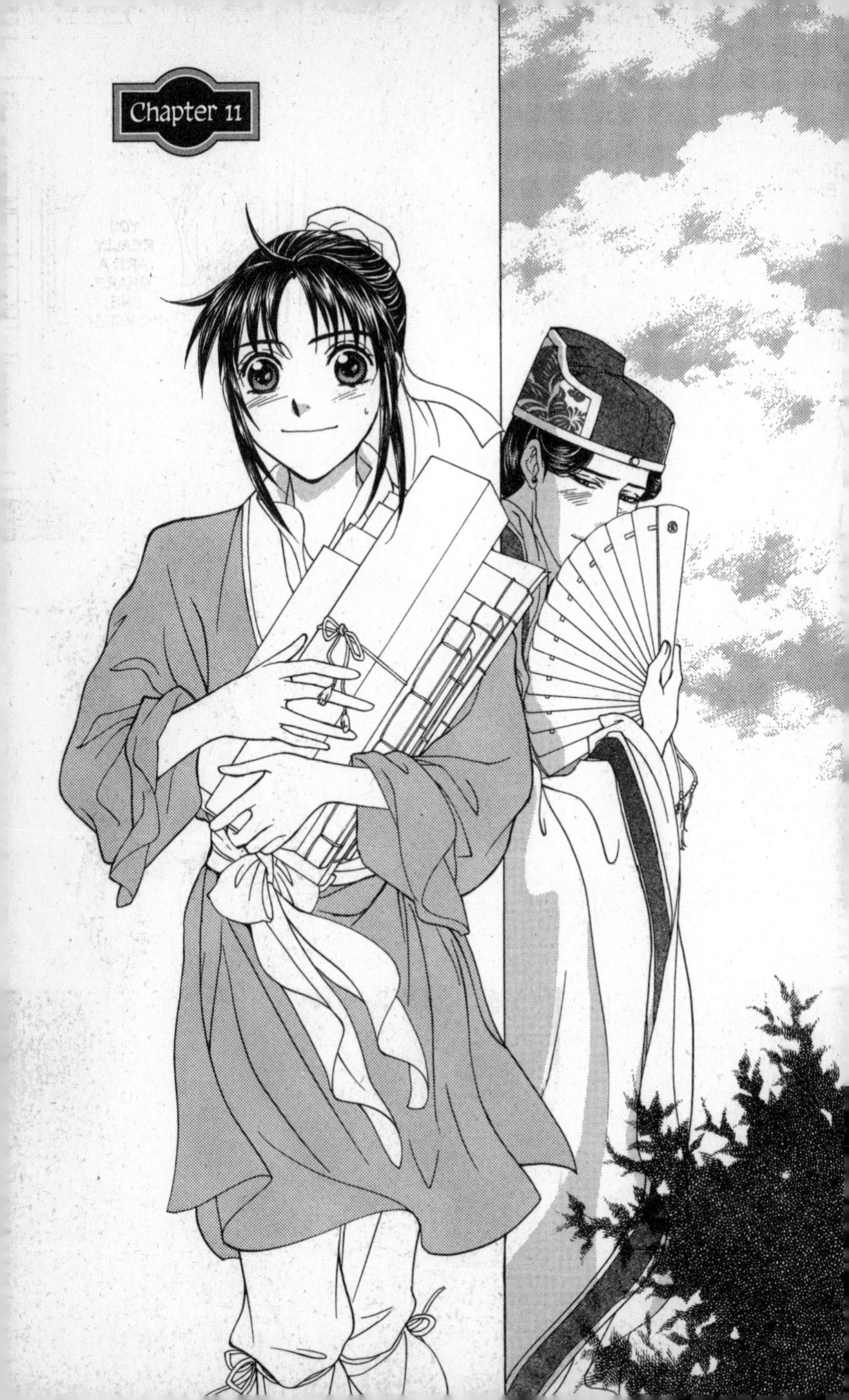
Chapter 11

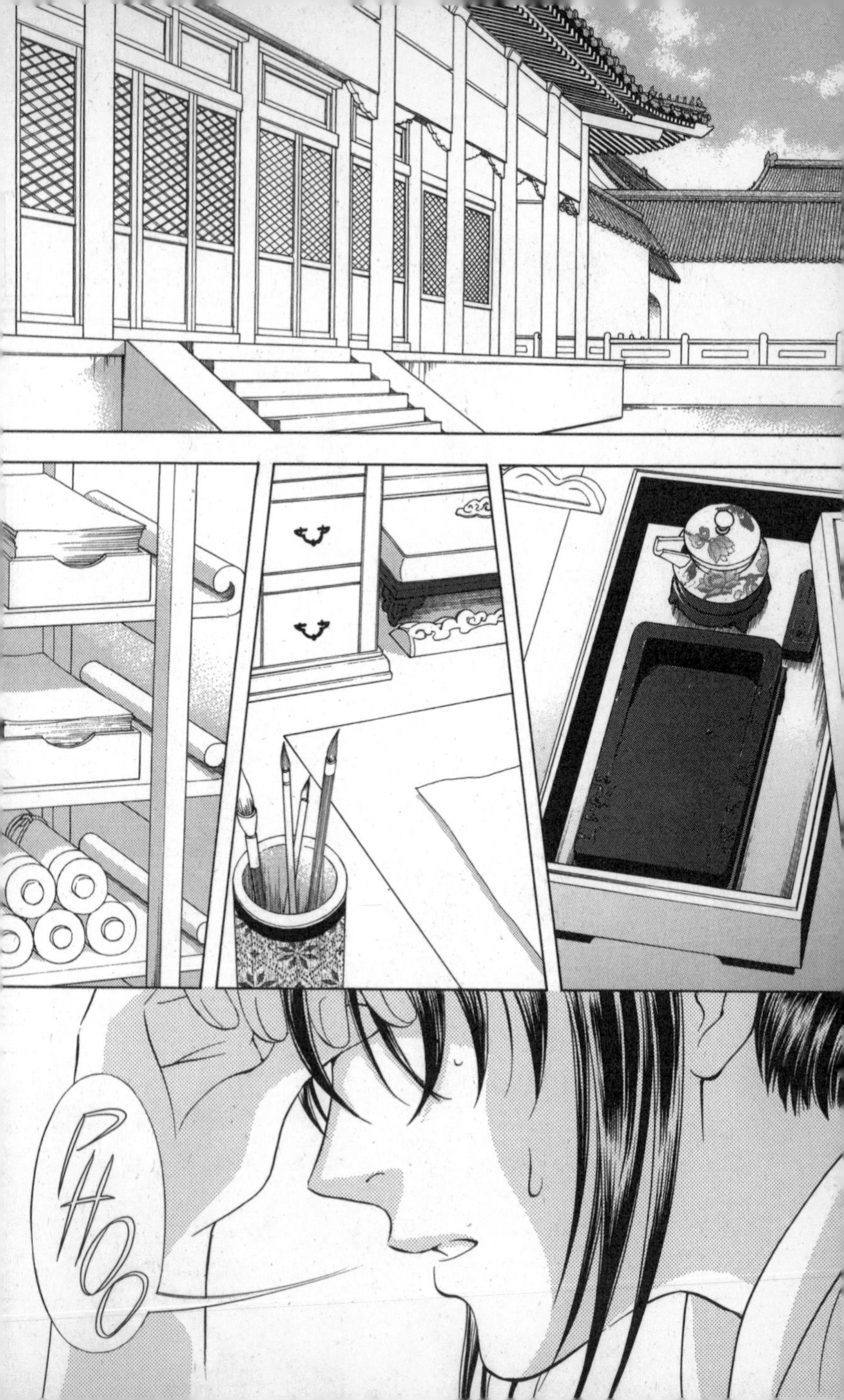
PHOO

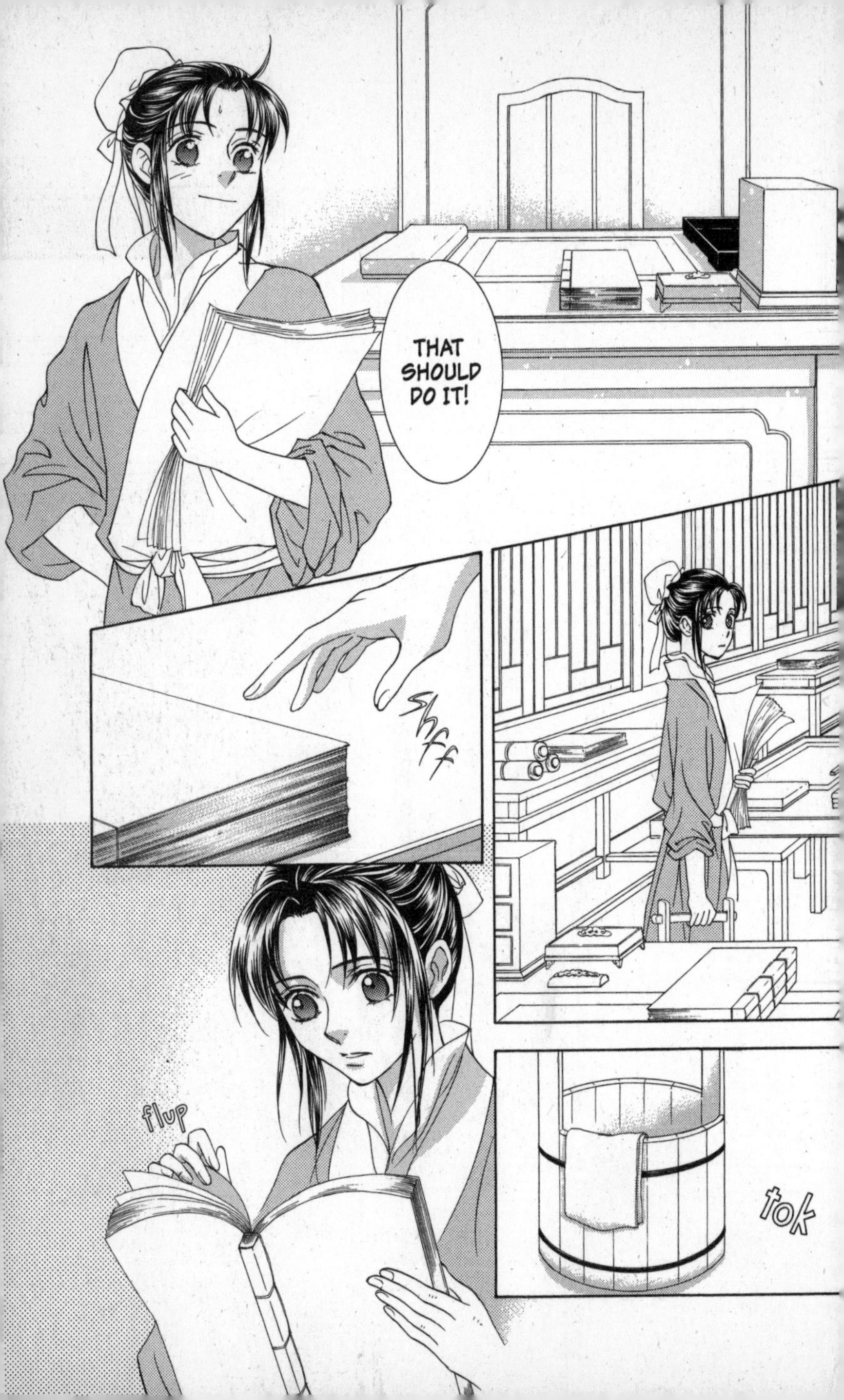
THAT SHOULD DO IT!
shff
tok
flup

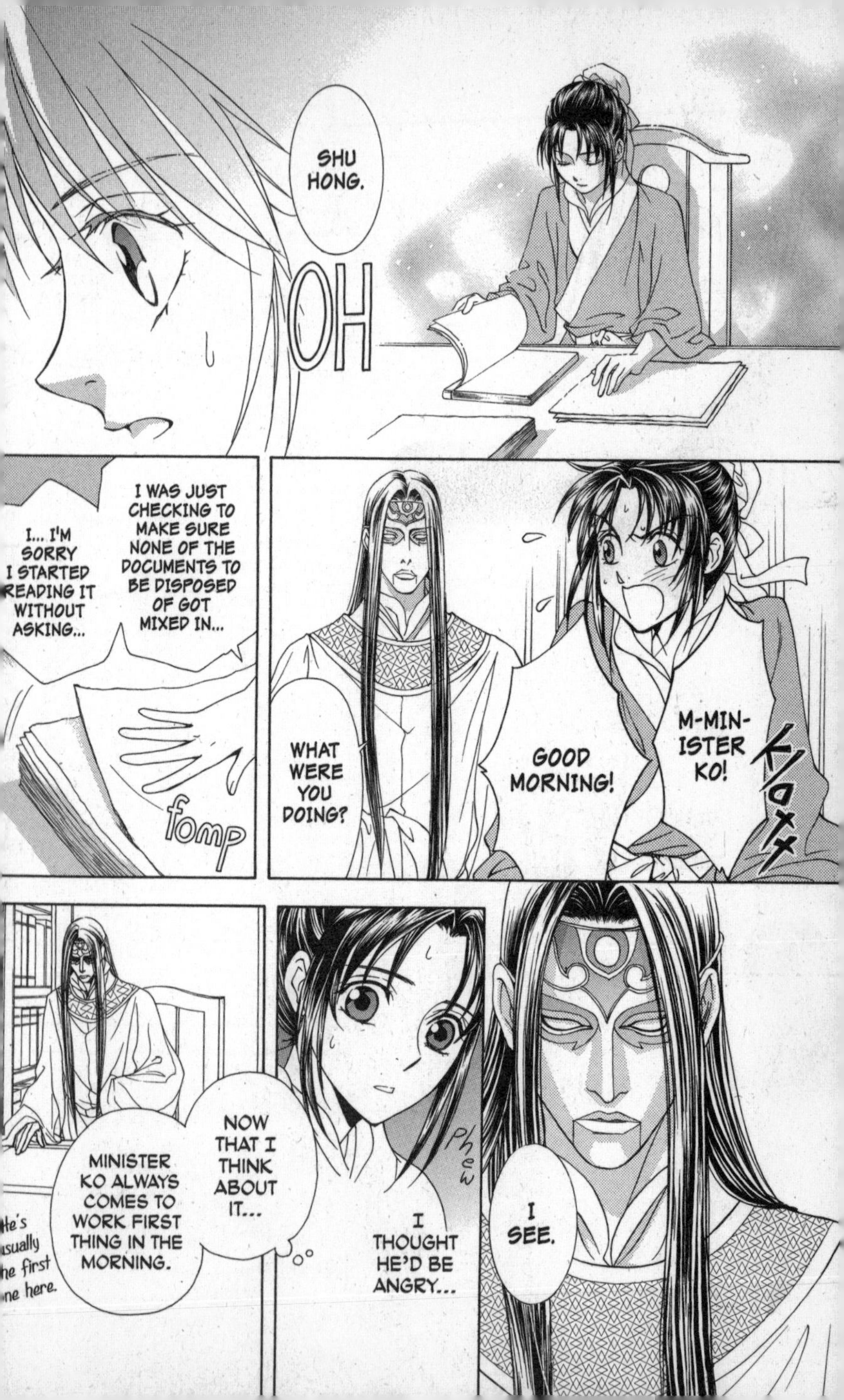
SHU HONG.
OH
M-MIN-ISTER KO!
Klatt
GOOD MORNING!
WHAT WERE YOU DOING?
I WAS JUST CHECKING TO MAKE SURE NONE OF THE DOCUMENTS TO BE DISPOSED OF GOT MIXED IN...
I... I'M SORRY I STARTED READING IT WITHOUT ASKING...
fomp
I SEE.
I THOUGHT HE'D BE ANGRY...
Phew
NOW THAT I THINK ABOUT IT...
MINISTER KO ALWAYS COMES TO WORK FIRST THING IN THE MORNING.
He's usually the first one here.

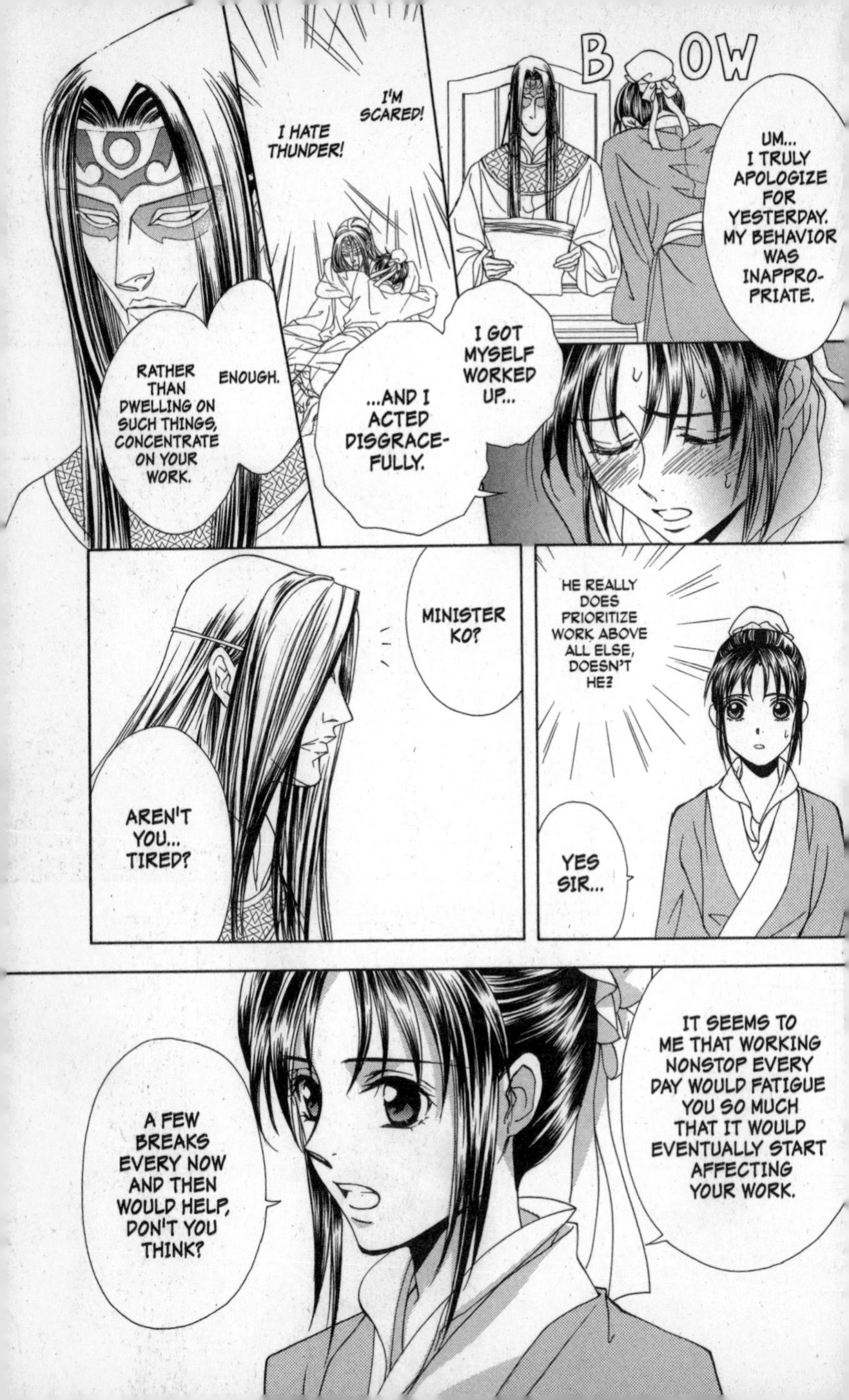
BOW
UM... I TRULY APOLOGIZE FOR YESTERDAY. MY BEHAVIOR WAS INAPPROPRIATE.
I GOT MYSELF WORKED UP...
...AND I ACTED DISGRACEFULLY.
I'M SCARED!
I HATE THUNDER!
ENOUGH.
RATHER THAN DWELLING ON SUCH THINGS, CONCENTRATE ON YOUR WORK.
HE REALLY DOES PRIORITIZE WORK ABOVE ALL ELSE, DOESN'T HE?
YES SIR...
MINISTER KO?
AREN'T YOU... TIRED?
IT SEEMS TO ME THAT WORKING NONSTOP EVERY DAY WOULD FATIGUE YOU SO MUCH THAT IT WOULD EVENTUALLY START AFFECTING YOUR WORK.
A FEW BREAKS EVERY NOW AND THEN WOULD HELP, DON'T YOU THINK?

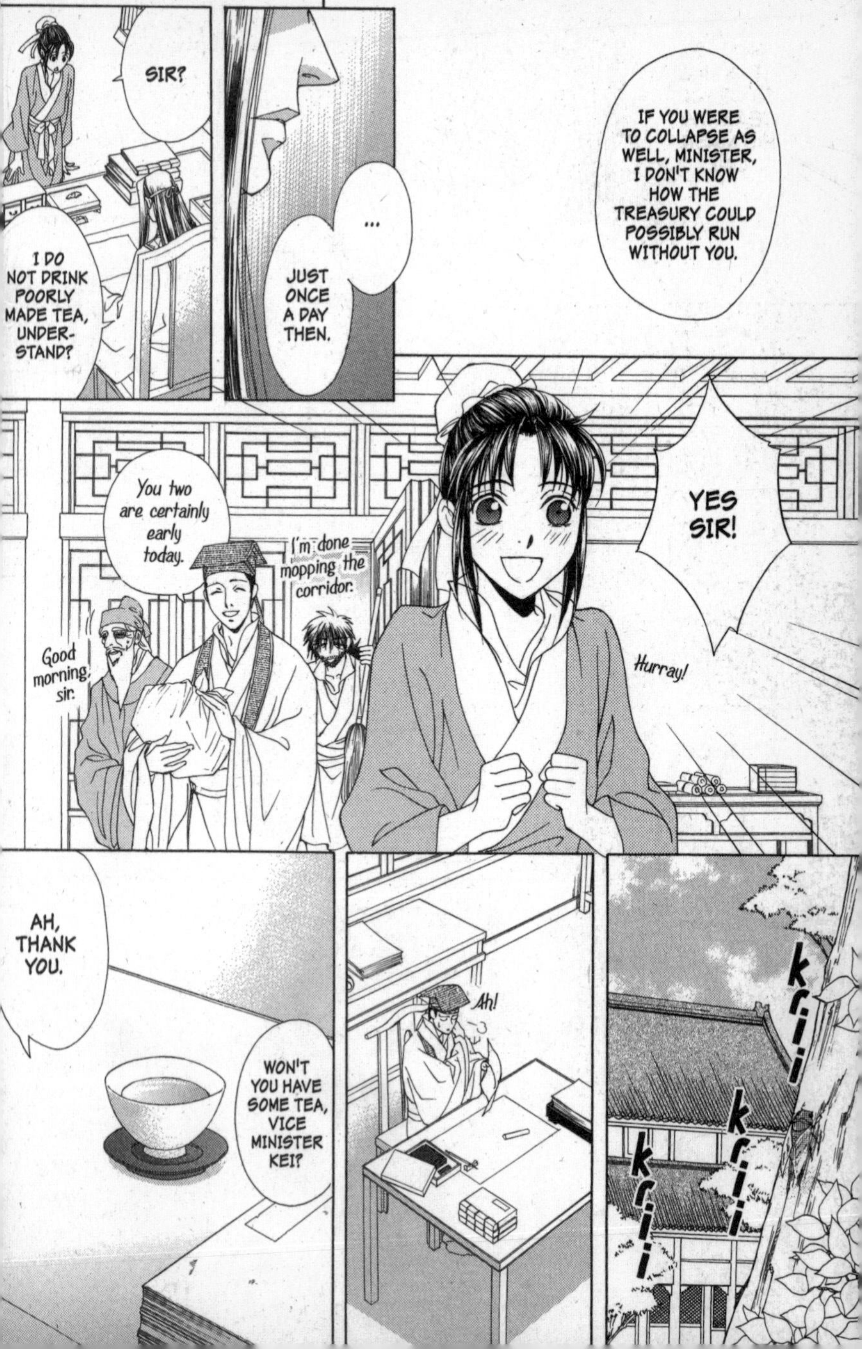
IF YOU WERE TO COLLAPSE AS WELL, MINISTER, I DON'T KNOW HOW THE TREASURY COULD POSSIBLY RUN WITHOUT YOU.
...
JUST ONCE A DAY THEN.
SIR?
I DO NOT DRINK POORLY MADE TEA, UNDERSTAND?
YES SIR!
Hurray!
I'm done mopping the corridor.
You two are certainly early today.
Good morning, sir.
kri
kri
kri
Ah!
WON'T YOU HAVE SOME TEA, VICE MINISTER KEI?
AH, THANK YOU.

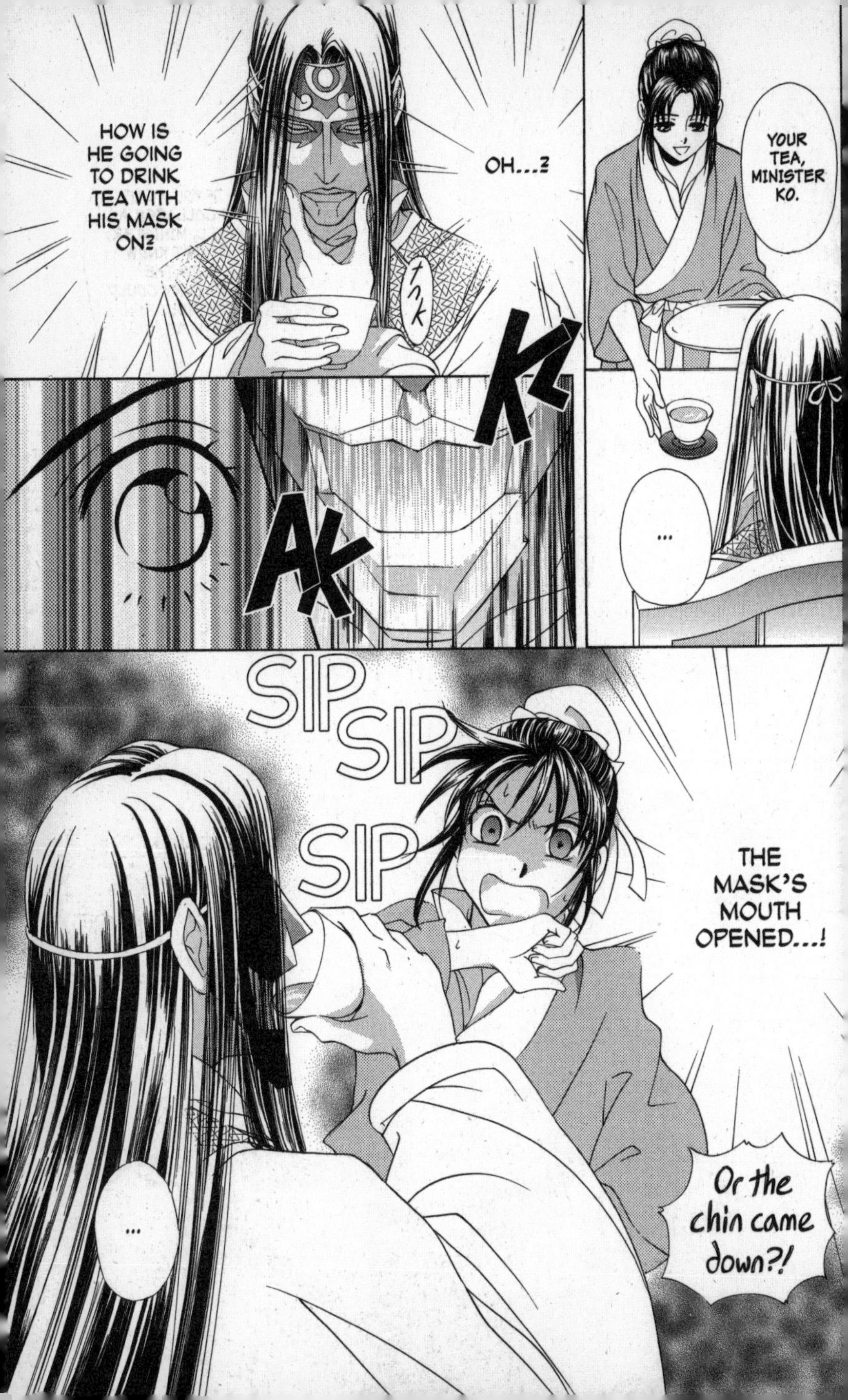
YOUR TEA, MINISTER KO.
OH...?
HOW IS HE GOING TO DRINK TEA WITH HIS MASK ON?
...
KL
AK
SIP
SIP
SIP
THE MASK'S MOUTH OPENED...!
Or the chin came down?!
...

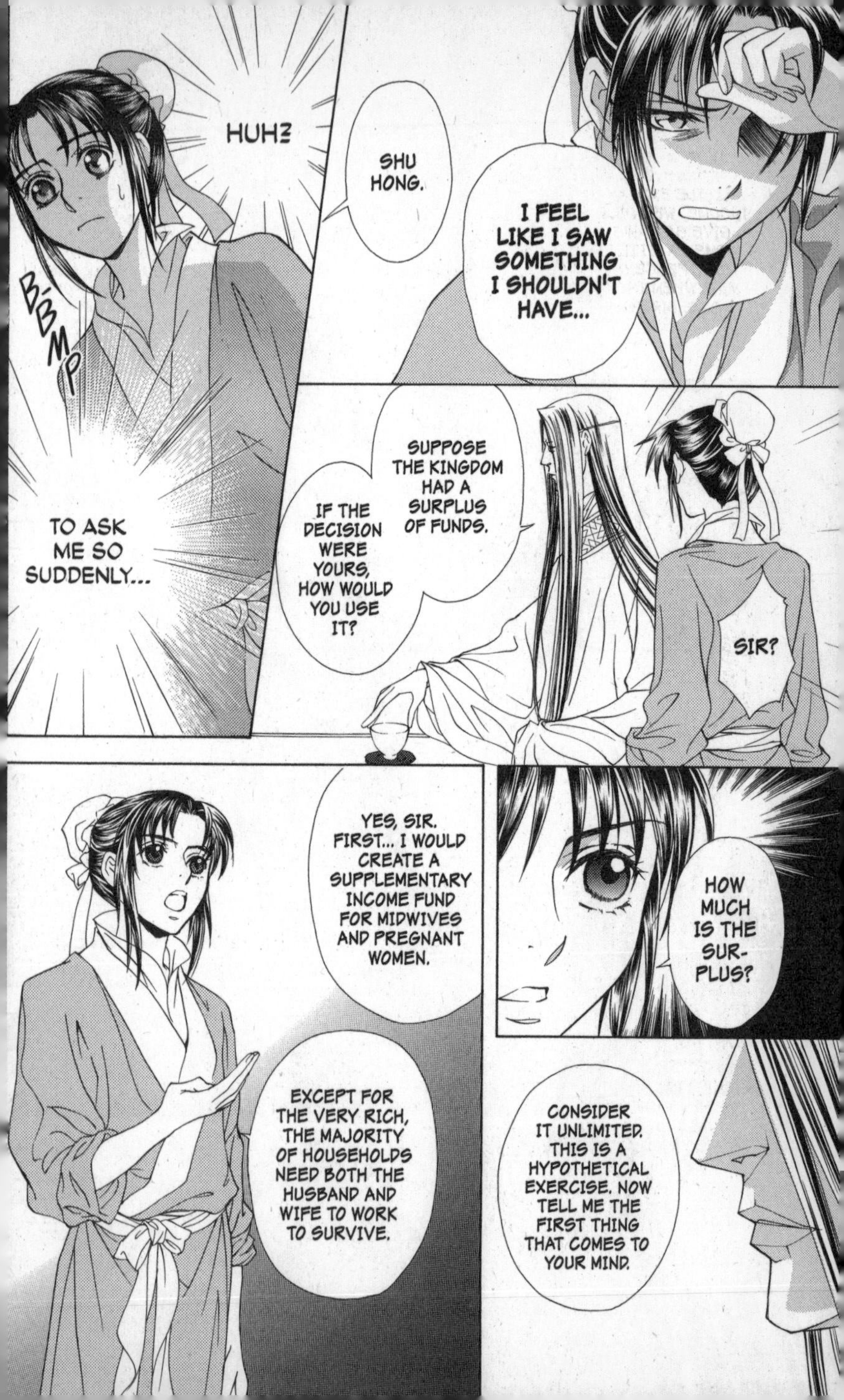
I FEEL LIKE I SAW SOMETHING I SHOULDN'T HAVE...
SHU HONG.
SIR?
SUPPOSE THE KINGDOM HAD A SURPLUS OF FUNDS.
IF THE DECISION WERE YOURS, HOW WOULD YOU USE IT?
HUH?
BBMP
TO ASK ME SO SUDDENLY...
HOW MUCH IS THE SUR-PLUS?
CONSIDER IT UNLIMITED. THIS IS A HYPOTHETICAL EXERCISE. NOW TELL ME THE FIRST THING THAT COMES TO YOUR MIND.
YES, SIR. FIRST... I WOULD CREATE A SUPPLEMENTARY INCOME FUND FOR MIDWIVES AND PREGNANT WOMEN.
EXCEPT FOR THE VERY RICH, THE MAJORITY OF HOUSEHOLDS NEED BOTH THE HUSBAND AND WIFE TO WORK TO SURVIVE.

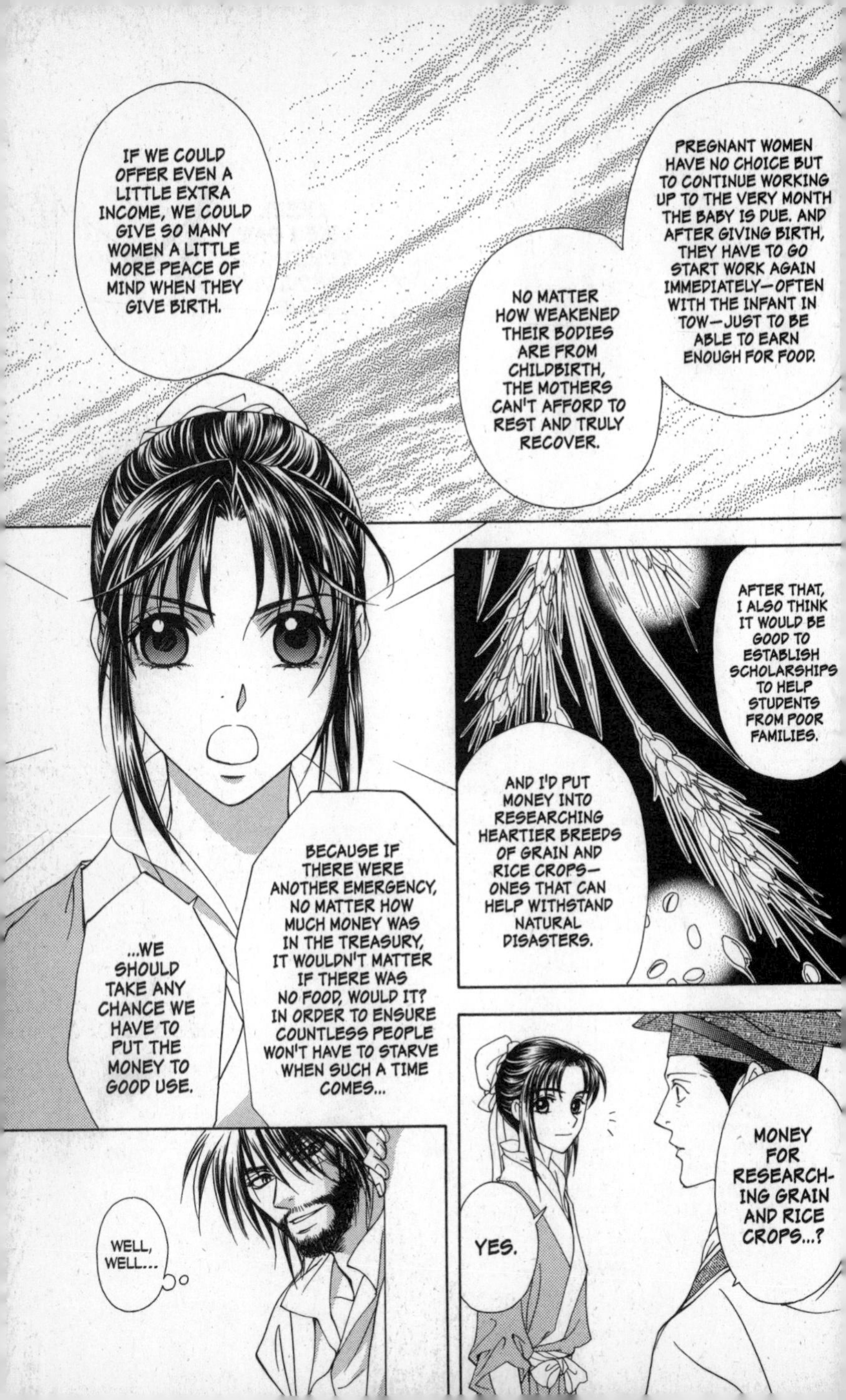
PREGNANT WOMEN HAVE NO CHOICE BUT TO CONTINUE WORKING UP TO THE VERY MONTH THE BABY IS DUE. AND AFTER GIVING BIRTH, THEY HAVE TO GO START WORK AGAIN IMMEDIATELY—OFTEN WITH THE INFANT IN TOW—JUST TO BE ABLE TO EARN ENOUGH FOR FOOD.
NO MATTER HOW WEAKENED THEIR BODIES ARE FROM CHILDBIRTH, THE MOTHERS CAN'T AFFORD TO REST AND TRULY RECOVER.
IF WE COULD OFFER EVEN A LITTLE EXTRA INCOME, WE COULD GIVE SO MANY WOMEN A LITTLE MORE PEACE OF MIND WHEN THEY GIVE BIRTH.
AFTER THAT, I ALSO THINK IT WOULD BE GOOD TO ESTABLISH SCHOLARSHIPS TO HELP STUDENTS FROM POOR FAMILIES.
AND I'D PUT MONEY INTO RESEARCHING HEARTIER BREEDS OF GRAIN AND RICE CROPS—ONES THAT CAN HELP WITHSTAND NATURAL DISASTERS.
BECAUSE IF THERE WERE ANOTHER EMERGENCY, NO MATTER HOW MUCH MONEY WAS IN THE TREASURY, IT WOULDN'T MATTER IF THERE WAS NO FOOD, WOULD IT? IN ORDER TO ENSURE COUNTLESS PEOPLE WON'T HAVE TO STARVE WHEN SUCH A TIME COMES...
...WE SHOULD TAKE ANY CHANCE WE HAVE TO PUT THE MONEY TO GOOD USE.
MONEY FOR RESEARCHING GRAIN AND RICE CROPS...?
YES.
WELL, WELL...

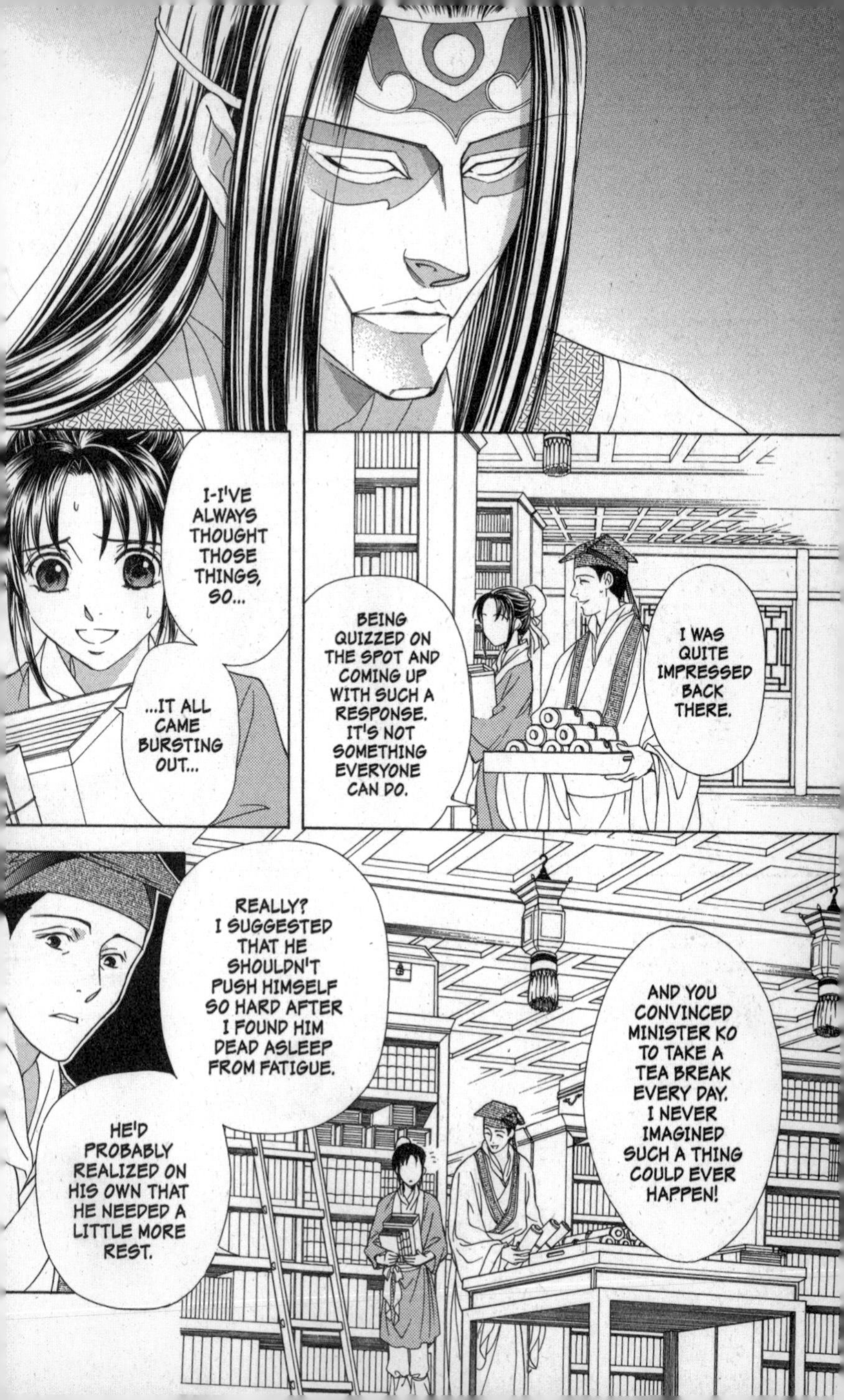
I WAS QUITE IMPRESSED BACK THERE.
BEING QUIZZED ON THE SPOT AND COMING UP WITH SUCH A RESPONSE. IT'S NOT SOMETHING EVERYONE CAN DO.
I-I'VE ALWAYS THOUGHT THOSE THINGS, SO...
...IT ALL CAME BURSTING OUT...
AND YOU CONVINCED MINISTER KO TO TAKE A TEA BREAK EVERY DAY. I NEVER IMAGINED SUCH A THING COULD EVER HAPPEN!
REALLY? I SUGGESTED THAT HE SHOULDN'T PUSH HIMSELF SO HARD AFTER I FOUND HIM DEAD ASLEEP FROM FATIGUE.
HE'D PROBABLY REALIZED ON HIS OWN THAT HE NEEDED A LITTLE MORE REST.

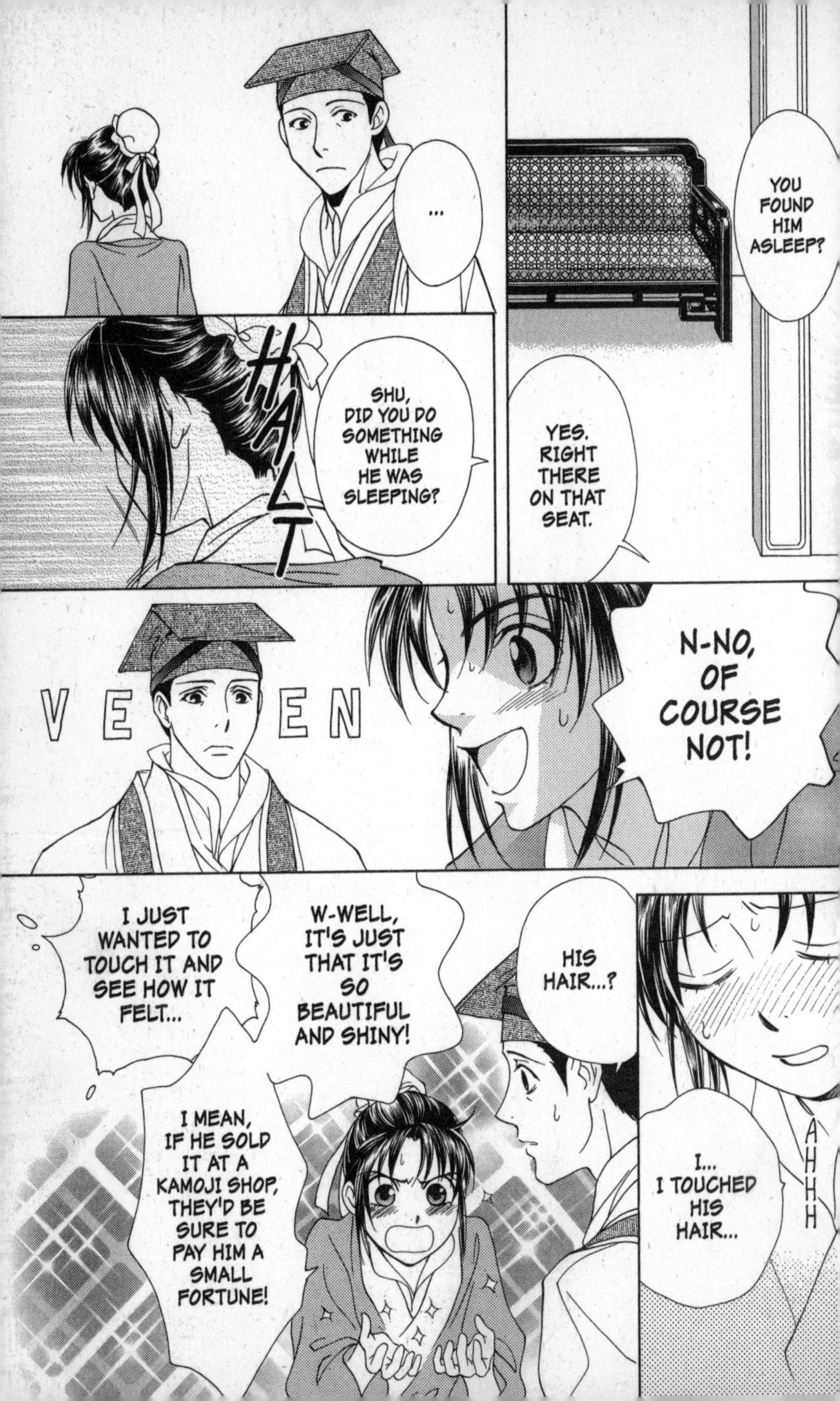
YOU FOUND HIM ASLEEP?
YES. RIGHT THERE ON THAT SEAT.
...
HALT
SHU, DID YOU DO SOMETHING WHILE HE WAS SLEEPING?
N-NO, OF COURSE NOT!
VEEN
AHHH
I... I TOUCHED HIS HAIR...
HIS HAIR...?
W-WELL, IT'S JUST THAT IT'S SO BEAUTIFUL AND SHINY!
I JUST WANTED TO TOUCH IT AND SEE HOW IT FELT...
I MEAN, IF HE SOLD IT AT A KAMOJI SHOP, THEY'D BE SURE TO PAY HIM A SMALL FORTUNE!

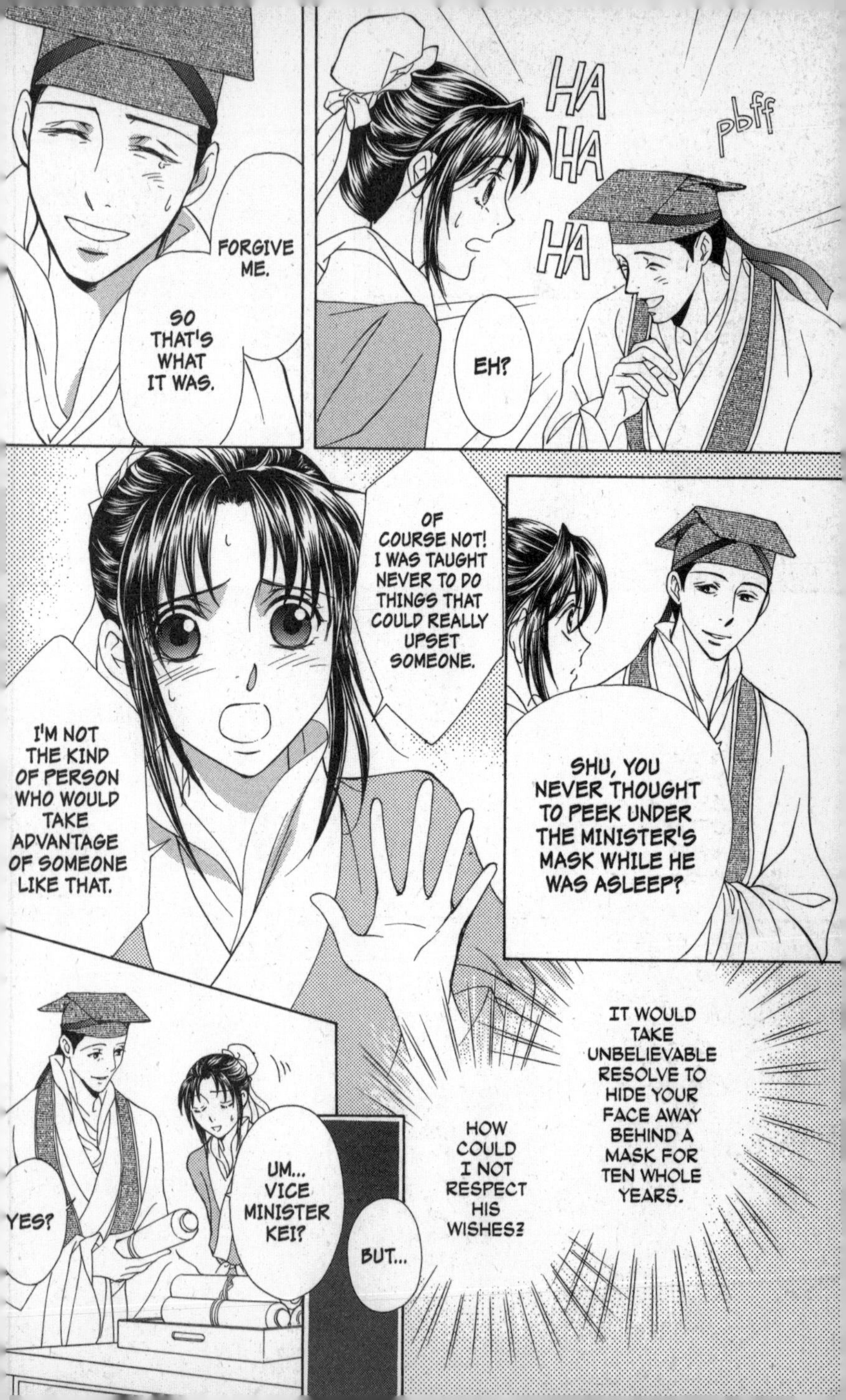
HA HA HA
pbff
EH?
FORGIVE ME.
SO THAT'S WHAT IT WAS.
SHU, YOU NEVER THOUGHT TO PEEK UNDER THE MINISTER'S MASK WHILE HE WAS ASLEEP?
OF COURSE NOT! I WAS TAUGHT NEVER TO DO THINGS THAT COULD REALLY UPSET SOMEONE.
I'M NOT THE KIND OF PERSON WHO WOULD TAKE ADVANTAGE OF SOMEONE LIKE THAT.
IT WOULD TAKE UNBELIEVABLE RESOLVE TO HIDE YOUR FACE AWAY BEHIND A MASK FOR TEN WHOLE YEARS.
HOW COULD I NOT RESPECT HIS WISHES?
BUT...
UM... VICE MINISTER KEI?
YES?

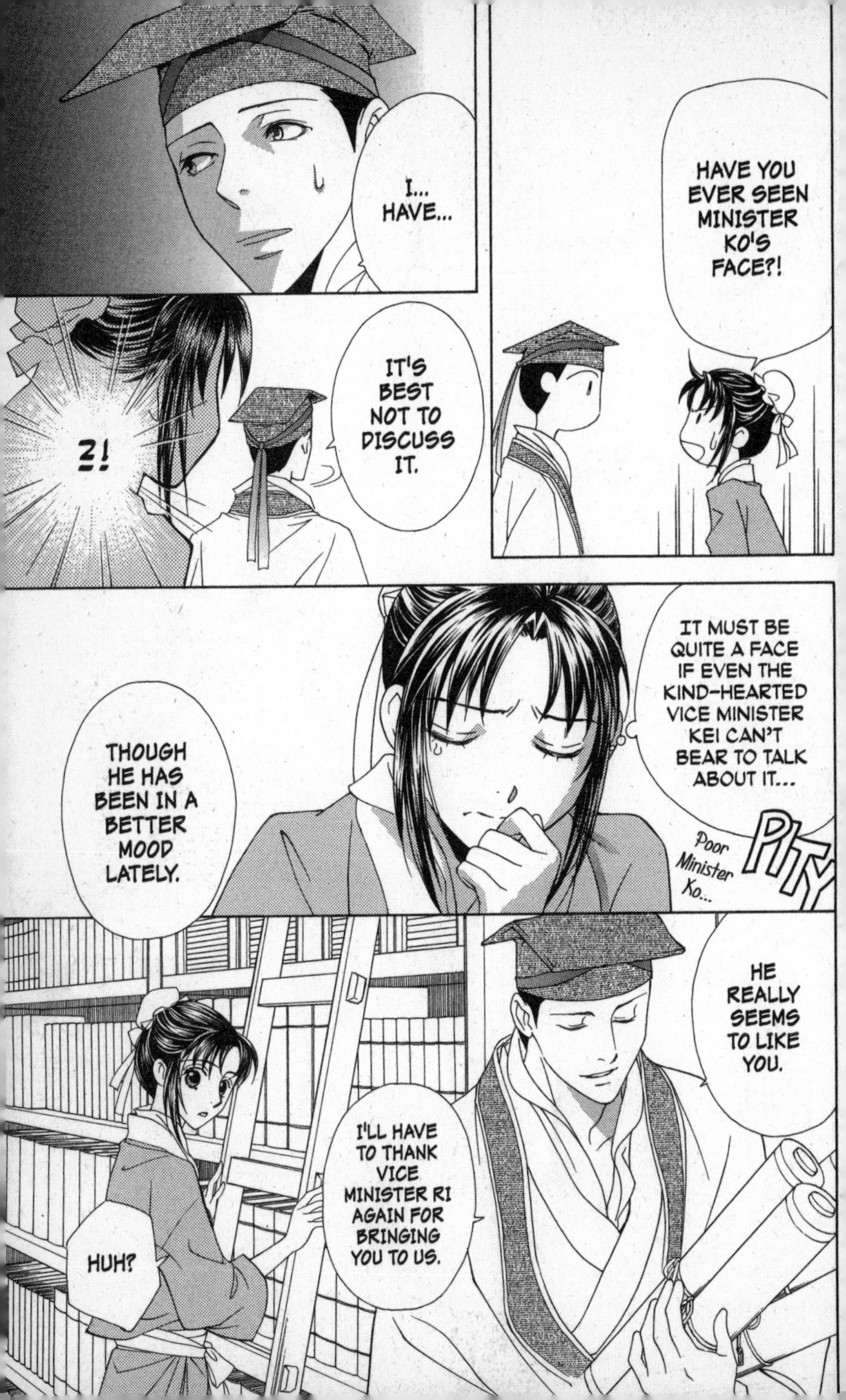
HAVE YOU EVER SEEN MINISTER KO'S FACE?!
I... HAVE...
IT'S BEST NOT TO DISCUSS IT.
Z!
IT MUST BE QUITE A FACE IF EVEN THE KIND-HEARTED VICE MINISTER KEI CAN'T BEAR TO TALK ABOUT IT...
PITY
Poor Minister Ko...
THOUGH HE HAS BEEN IN A BETTER MOOD LATELY.
HE REALLY SEEMS TO LIKE YOU.
I'LL HAVE TO THANK VICE MINISTER RI AGAIN FOR BRINGING YOU TO US.
HUH?

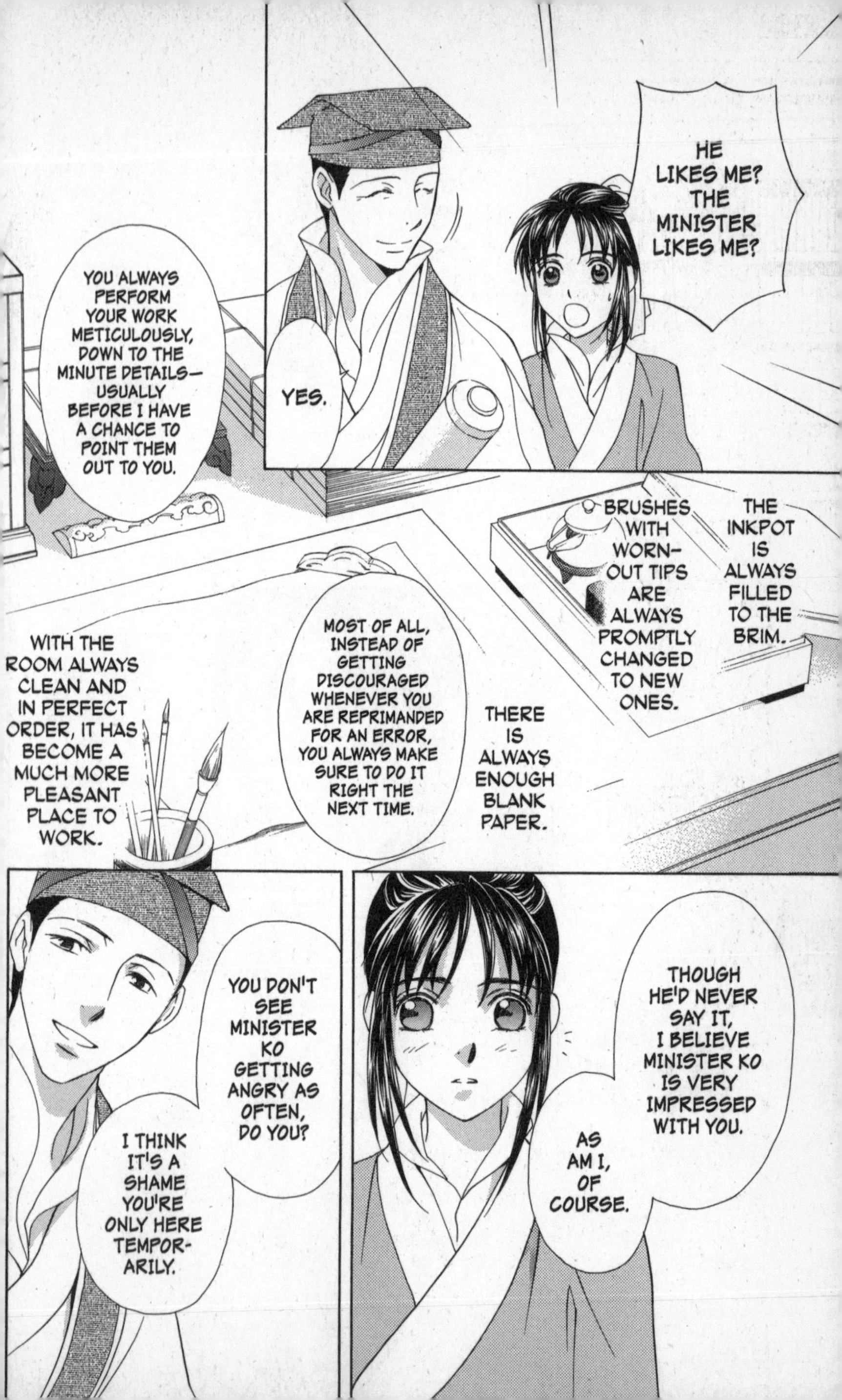
HE LIKES ME? THE MINISTER LIKES ME?
YES.
YOU ALWAYS PERFORM YOUR WORK METICULOUSLY, DOWN TO THE MINUTE DETAILS—USUALLY BEFORE I HAVE A CHANCE TO POINT THEM OUT TO YOU.
THE INKPOT IS ALWAYS FILLED TO THE BRIM.
BRUSHES WITH WORN-OUT TIPS ARE ALWAYS PROMPTLY CHANGED TO NEW ONES.
THERE IS ALWAYS ENOUGH BLANK PAPER.
MOST OF ALL, INSTEAD OF GETTING DISCOURAGED WHENEVER YOU ARE REPRIMANDED FOR AN ERROR, YOU ALWAYS MAKE SURE TO DO IT RIGHT THE NEXT TIME.
WITH THE ROOM ALWAYS CLEAN AND IN PERFECT ORDER, IT HAS BECOME A MUCH MORE PLEASANT PLACE TO WORK.
THOUGH HE'D NEVER SAY IT, I BELIEVE MINISTER KO IS VERY IMPRESSED WITH YOU.
AS AM I, OF COURSE.
YOU DON'T SEE MINISTER KO GETTING ANGRY AS OFTEN, DO YOU?
I THINK IT'S A SHAME YOU'RE ONLY HERE TEMPOR-ARILY.

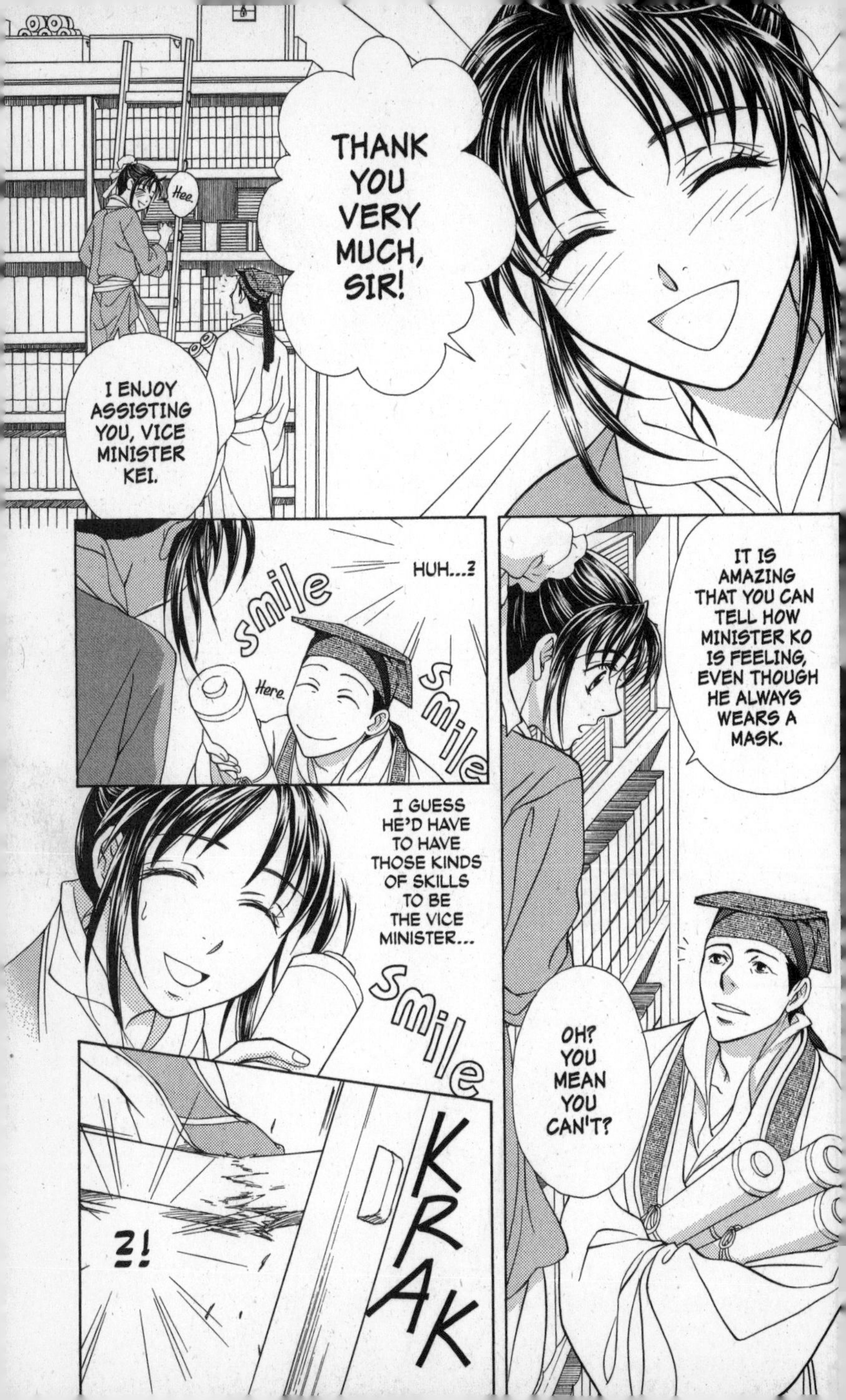
THANK YOU VERY MUCH, SIR!
Hee...
I ENJOY ASSISTING YOU, VICE MINISTER KEI.
IT IS AMAZING THAT YOU CAN TELL HOW MINISTER KO IS FEELING, EVEN THOUGH HE ALWAYS WEARS A MASK.
OH? YOU MEAN YOU CAN'T?
HUH...?
smile
Here.
smile
I GUESS HE'D HAVE TO HAVE THOSE KINDS OF SKILLS TO BE THE VICE MINISTER...
Smile
KRAK
?!

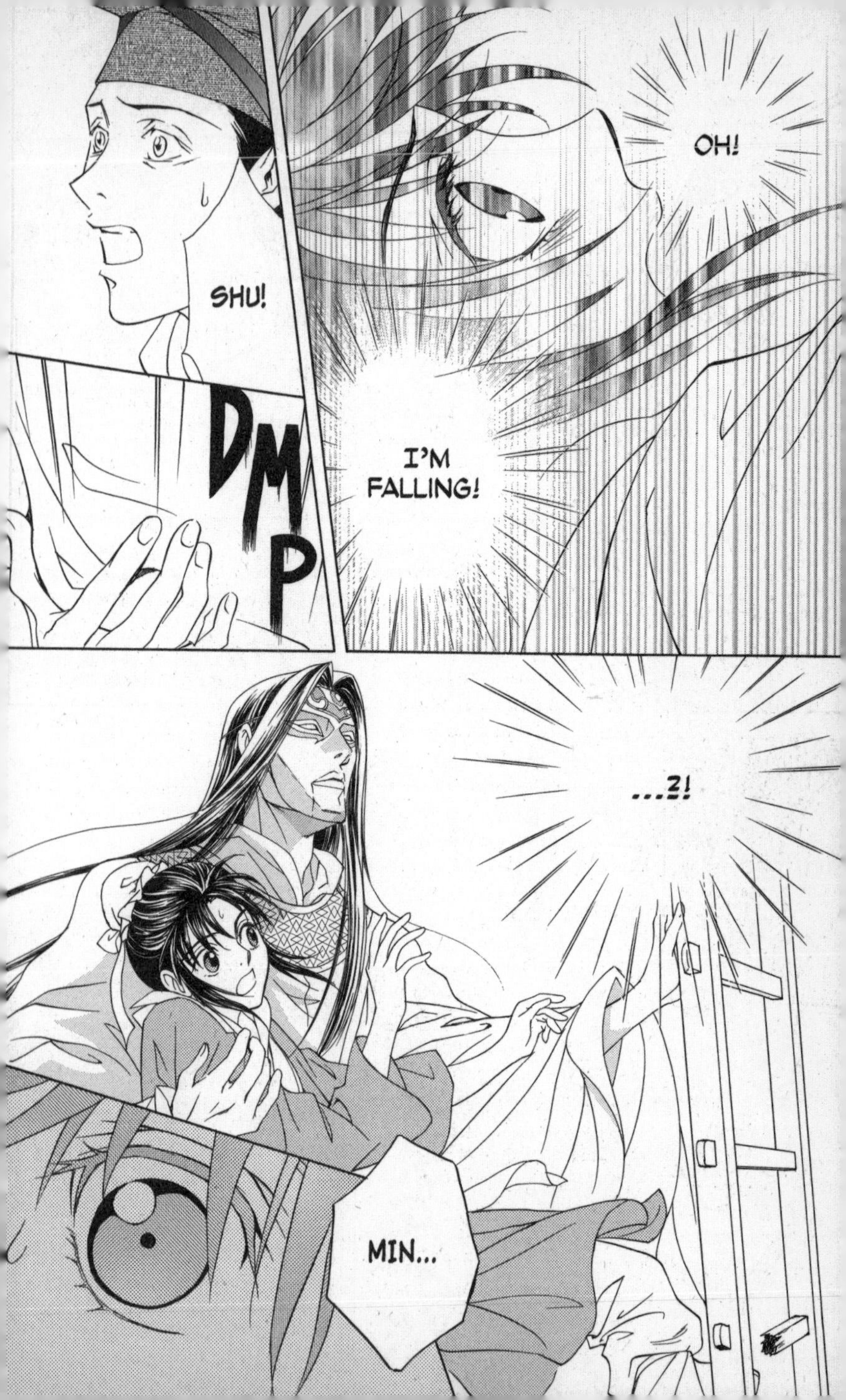
OH!
I'M FALLING!
SHU!
DMP
...?!
MIN...

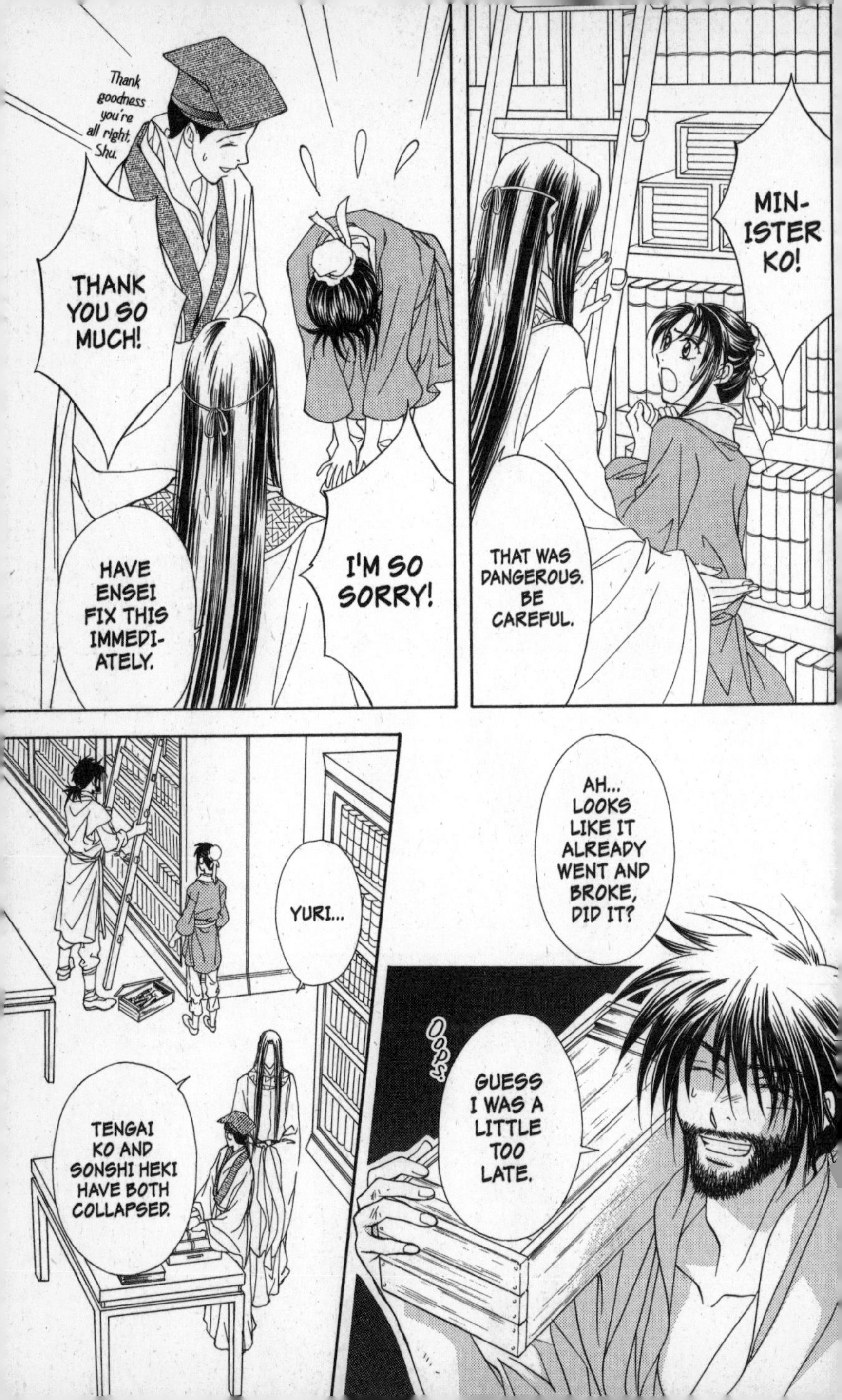
MIN-ISTER KO!
THAT WAS DANGEROUS. BE CAREFUL.
I'M SO SORRY!
Thank goodness you're all right, Shu.
THANK YOU SO MUCH!
HAVE ENSEI FIX THIS IMMEDI-ATELY.
AH... LOOKS LIKE IT ALREADY WENT AND BROKE, DID IT?
Oops.
GUESS I WAS A LITTLE TOO LATE.
YURI...
TENGAI KO AND SONSHI HEKI HAVE BOTH COLLAPSED.

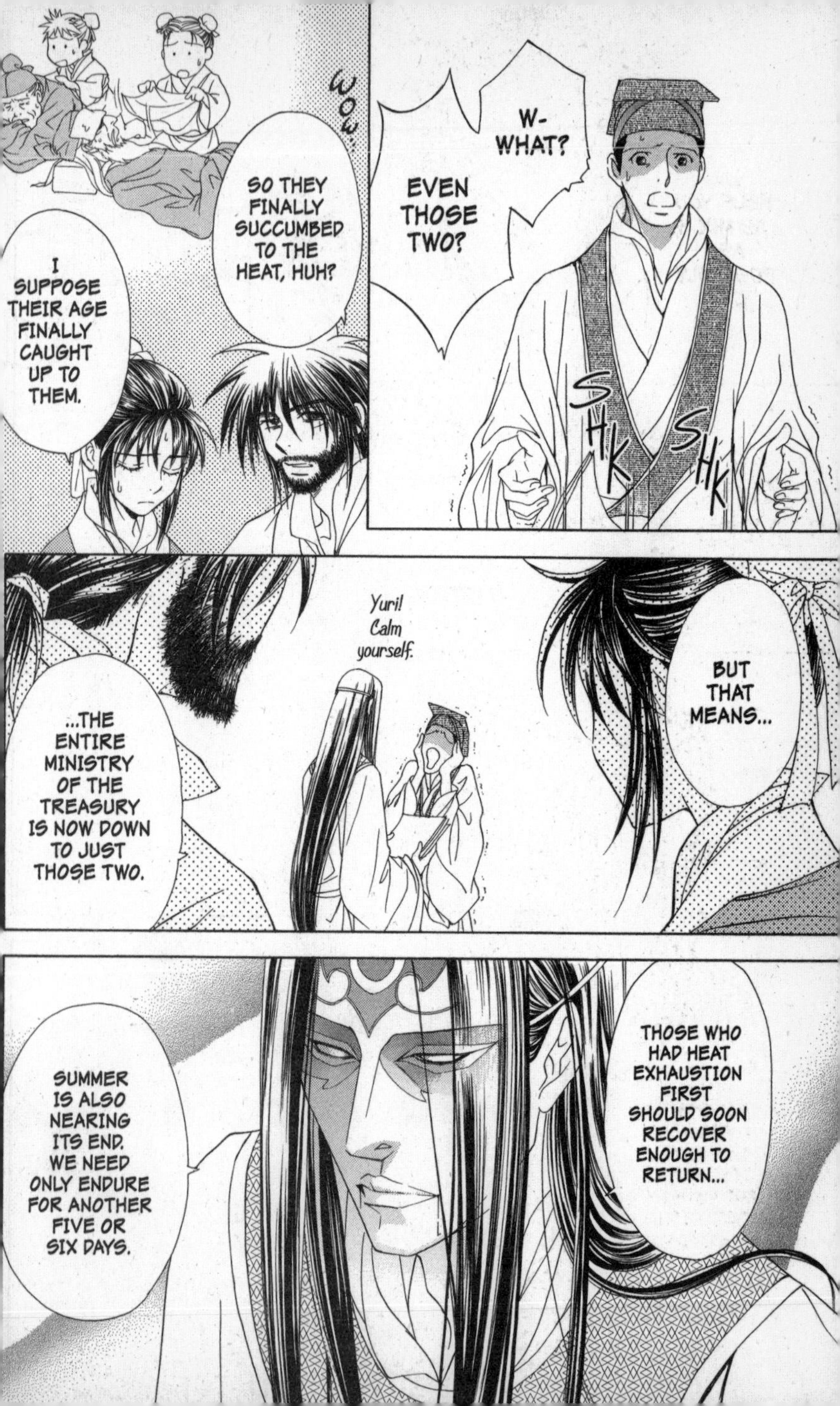
W-WHAT?
EVEN THOSE TWO?
SHK SHK
WOW...
SO THEY FINALLY SUCCUMBED TO THE HEAT, HUH?
I SUPPOSE THEIR AGE FINALLY CAUGHT UP TO THEM.
BUT THAT MEANS...
Yuri! Calm yourself.
...THE ENTIRE MINISTRY OF THE TREASURY IS NOW DOWN TO JUST THOSE TWO.
THOSE WHO HAD HEAT EXHAUSTION FIRST SHOULD SOON RECOVER ENOUGH TO RETURN...
SUMMER IS ALSO NEARING ITS END. WE NEED ONLY ENDURE FOR ANOTHER FIVE OR SIX DAYS.

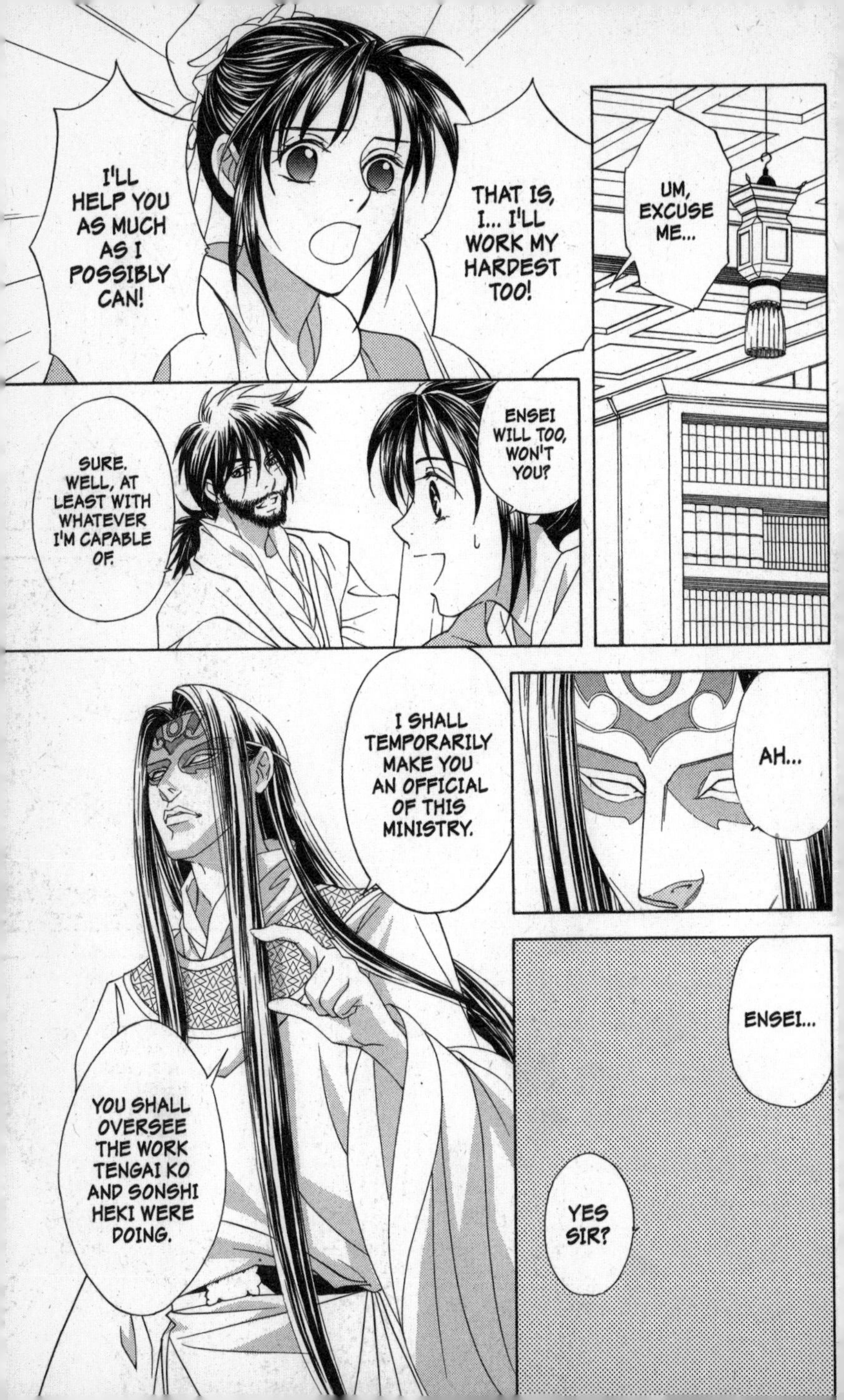
UM, EXCUSE ME...
THAT IS, I... I'LL WORK MY HARDEST TOO!
I'LL HELP YOU AS MUCH AS I POSSIBLY CAN!
ENSEI WILL TOO, WON'T YOU?
SURE. WELL, AT LEAST WITH WHATEVER I'M CAPABLE OF.
AH...
ENSEI...
YES SIR?
I SHALL TEMPORARILY MAKE YOU AN OFFICIAL OF THIS MINISTRY.
YOU SHALL OVERSEE THE WORK TENGAI KO AND SONSHI HEKI WERE DOING.

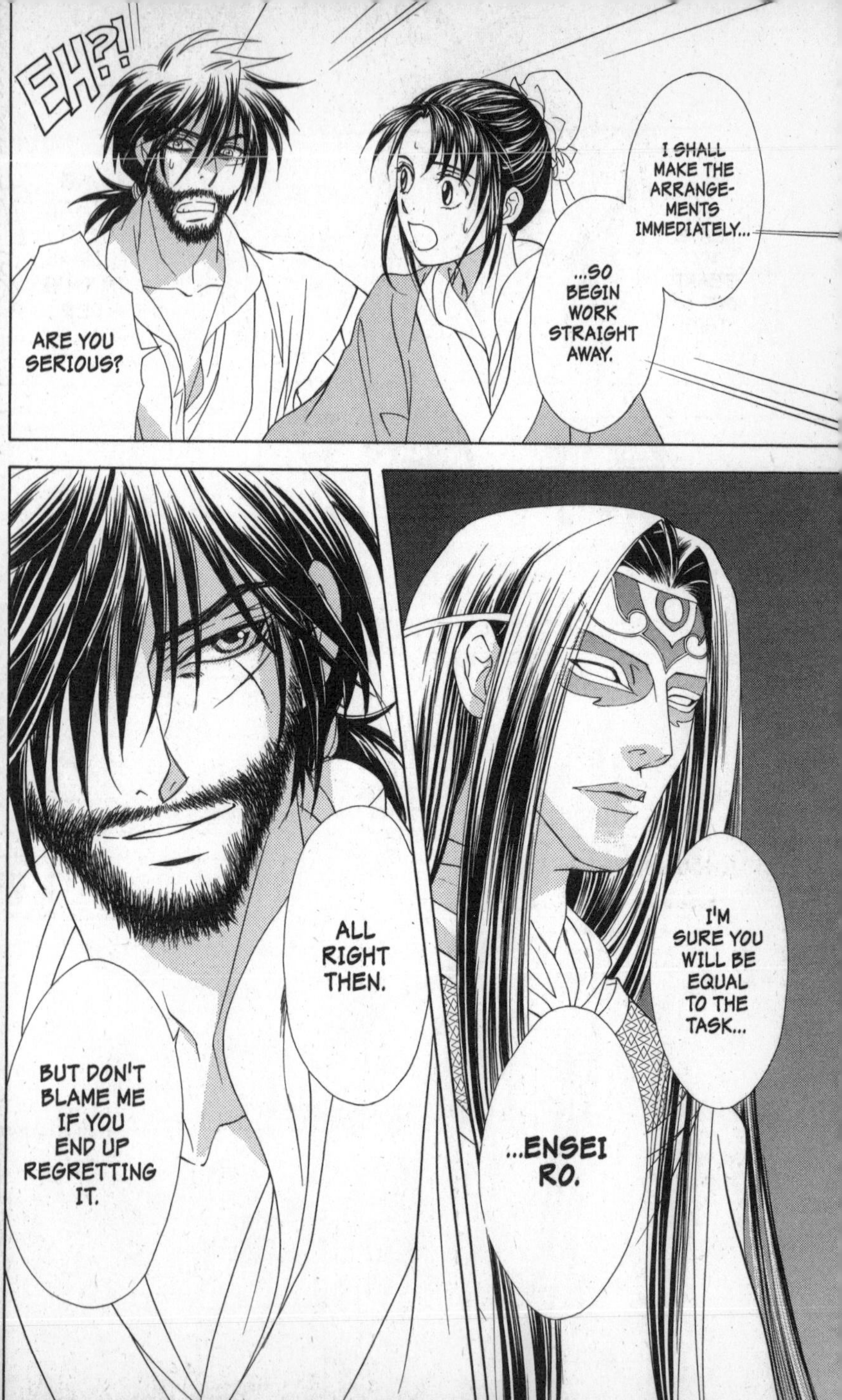
I SHALL MAKE THE ARRANGE-MENTS IMMEDIATELY...
...SO BEGIN WORK STRAIGHT AWAY.
EH?!
ARE YOU SERIOUS?
I'M SURE YOU WILL BE EQUAL TO THE TASK...
...ENSEI RO.
ALL RIGHT THEN.
BUT DON'T BLAME ME IF YOU END UP REGRETTING IT.

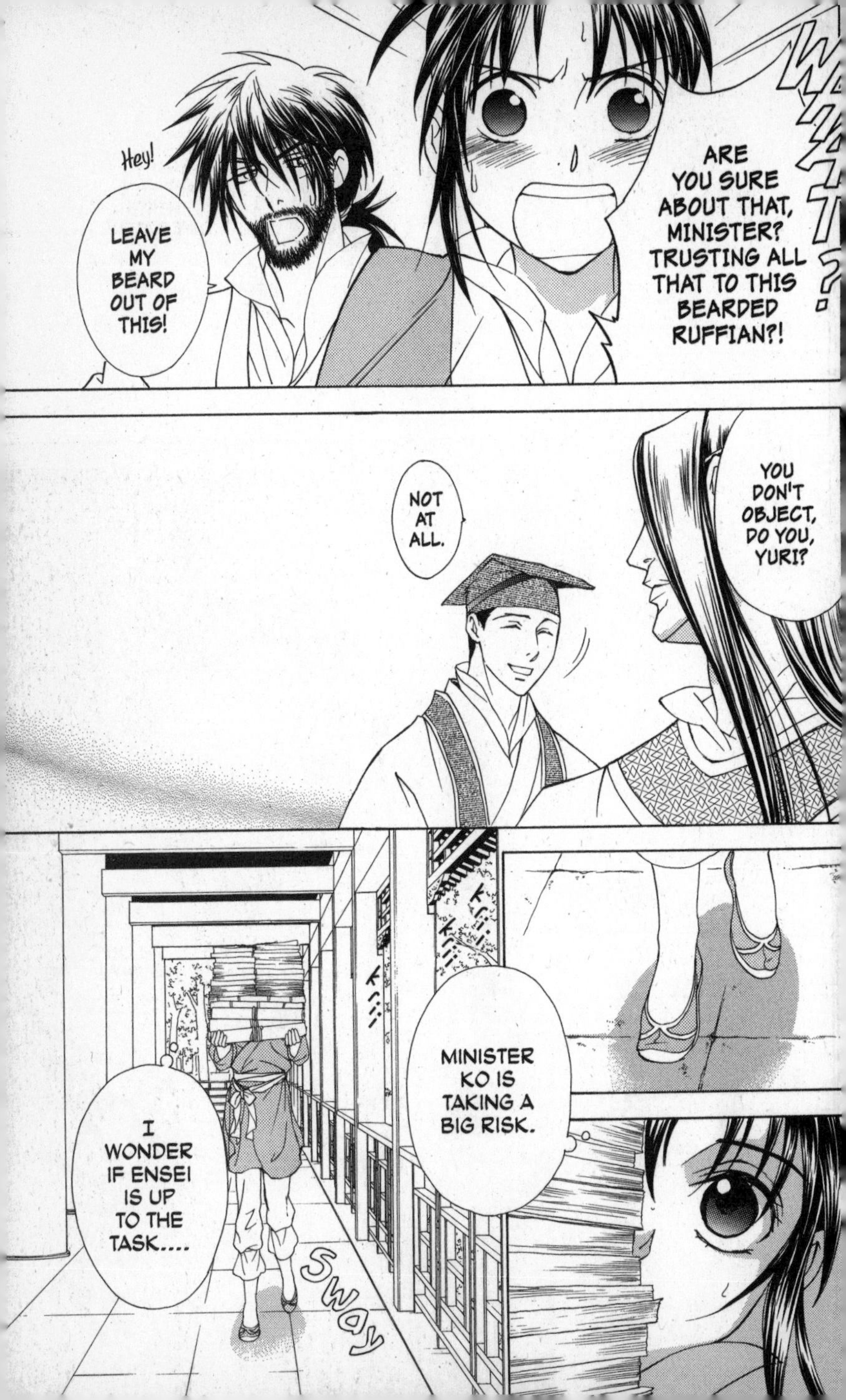
WHAT?
ARE YOU SURE ABOUT THAT, MINISTER? TRUSTING ALL THAT TO THIS BEARDED RUFFIAN?!
Hey!
LEAVE MY BEARD OUT OF THIS!
YOU DON'T OBJECT, DO YOU, YURI?
NOT AT ALL.
MINISTER KO IS TAKING A BIG RISK.
Kriii
Kriii
Kriii
I WONDER IF ENSEI IS UP TO THE TASK....
SWAY

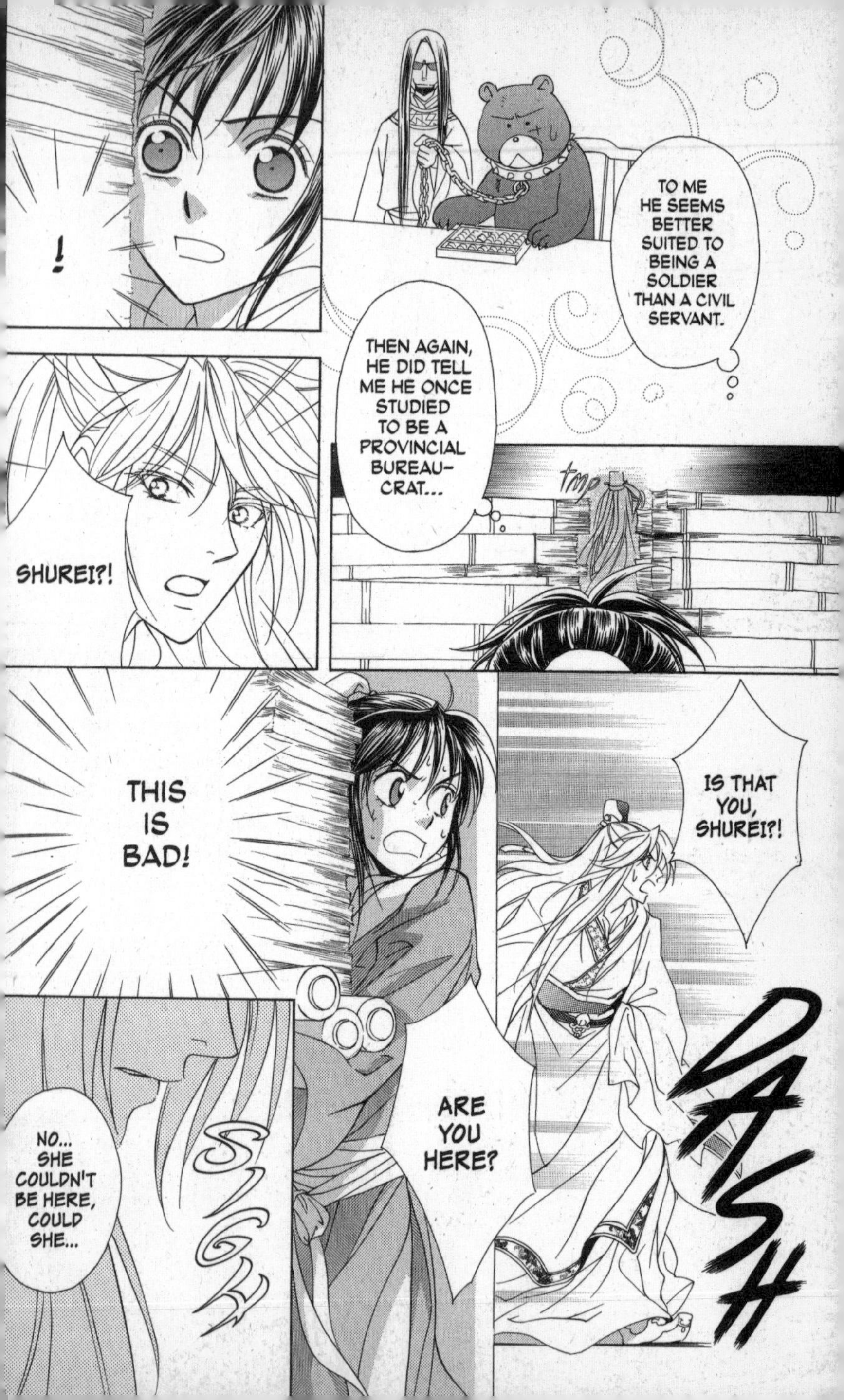
TO ME HE SEEMS BETTER SUITED TO BEING A SOLDIER THAN A CIVIL SERVANT.
THEN AGAIN, HE DID TELL ME HE ONCE STUDIED TO BE A PROVINCIAL BUREAU-CRAT...
!
tmp
SHUREI?!
IS THAT YOU, SHUREI?!
ARE YOU HERE?
DASH
THIS IS BAD!
NO... SHE COULDN'T BE HERE, COULD SHE...
SIGH

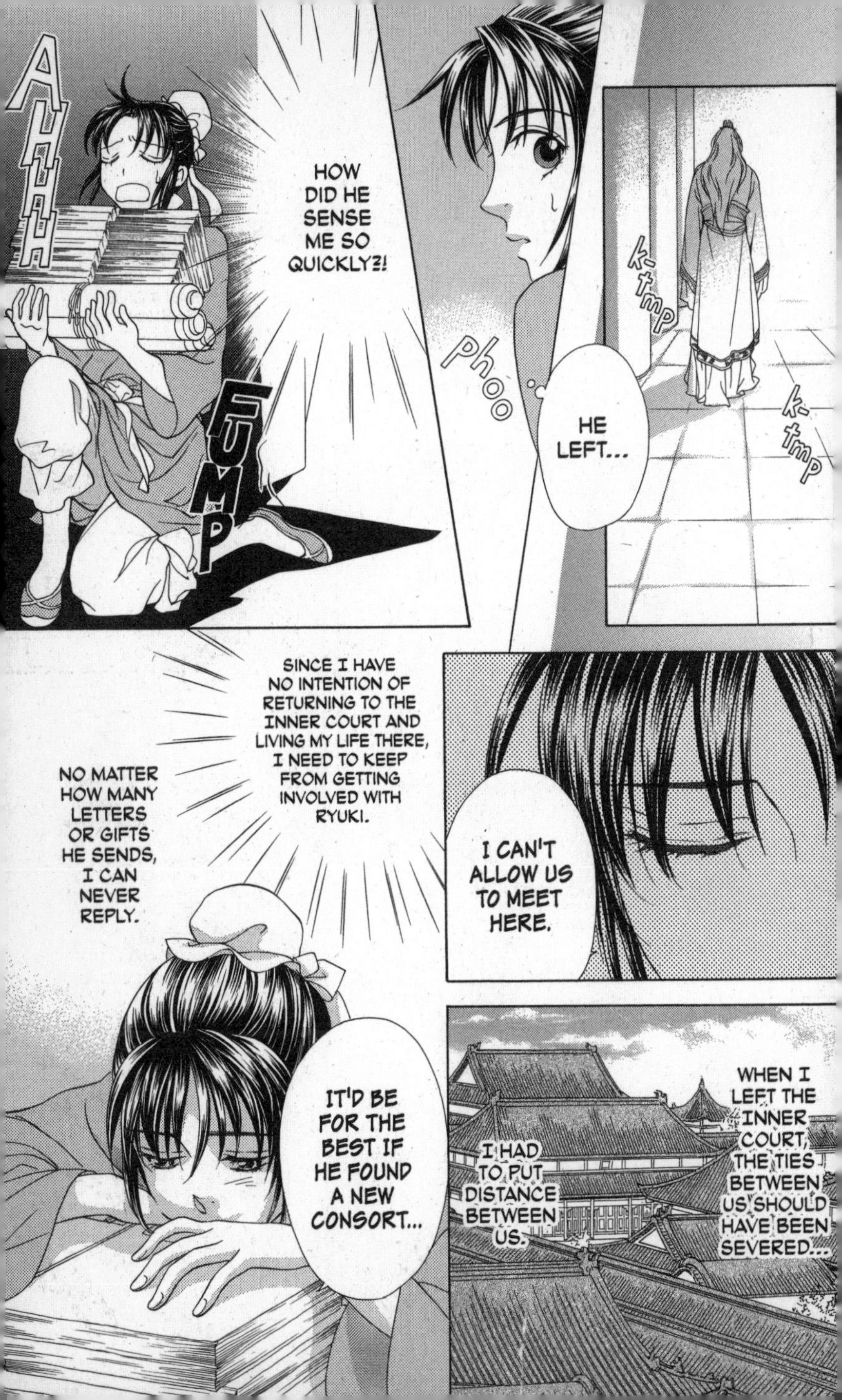
k-tmp
k-tmp
Phoo
HE LEFT...
AHHHHH
HOW DID HE SENSE ME SO QUICKLY?!
FUMP
I CAN'T ALLOW US TO MEET HERE.
WHEN I LEFT THE INNER COURT, THE TIES BETWEEN US SHOULD HAVE BEEN SEVERED...
I HAD TO PUT DISTANCE BETWEEN US.
SINCE I HAVE NO INTENTION OF RETURNING TO THE INNER COURT AND LIVING MY LIFE THERE, I NEED TO KEEP FROM GETTING INVOLVED WITH RYUKI.
NO MATTER HOW MANY LETTERS OR GIFTS HE SENDS, I CAN NEVER REPLY.
IT'D BE FOR THE BEST IF HE FOUND A NEW CONSORT...

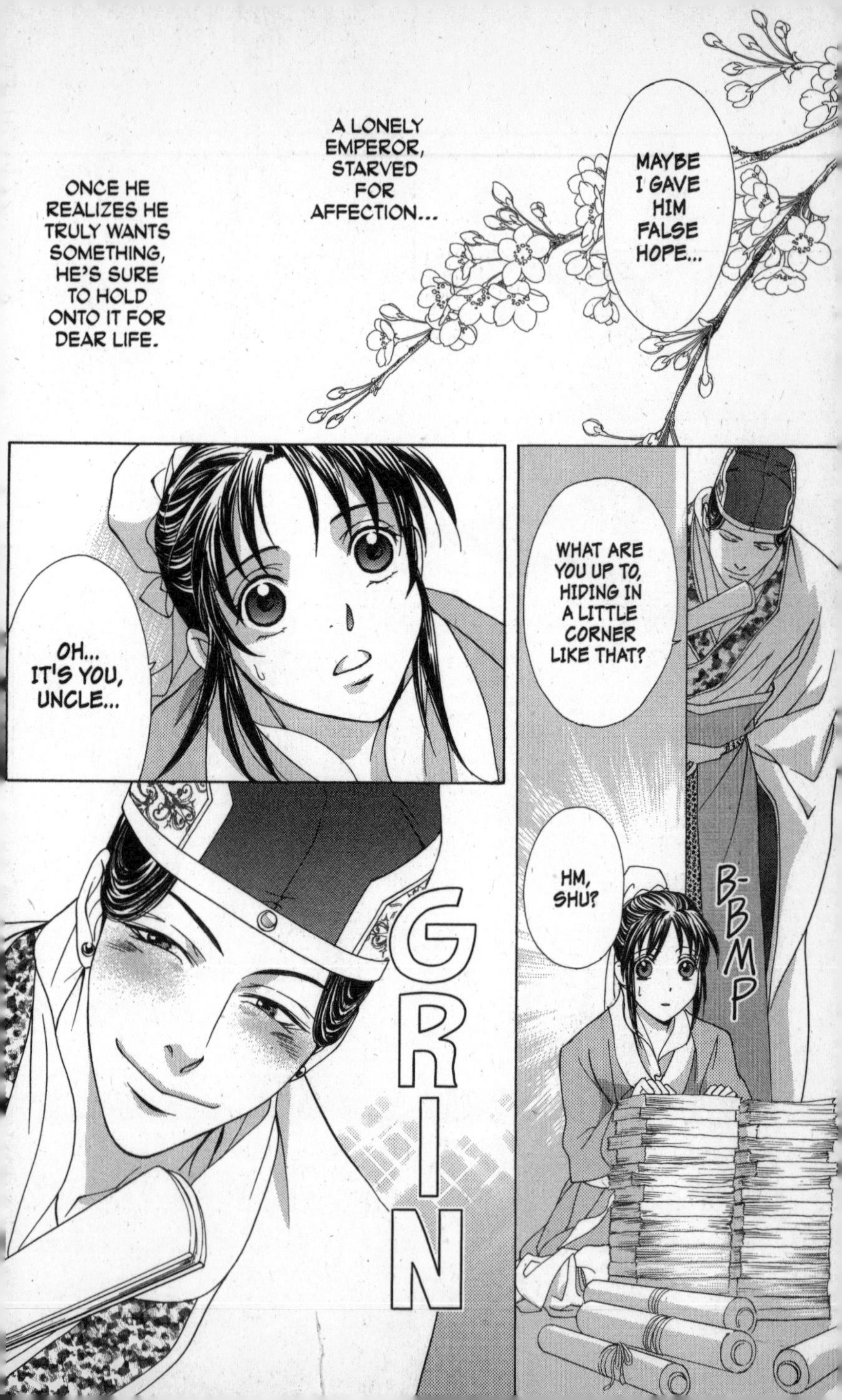
MAYBE I GAVE HIM FALSE HOPE...
A LONELY EMPEROR, STARVED FOR AFFECTION...
ONCE HE REALIZES HE TRULY WANTS SOMETHING, HE'S SURE TO HOLD ONTO IT FOR DEAR LIFE.
WHAT ARE YOU UP TO, HIDING IN A LITTLE CORNER LIKE THAT?
HM, SHU?
B-BMP
OH... IT'S YOU, UNCLE...
GRIN

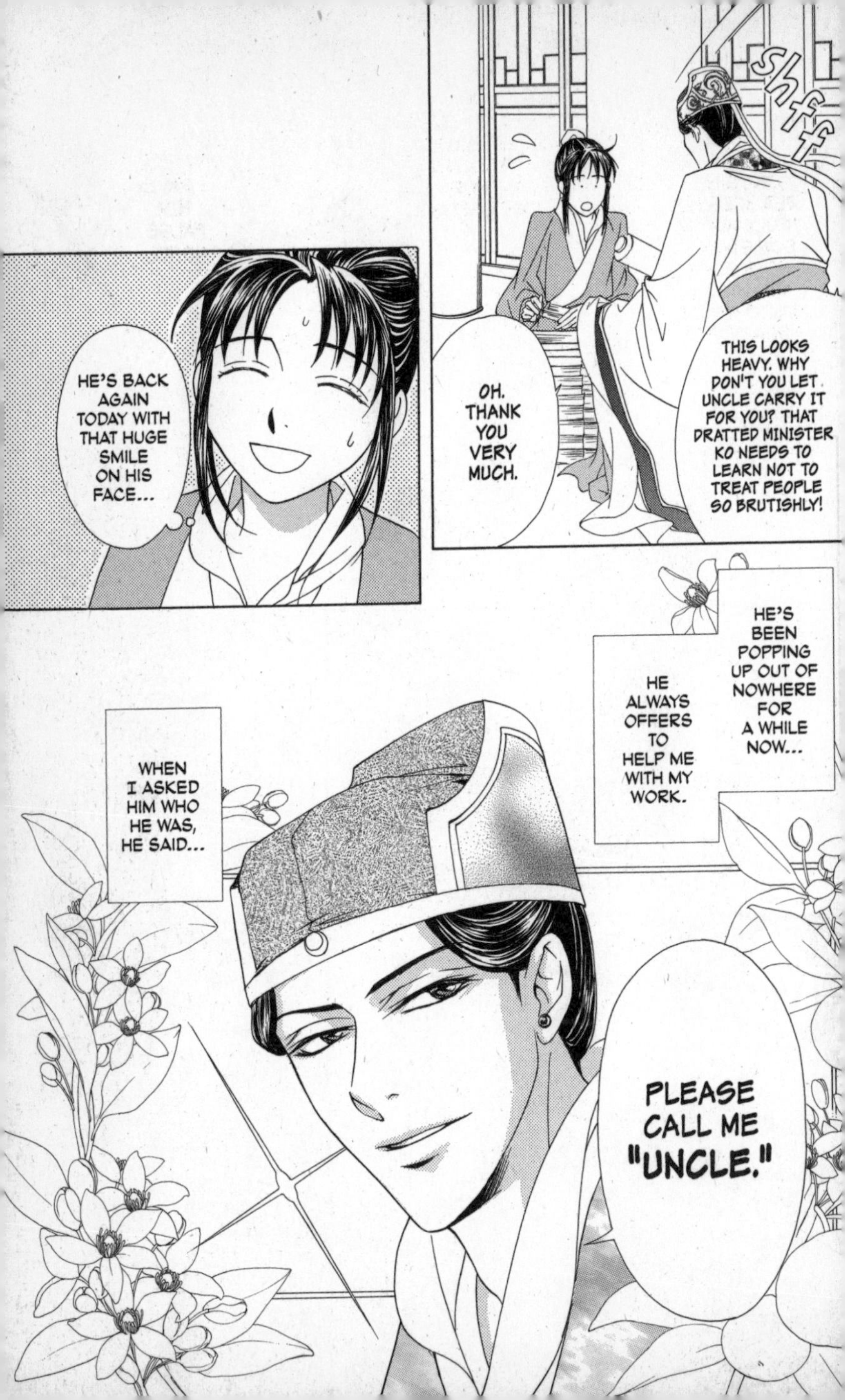
shff
THIS LOOKS HEAVY. WHY DON'T YOU LET UNCLE CARRY IT FOR YOU? THAT DRATTED MINISTER KO NEEDS TO LEARN NOT TO TREAT PEOPLE SO BRUTISHLY!
OH. THANK YOU VERY MUCH.
HE'S BACK AGAIN TODAY WITH THAT HUGE SMILE ON HIS FACE...
HE'S BEEN POPPING UP OUT OF NOWHERE FOR A WHILE NOW...
HE ALWAYS OFFERS TO HELP ME WITH MY WORK.
WHEN I ASKED HIM WHO HE WAS, HE SAID...
PLEASE CALL ME "UNCLE."

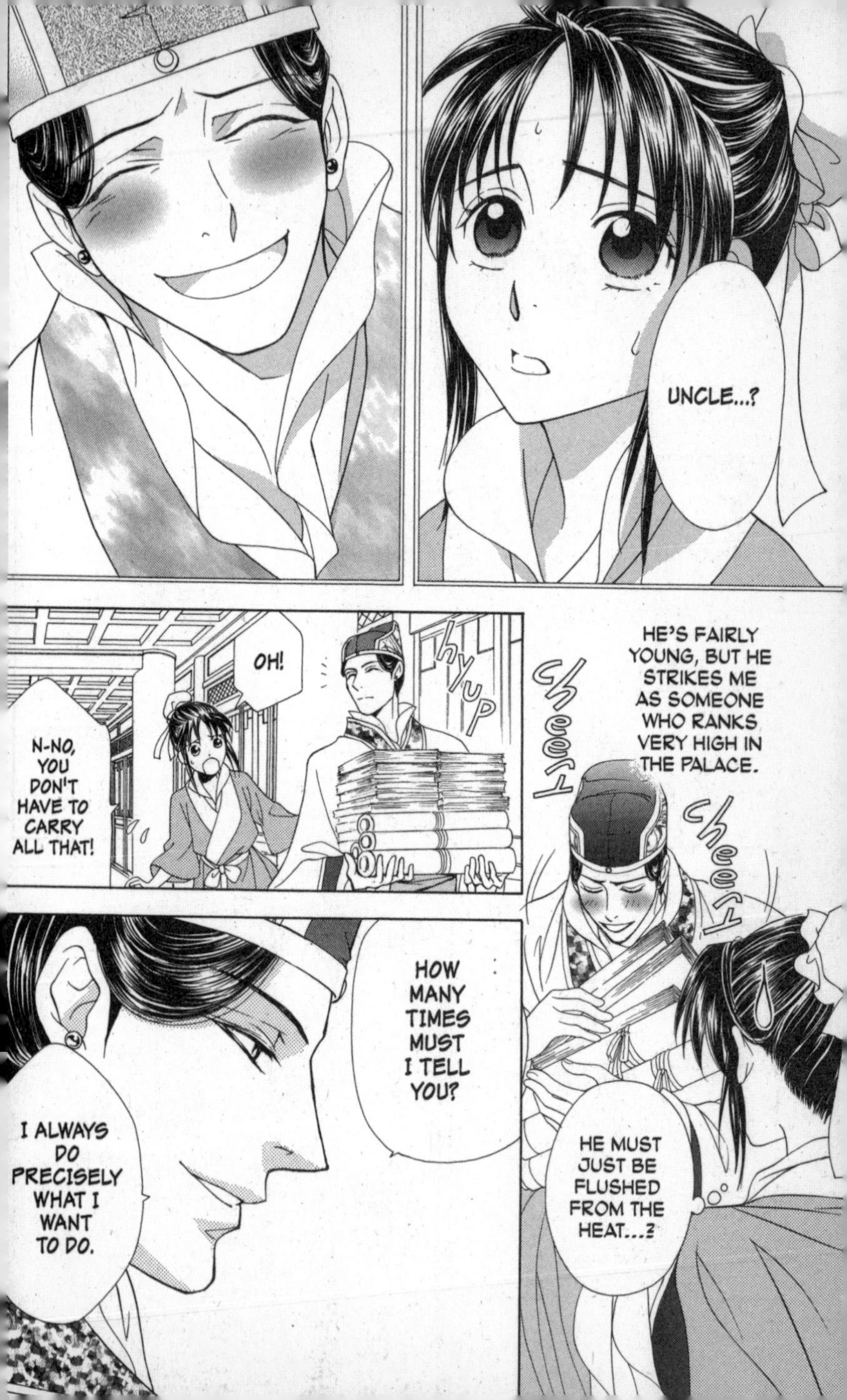
UNCLE...?
cheery
cheery
HE'S FAIRLY YOUNG, BUT HE STRIKES ME AS SOMEONE WHO RANKS VERY HIGH IN THE PALACE.
HE MUST JUST BE FLUSHED FROM THE HEAT...?
OH!
hyup
N-NO, YOU DON'T HAVE TO CARRY ALL THAT!
HOW MANY TIMES MUST I TELL YOU?
I ALWAYS DO PRECISELY WHAT I WANT TO DO.

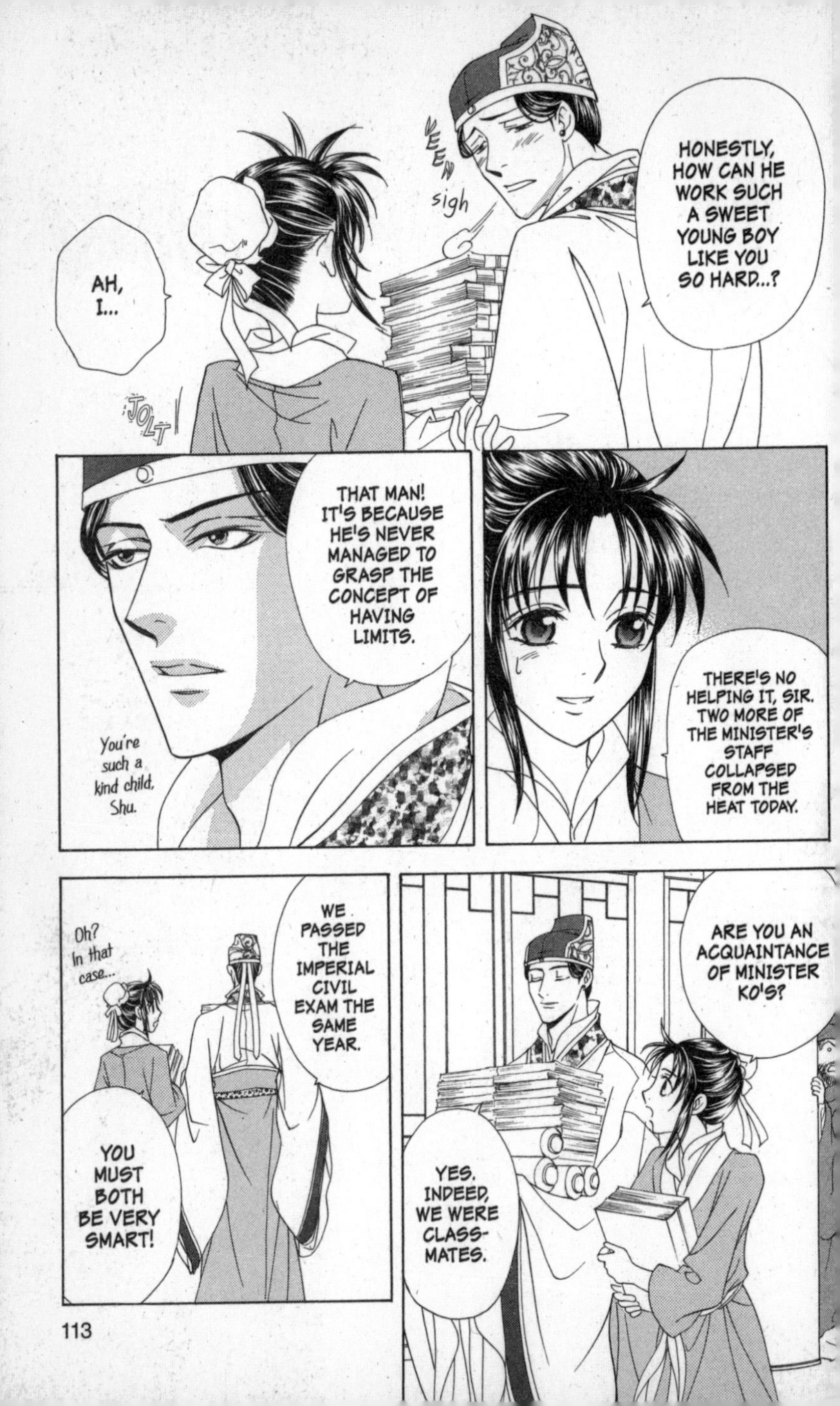
VEEN
sigh
HONESTLY, HOW CAN HE WORK SUCH A SWEET YOUNG BOY LIKE YOU SO HARD...?
AH, I...
JOLT
THERE'S NO HELPING IT, SIR. TWO MORE OF THE MINISTER'S STAFF COLLAPSED FROM THE HEAT TODAY.
THAT MAN! IT'S BECAUSE HE'S NEVER MANAGED TO GRASP THE CONCEPT OF HAVING LIMITS.
You're such a kind child, Shu.
ARE YOU AN ACQUAINTANCE OF MINISTER KO'S?
YES. INDEED, WE WERE CLASS-MATES.
WE PASSED THE IMPERIAL CIVIL EXAM THE SAME YEAR.
Oh? In that case...
YOU MUST BOTH BE VERY SMART!

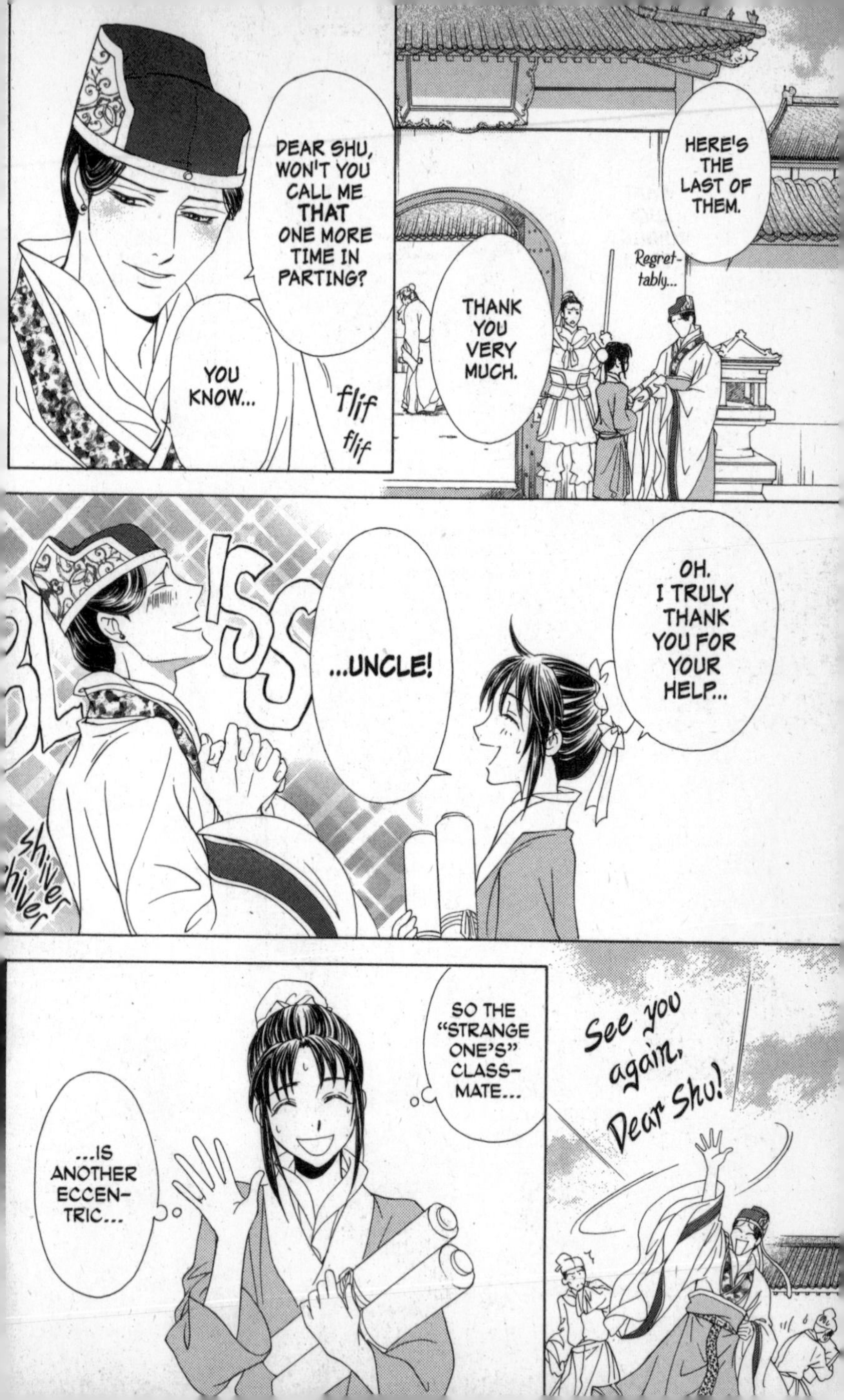
HERE'S THE LAST OF THEM.
Regret-tably...
THANK YOU VERY MUCH.
DEAR SHU, WON'T YOU CALL ME THAT ONE MORE TIME IN PARTING?
YOU KNOW...
flif flif
OH. I TRULY THANK YOU FOR YOUR HELP...
...UNCLE!
shiver shiver
See you again, Dear Shu!
SO THE "STRANGE ONE'S" CLASS-MATE...
...IS ANOTHER ECCEN-TRIC...

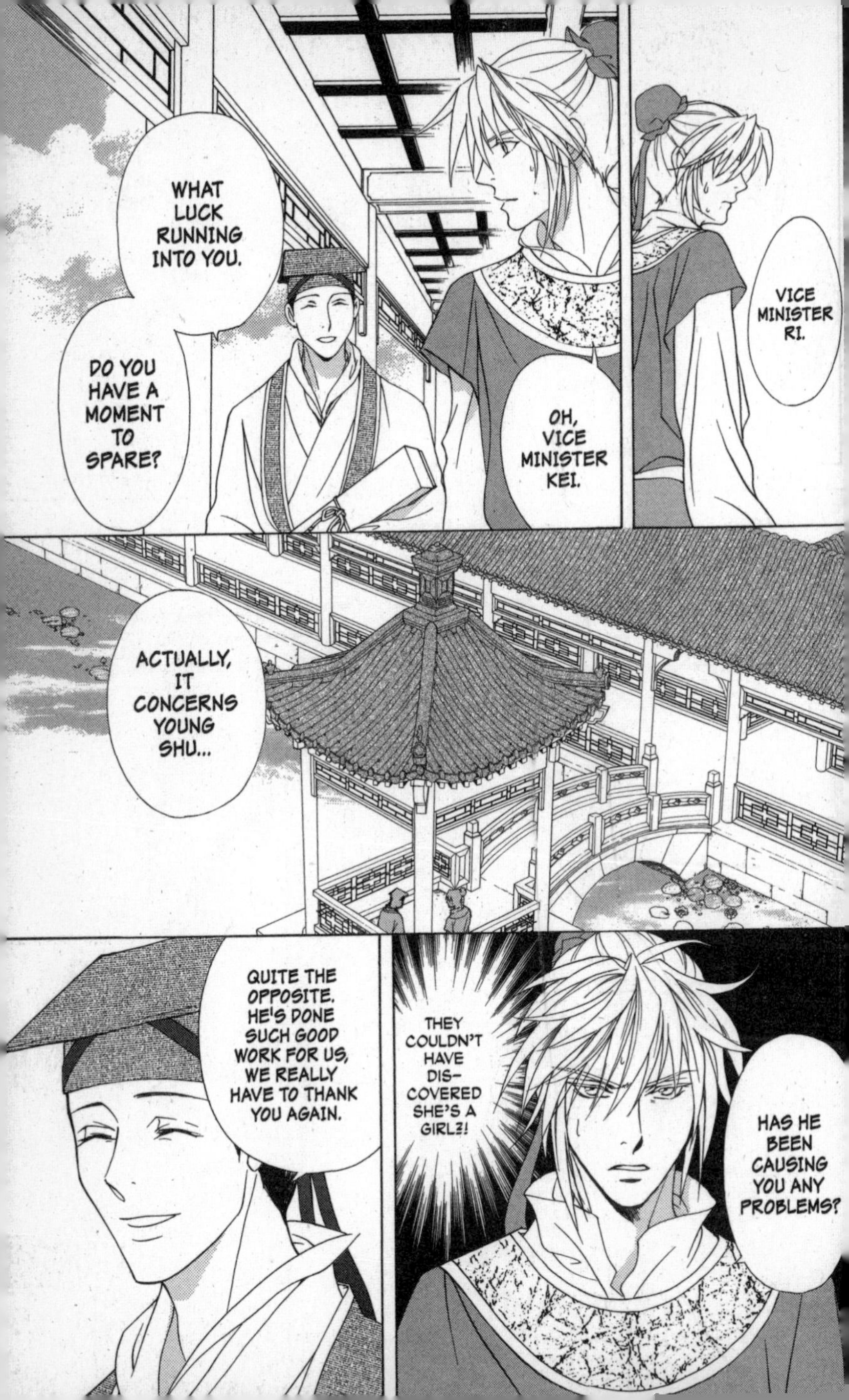
VICE MINISTER RI.
OH, VICE MINISTER KEI.
WHAT LUCK RUNNING INTO YOU.
DO YOU HAVE A MOMENT TO SPARE?
ACTUALLY, IT CONCERNS YOUNG SHU...
HAS HE BEEN CAUSING YOU ANY PROBLEMS?
THEY COULDN'T HAVE DIS-COVERED SHE'S A GIRL?!
QUITE THE OPPOSITE. HE'S DONE SUCH GOOD WORK FOR US, WE REALLY HAVE TO THANK YOU AGAIN.

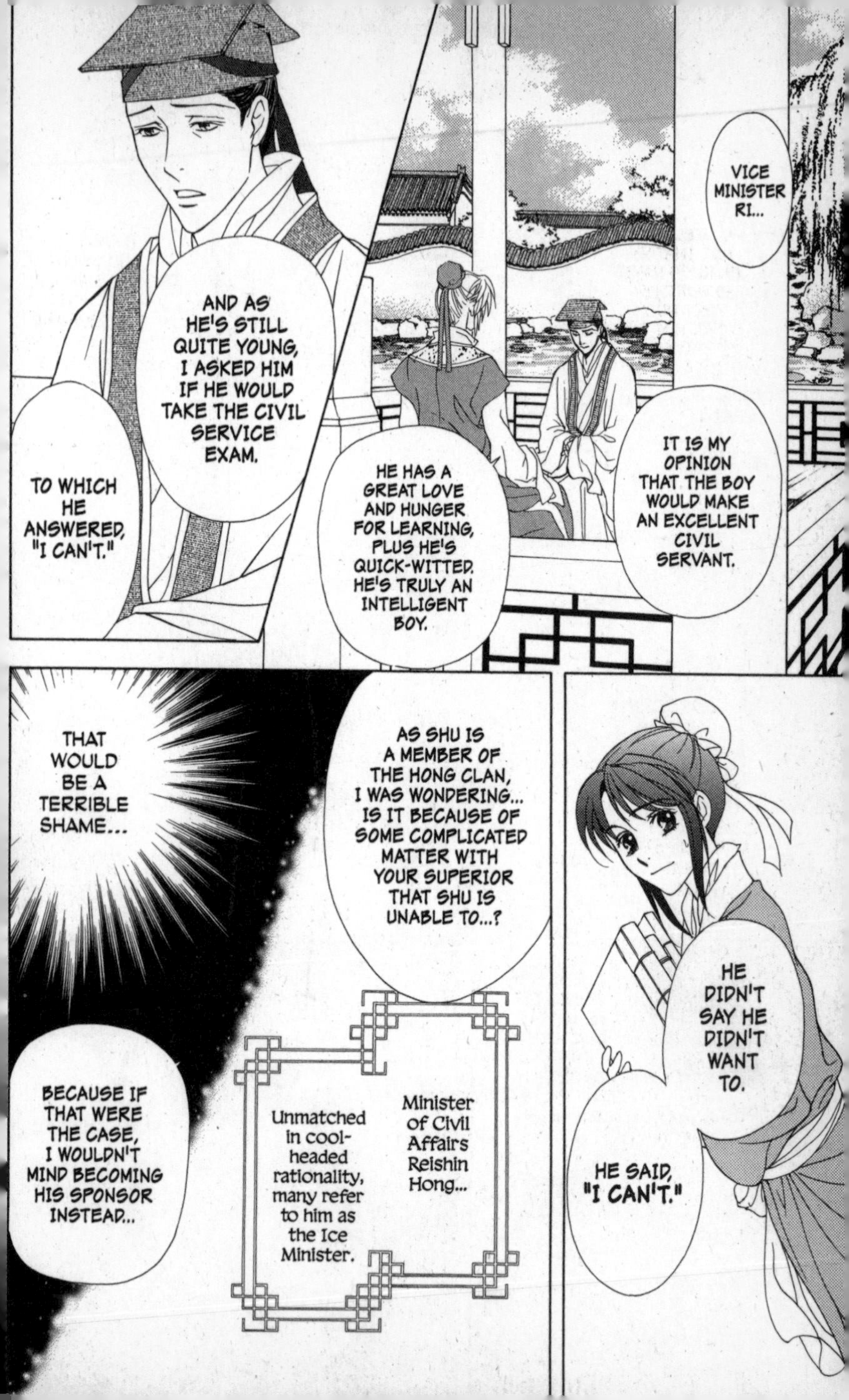
VICE MINISTER RI...
IT IS MY OPINION THAT THE BOY WOULD MAKE AN EXCELLENT CIVIL SERVANT.
HE HAS A GREAT LOVE AND HUNGER FOR LEARNING, PLUS HE'S QUICK-WITTED. HE'S TRULY AN INTELLIGENT BOY.
AND AS HE'S STILL QUITE YOUNG, I ASKED HIM IF HE WOULD TAKE THE CIVIL SERVICE EXAM.
TO WHICH HE ANSWERED, "I CAN'T."
HE DIDN'T SAY HE DIDN'T WANT TO.
HE SAID, "I CAN'T."
AS SHU IS A MEMBER OF THE HONG CLAN, I WAS WONDERING... IS IT BECAUSE OF SOME COMPLICATED MATTER WITH YOUR SUPERIOR THAT SHU IS UNABLE TO...?
THAT WOULD BE A TERRIBLE SHAME...
Minister of Civil Affairs Reishin Hong...
Unmatched in cool-headed rationality, many refer to him as the Ice Minister.
BECAUSE IF THAT WERE THE CASE, I WOULDN'T MIND BECOMING HIS SPONSOR INSTEAD...

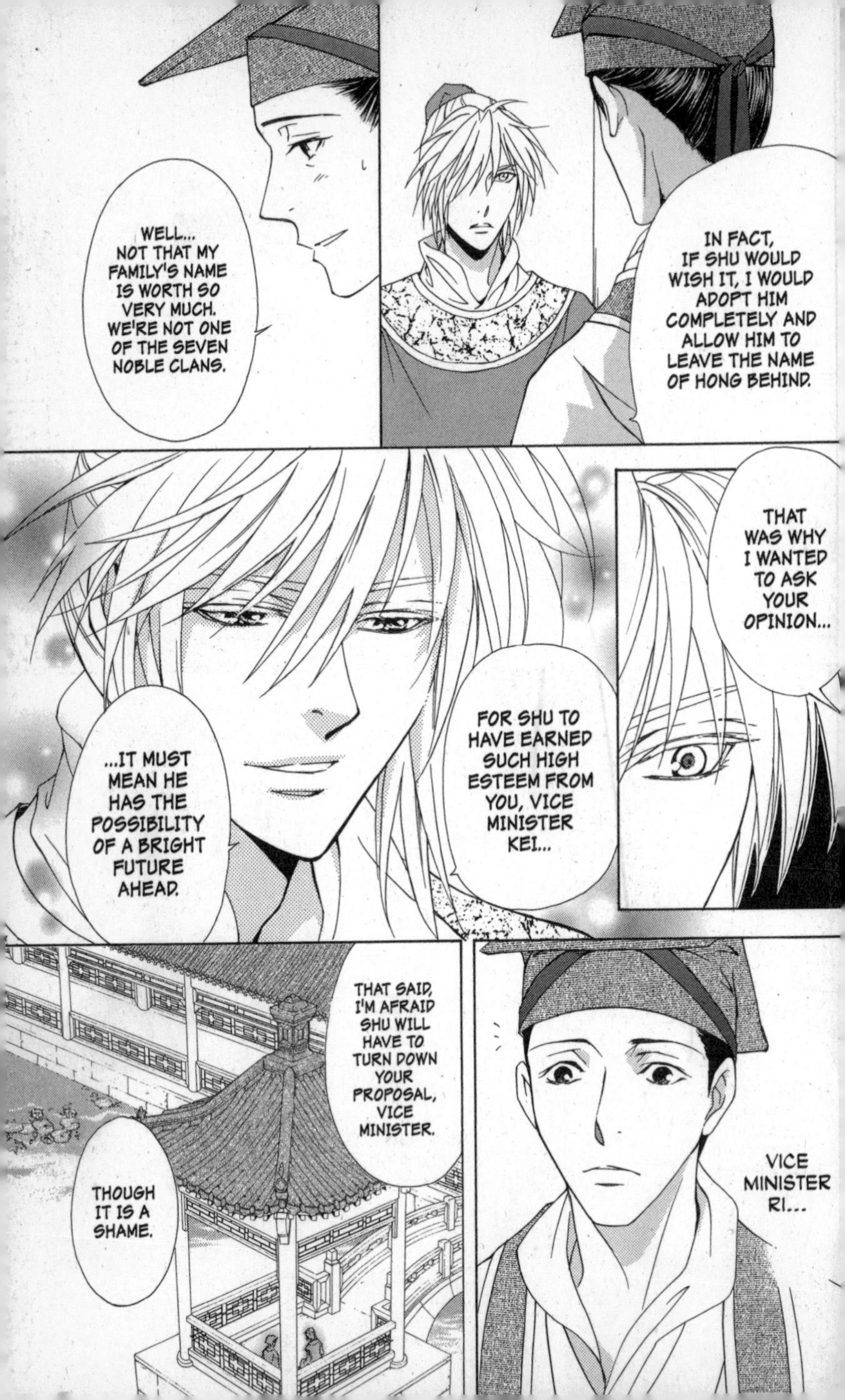
IN FACT, IF SHU WOULD WISH IT, I WOULD ADOPT HIM COMPLETELY AND ALLOW HIM TO LEAVE THE NAME OF HONG BEHIND.
WELL... NOT THAT MY FAMILY'S NAME IS WORTH SO VERY MUCH. WE'RE NOT ONE OF THE SEVEN NOBLE CLANS.
THAT WAS WHY I WANTED TO ASK YOUR OPINION...
FOR SHU TO HAVE EARNED SUCH HIGH ESTEEM FROM YOU, VICE MINISTER KEI...
...IT MUST MEAN HE HAS THE POSSIBILITY OF A BRIGHT FUTURE AHEAD.
VICE MINISTER RI...
THAT SAID, I'M AFRAID SHU WILL HAVE TO TURN DOWN YOUR PROPOSAL, VICE MINISTER.
THOUGH IT IS A SHAME.

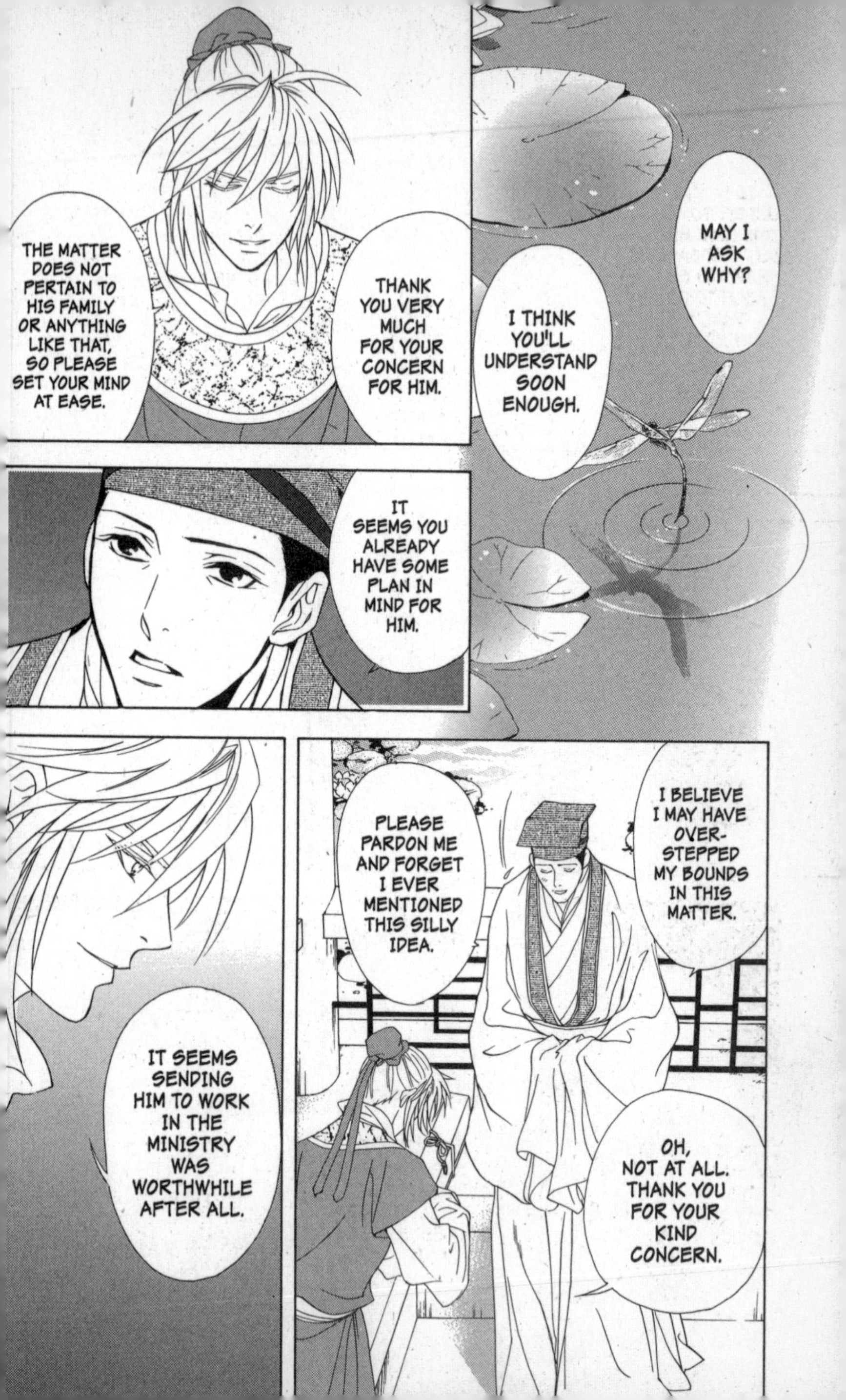
MAY I ASK WHY?
I THINK YOU'LL UNDERSTAND SOON ENOUGH.
THANK YOU VERY MUCH FOR YOUR CONCERN FOR HIM.
THE MATTER DOES NOT PERTAIN TO HIS FAMILY OR ANYTHING LIKE THAT, SO PLEASE SET YOUR MIND AT EASE.
IT SEEMS YOU ALREADY HAVE SOME PLAN IN MIND FOR HIM.
I BELIEVE I MAY HAVE OVER-STEPPED MY BOUNDS IN THIS MATTER.
PLEASE PARDON ME AND FORGET I EVER MENTIONED THIS SILLY IDEA.
OH, NOT AT ALL. THANK YOU FOR YOUR KIND CONCERN.
IT SEEMS SENDING HIM TO WORK IN THE MINISTRY WAS WORTHWHILE AFTER ALL.

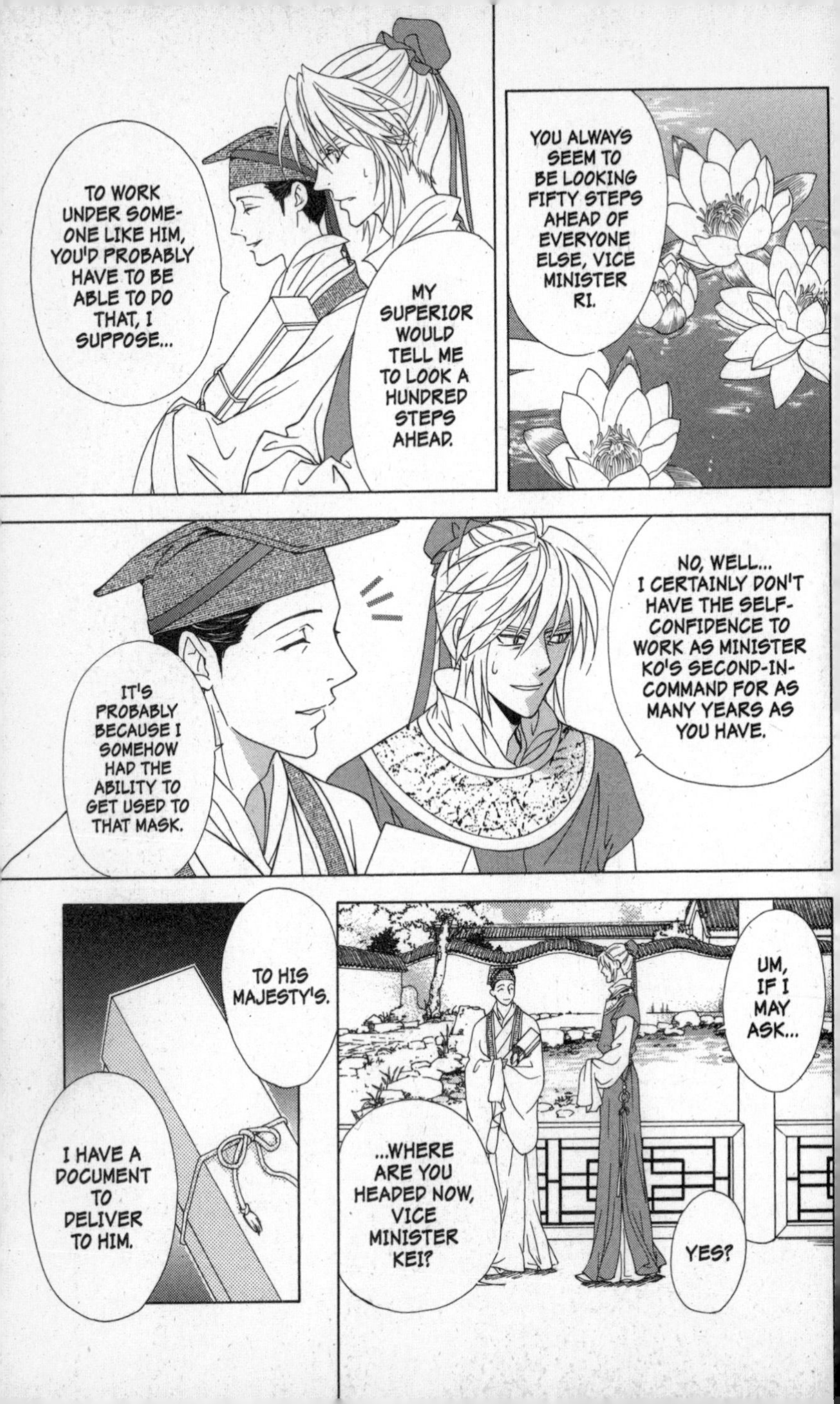
YOU ALWAYS SEEM TO BE LOOKING FIFTY STEPS AHEAD OF EVERYONE ELSE, VICE MINISTER RI.
MY SUPERIOR WOULD TELL ME TO LOOK A HUNDRED STEPS AHEAD.
TO WORK UNDER SOME-ONE LIKE HIM, YOU'D PROBABLY HAVE TO BE ABLE TO DO THAT, I SUPPOSE...
NO, WELL... I CERTAINLY DON'T HAVE THE SELF-CONFIDENCE TO WORK AS MINISTER KO'S SECOND-IN-COMMAND FOR AS MANY YEARS AS YOU HAVE.
IT'S PROBABLY BECAUSE I SOMEHOW HAD THE ABILITY TO GET USED TO THAT MASK.
UM, IF I MAY ASK...
YES?
...WHERE ARE YOU HEADED NOW, VICE MINISTER KEI?
TO HIS MAJESTY'S.
I HAVE A DOCUMENT TO DELIVER TO HIM.

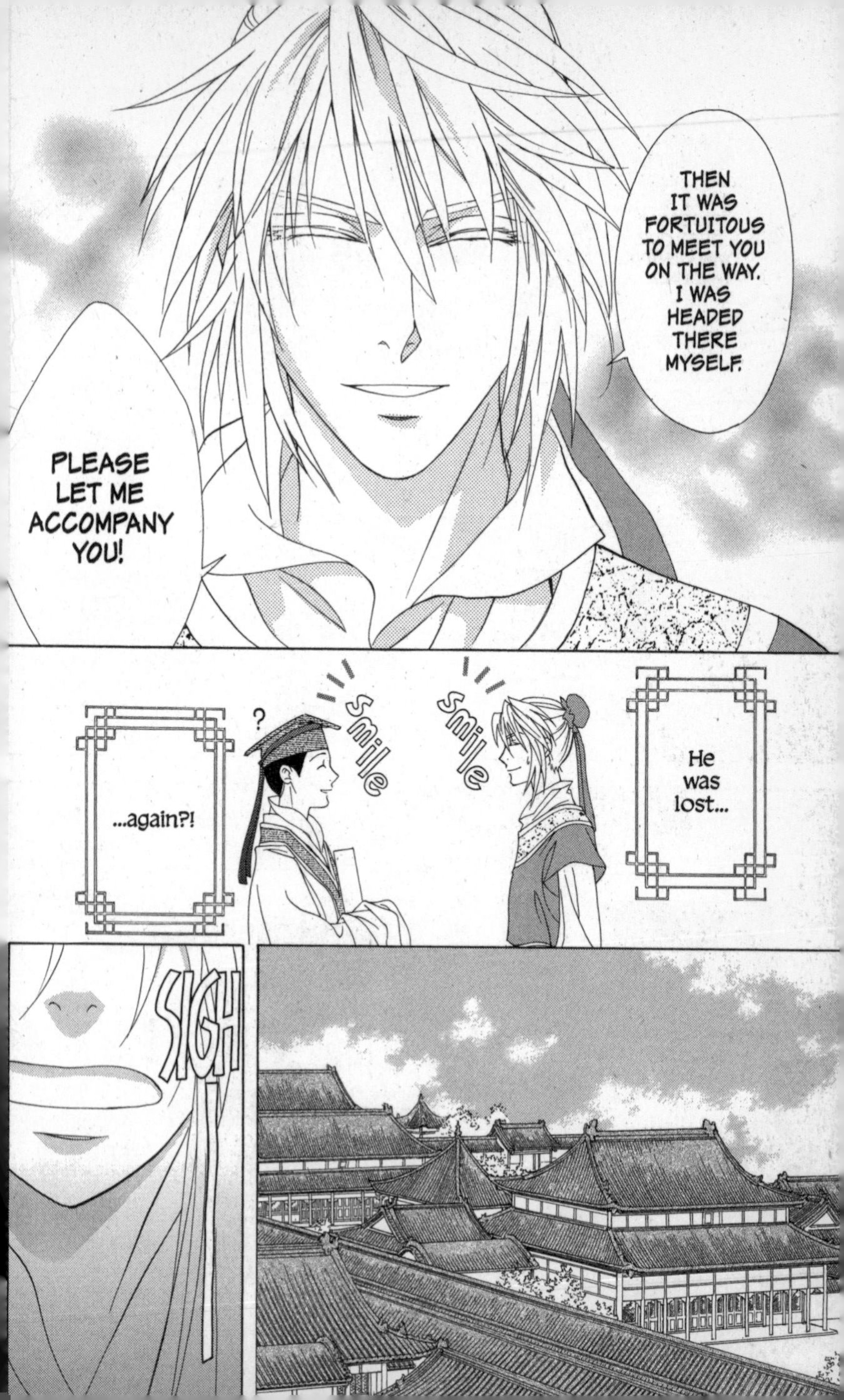
THEN IT WAS FORTUITOUS TO MEET YOU ON THE WAY. I WAS HEADED THERE MYSELF.
PLEASE LET ME ACCOMPANY YOU!
He was lost...
smile
smile
?
...again?!
SIGH

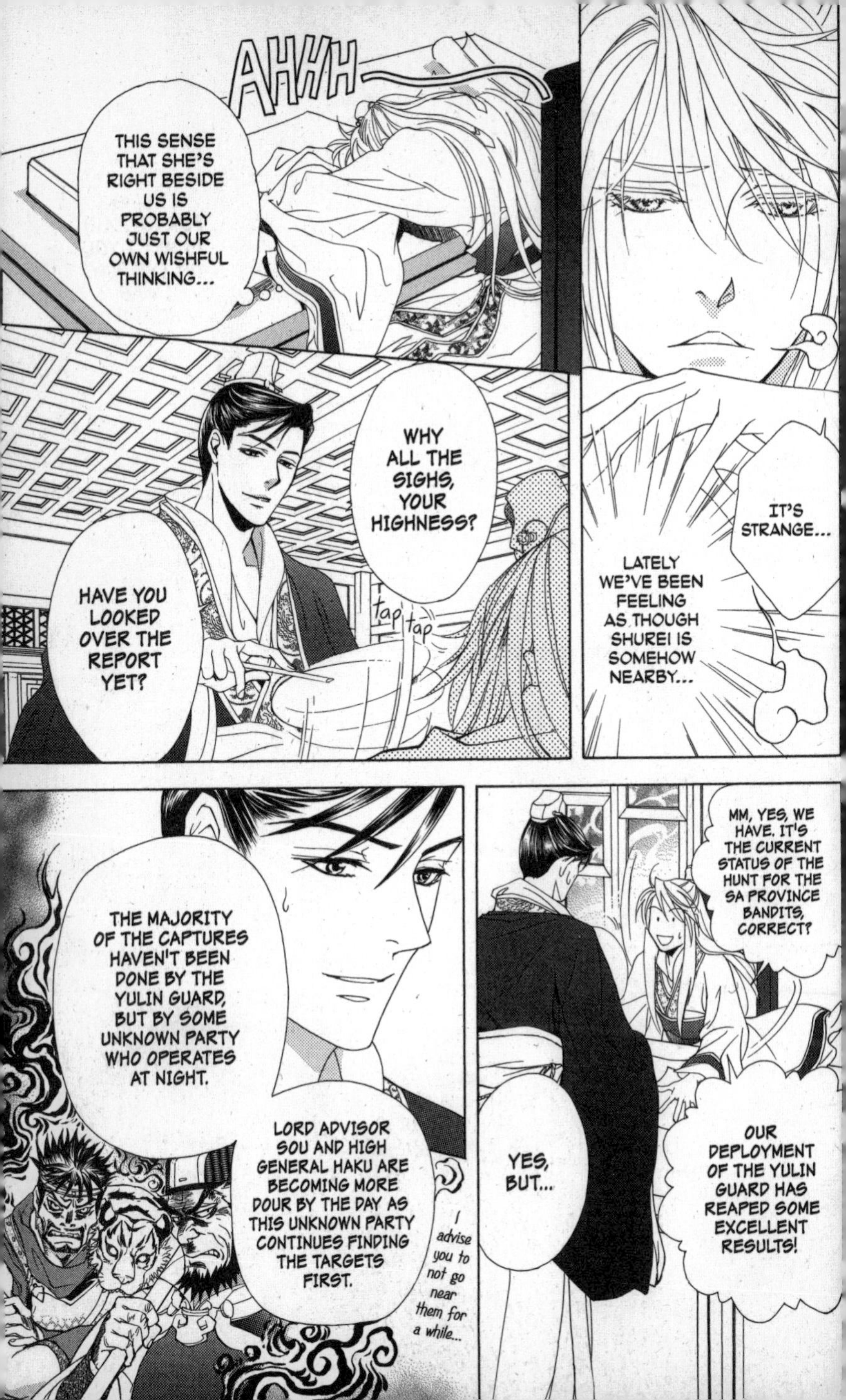
IT'S STRANGE...
LATELY WE'VE BEEN FEELING AS THOUGH SHUREI IS SOMEHOW NEARBY...
THIS SENSE THAT SHE'S RIGHT BESIDE US IS PROBABLY JUST OUR OWN WISHFUL THINKING...
AHHH
WHY ALL THE SIGHS, YOUR HIGHNESS?
HAVE YOU LOOKED OVER THE REPORT YET?
tap tap
MM, YES, WE HAVE. IT'S THE CURRENT STATUS OF THE HUNT FOR THE SA PROVINCE BANDITS, CORRECT?
OUR DEPLOYMENT OF THE YULIN GUARD HAS REAPED SOME EXCELLENT RESULTS!
YES, BUT...
THE MAJORITY OF THE CAPTURES HAVEN'T BEEN DONE BY THE YULIN GUARD, BUT BY SOME UNKNOWN PARTY WHO OPERATES AT NIGHT.
LORD ADVISOR SOU AND HIGH GENERAL HAKU ARE BECOMING MORE DOUR BY THE DAY AS THIS UNKNOWN PARTY CONTINUES FINDING THE TARGETS FIRST.
I advise you to not go near them for a while...

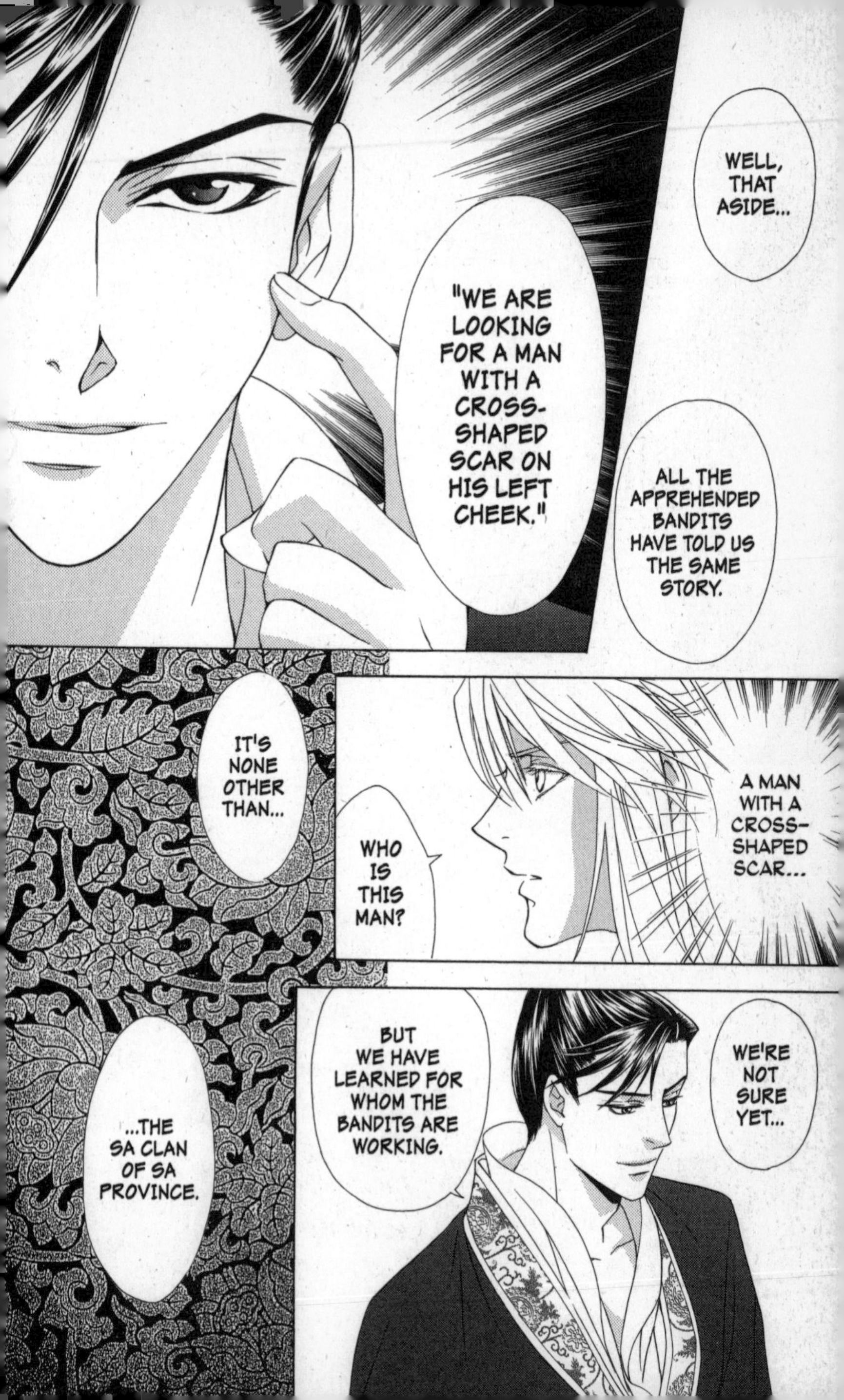
WELL, THAT ASIDE...
ALL THE APPREHENDED BANDITS HAVE TOLD US THE SAME STORY.
"WE ARE LOOKING FOR A MAN WITH A CROSS-SHAPED SCAR ON HIS LEFT CHEEK."
A MAN WITH A CROSS-SHAPED SCAR...
WHO IS THIS MAN?
WE'RE NOT SURE YET...
BUT WE HAVE LEARNED FOR WHOM THE BANDITS ARE WORKING.
IT'S NONE OTHER THAN...
...THE SA CLAN OF SA PROVINCE.

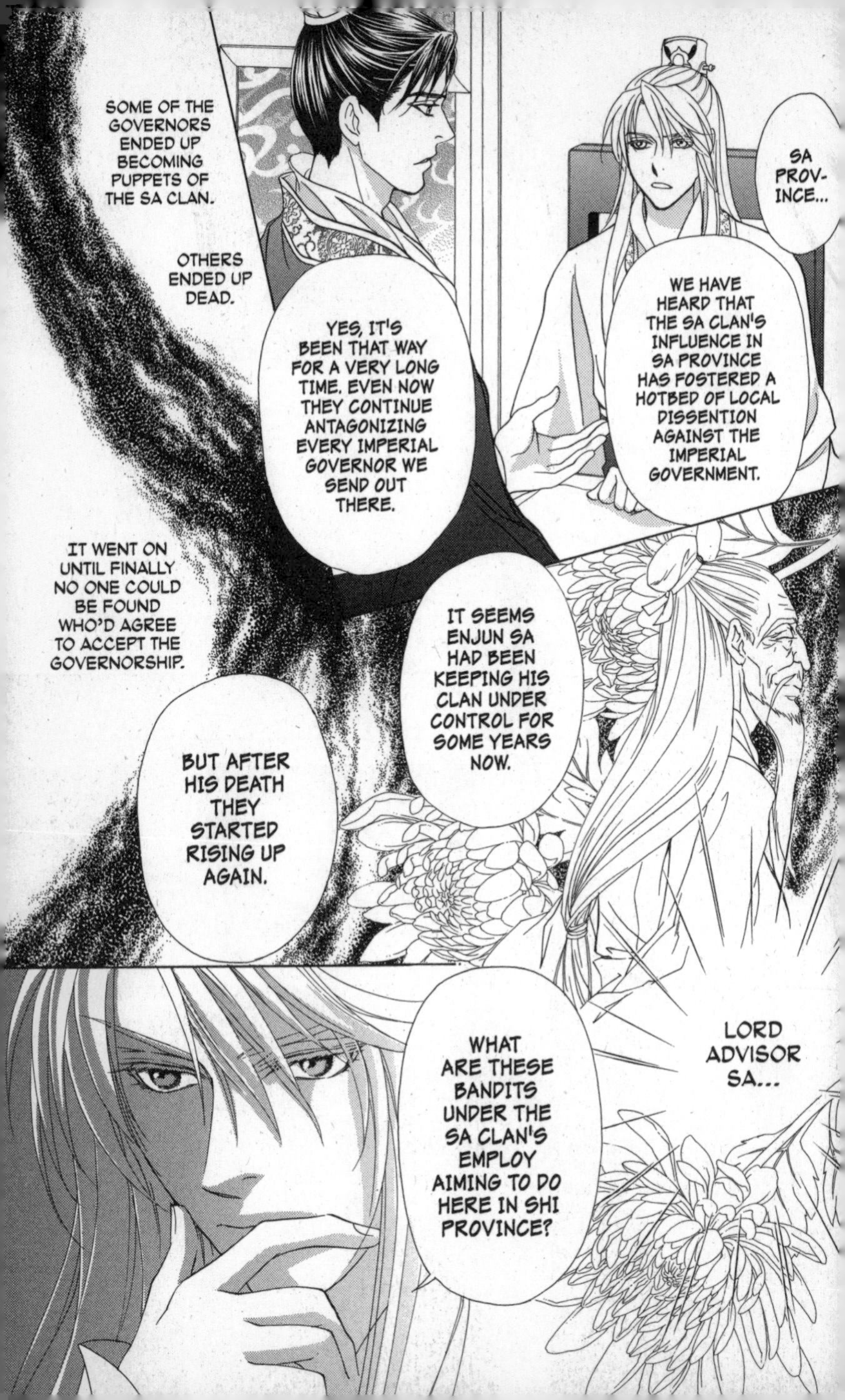
SA PROVINCE...
WE HAVE HEARD THAT THE SA CLAN'S INFLUENCE IN SA PROVINCE HAS FOSTERED A HOTBED OF LOCAL DISSENTION AGAINST THE IMPERIAL GOVERNMENT.
YES, IT'S BEEN THAT WAY FOR A VERY LONG TIME. EVEN NOW THEY CONTINUE ANTAGONIZING EVERY IMPERIAL GOVERNOR WE SEND OUT THERE.
SOME OF THE GOVERNORS ENDED UP BECOMING PUPPETS OF THE SA CLAN.
OTHERS ENDED UP DEAD.
IT WENT ON UNTIL FINALLY NO ONE COULD BE FOUND WHO'D AGREE TO ACCEPT THE GOVERNORSHIP.
IT SEEMS ENJUN SA HAD BEEN KEEPING HIS CLAN UNDER CONTROL FOR SOME YEARS NOW.
BUT AFTER HIS DEATH THEY STARTED RISING UP AGAIN.
LORD ADVISOR SA...
WHAT ARE THESE BANDITS UNDER THE SA CLAN'S EMPLOY AIMING TO DO HERE IN SHI PROVINCE?

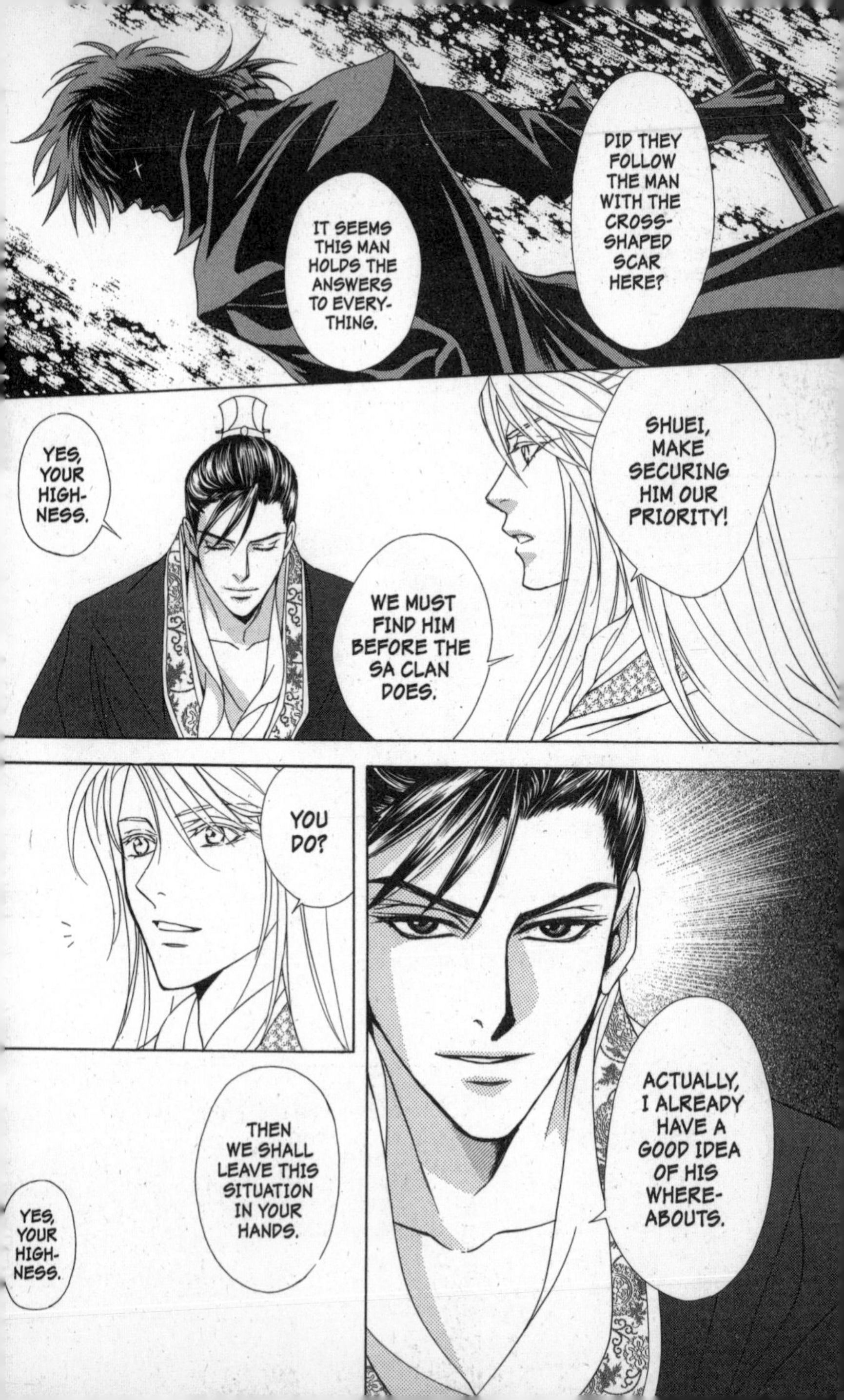
DID THEY FOLLOW THE MAN WITH THE CROSS-SHAPED SCAR HERE?
IT SEEMS THIS MAN HOLDS THE ANSWERS TO EVERY-THING.
SHUEI, MAKE SECURING HIM OUR PRIORITY!
WE MUST FIND HIM BEFORE THE SA CLAN DOES.
YES, YOUR HIGH-NESS.
ACTUALLY, I ALREADY HAVE A GOOD IDEA OF HIS WHERE-ABOUTS.
YOU DO?
THEN WE SHALL LEAVE THIS SITUATION IN YOUR HANDS.
YES, YOUR HIGH-NESS.

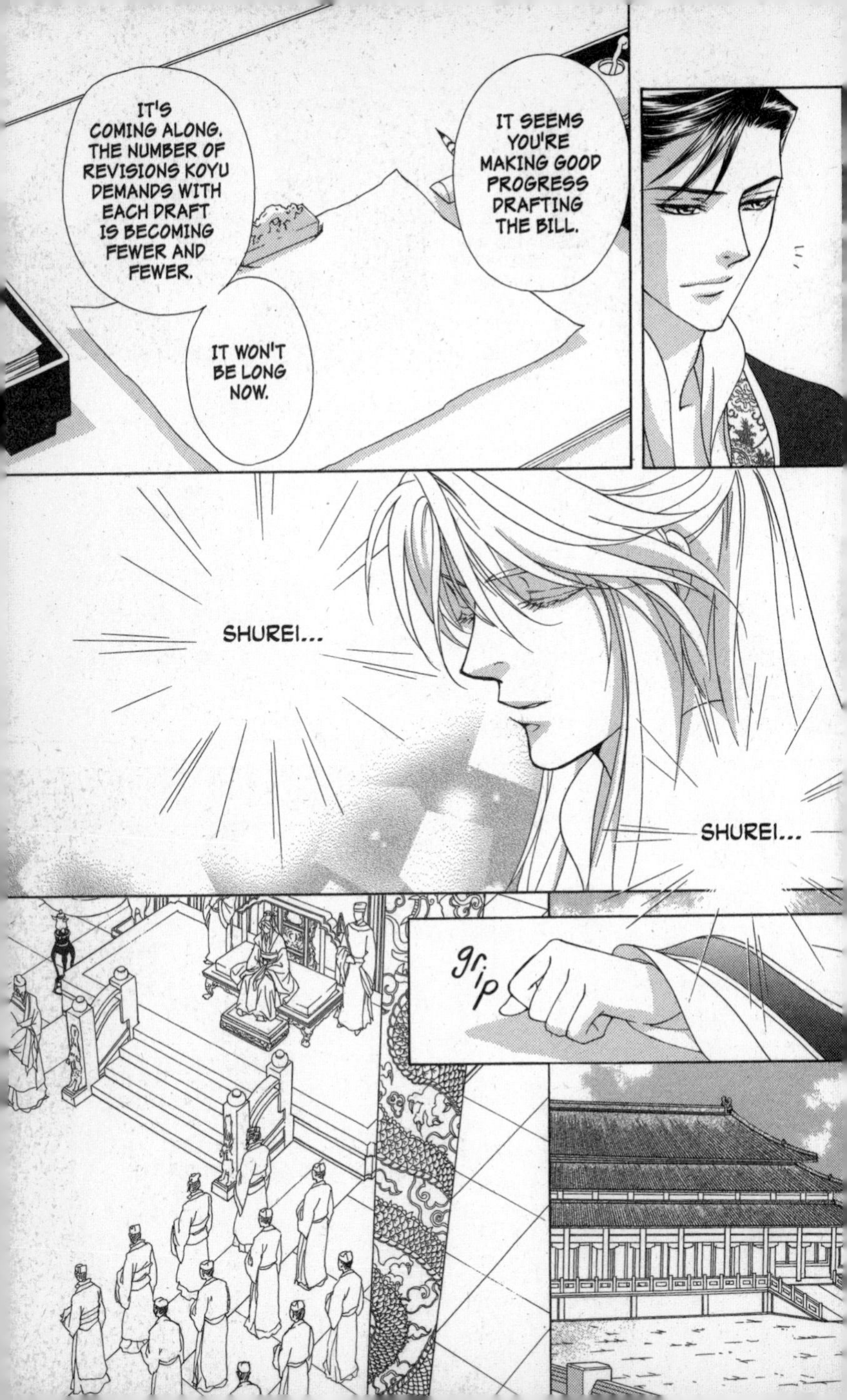
IT SEEMS YOU'RE MAKING GOOD PROGRESS DRAFTING THE BILL.
IT'S COMING ALONG. THE NUMBER OF REVISIONS KOYU DEMANDS WITH EACH DRAFT IS BECOMING FEWER AND FEWER.
IT WON'T BE LONG NOW.
SHUREI...
SHUREI...
grip

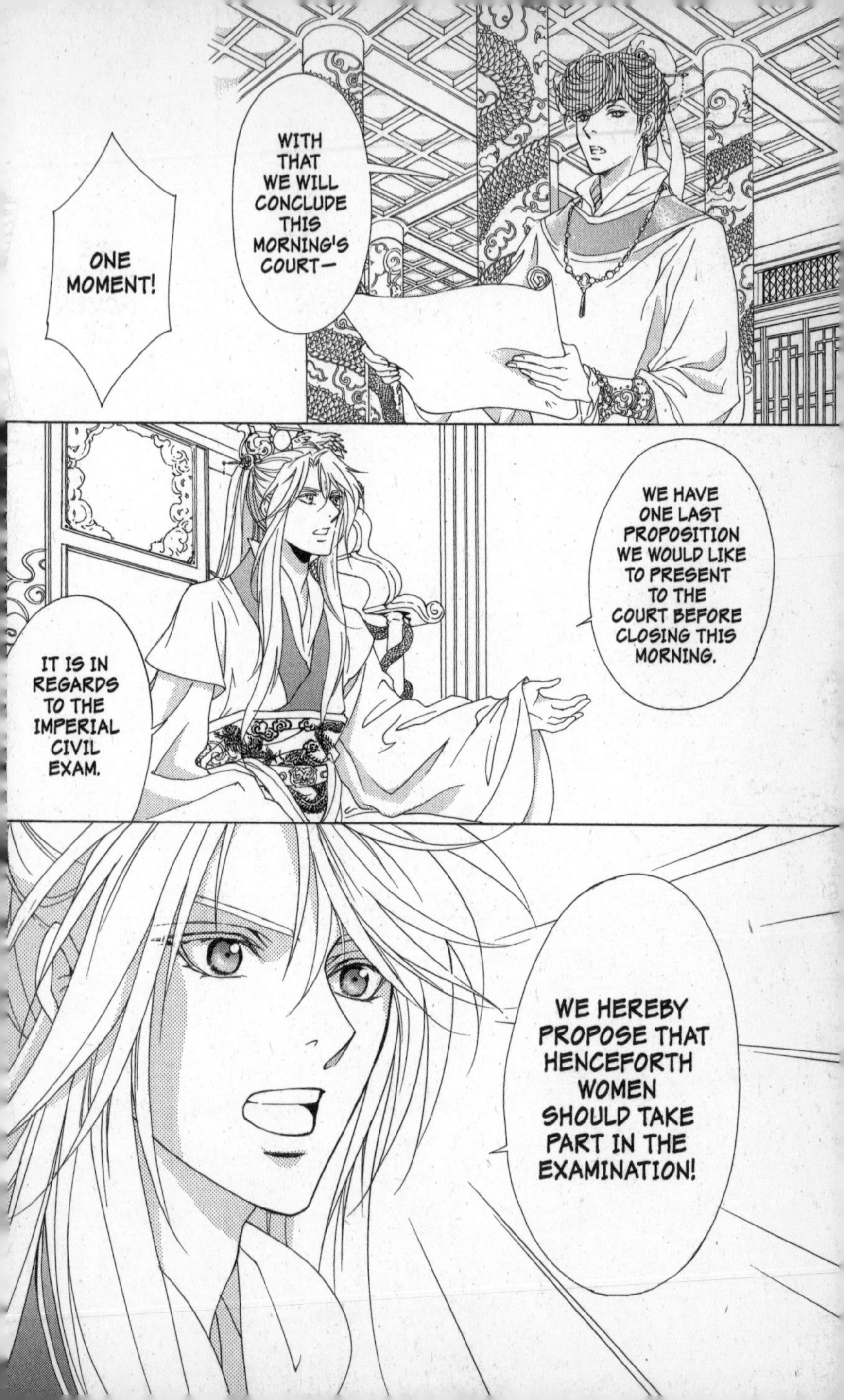
WITH THAT WE WILL CONCLUDE THIS MORNING'S COURT—
ONE MOMENT!
WE HAVE ONE LAST PROPOSITION WE WOULD LIKE TO PRESENT TO THE COURT BEFORE CLOSING THIS MORNING.
IT IS IN REGARDS TO THE IMPERIAL CIVIL EXAM.
WE HEREBY PROPOSE THAT HENCEFORTH WOMEN SHOULD TAKE PART IN THE EXAMINATION!

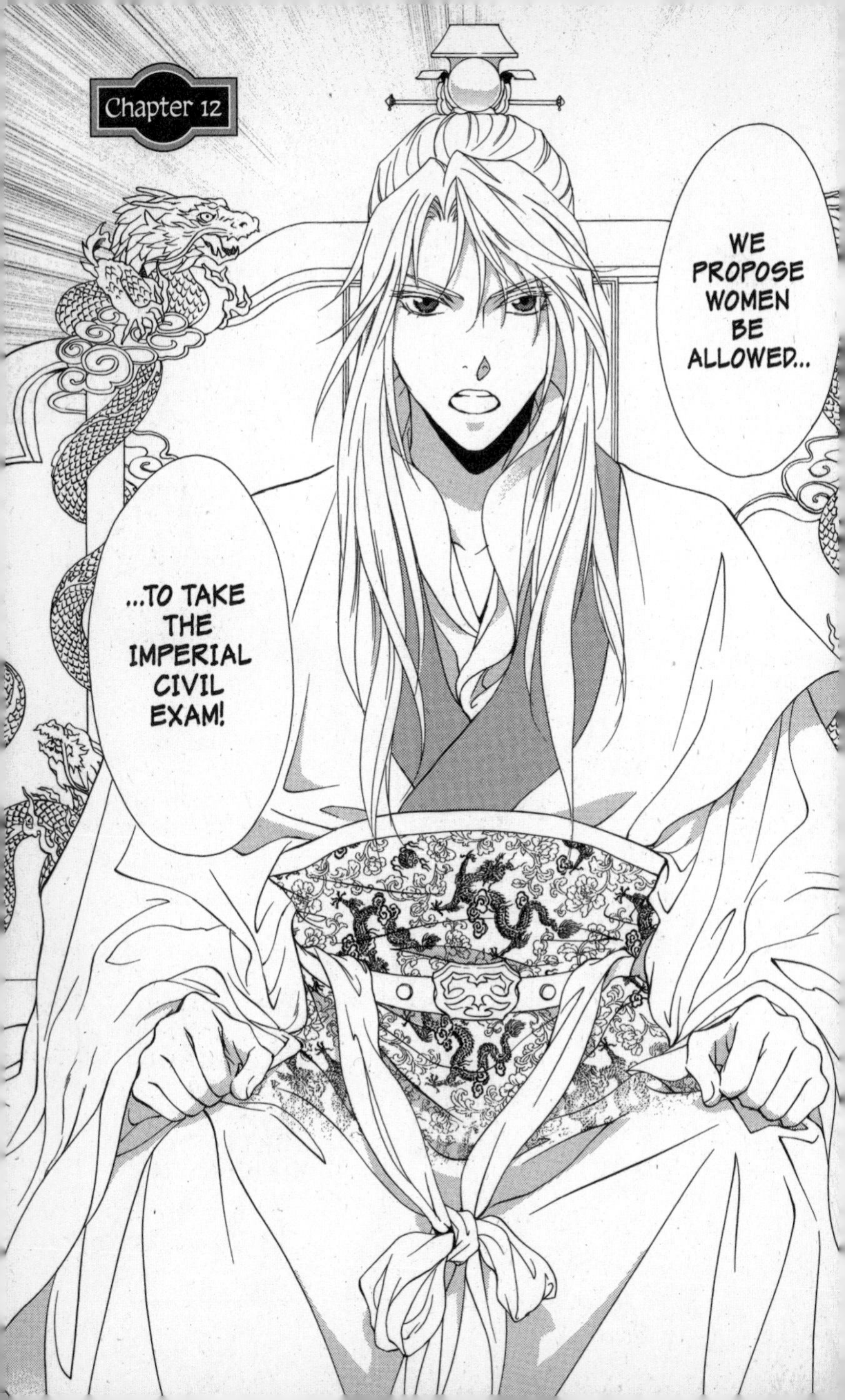
Chapter 12
WE PROPOSE WOMEN BE ALLOWED...
...TO TAKE THE IMPERIAL CIVIL EXAM!

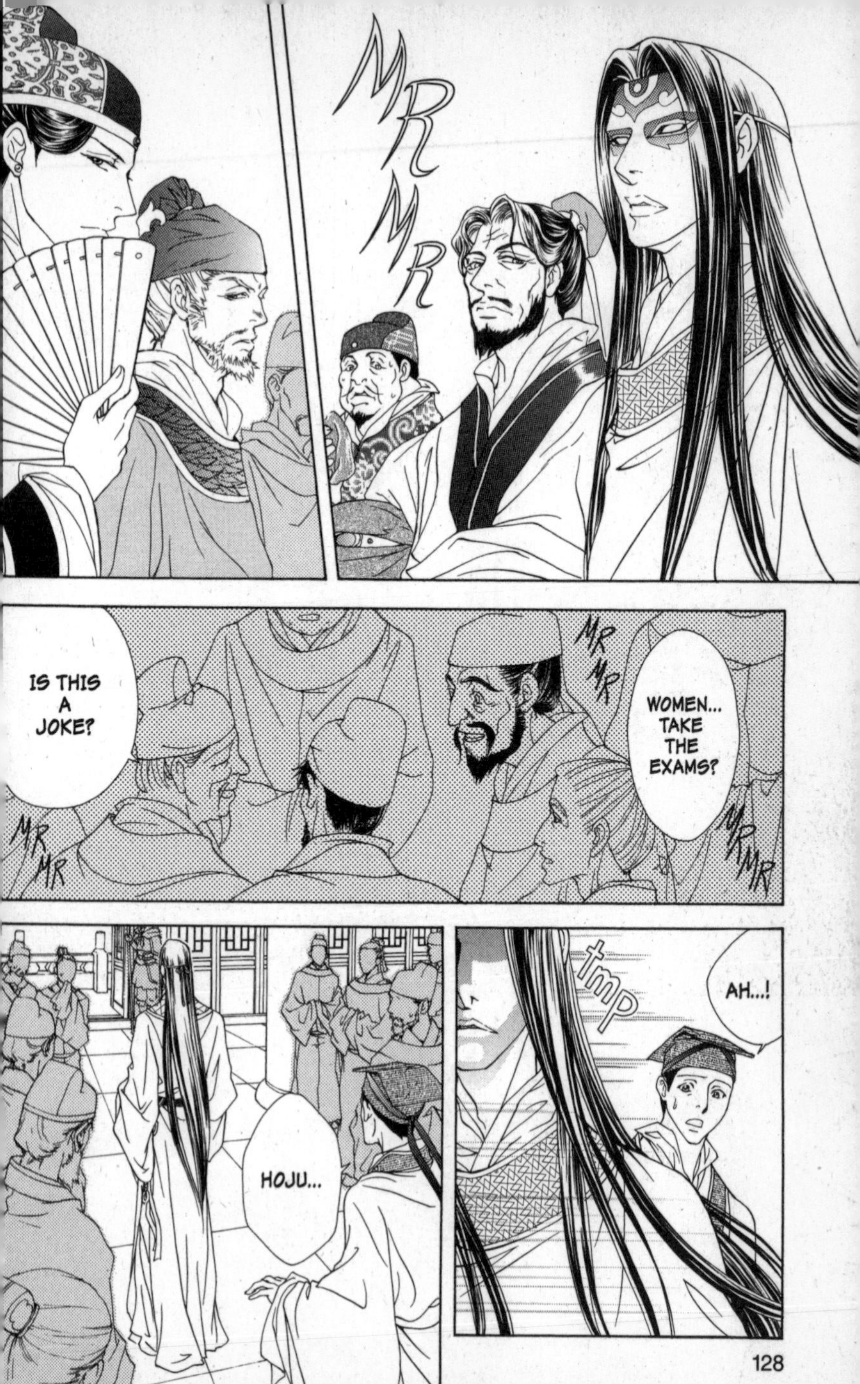
MRMR
MRMR
WOMEN... TAKE THE EXAMS?
MRMR
IS THIS A JOKE?
MR MR
tmp
AH...!
HOJU...

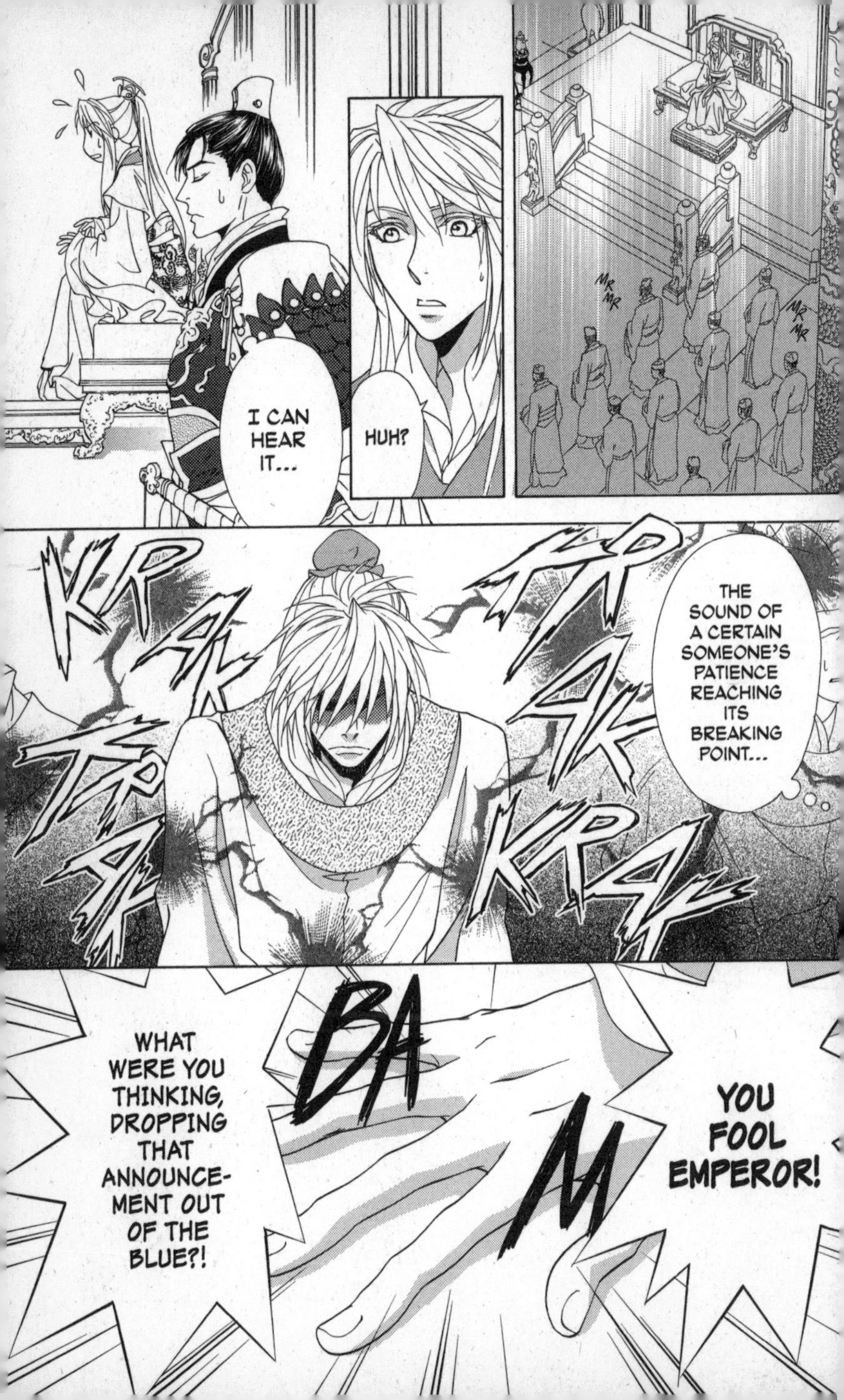

MR MR
MR MR
HUH?
I CAN HEAR IT...
THE SOUND OF A CERTAIN SOMEONE'S PATIENCE REACHING ITS BREAKING POINT...
KRAK
KRAK
KRAK
TRAK
YOU FOOL EMPEROR!
BAM
WHAT WERE YOU THINKING, DROPPING THAT ANNOUNCEMENT OUT OF THE BLUE?!

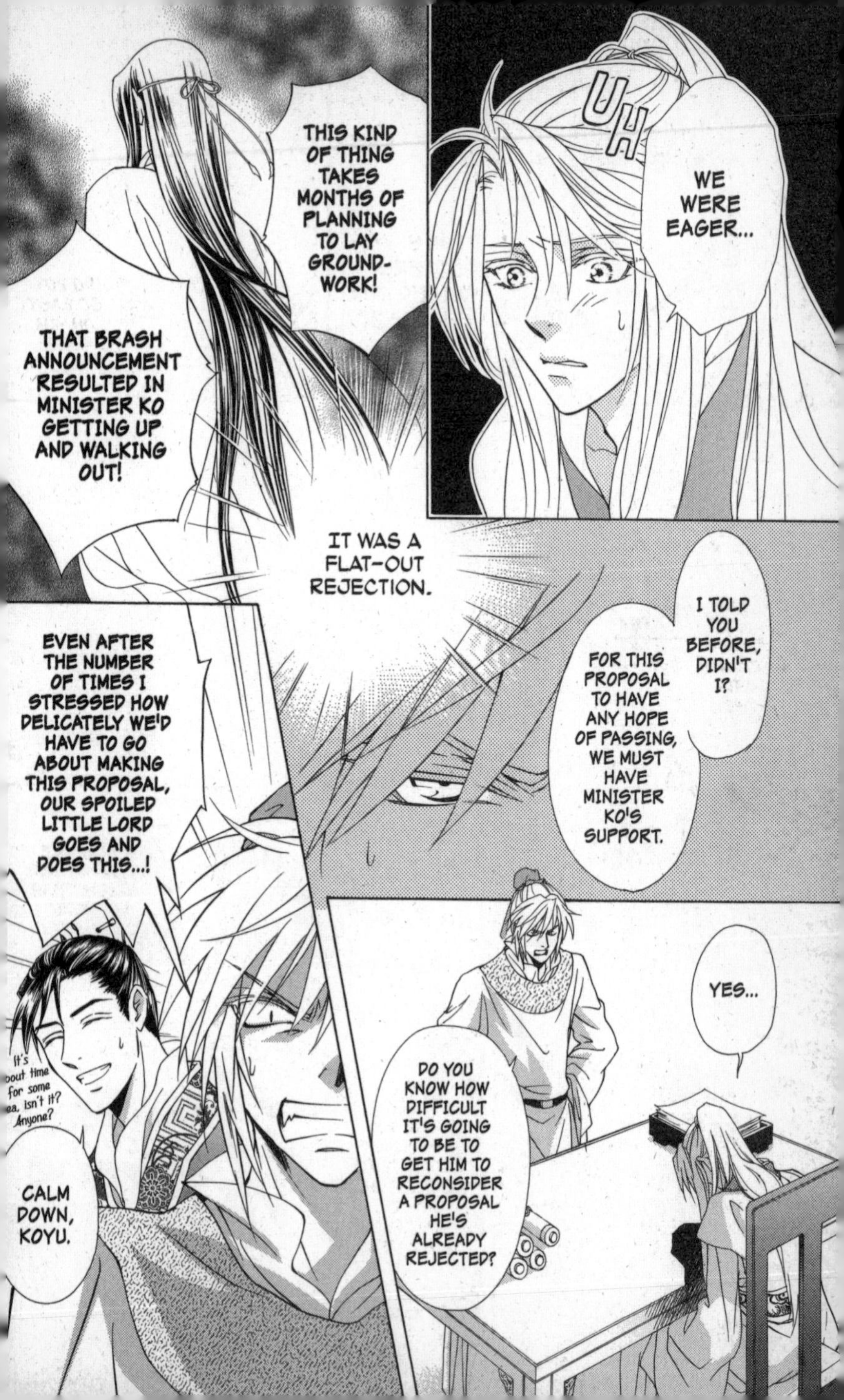
UH
WE WERE EAGER...
THIS KIND OF THING TAKES MONTHS OF PLANNING TO LAY GROUND-WORK!
THAT BRASH ANNOUNCEMENT RESULTED IN MINISTER KO GETTING UP AND WALKING OUT!
IT WAS A FLAT-OUT REJECTION.
I TOLD YOU BEFORE, DIDN'T I?
FOR THIS PROPOSAL TO HAVE ANY HOPE OF PASSING, WE MUST HAVE MINISTER KO'S SUPPORT.
YES...
DO YOU KNOW HOW DIFFICULT IT'S GOING TO BE TO GET HIM TO RECONSIDER A PROPOSAL HE'S ALREADY REJECTED?
EVEN AFTER THE NUMBER OF TIMES I STRESSED HOW DELICATELY WE'D HAVE TO GO ABOUT MAKING THIS PROPOSAL, OUR SPOILED LITTLE LORD GOES AND DOES THIS...!
It's about time for some tea, isn't it? Anyone?
CALM DOWN, KOYU.

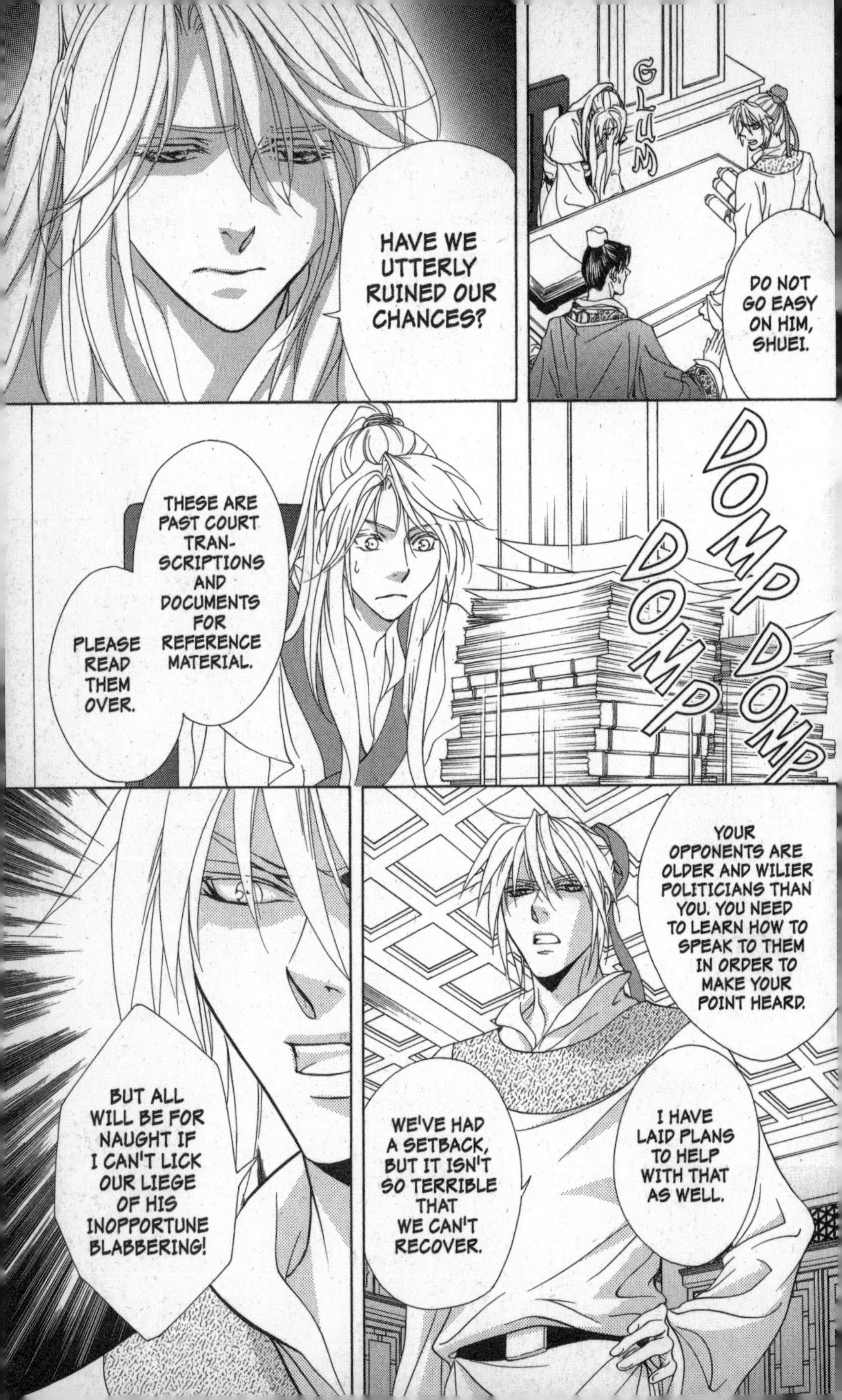
GLUM
DO NOT GO EASY ON HIM, SHUEI.
HAVE WE UTTERLY RUINED OUR CHANCES?
DOMP DOMP
DOMP
THESE ARE PAST COURT TRAN-SCRIPTIONS AND DOCUMENTS FOR REFERENCE MATERIAL.
PLEASE READ THEM OVER.
YOUR OPPONENTS ARE OLDER AND WILIER POLITICIANS THAN YOU. YOU NEED TO LEARN HOW TO SPEAK TO THEM IN ORDER TO MAKE YOUR POINT HEARD.
I HAVE LAID PLANS TO HELP WITH THAT AS WELL.
WE'VE HAD A SETBACK, BUT IT ISN'T SO TERRIBLE THAT WE CAN'T RECOVER.
BUT ALL WILL BE FOR NAUGHT IF I CAN'T LICK OUR LIEGE OF HIS INOPPORTUNE BLABBERING!

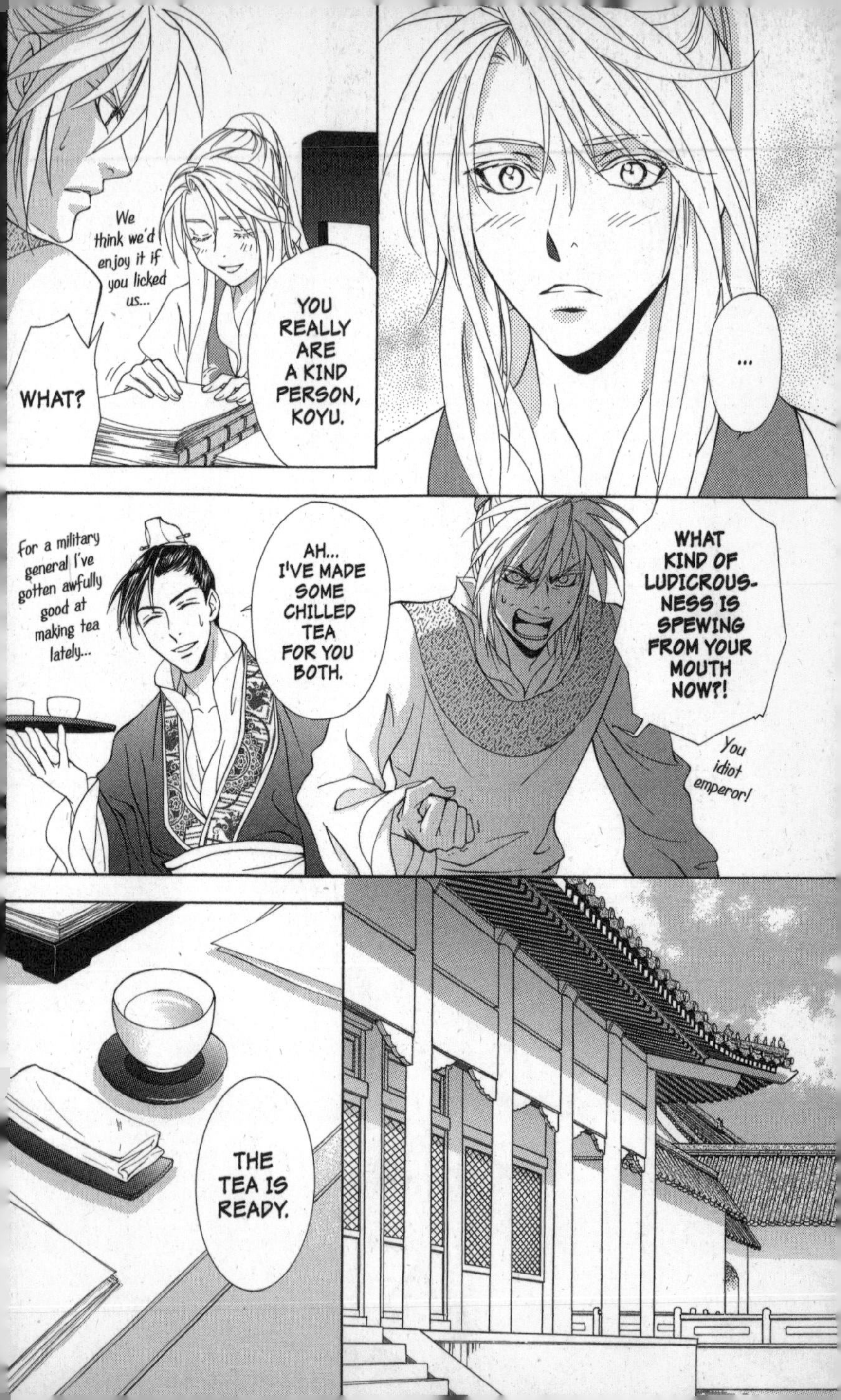
...
YOU REALLY ARE A KIND PERSON, KOYU.
We think we'd enjoy it if you licked us...
WHAT?
WHAT KIND OF LUDICROUSNESS IS SPEWING FROM YOUR MOUTH NOW?!
You idiot emperor!
AH... I'VE MADE SOME CHILLED TEA FOR YOU BOTH.
For a military general I've gotten awfully good at making tea lately...
THE TEA IS READY.

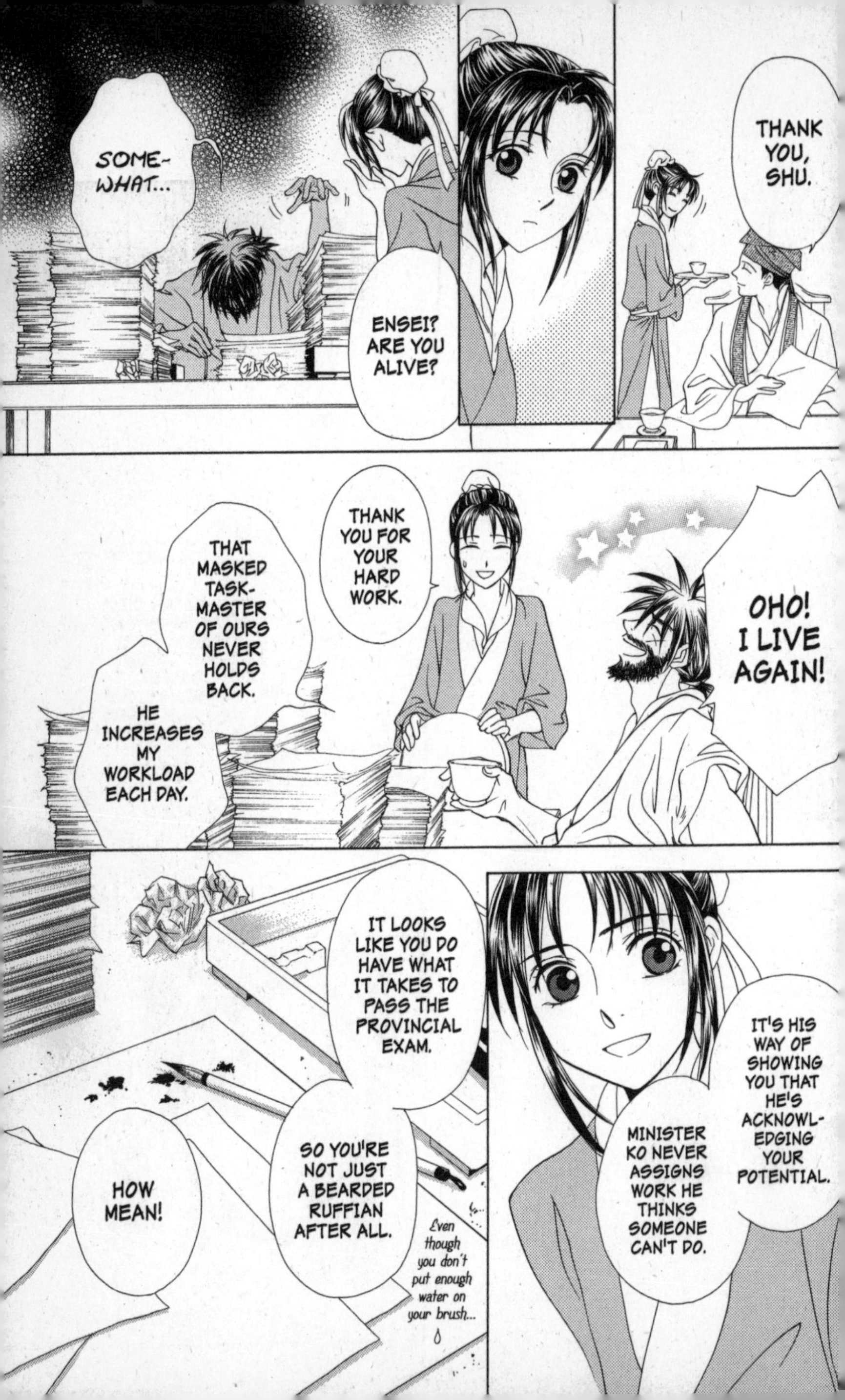
THANK YOU, SHU.
ENSEI? ARE YOU ALIVE?
SOME-WHAT...
OHO! I LIVE AGAIN!
THANK YOU FOR YOUR HARD WORK.
THAT MASKED TASK-MASTER OF OURS NEVER HOLDS BACK.
HE INCREASES MY WORKLOAD EACH DAY.
MINISTER KO NEVER ASSIGNS WORK HE THINKS SOMEONE CAN'T DO.
IT'S HIS WAY OF SHOWING YOU THAT HE'S ACKNOWL-EDGING YOUR POTENTIAL.
IT LOOKS LIKE YOU DO HAVE WHAT IT TAKES TO PASS THE PROVINCIAL EXAM.
SO YOU'RE NOT JUST A BEARDED RUFFIAN AFTER ALL.
Even though you don't put enough water on your brush...
HOW MEAN!

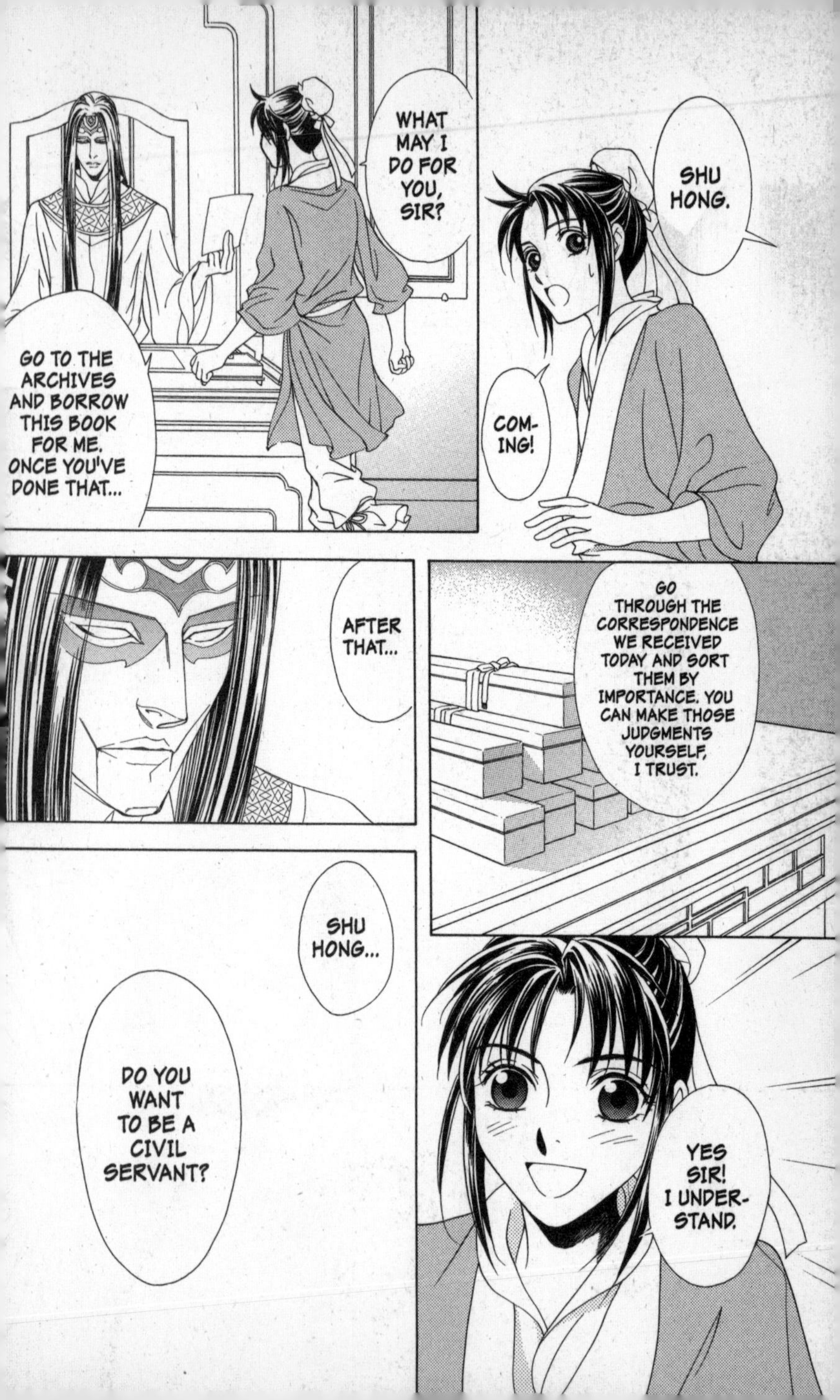
SHU HONG.
COM-ING!
WHAT MAY I DO FOR YOU, SIR?
GO TO THE ARCHIVES AND BORROW THIS BOOK FOR ME. ONCE YOU'VE DONE THAT...
GO THROUGH THE CORRESPONDENCE WE RECEIVED TODAY AND SORT THEM BY IMPORTANCE. YOU CAN MAKE THOSE JUDGMENTS YOURSELF, I TRUST.
AFTER THAT...
YES SIR! I UNDER-STAND.
SHU HONG...
DO YOU WANT TO BE A CIVIL SERVANT?

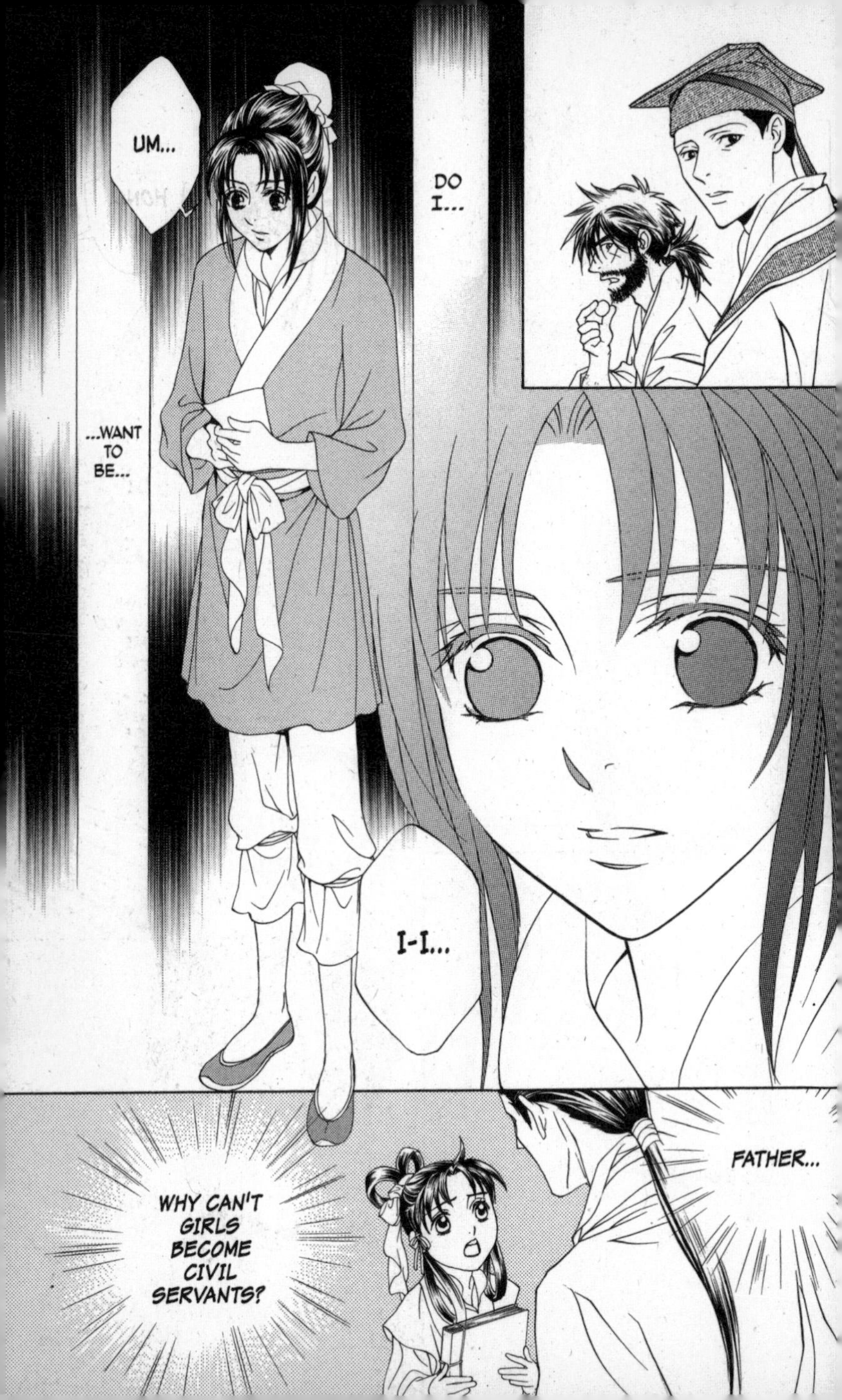
UM...
DO I...
...WANT TO BE...
I-I...
FATHER...
WHY CAN'T GIRLS BECOME CIVIL SERVANTS?

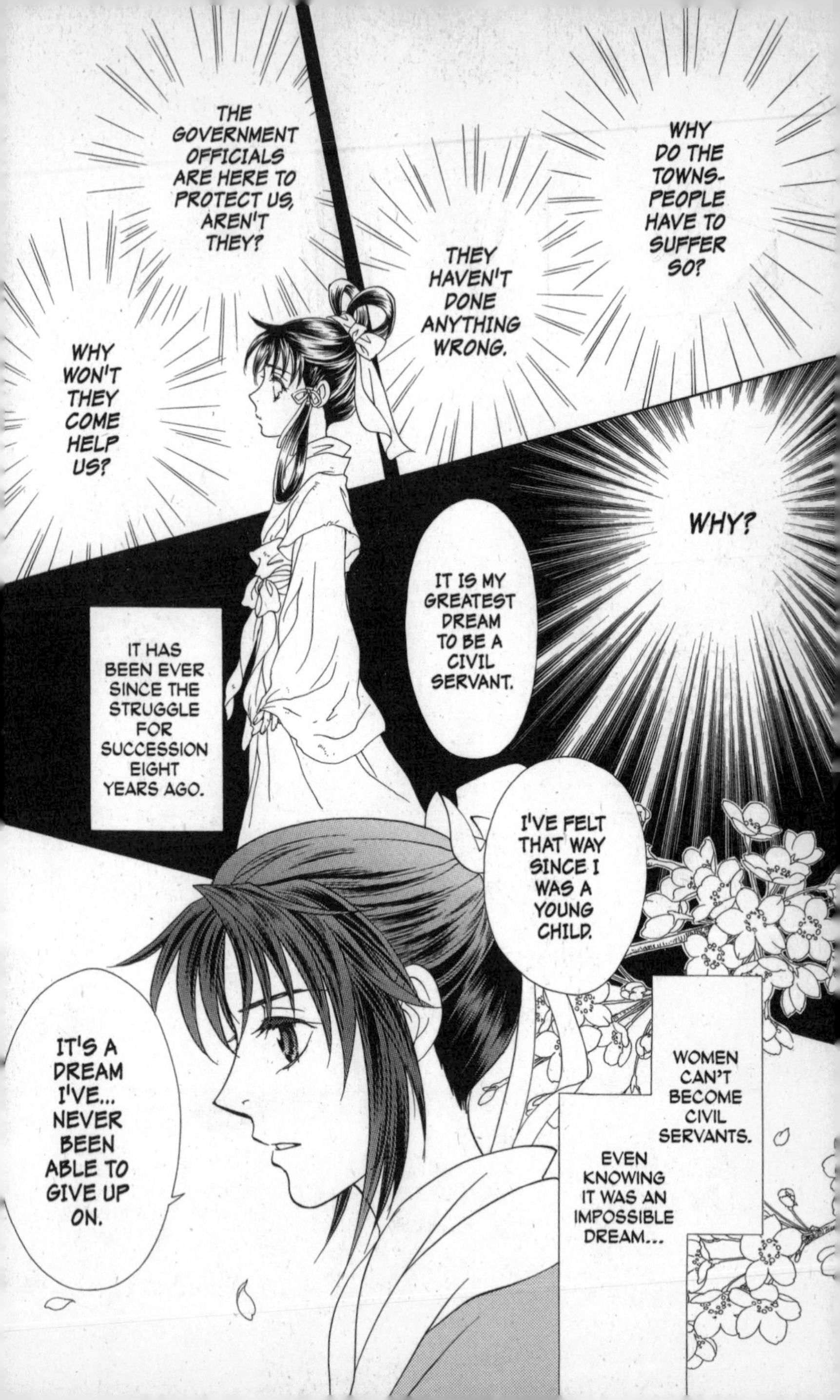
WHY DO THE TOWNS-PEOPLE HAVE TO SUFFER SO?
THEY HAVEN'T DONE ANYTHING WRONG.
THE GOVERNMENT OFFICIALS ARE HERE TO PROTECT US, AREN'T THEY?
WHY WON'T THEY COME HELP US?
WHY?
IT HAS BEEN EVER SINCE THE STRUGGLE FOR SUCCESSION EIGHT YEARS AGO.
IT IS MY GREATEST DREAM TO BE A CIVIL SERVANT.
I'VE FELT THAT WAY SINCE I WAS A YOUNG CHILD.
WOMEN CAN'T BECOME CIVIL SERVANTS.
EVEN KNOWING IT WAS AN IMPOSSIBLE DREAM...
IT'S A DREAM I'VE... NEVER BEEN ABLE TO GIVE UP ON.

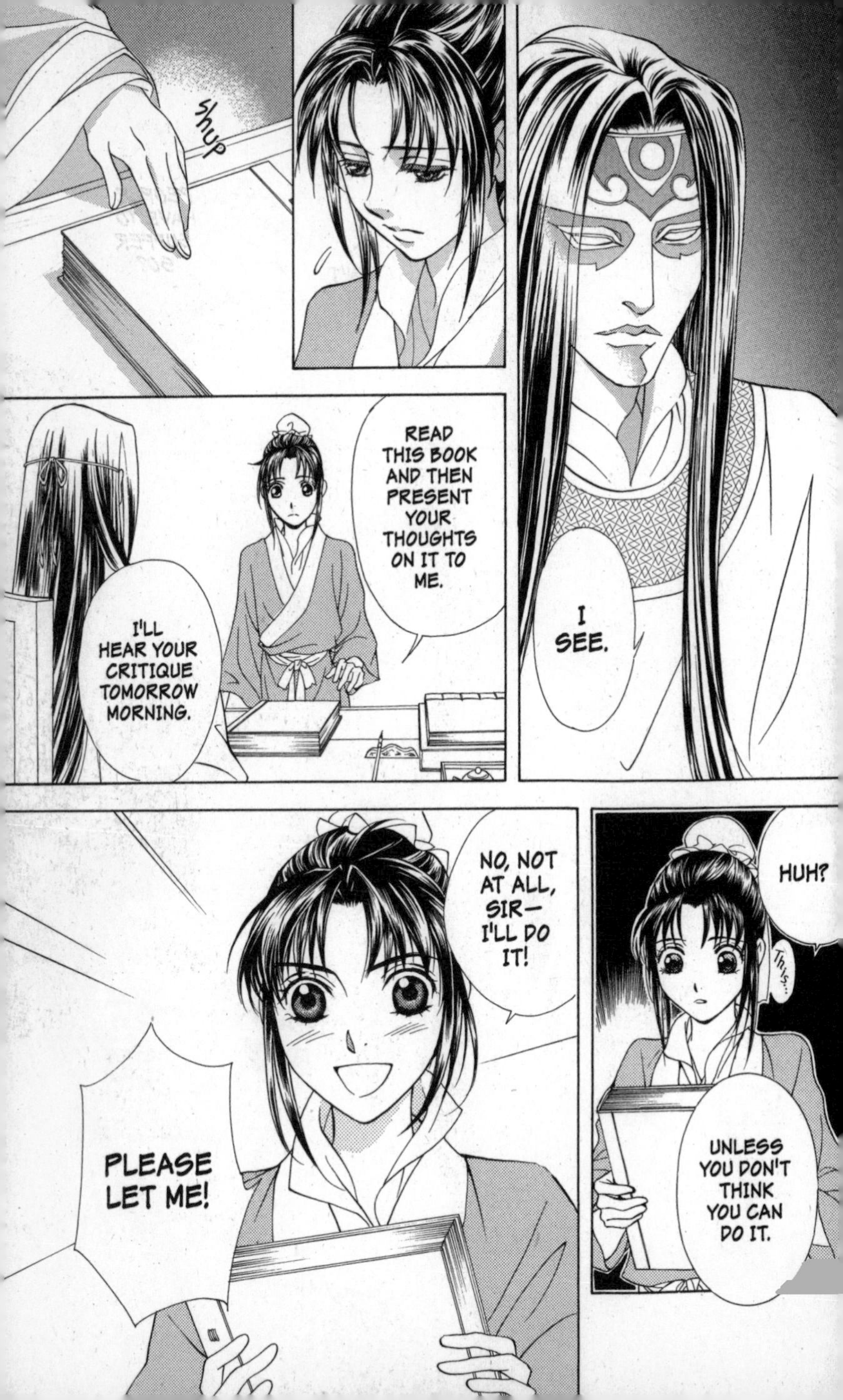
I SEE.
shup
READ THIS BOOK AND THEN PRESENT YOUR THOUGHTS ON IT TO ME.
I'LL HEAR YOUR CRITIQUE TOMORROW MORNING.
HUH?
This...
UNLESS YOU DON'T THINK YOU CAN DO IT.
NO, NOT AT ALL, SIR— I'LL DO IT!
PLEASE LET ME!

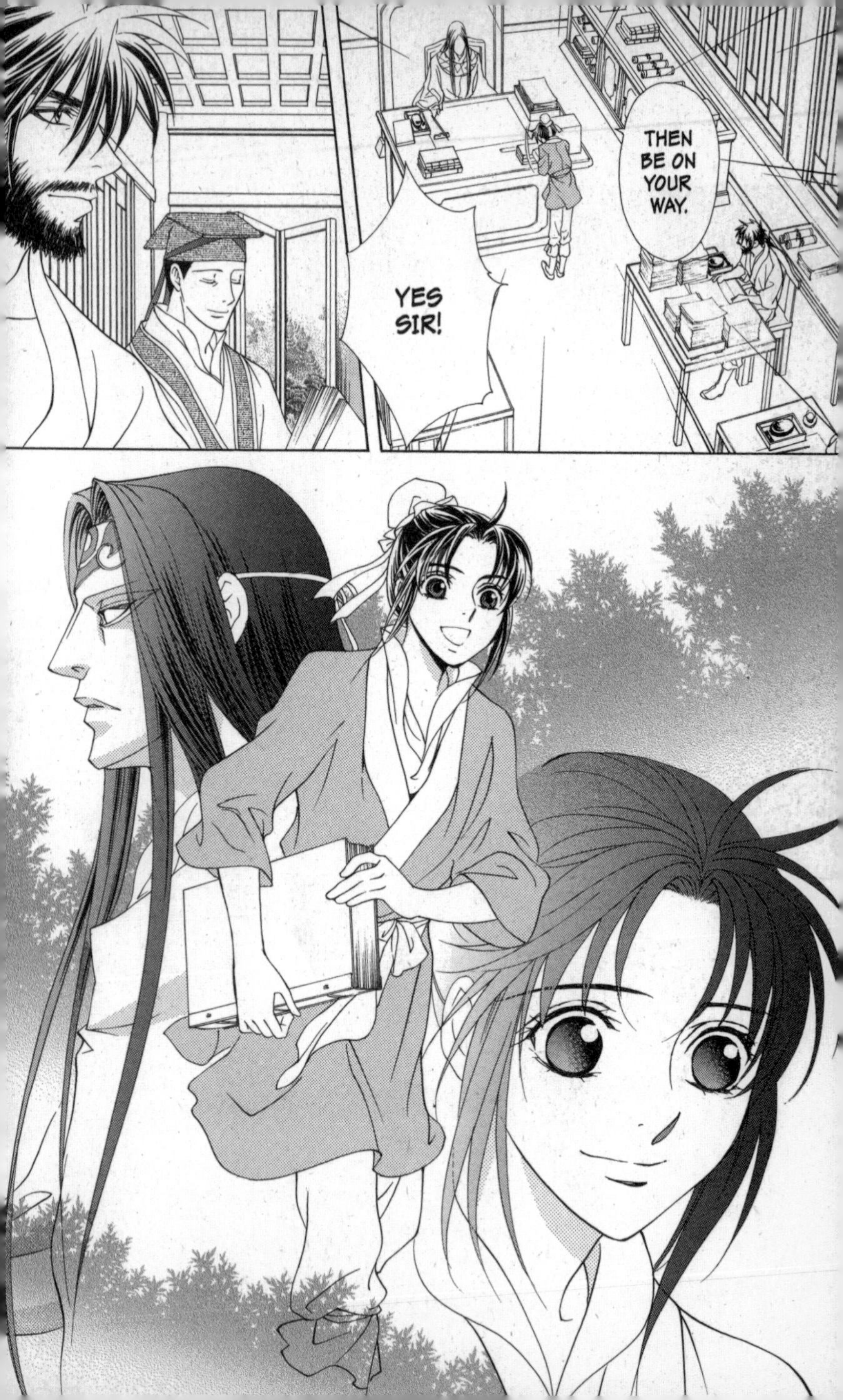
THEN BE ON YOUR WAY.
YES SIR!

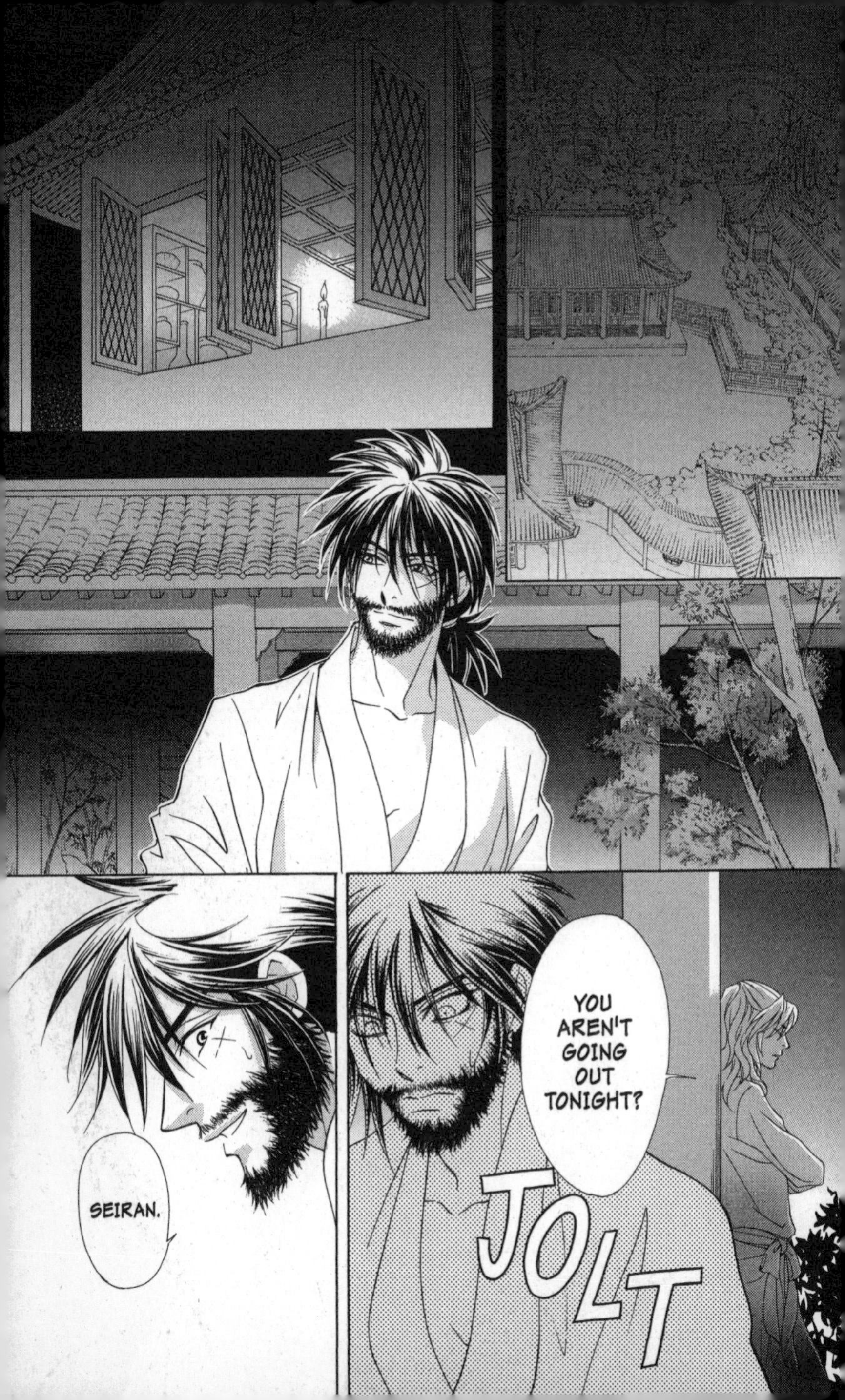
YOU AREN'T GOING OUT TONIGHT?
JOLT
SEIRAN.

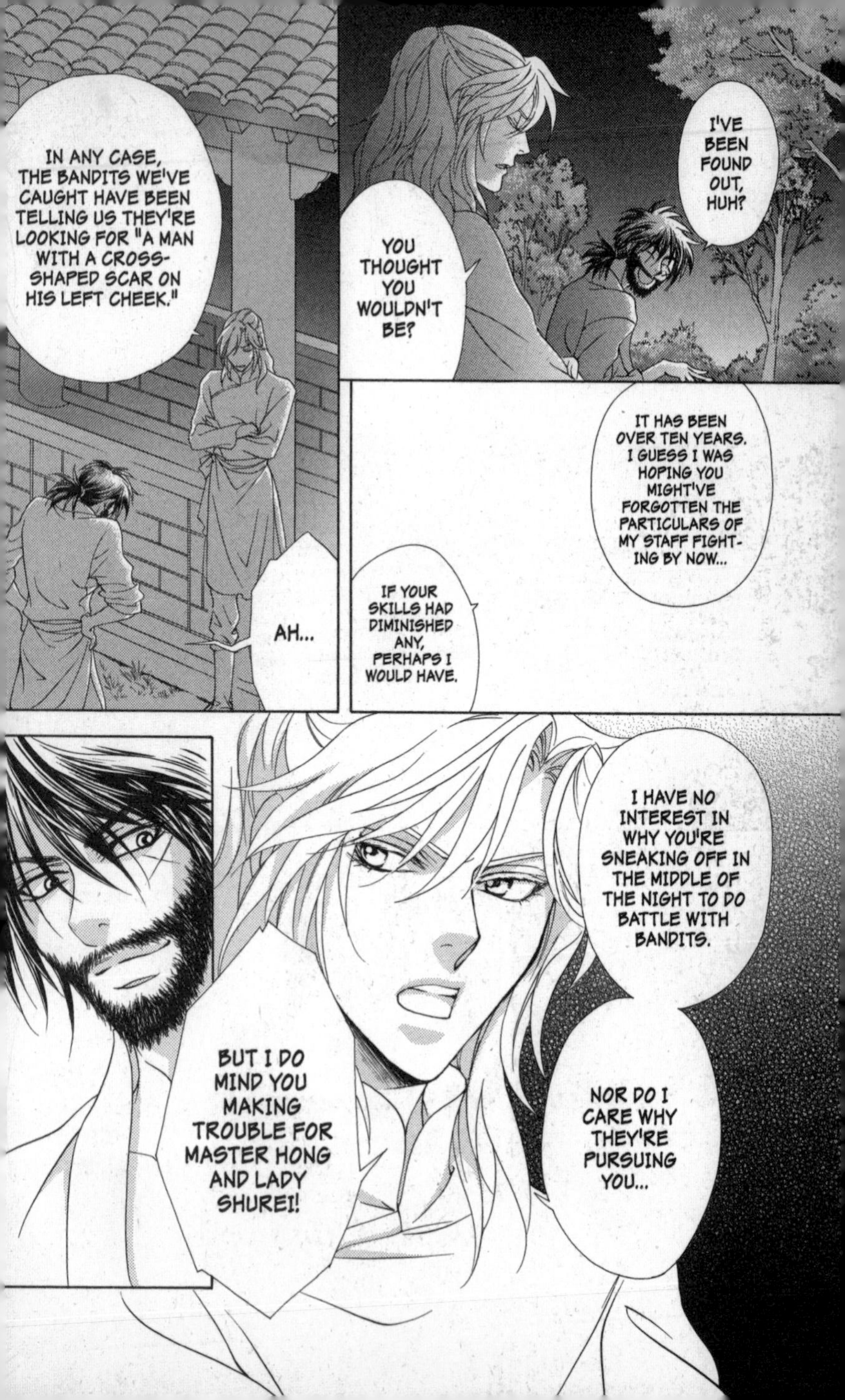
I'VE BEEN FOUND OUT, HUH?
YOU THOUGHT YOU WOULDN'T BE?
IT HAS BEEN OVER TEN YEARS. I GUESS I WAS HOPING YOU MIGHT'VE FORGOTTEN THE PARTICULARS OF MY STAFF FIGHTING BY NOW...
IF YOUR SKILLS HAD DIMINISHED ANY, PERHAPS I WOULD HAVE.
IN ANY CASE, THE BANDITS WE'VE CAUGHT HAVE BEEN TELLING US THEY'RE LOOKING FOR "A MAN WITH A CROSS-SHAPED SCAR ON HIS LEFT CHEEK."
AH...
I HAVE NO INTEREST IN WHY YOU'RE SNEAKING OFF IN THE MIDDLE OF THE NIGHT TO DO BATTLE WITH BANDITS.
NOR DO I CARE WHY THEY'RE PURSUING YOU...
BUT I DO MIND YOU MAKING TROUBLE FOR MASTER HONG AND LADY SHUREI!

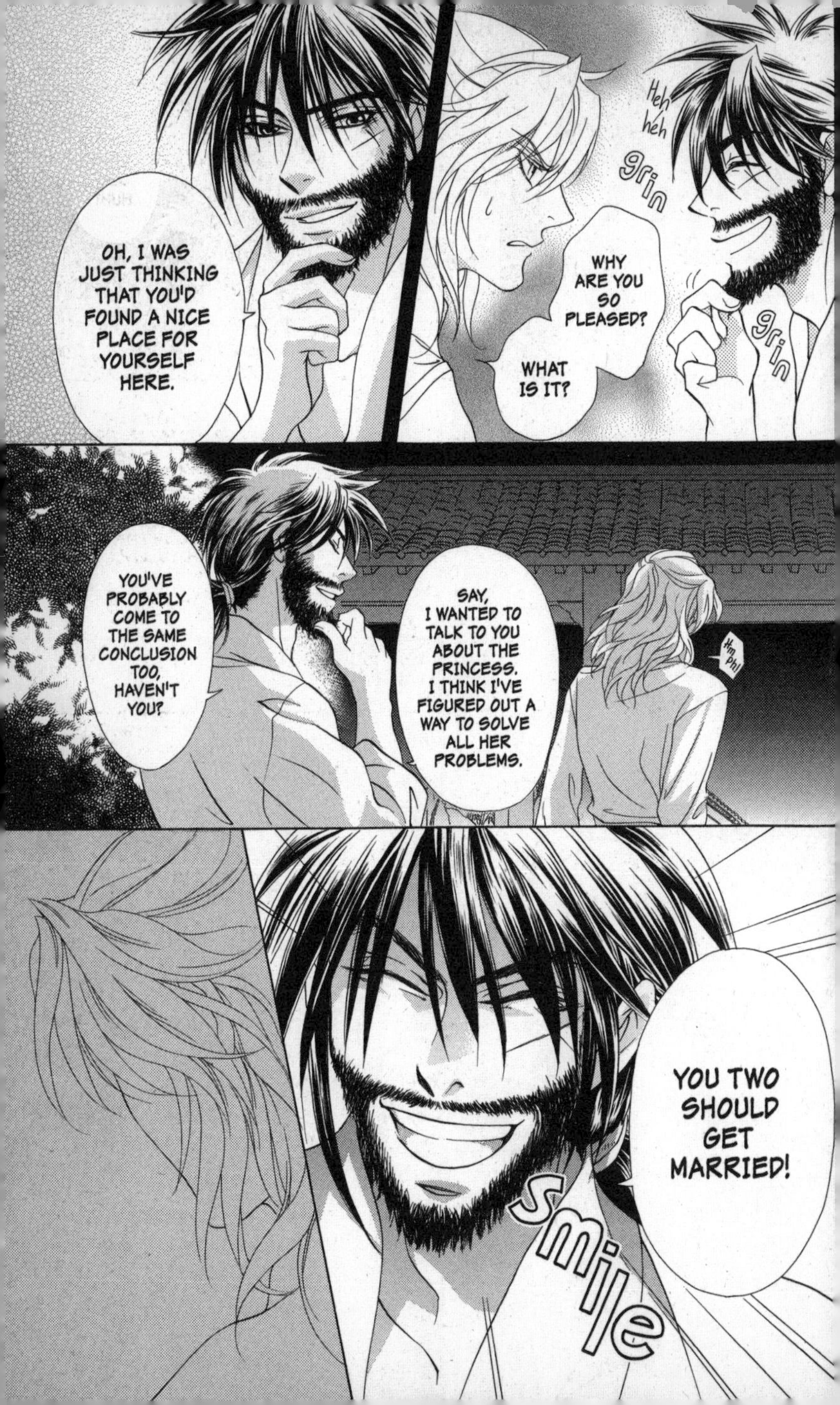
Heh heh
grin
grin
WHY ARE YOU SO PLEASED?
WHAT IS IT?
OH, I WAS JUST THINKING THAT YOU'D FOUND A NICE PLACE FOR YOURSELF HERE.
Hmph!
SAY, I WANTED TO TALK TO YOU ABOUT THE PRINCESS. I THINK I'VE FIGURED OUT A WAY TO SOLVE ALL HER PROBLEMS.
YOU'VE PROBABLY COME TO THE SAME CONCLUSION TOO, HAVEN'T YOU?
YOU TWO SHOULD GET MARRIED!
smile

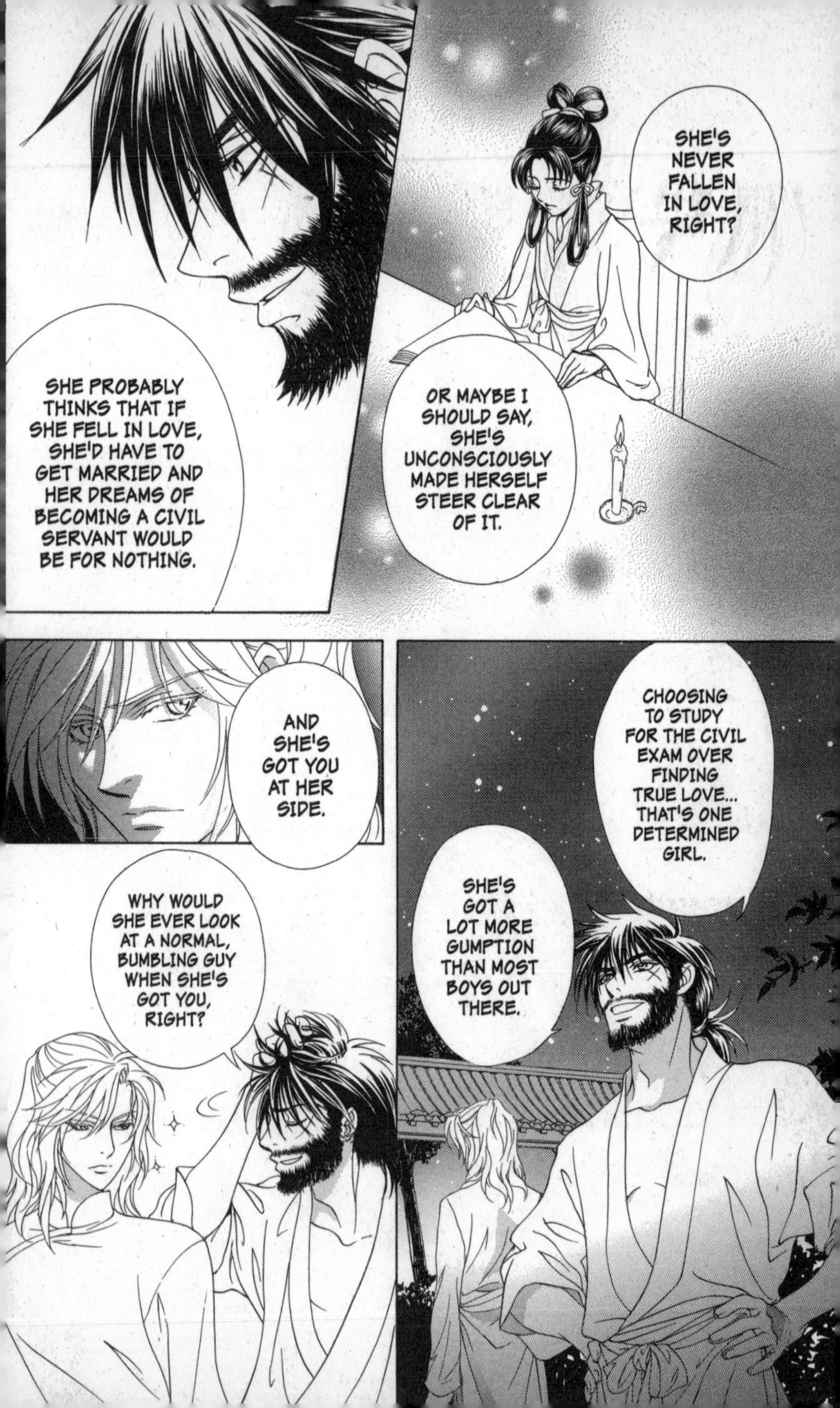
SHE'S NEVER FALLEN IN LOVE, RIGHT?
OR MAYBE I SHOULD SAY, SHE'S UNCONSCIOUSLY MADE HERSELF STEER CLEAR OF IT.
SHE PROBABLY THINKS THAT IF SHE FELL IN LOVE, SHE'D HAVE TO GET MARRIED AND HER DREAMS OF BECOMING A CIVIL SERVANT WOULD BE FOR NOTHING.
CHOOSING TO STUDY FOR THE CIVIL EXAM OVER FINDING TRUE LOVE... THAT'S ONE DETERMINED GIRL.
SHE'S GOT A LOT MORE GUMPTION THAN MOST BOYS OUT THERE.
AND SHE'S GOT YOU AT HER SIDE.
WHY WOULD SHE EVER LOOK AT A NORMAL, BUMBLING GUY WHEN SHE'S GOT YOU, RIGHT?

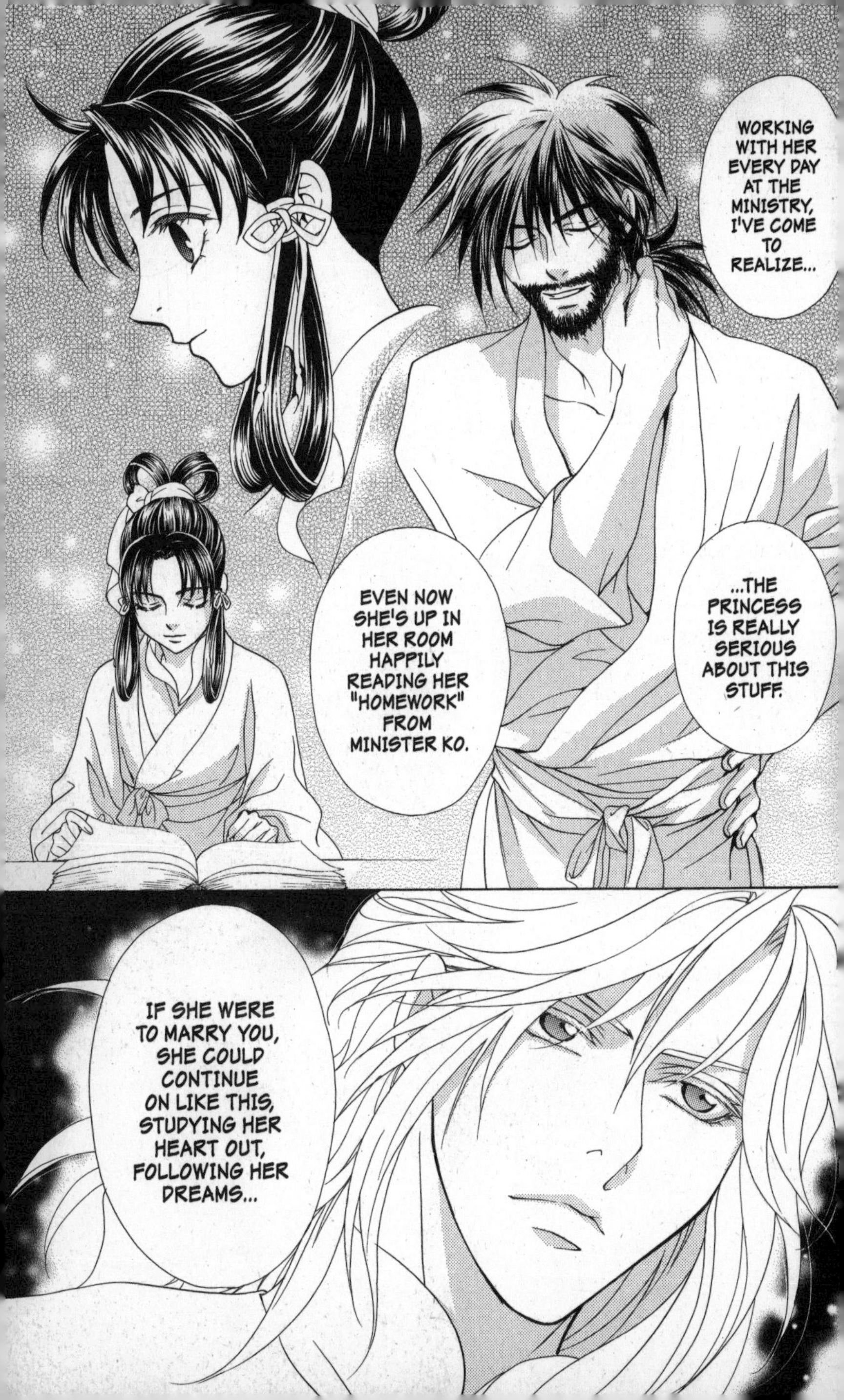
WORKING WITH HER EVERY DAY AT THE MINISTRY, I'VE COME TO REALIZE...
...THE PRINCESS IS REALLY SERIOUS ABOUT THIS STUFF.
EVEN NOW SHE'S UP IN HER ROOM HAPPILY READING HER "HOMEWORK" FROM MINISTER KO.
IF SHE WERE TO MARRY YOU, SHE COULD CONTINUE ON LIKE THIS, STUDYING HER HEART OUT, FOLLOWING HER DREAMS...

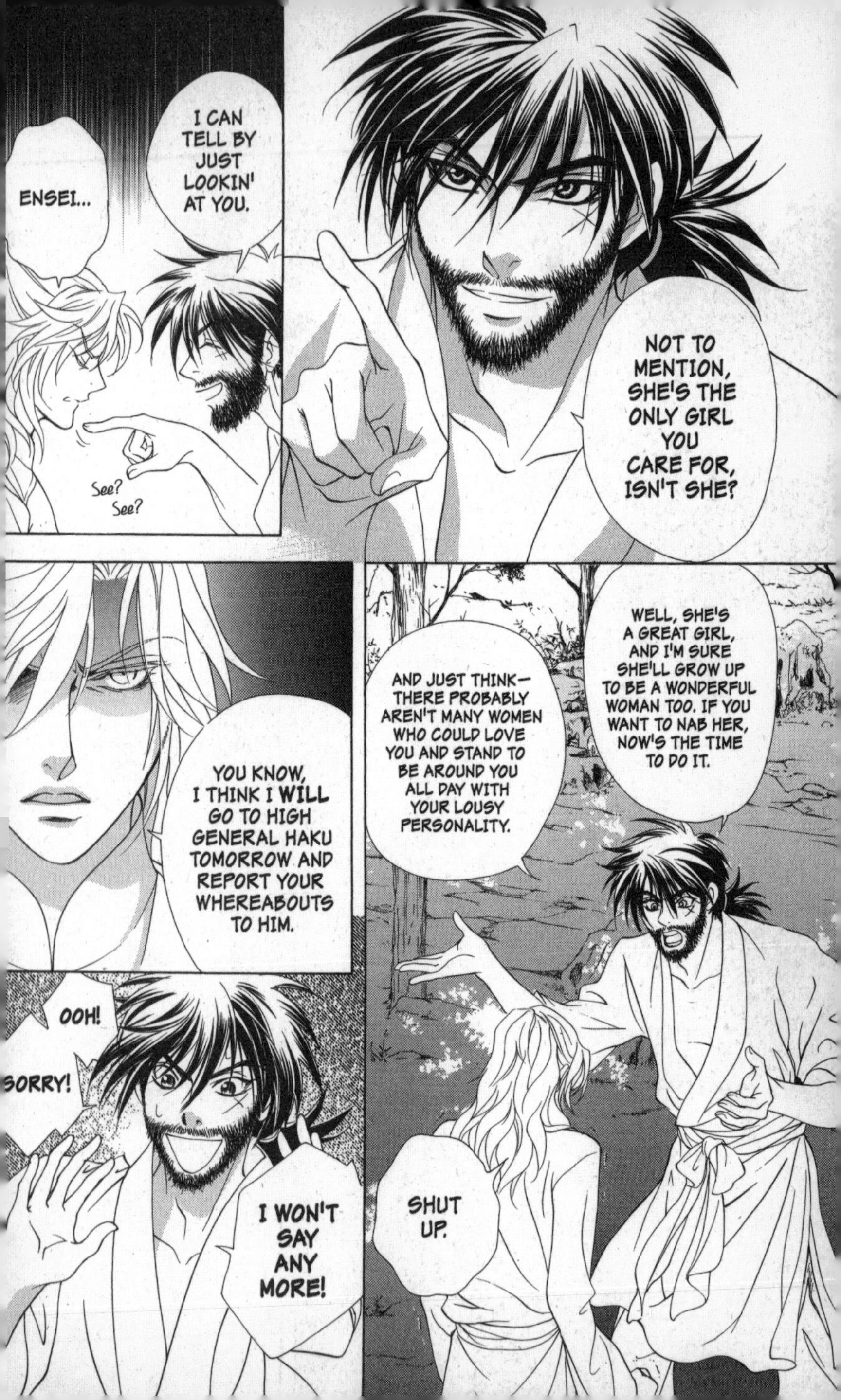
NOT TO MENTION, SHE'S THE ONLY GIRL YOU CARE FOR, ISN'T SHE?
I CAN TELL BY JUST LOOKIN' AT YOU.
ENSEI...
See? See?
WELL, SHE'S A GREAT GIRL, AND I'M SURE SHE'LL GROW UP TO BE A WONDERFUL WOMAN TOO. IF YOU WANT TO NAB HER, NOW'S THE TIME TO DO IT.
AND JUST THINK—THERE PROBABLY AREN'T MANY WOMEN WHO COULD LOVE YOU AND STAND TO BE AROUND YOU ALL DAY WITH YOUR LOUSY PERSONALITY.
SHUT UP.
YOU KNOW, I THINK I **WILL** GO TO HIGH GENERAL HAKU TOMORROW AND REPORT YOUR WHEREABOUTS TO HIM.
OOH!
SORRY!
I WON'T SAY ANY MORE!

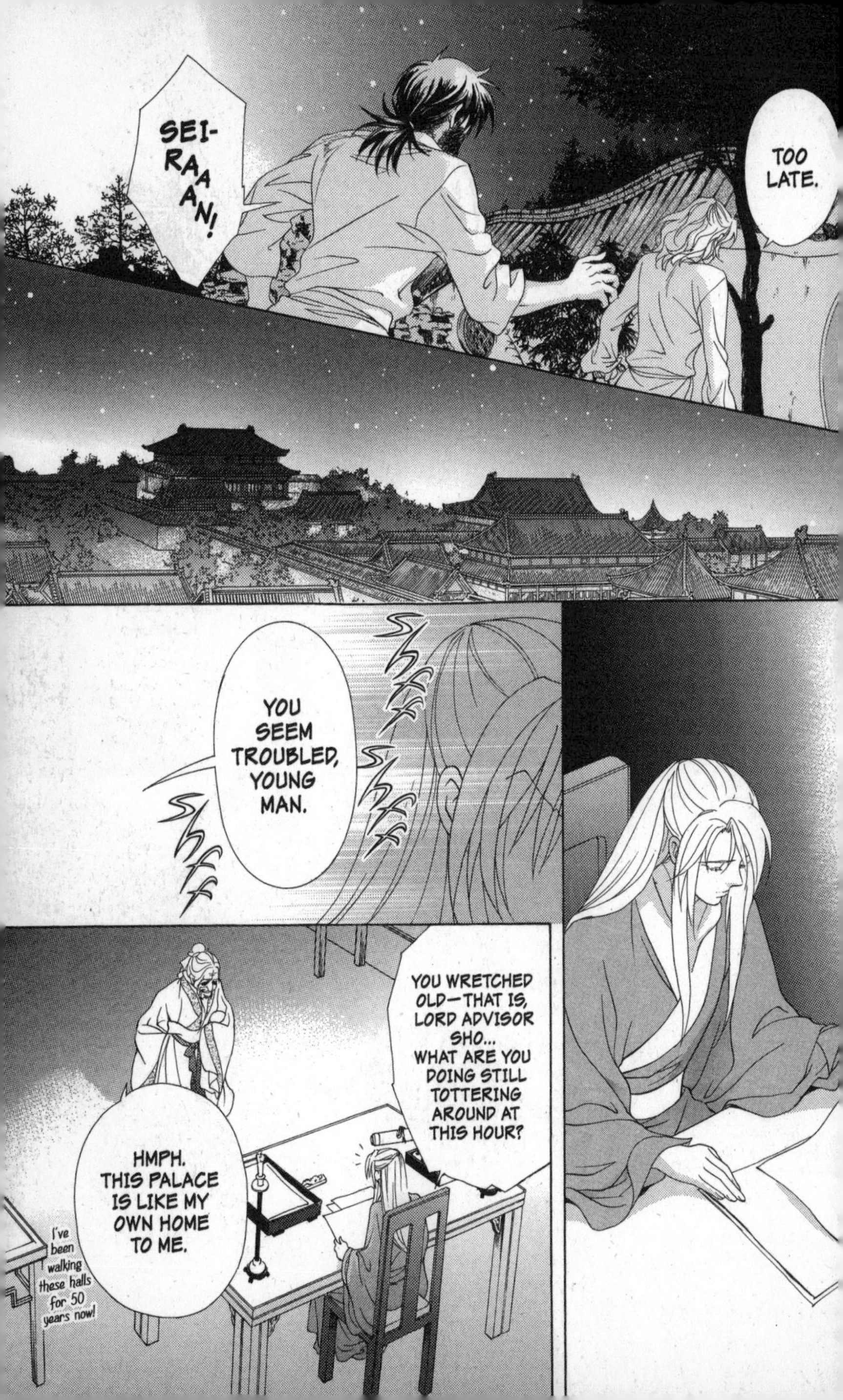
TOO LATE.
SEI-RAAAAN!
SHFF SHFF SHFF
YOU SEEM TROUBLED, YOUNG MAN.
SHFF
YOU WRETCHED OLD—THAT IS, LORD ADVISOR SHO... WHAT ARE YOU DOING STILL TOTTERING AROUND AT THIS HOUR?
HMPH. THIS PALACE IS LIKE MY OWN HOME TO ME.
I've been walking these halls for 50 years now!

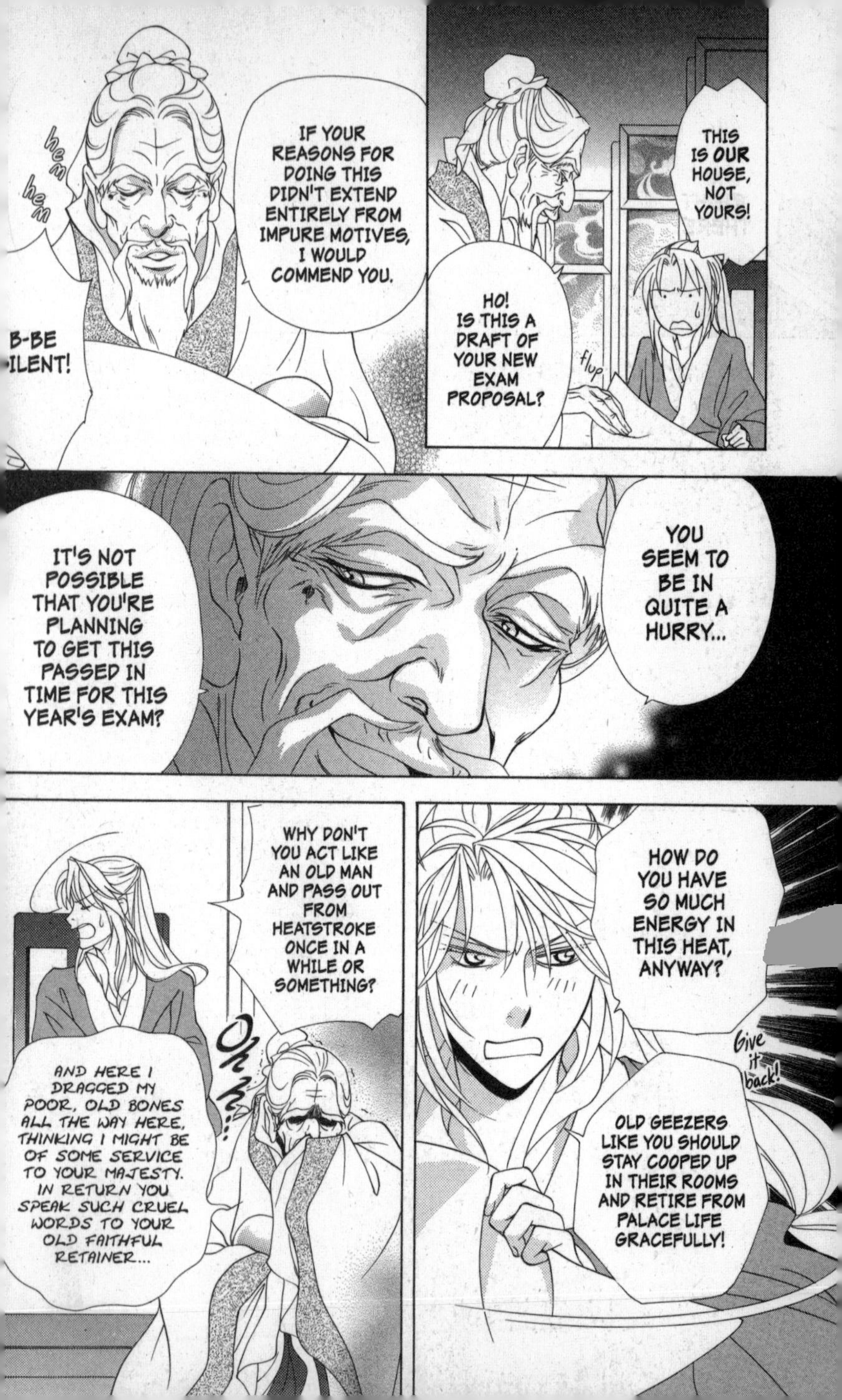
THIS IS OUR HOUSE, NOT YOURS!
HO! IS THIS A DRAFT OF YOUR NEW EXAM PROPOSAL?
flup
hem hem
IF YOUR REASONS FOR DOING THIS DIDN'T EXTEND ENTIRELY FROM IMPURE MOTIVES, I WOULD COMMEND YOU.
B-BE ILENT!
YOU SEEM TO BE IN QUITE A HURRY...
IT'S NOT POSSIBLE THAT YOU'RE PLANNING TO GET THIS PASSED IN TIME FOR THIS YEAR'S EXAM?
HOW DO YOU HAVE SO MUCH ENERGY IN THIS HEAT, ANYWAY?
Give it back!
OLD GEEZERS LIKE YOU SHOULD STAY COOPED UP IN THEIR ROOMS AND RETIRE FROM PALACE LIFE GRACEFULLY!
WHY DON'T YOU ACT LIKE AN OLD MAN AND PASS OUT FROM HEATSTROKE ONCE IN A WHILE OR SOMETHING?
Oh h...
AND HERE I DRAGGED MY POOR, OLD BONES ALL THE WAY HERE, THINKING I MIGHT BE OF SOME SERVICE TO YOUR MAJESTY. IN RETURN YOU SPEAK SUCH CRUEL WORDS TO YOUR OLD FAITHFUL RETAINER...

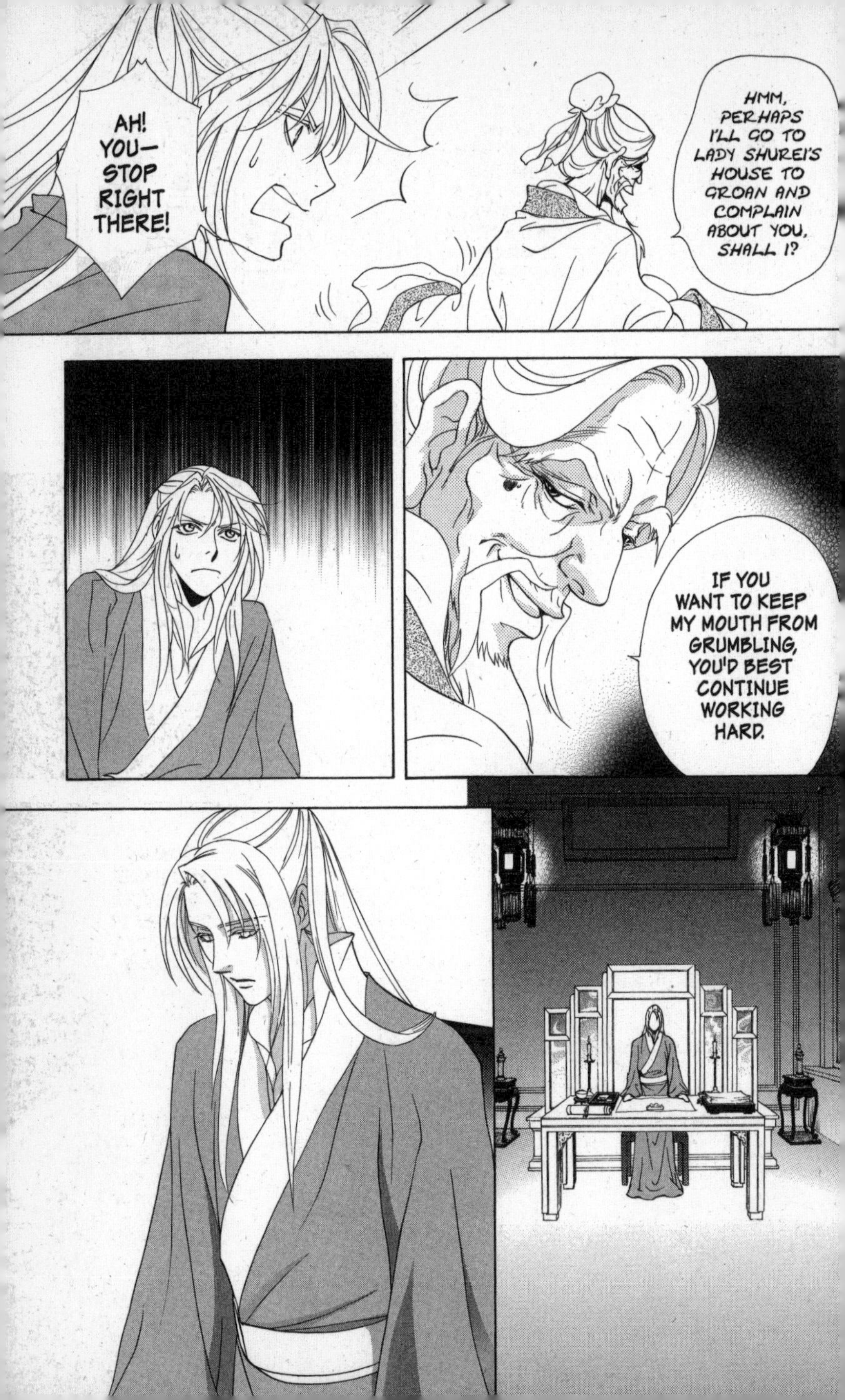
HMM, PERHAPS I'LL GO TO LADY SHUREI'S HOUSE TO GROAN AND COMPLAIN ABOUT YOU, SHALL I?
AH! YOU—STOP RIGHT THERE!
IF YOU WANT TO KEEP MY MOUTH FROM GRUMBLING, YOU'D BEST CONTINUE WORKING HARD.

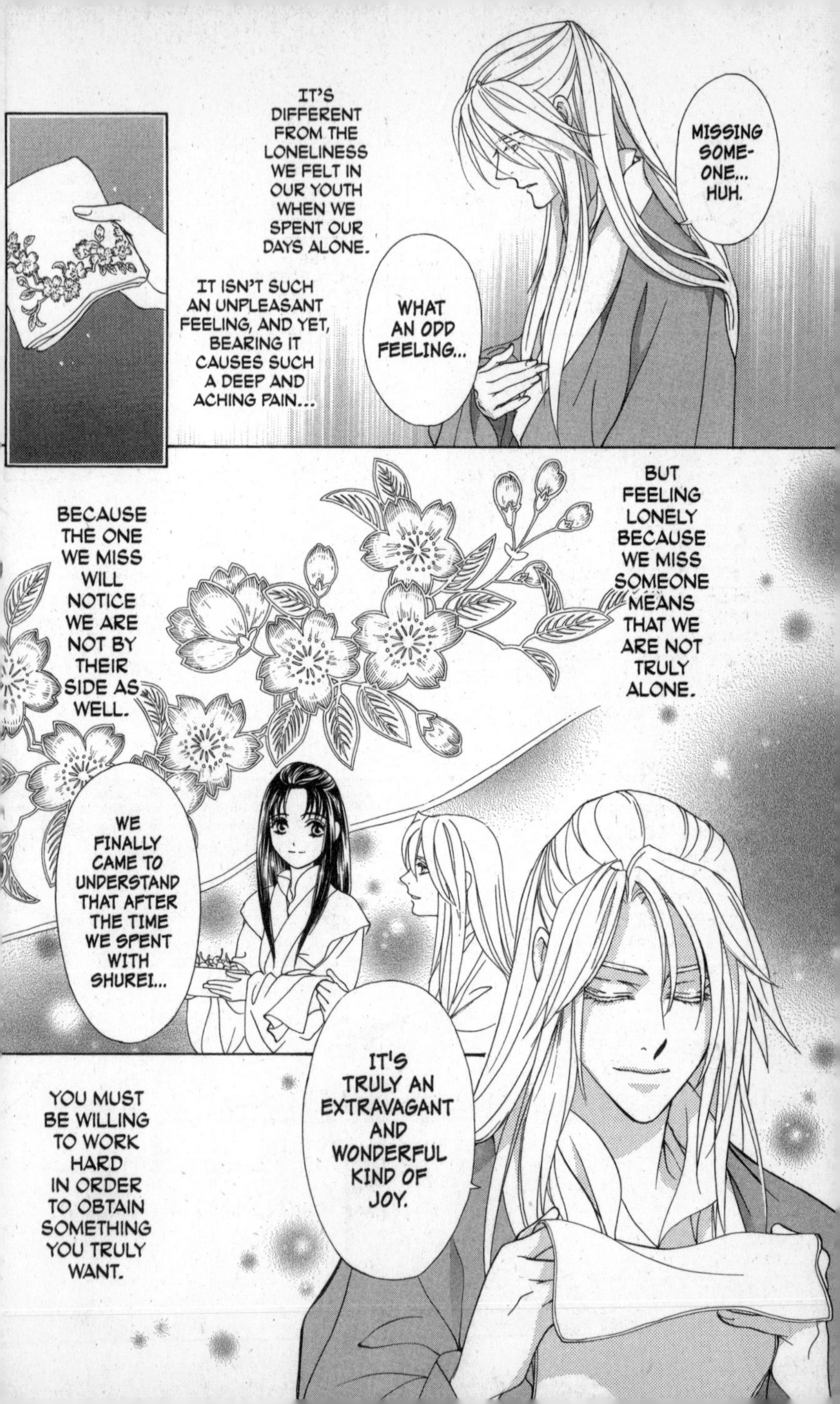
MISSING SOME-ONE... HUH.
WHAT AN ODD FEELING...
IT'S DIFFERENT FROM THE LONELINESS WE FELT IN OUR YOUTH WHEN WE SPENT OUR DAYS ALONE.
IT ISN'T SUCH AN UNPLEASANT FEELING, AND YET, BEARING IT CAUSES SUCH A DEEP AND ACHING PAIN...
BUT FEELING LONELY BECAUSE WE MISS SOMEONE MEANS THAT WE ARE NOT TRULY ALONE.
BECAUSE THE ONE WE MISS WILL NOTICE WE ARE NOT BY THEIR SIDE AS WELL.
WE FINALLY CAME TO UNDERSTAND THAT AFTER THE TIME WE SPENT WITH SHUREI...
IT'S TRULY AN EXTRAVAGANT AND WONDERFUL KIND OF JOY.
YOU MUST BE WILLING TO WORK HARD IN ORDER TO OBTAIN SOMETHING YOU TRULY WANT.

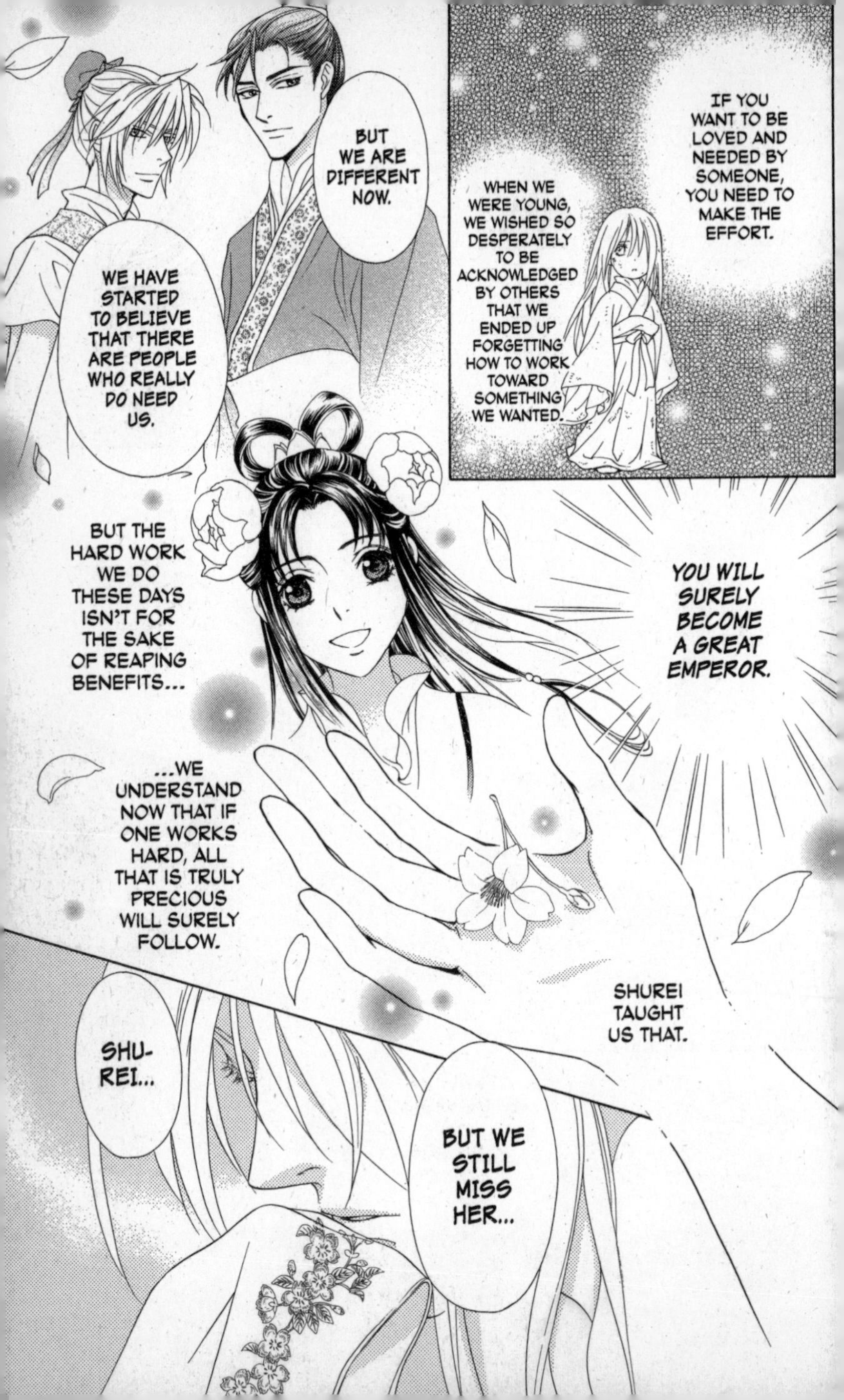
IF YOU WANT TO BE LOVED AND NEEDED BY SOMEONE, YOU NEED TO MAKE THE EFFORT.
WHEN WE WERE YOUNG, WE WISHED SO DESPERATELY TO BE ACKNOWLEDGED BY OTHERS THAT WE ENDED UP FORGETTING HOW TO WORK TOWARD SOMETHING WE WANTED.
BUT WE ARE DIFFERENT NOW.
WE HAVE STARTED TO BELIEVE THAT THERE ARE PEOPLE WHO REALLY DO NEED US.
YOU WILL SURELY BECOME A GREAT EMPEROR.
BUT THE HARD WORK WE DO THESE DAYS ISN'T FOR THE SAKE OF REAPING BENEFITS...
...WE UNDERSTAND NOW THAT IF ONE WORKS HARD, ALL THAT IS TRULY PRECIOUS WILL SURELY FOLLOW.
SHUREI TAUGHT US THAT.
BUT WE STILL MISS HER...
SHU-REI...

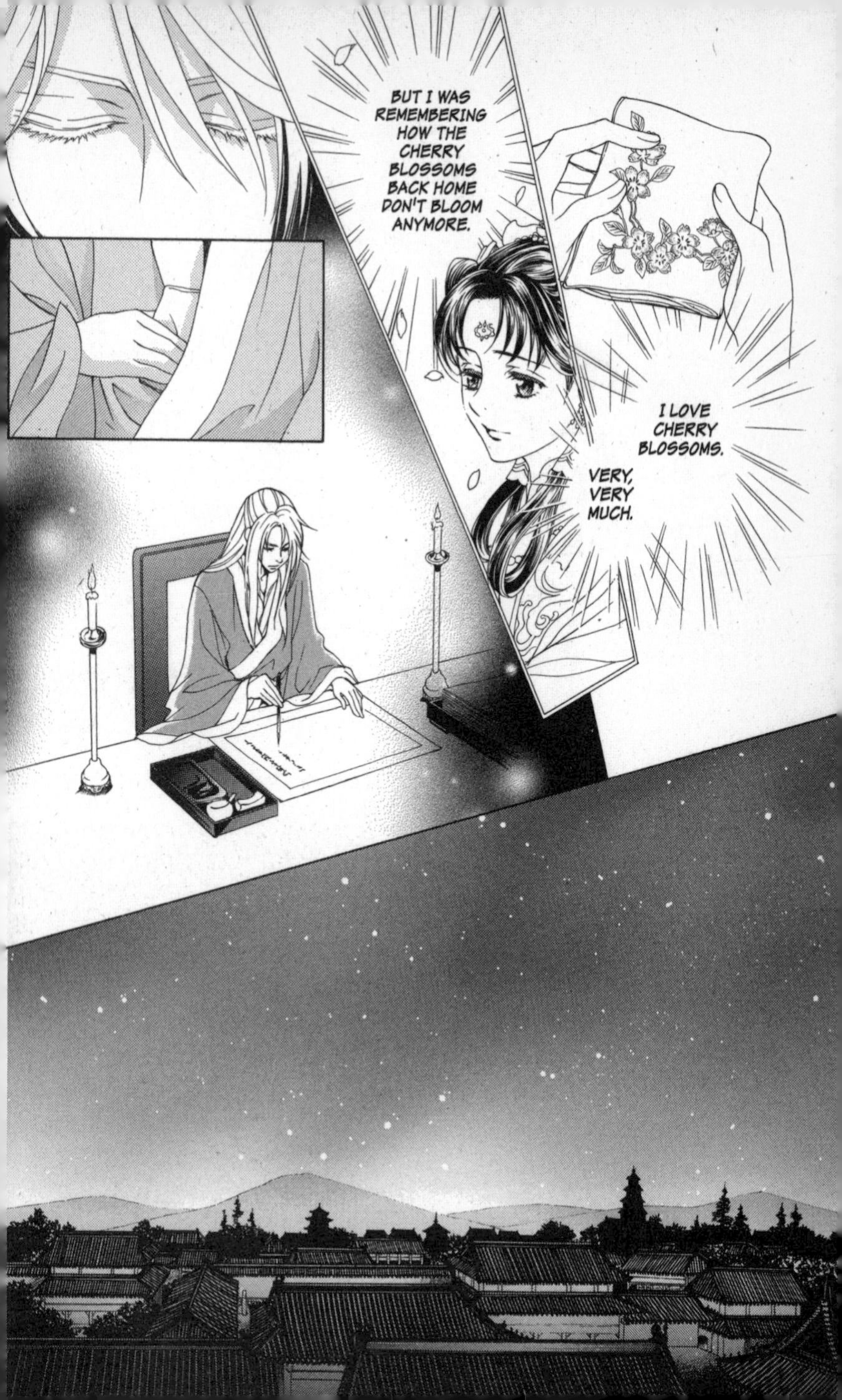
BUT I WAS REMEMBERING HOW THE CHERRY BLOSSOMS BACK HOME DON'T BLOOM ANYMORE.
I LOVE CHERRY BLOSSOMS.
VERY, VERY MUCH.

I DON'T HAVE MANY GOOD MEMORIES OF SUMMER.

ESPECIALLY WHEN THUNDER-STORMS COME...

Side Story

The Proper Way to Pass a Stormy Evening

WAIT...

DON'T START YET...!

tremble

tremble

B-BUMP

OH NO!

RUMBLE RUMBLE

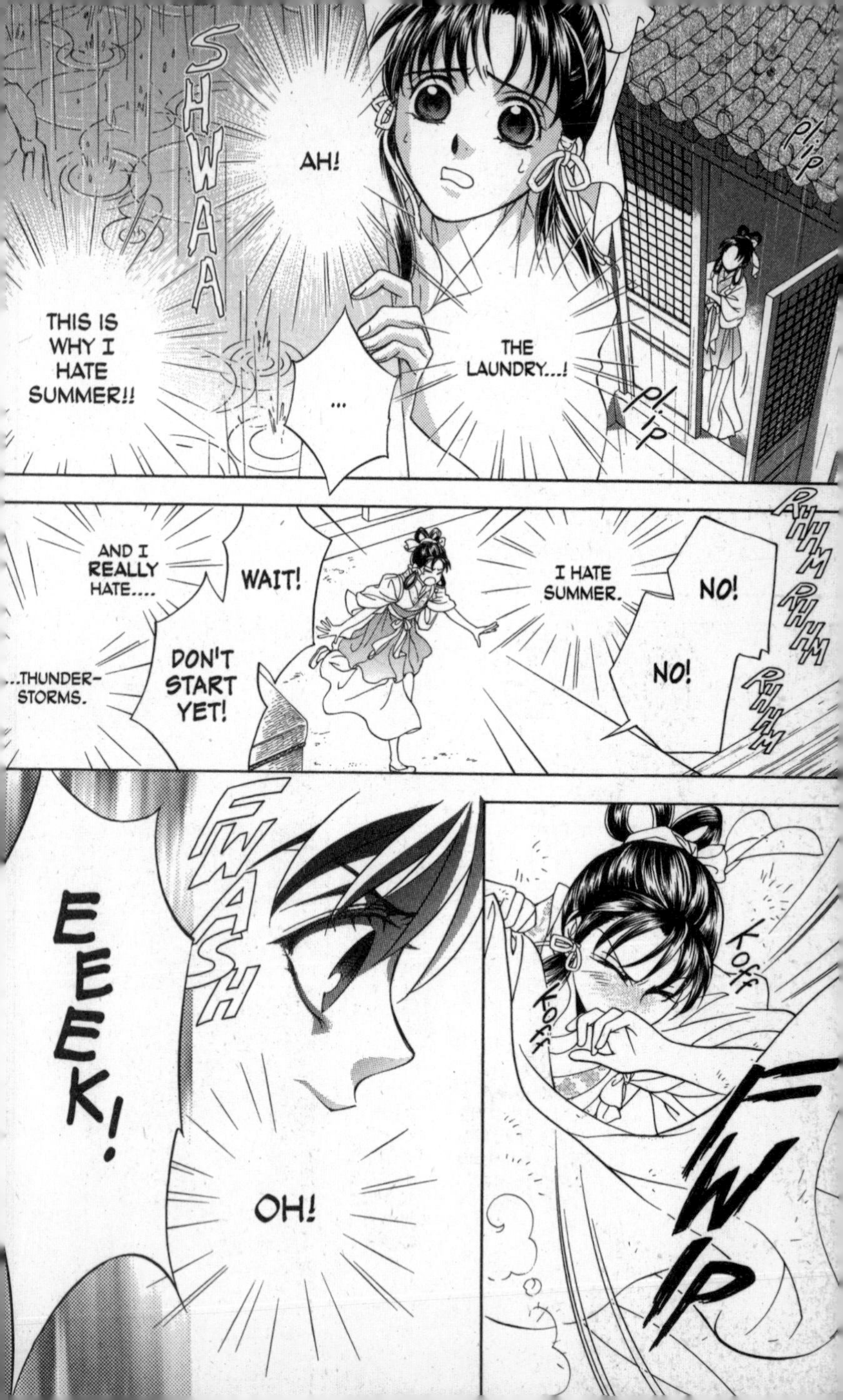
plip
AH!
THE LAUNDRY...!
plip
SHWAA
...
THIS IS WHY I HATE SUMMER!!
RHHM RHHM RHHM
NO!
NO!
I HATE SUMMER.
WAIT!
DON'T START YET!
AND I REALLY HATE....
...THUNDER-STORMS.
koff
koff
FWIP
FWASH
OH!
EEEK!

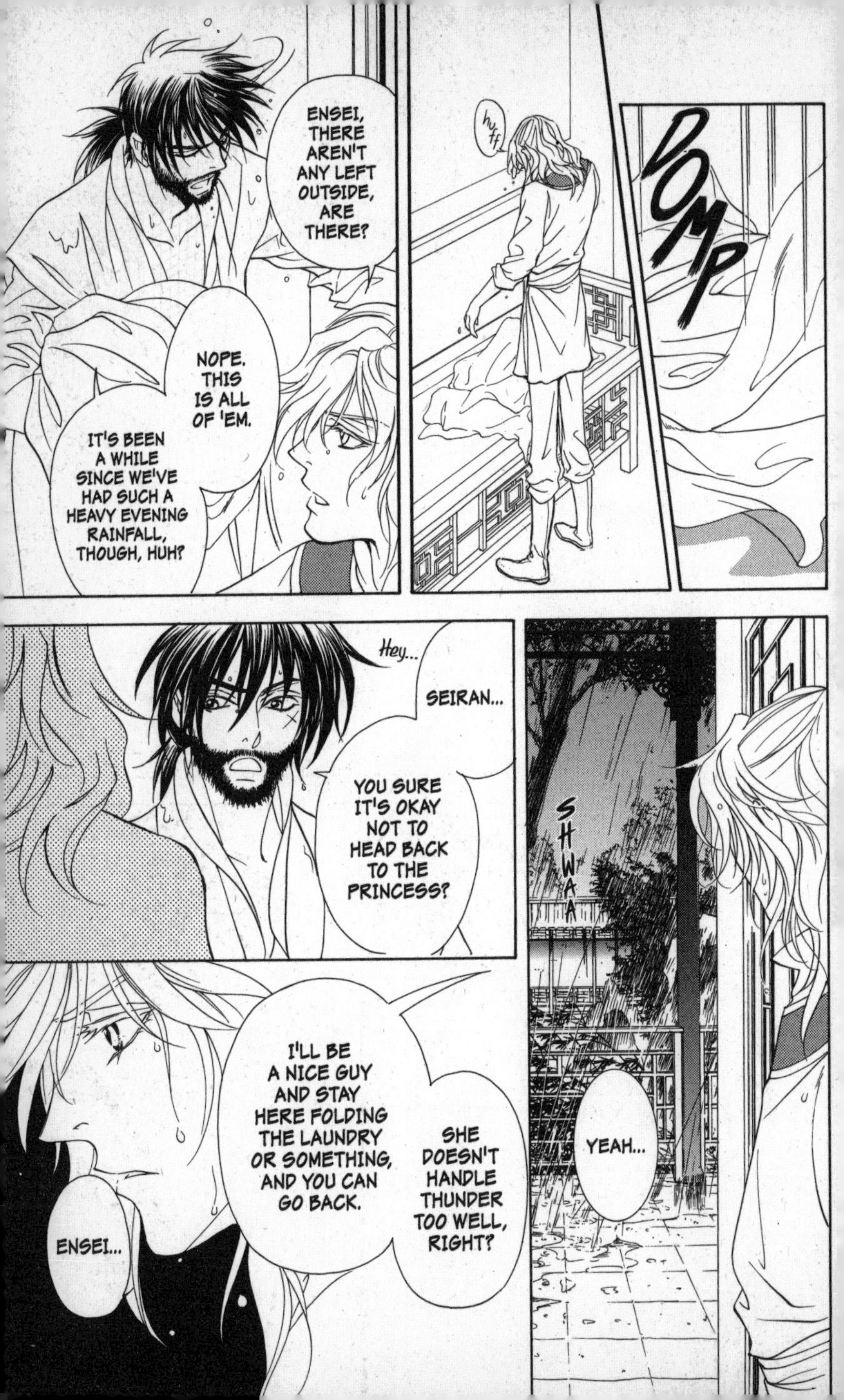
DOMP
huff
ENSEI, THERE AREN'T ANY LEFT OUTSIDE, ARE THERE?
NOPE. THIS IS ALL OF 'EM.
IT'S BEEN A WHILE SINCE WE'VE HAD SUCH A HEAVY EVENING RAINFALL, THOUGH, HUH?
SHWAA
Hey...
SEIRAN...
YOU SURE IT'S OKAY NOT TO HEAD BACK TO THE PRINCESS?
SHE DOESN'T HANDLE THUNDER TOO WELL, RIGHT?
YEAH...
I'LL BE A NICE GUY AND STAY HERE FOLDING THE LAUNDRY OR SOMETHING, AND YOU CAN GO BACK.
ENSEI...

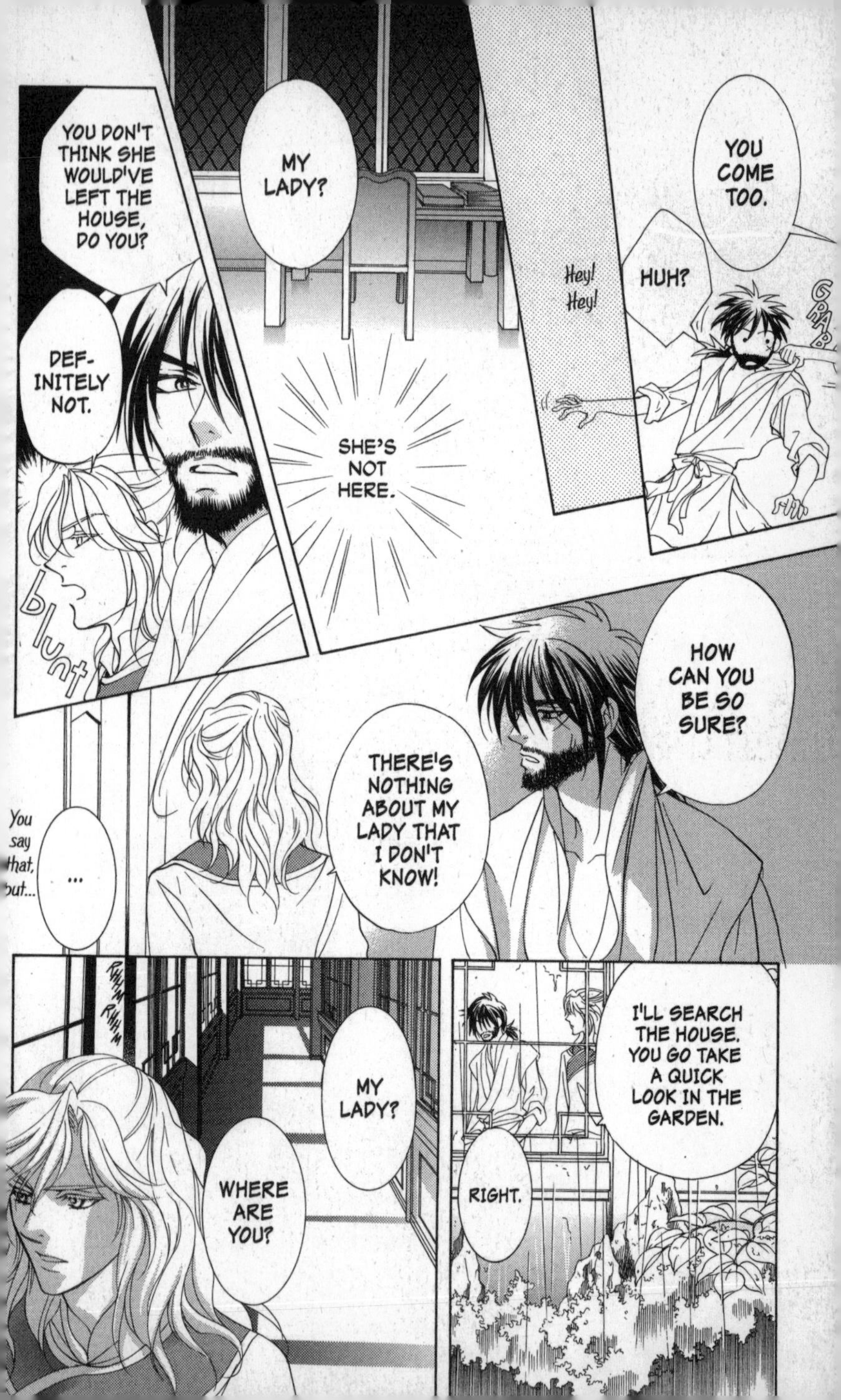
YOU COME TOO.
HUH?
Hey! Hey!
GRAB
MY LADY?
SHE'S NOT HERE.
YOU DON'T THINK SHE WOULD'VE LEFT THE HOUSE, DO YOU?
DEF-INITELY NOT.
blunt
HOW CAN YOU BE SO SURE?
THERE'S NOTHING ABOUT MY LADY THAT I DON'T KNOW!
...
You say that, but...
I'LL SEARCH THE HOUSE. YOU GO TAKE A QUICK LOOK IN THE GARDEN.
RIGHT.
MY LADY?
WHERE ARE YOU?

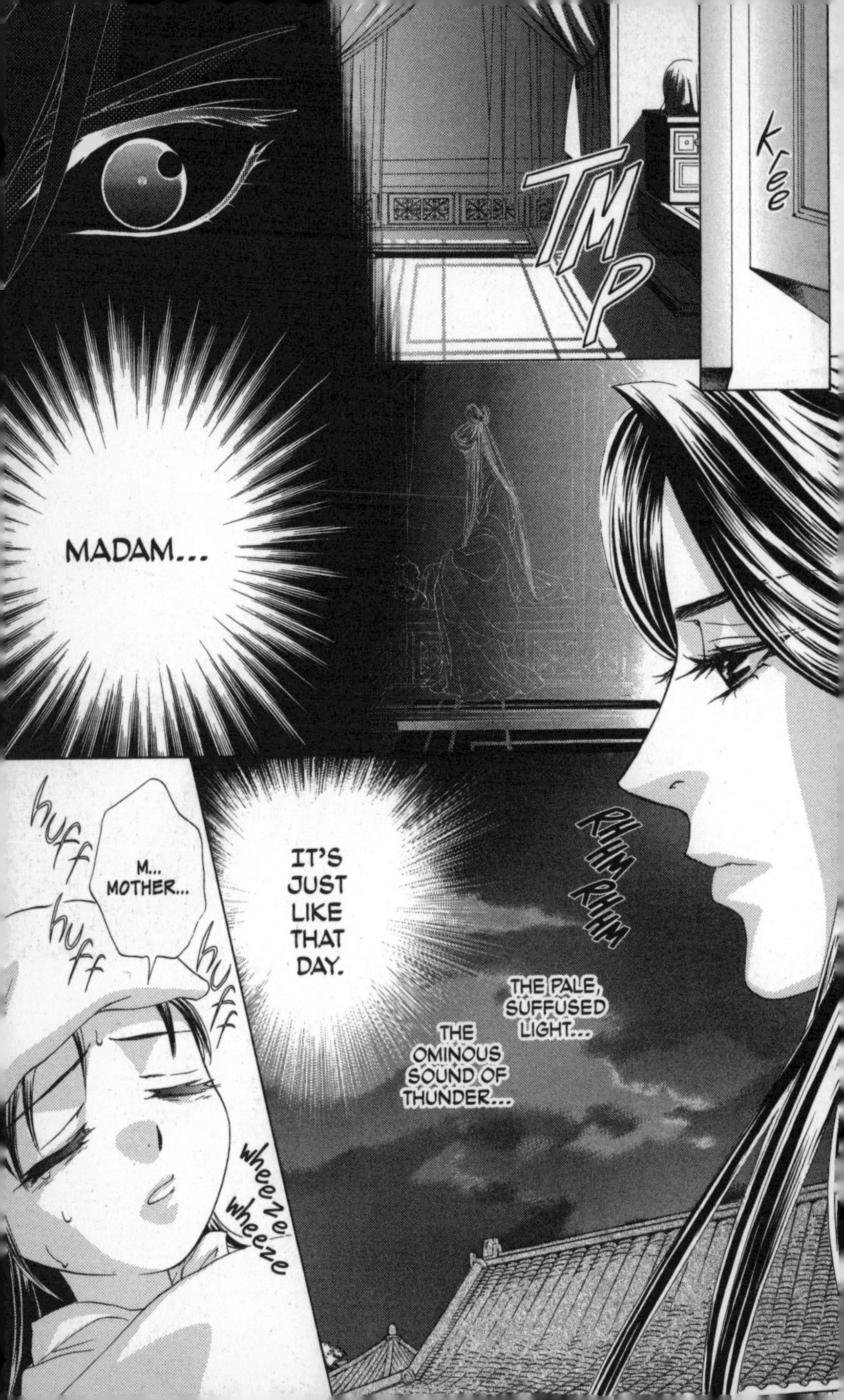
Kree
TMP
MADAM...
RHHM RHHM
THE PALE, SUFFUSED LIGHT...
THE OMINOUS SOUND OF THUNDER...
IT'S JUST LIKE THAT DAY.
M... MOTHER...
huff huff huff
wheeze wheeze wheeze

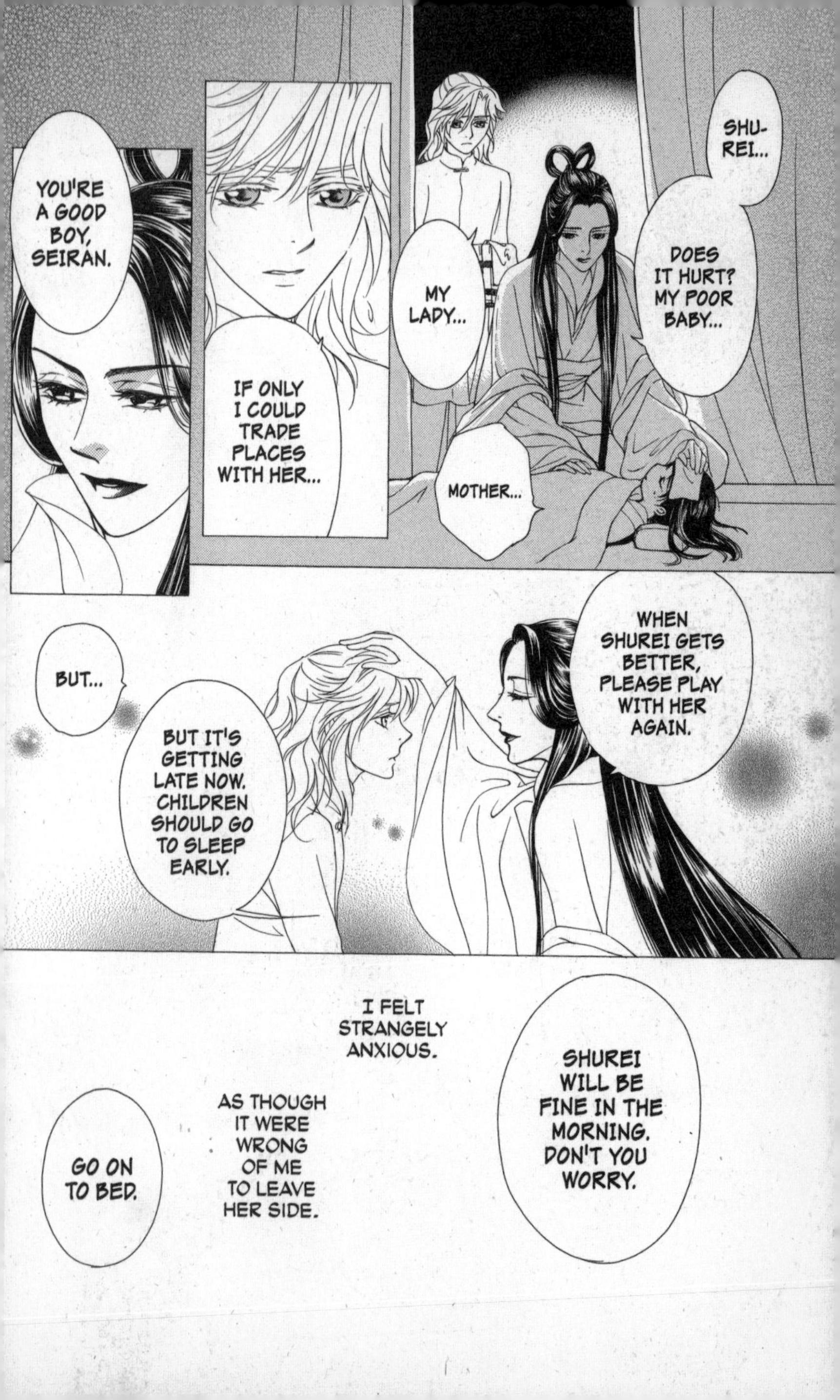
SHU-REI...
DOES IT HURT? MY POOR BABY...
MY LADY...
MOTHER...
IF ONLY I COULD TRADE PLACES WITH HER...
YOU'RE A GOOD BOY, SEIRAN.
WHEN SHUREI GETS BETTER, PLEASE PLAY WITH HER AGAIN.
BUT IT'S GETTING LATE NOW. CHILDREN SHOULD GO TO SLEEP EARLY.
BUT...
SHUREI WILL BE FINE IN THE MORNING. DON'T YOU WORRY.
I FELT STRANGELY ANXIOUS.
AS THOUGH IT WERE WRONG OF ME TO LEAVE HER SIDE.
GO ON TO BED.

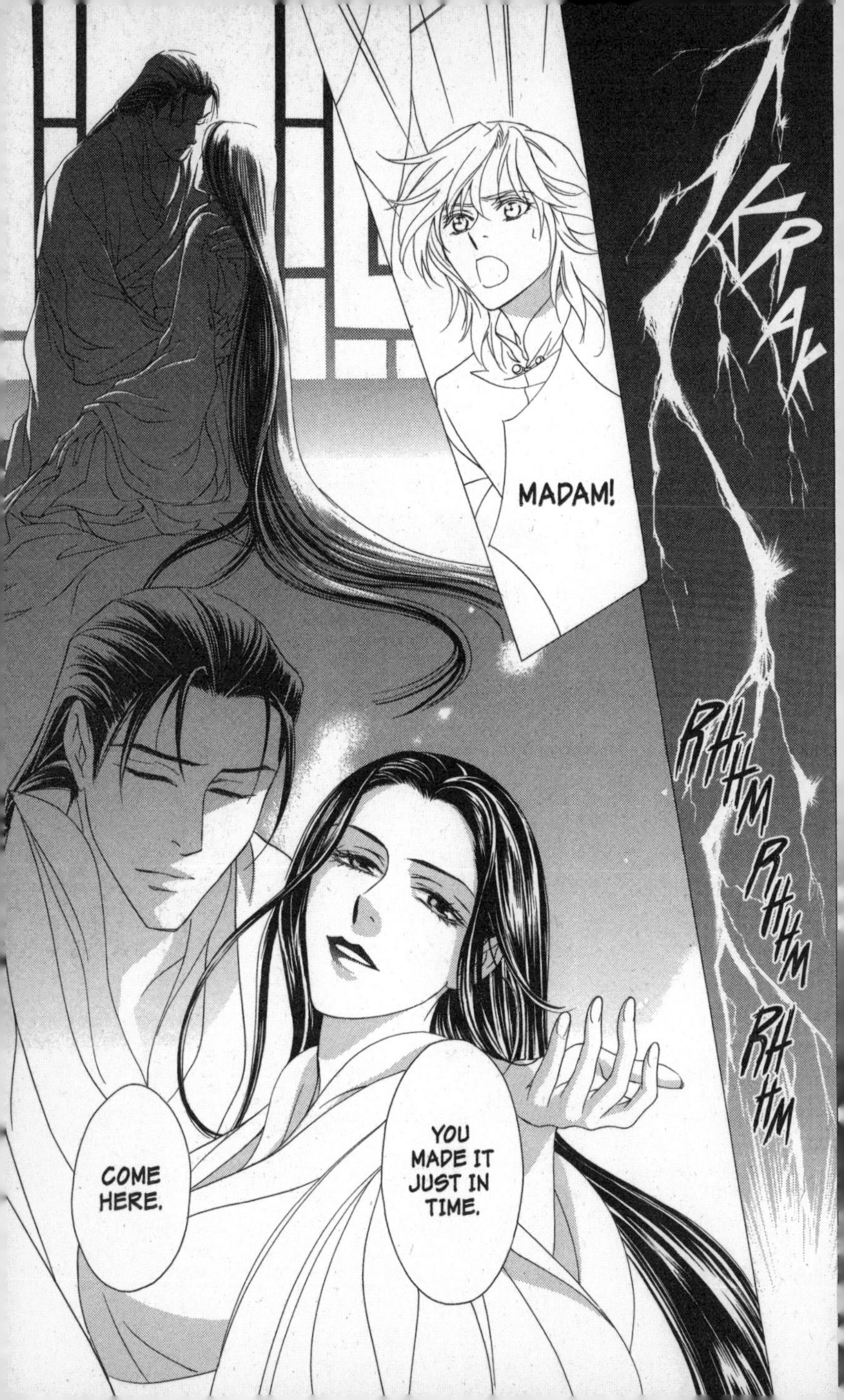
KRAK
RHHM RHHM RHHM
MADAM!
YOU MADE IT JUST IN TIME.
COME HERE.

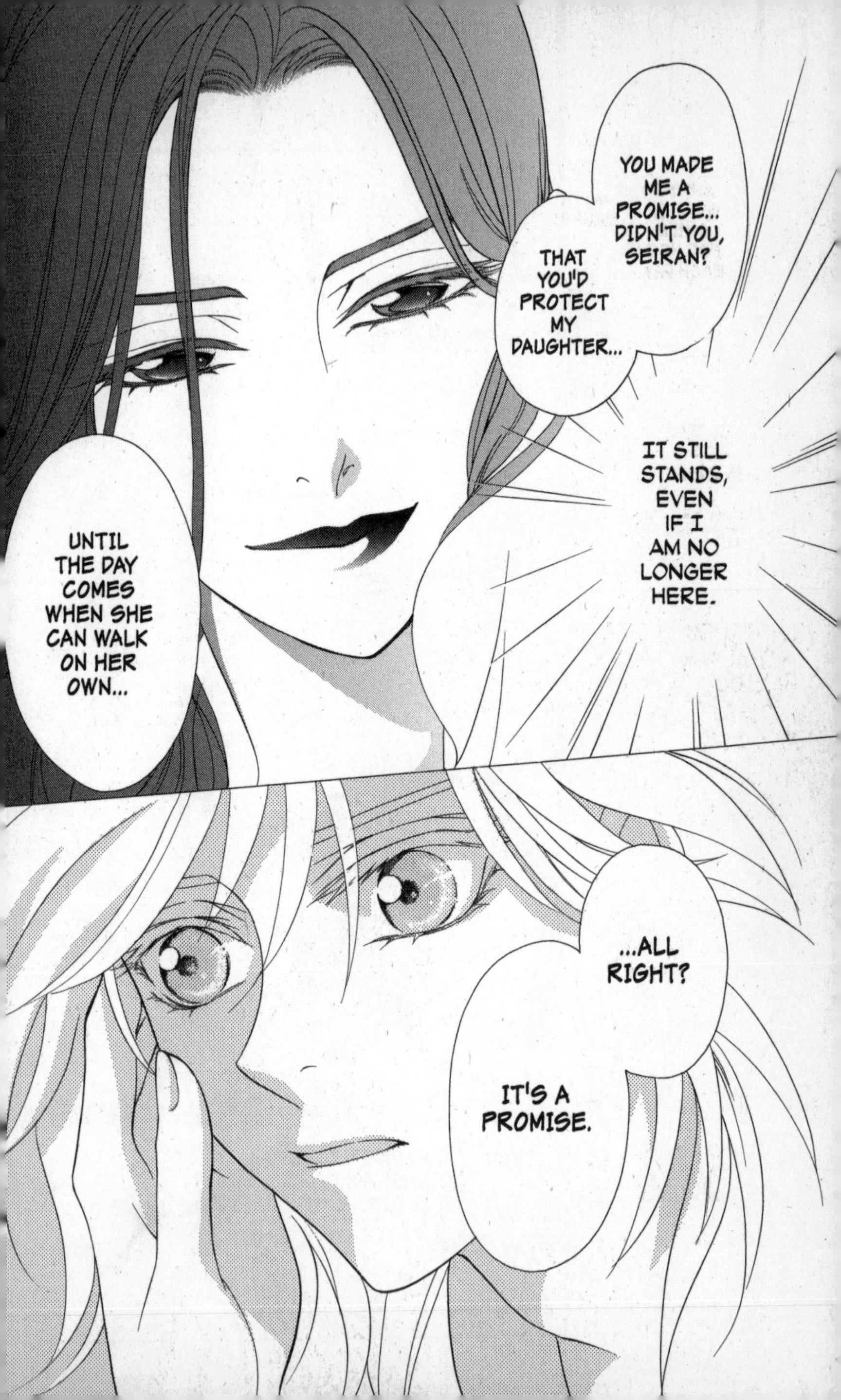
YOU MADE ME A PROMISE... DIDN'T YOU, SEIRAN?
THAT YOU'D PROTECT MY DAUGHTER...
IT STILL STANDS, EVEN IF I AM NO LONGER HERE.
UNTIL THE DAY COMES WHEN SHE CAN WALK ON HER OWN...
...ALL RIGHT?
IT'S A PROMISE.

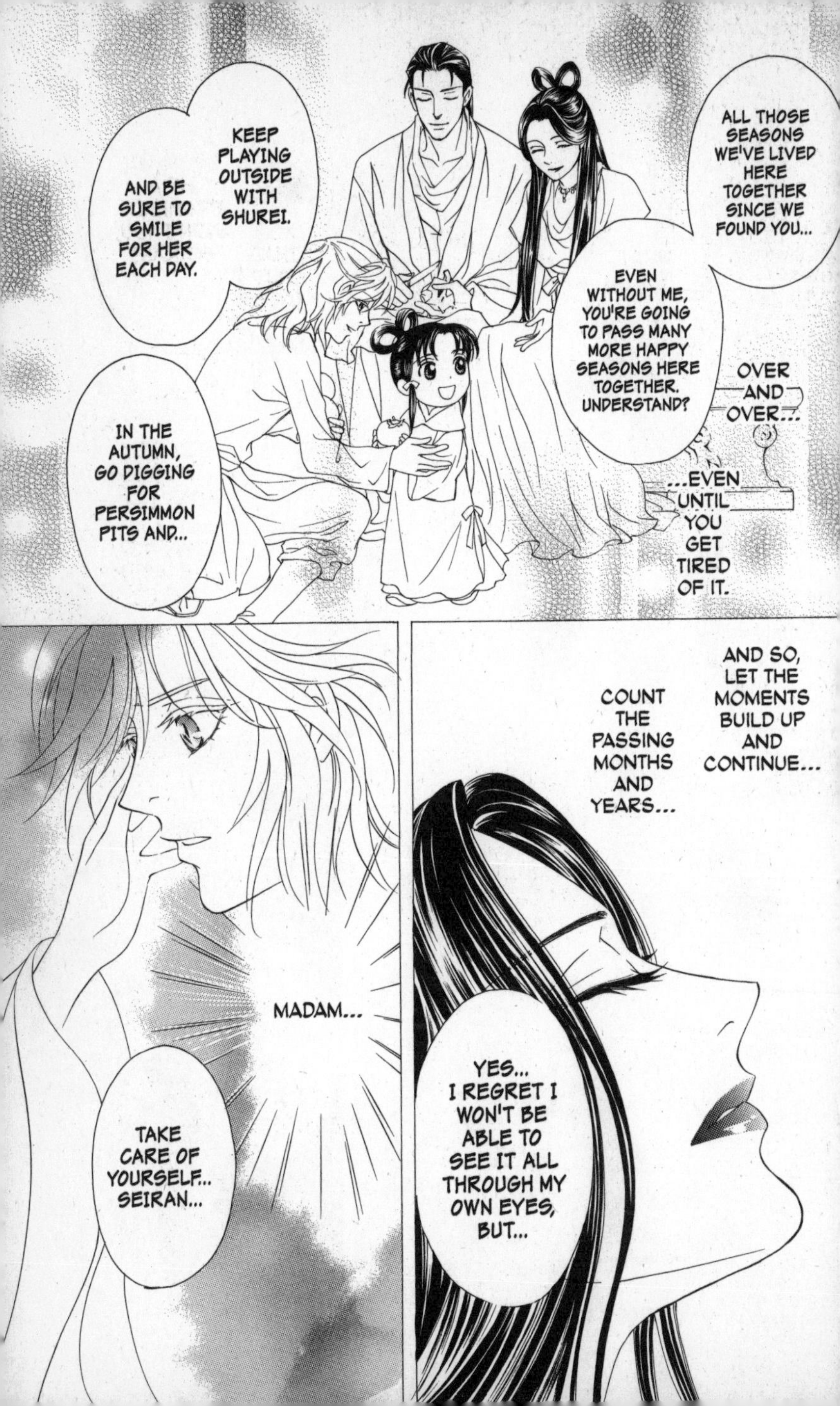
ALL THOSE SEASONS WE'VE LIVED HERE TOGETHER SINCE WE FOUND YOU...
EVEN WITHOUT ME, YOU'RE GOING TO PASS MANY MORE HAPPY SEASONS HERE TOGETHER. UNDERSTAND?
OVER AND OVER...
...EVEN UNTIL YOU GET TIRED OF IT.
KEEP PLAYING OUTSIDE WITH SHUREI.
AND BE SURE TO SMILE FOR HER EACH DAY.
IN THE AUTUMN, GO DIGGING FOR PERSIMMON PITS AND...
AND SO, LET THE MOMENTS BUILD UP AND CONTINUE...
COUNT THE PASSING MONTHS AND YEARS...
YES... I REGRET I WON'T BE ABLE TO SEE IT ALL THROUGH MY OWN EYES, BUT...
MADAM...
TAKE CARE OF YOURSELF... SEIRAN...

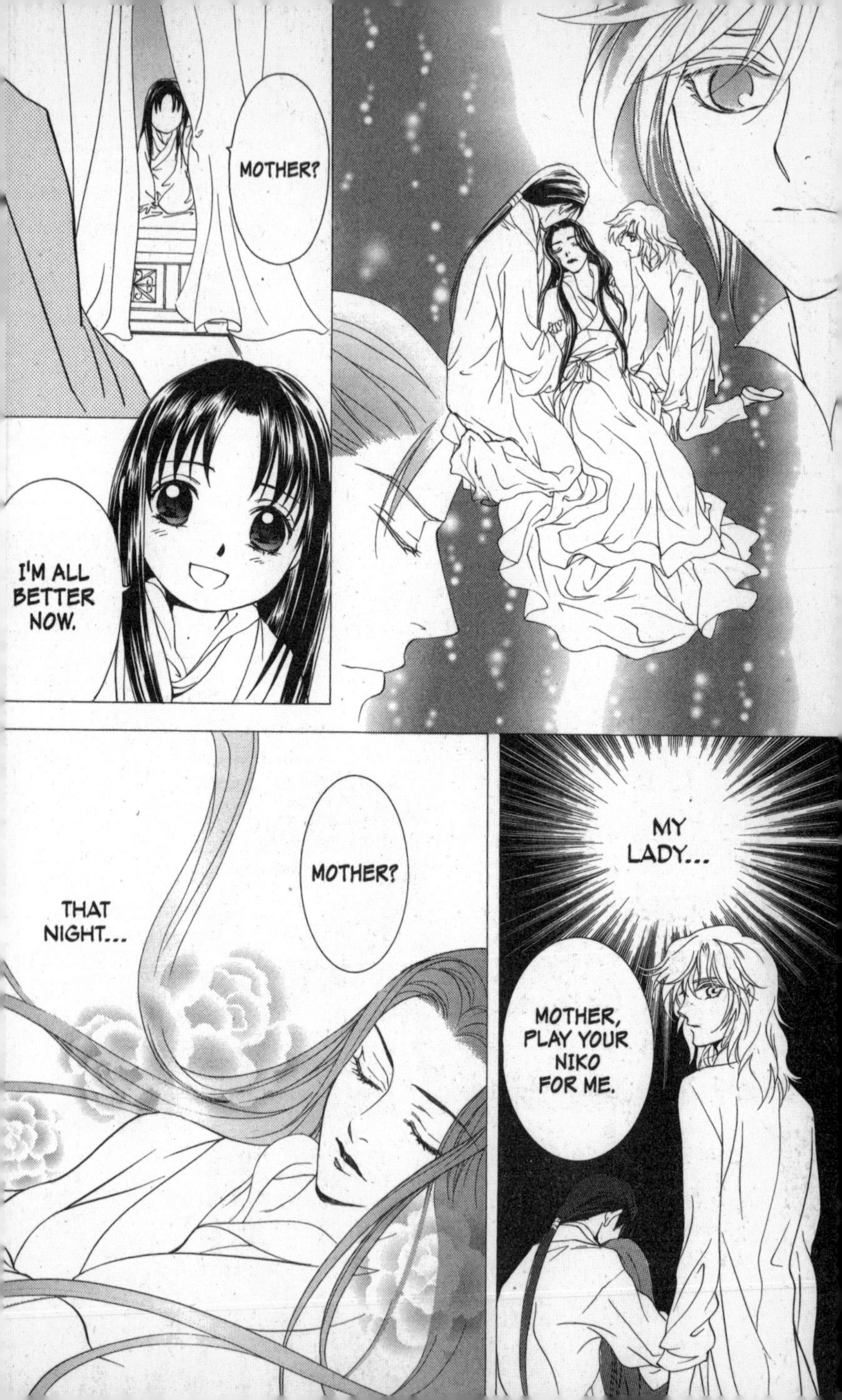
MOTHER?
I'M ALL BETTER NOW.
MY LADY...
MOTHER, PLAY YOUR NIKO FOR ME.
MOTHER?
THAT NIGHT...

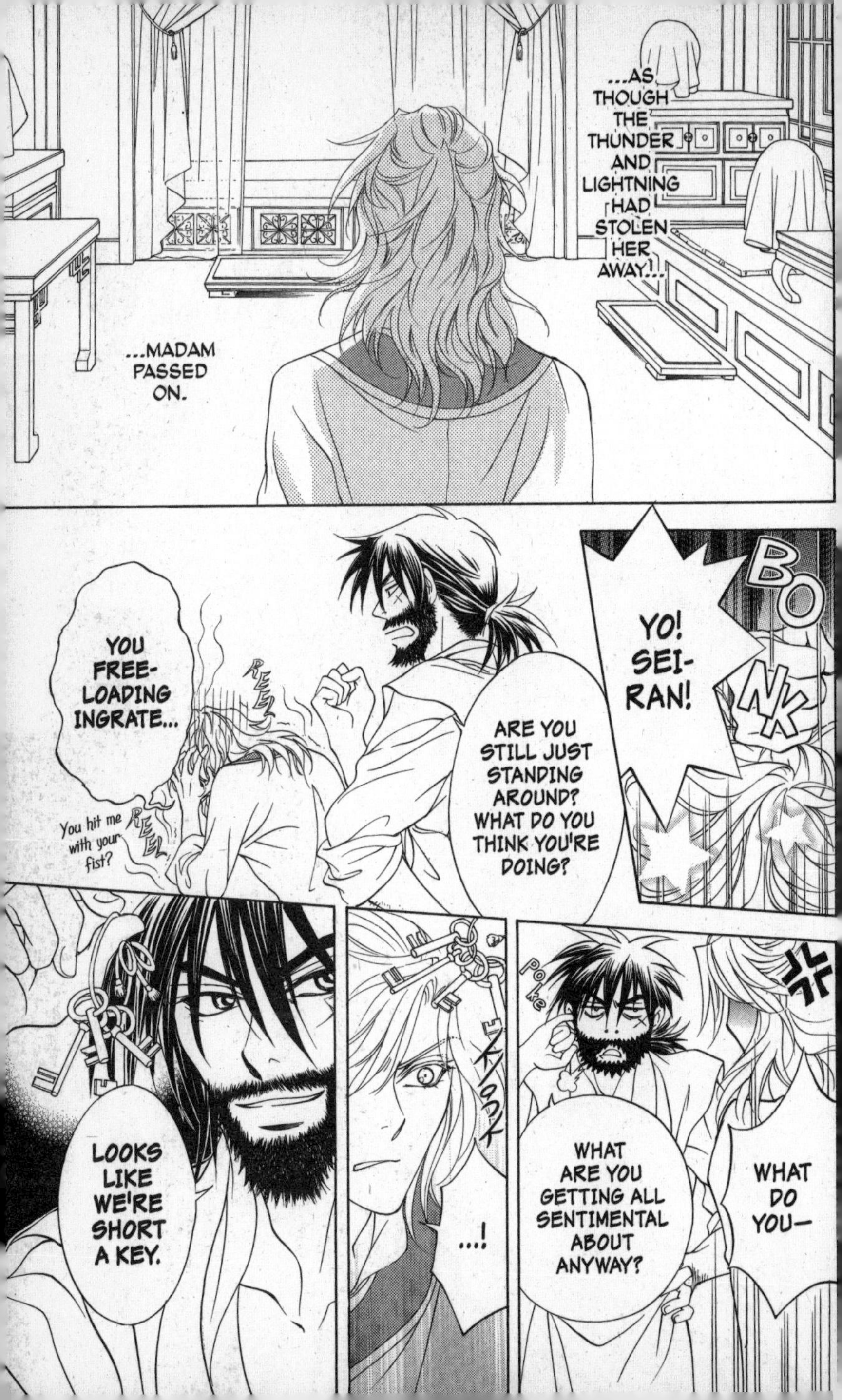
...AS THOUGH THE THUNDER AND LIGHTNING HAD STOLEN HER AWAY...
...MADAM PASSED ON.
BONK
YO! SEI-RAN!
ARE YOU STILL JUST STANDING AROUND? WHAT DO YOU THINK YOU'RE DOING?
REEL
REEL
YOU FREE-LOADING INGRATE...
You hit me with your fist?
Poke
WHAT ARE YOU GETTING ALL SENTIMENTAL ABOUT ANYWAY?
WHAT DO YOU—
...!
LOOKS LIKE WE'RE SHORT A KEY.

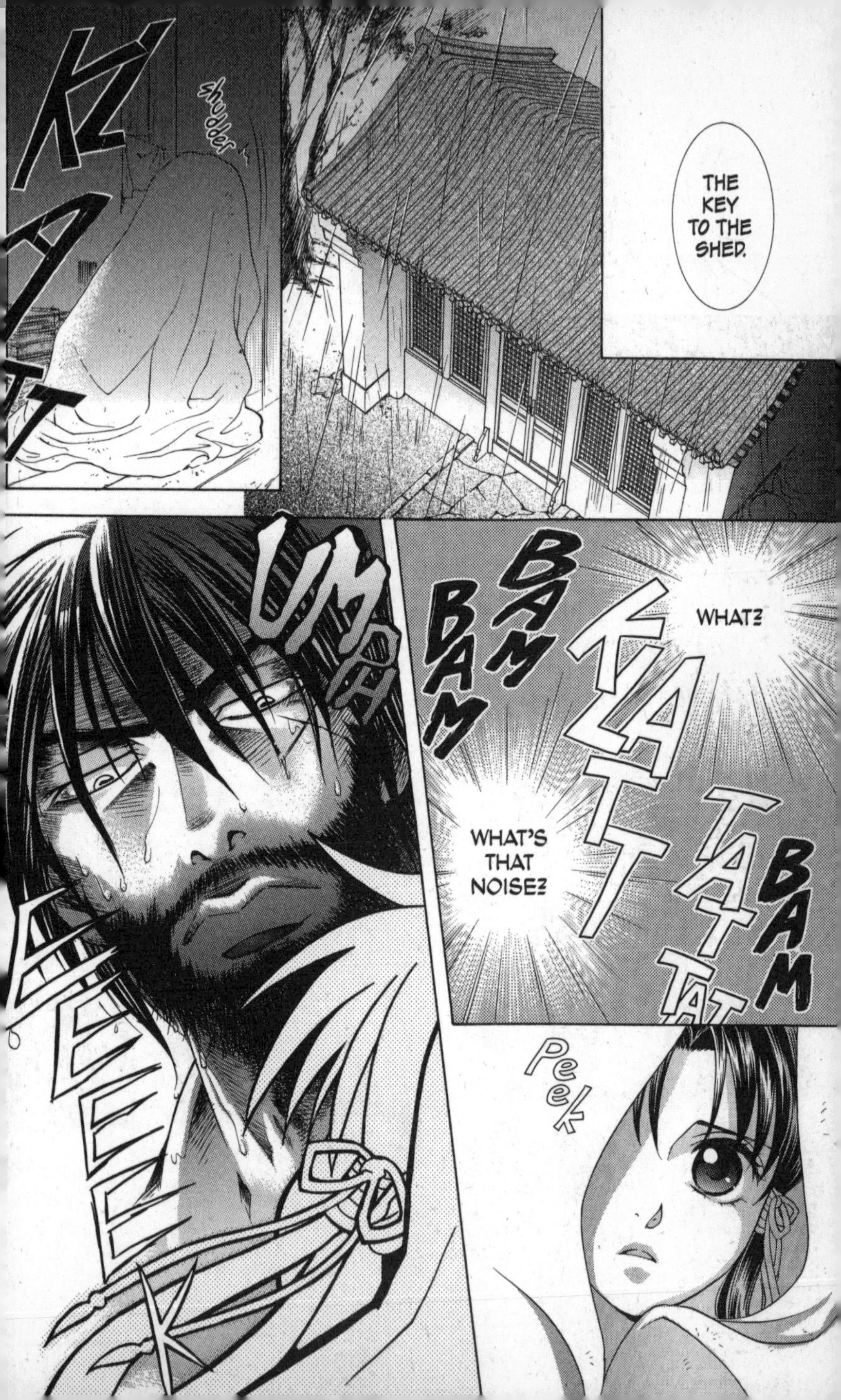

THE KEY TO THE SHED.
KLATT
shudder
WHAT?
BAM BAM
BAM BAM
KLATT
WHAT'S THAT NOISE?
TAT TAT
BAM BAM
UMPH
Peek
EEEEEEEK

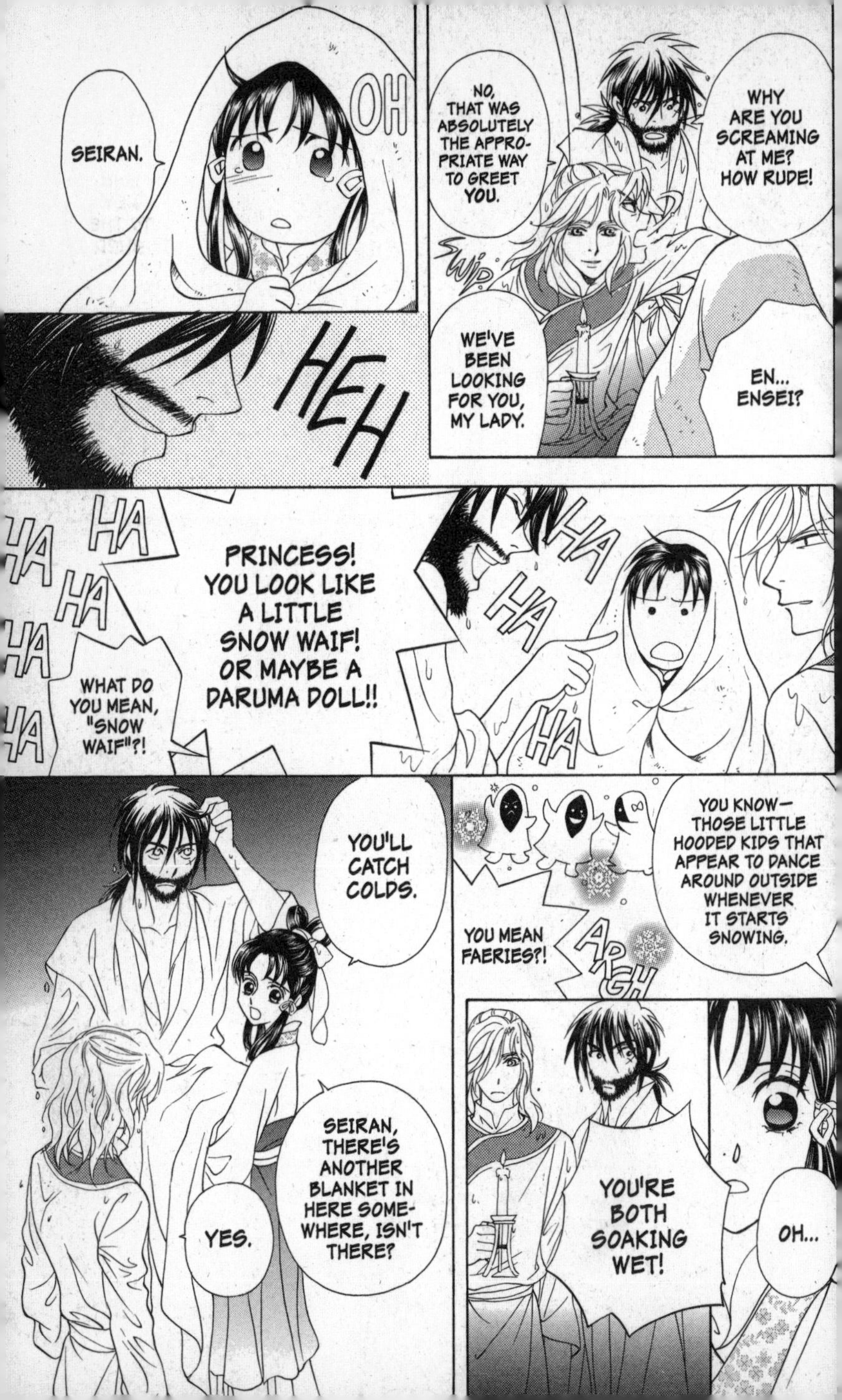
WHY ARE YOU SCREAMING AT ME? HOW RUDE!
NO, THAT WAS ABSOLUTELY THE APPROPRIATE WAY TO GREET YOU.
SWIP
EN... ENSEI?
WE'VE BEEN LOOKING FOR YOU, MY LADY.
OH
SEIRAN.
HEH
HA HA HA
PRINCESS! YOU LOOK LIKE A LITTLE SNOW WAIF! OR MAYBE A DARUMA DOLL!!
HA HA HA HA HA HA
WHAT DO YOU MEAN, "SNOW WAIF"?!
YOU KNOW—THOSE LITTLE HOODED KIDS THAT APPEAR TO DANCE AROUND OUTSIDE WHENEVER IT STARTS SNOWING.
ARGH
YOU MEAN FAERIES?!
OH...
YOU'RE BOTH SOAKING WET!
YOU'LL CATCH COLDS.
SEIRAN, THERE'S ANOTHER BLANKET IN HERE SOMEWHERE, ISN'T THERE?
YES.

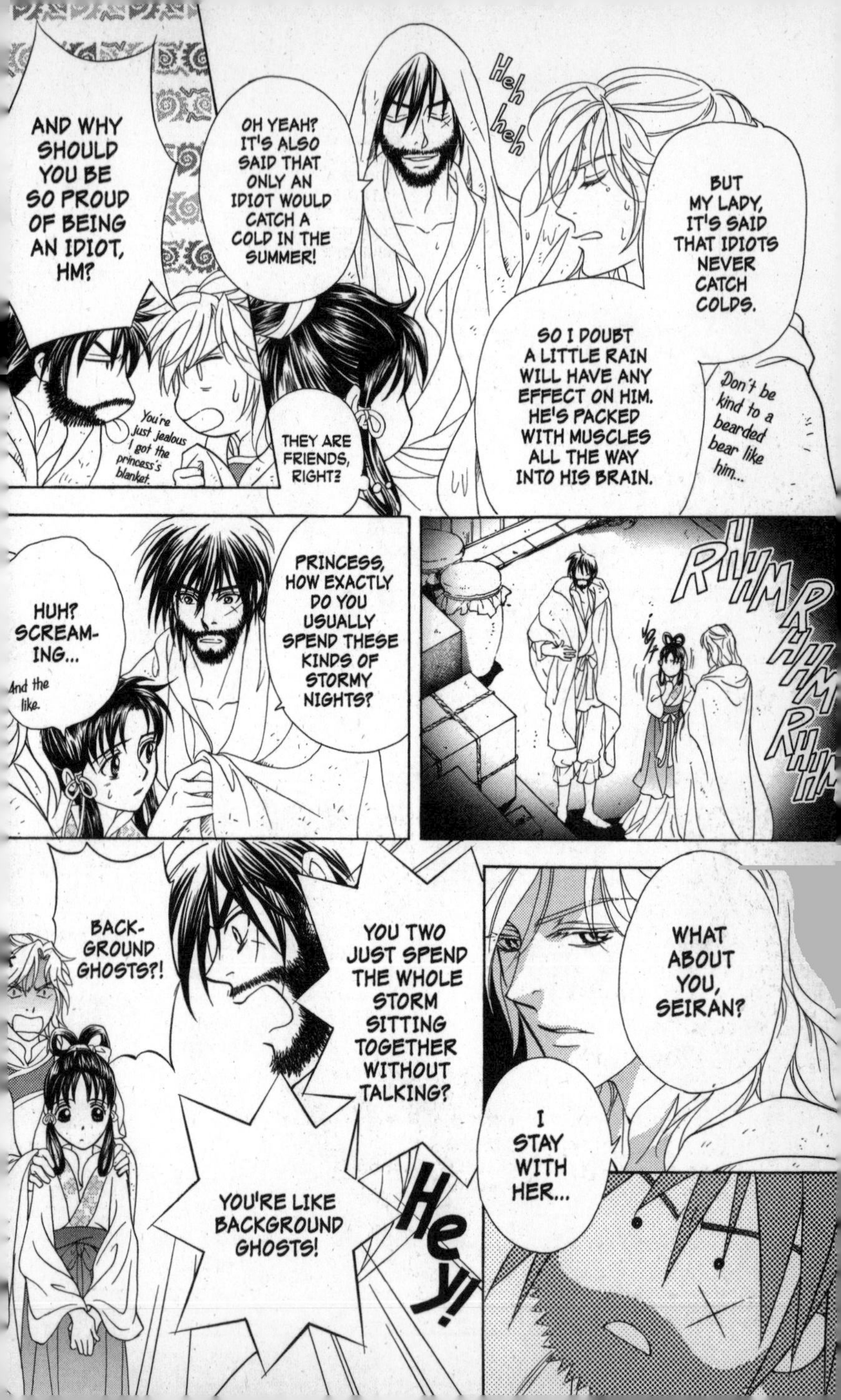
BUT MY LADY, IT'S SAID THAT IDIOTS NEVER CATCH COLDS.
Heh heh
Don't be kind to a bearded bear like him...
SO I DOUBT A LITTLE RAIN WILL HAVE ANY EFFECT ON HIM. HE'S PACKED WITH MUSCLES ALL THE WAY INTO HIS BRAIN.
OH YEAH? IT'S ALSO SAID THAT ONLY AN IDIOT WOULD CATCH A COLD IN THE SUMMER!
AND WHY SHOULD YOU BE SO PROUD OF BEING AN IDIOT, HM?
THEY ARE FRIENDS, RIGHT?
You're just jealous I got the princess's blanket.
RHHM RHHM RHHM
PRINCESS, HOW EXACTLY DO YOU USUALLY SPEND THESE KINDS OF STORMY NIGHTS?
HUH? SCREAM-ING...
And the like.
WHAT ABOUT YOU, SEIRAN?
I STAY WITH HER...
Hey!
YOU TWO JUST SPEND THE WHOLE STORM SITTING TOGETHER WITHOUT TALKING?
YOU'RE LIKE BACKGROUND GHOSTS!
BACK-GROUND GHOSTS?!

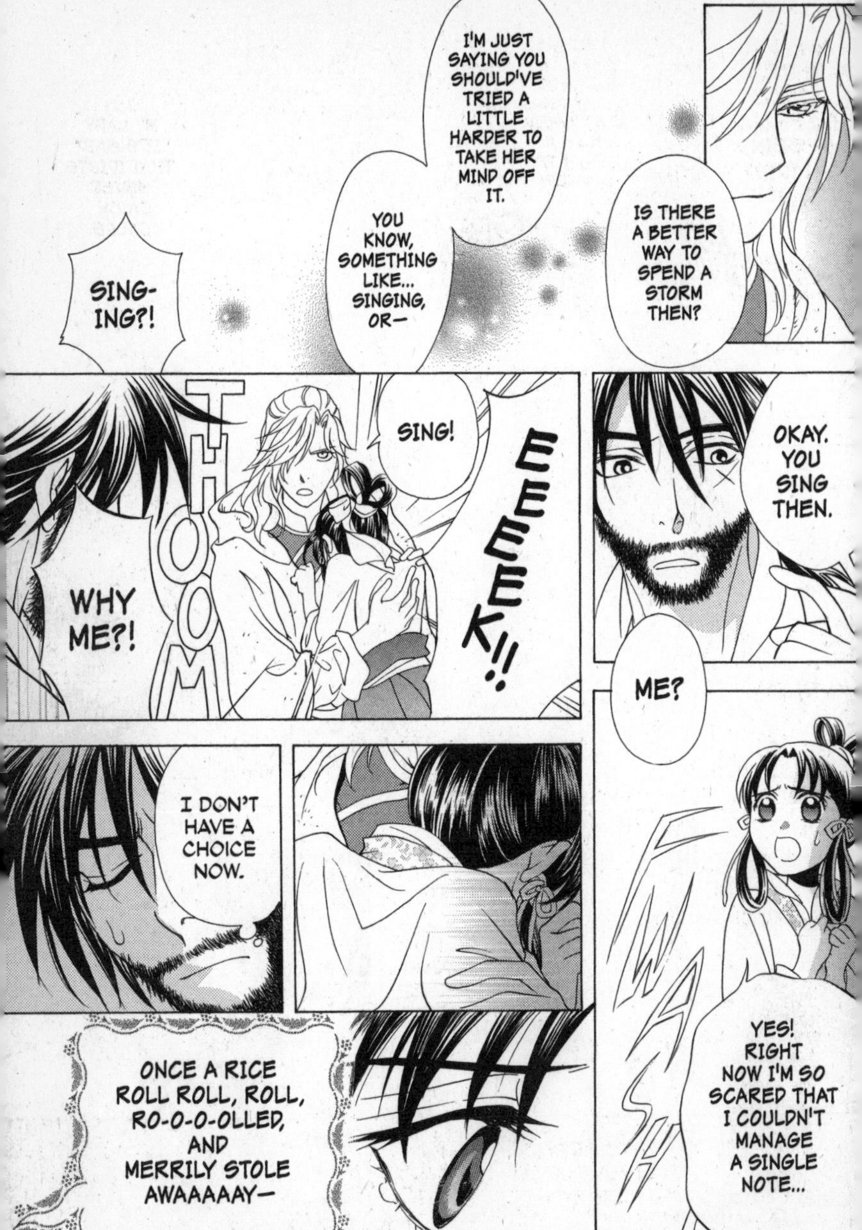
IS THERE A BETTER WAY TO SPEND A STORM THEN?
I'M JUST SAYING YOU SHOULD'VE TRIED A LITTLE HARDER TO TAKE HER MIND OFF IT.
YOU KNOW, SOMETHING LIKE... SINGING, OR—
SING-ING?!
OKAY. YOU SING THEN.
SING!
EEEEK!!
THOOM
WHY ME?!
ME?
WHASH
YES! RIGHT NOW I'M SO SCARED THAT I COULDN'T MANAGE A SINGLE NOTE...
I DON'T HAVE A CHOICE NOW.
ONCE A RICE ROLL ROLL, ROLL, RO-O-O-OLLED, AND MERRILY STOLE AWAAAAAY—

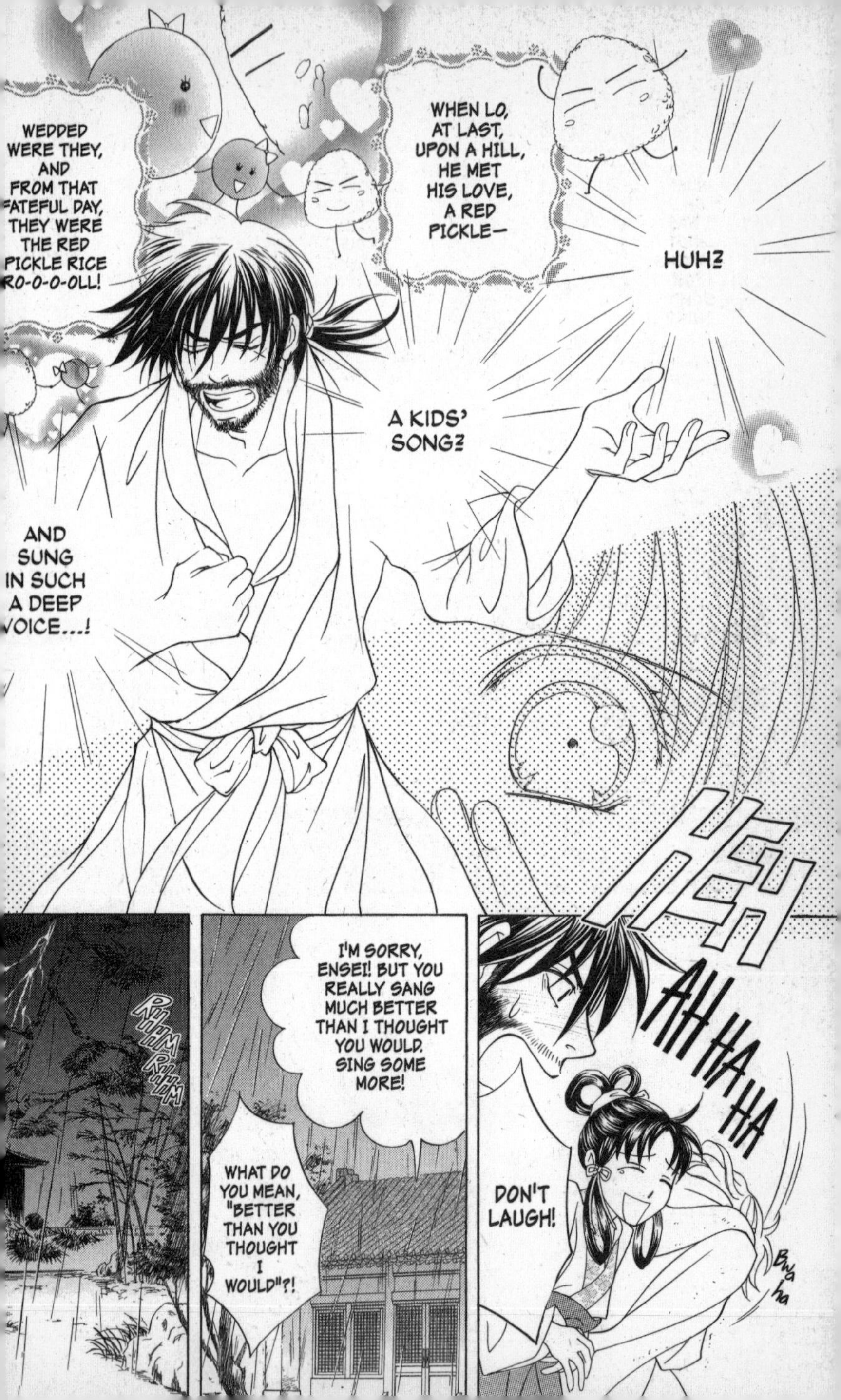
WHEN LO, AT LAST, UPON A HILL, HE MET HIS LOVE, A RED PICKLE—
WEDDED WERE THEY, AND FROM THAT FATEFUL DAY, THEY WERE THE RED PICKLE RICE RO-O-O-OLL!
HUH?
A KIDS' SONG?
AND SUNG IN SUCH A DEEP VOICE...!
HEH
AH HA HA HA
DON'T LAUGH!
Bwa ha
I'M SORRY, ENSEI! BUT YOU REALLY SANG MUCH BETTER THAN I THOUGHT YOU WOULD. SING SOME MORE!
WHAT DO YOU MEAN, "BETTER THAN YOU THOUGHT I WOULD"?!
RHM RHM

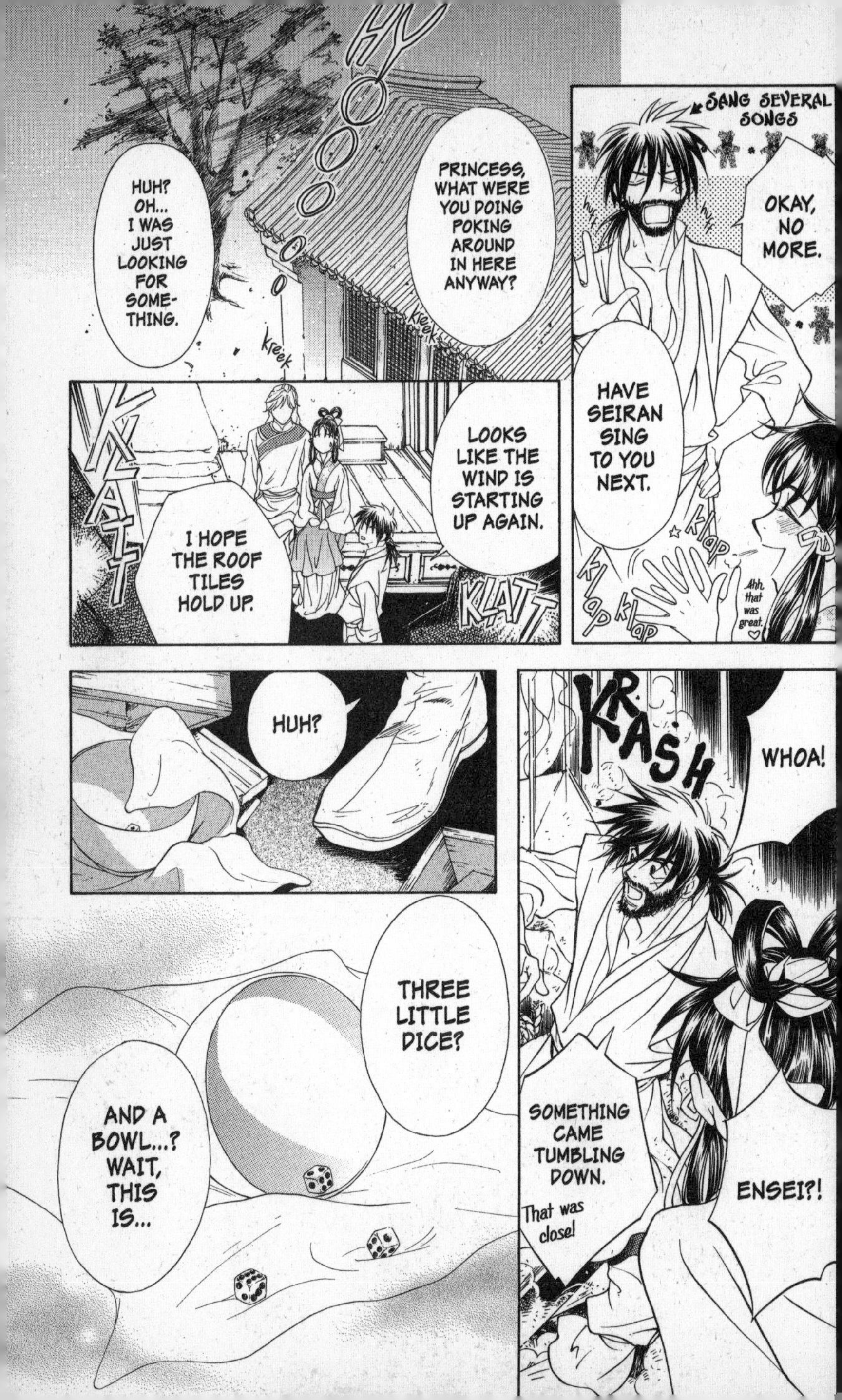

SANG SEVERAL SONGS
OKAY, NO MORE.
HAVE SEIRAN SING TO YOU NEXT.
klap klap klap klap
Ahh, that was great. ♡
HYOOOOOOOO
PRINCESS, WHAT WERE YOU DOING POKING AROUND IN HERE ANYWAY?
kreek kreek
HUH? OH... I WAS JUST LOOKING FOR SOME-THING.
KLATT
LOOKS LIKE THE WIND IS STARTING UP AGAIN.
I HOPE THE ROOF TILES HOLD UP.
KLATT
KRASH
WHOA!
SOMETHING CAME TUMBLING DOWN.
That was close!
ENSEI?!
HUH?
THREE LITTLE DICE?
AND A BOWL...? WAIT, THIS IS...

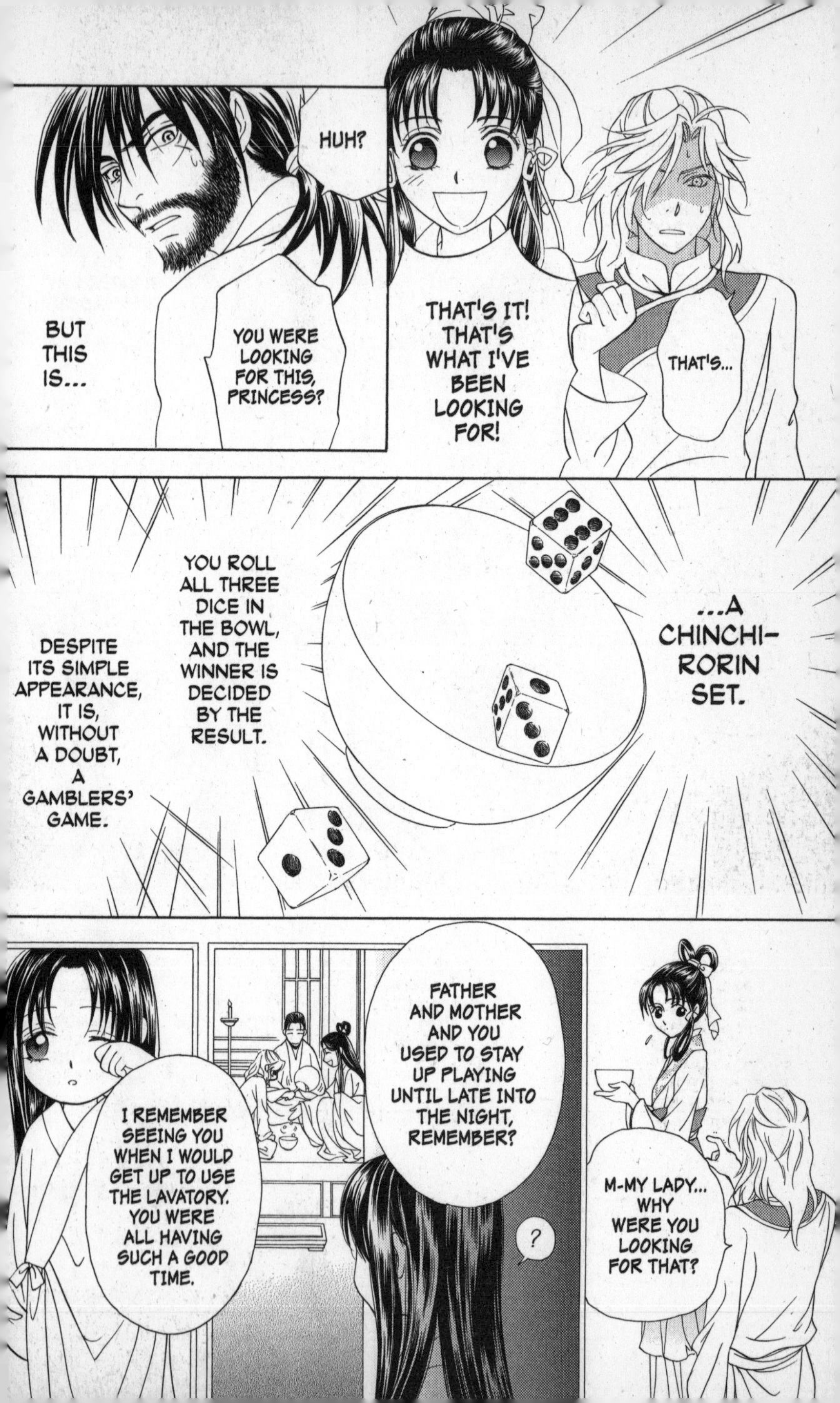
THAT'S IT! THAT'S WHAT I'VE BEEN LOOKING FOR!
THAT'S...
HUH?
YOU WERE LOOKING FOR THIS, PRINCESS?
BUT THIS IS...
...A CHINCHI-RORIN SET.
YOU ROLL ALL THREE DICE IN THE BOWL, AND THE WINNER IS DECIDED BY THE RESULT.
DESPITE ITS SIMPLE APPEARANCE, IT IS, WITHOUT A DOUBT, A GAMBLERS' GAME.
M-MY LADY... WHY WERE YOU LOOKING FOR THAT?
?
FATHER AND MOTHER AND YOU USED TO STAY UP PLAYING UNTIL LATE INTO THE NIGHT, REMEMBER?
I REMEMBER SEEING YOU WHEN I WOULD GET UP TO USE THE LAVATORY. YOU WERE ALL HAVING SUCH A GOOD TIME.

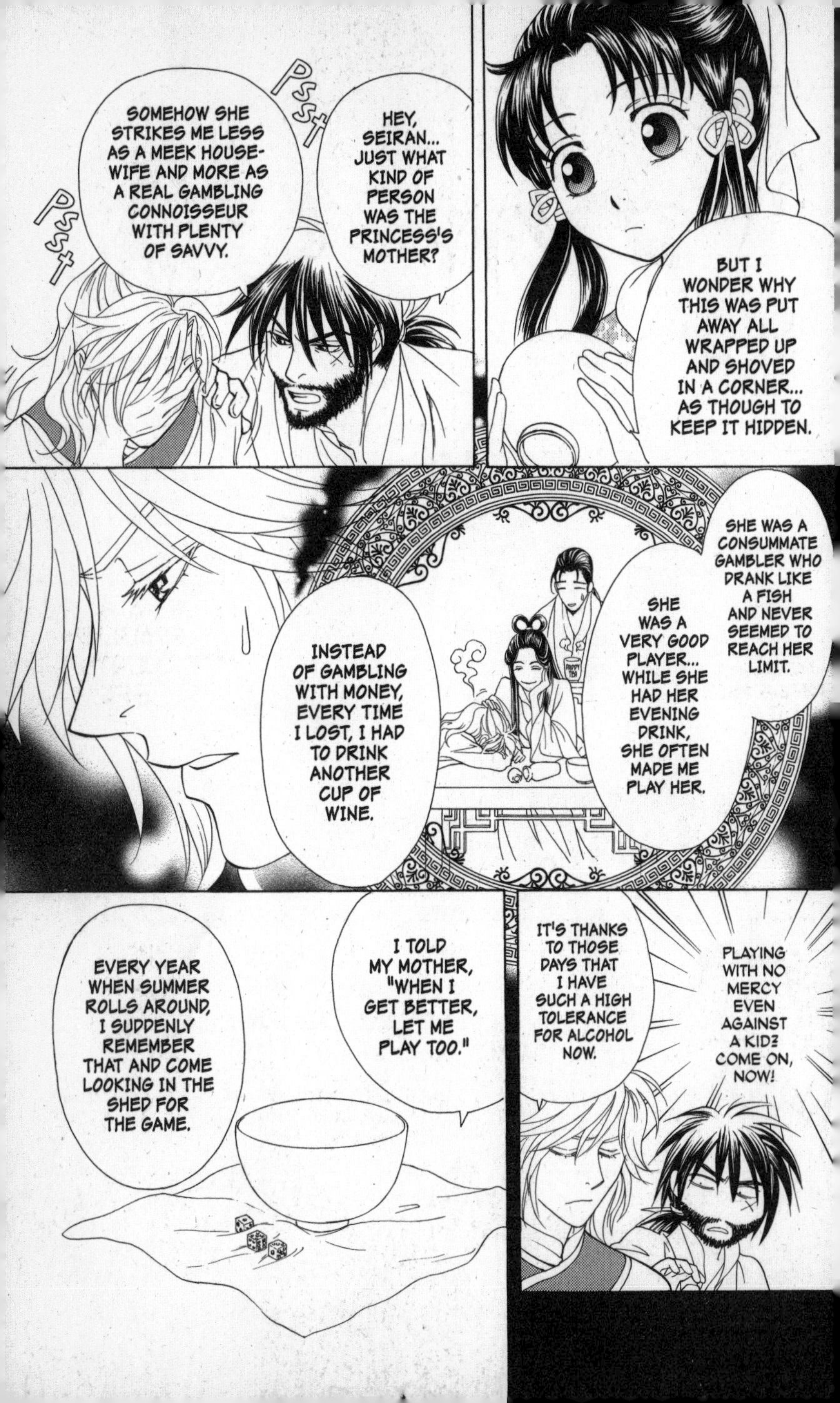
BUT I WONDER WHY THIS WAS PUT AWAY ALL WRAPPED UP AND SHOVED IN A CORNER... AS THOUGH TO KEEP IT HIDDEN.
PSST
HEY, SEIRAN... JUST WHAT KIND OF PERSON WAS THE PRINCESS'S MOTHER?
SOMEHOW SHE STRIKES ME LESS AS A MEEK HOUSE-WIFE AND MORE AS A REAL GAMBLING CONNOISSEUR WITH PLENTY OF SAVVY.
PSST
SHE WAS A CONSUMMATE GAMBLER WHO DRANK LIKE A FISH AND NEVER SEEMED TO REACH HER LIMIT.
SHE WAS A VERY GOOD PLAYER... WHILE SHE HAD HER EVENING DRINK, SHE OFTEN MADE ME PLAY HER.
INSTEAD OF GAMBLING WITH MONEY, EVERY TIME I LOST, I HAD TO DRINK ANOTHER CUP OF WINE.
PLAYING WITH NO MERCY EVEN AGAINST A KID? COME ON, NOW!
IT'S THANKS TO THOSE DAYS THAT I HAVE SUCH A HIGH TOLERANCE FOR ALCOHOL NOW.
I TOLD MY MOTHER, "WHEN I GET BETTER, LET ME PLAY TOO."
EVERY YEAR WHEN SUMMER ROLLS AROUND, I SUDDENLY REMEMBER THAT AND COME LOOKING IN THE SHED FOR THE GAME.

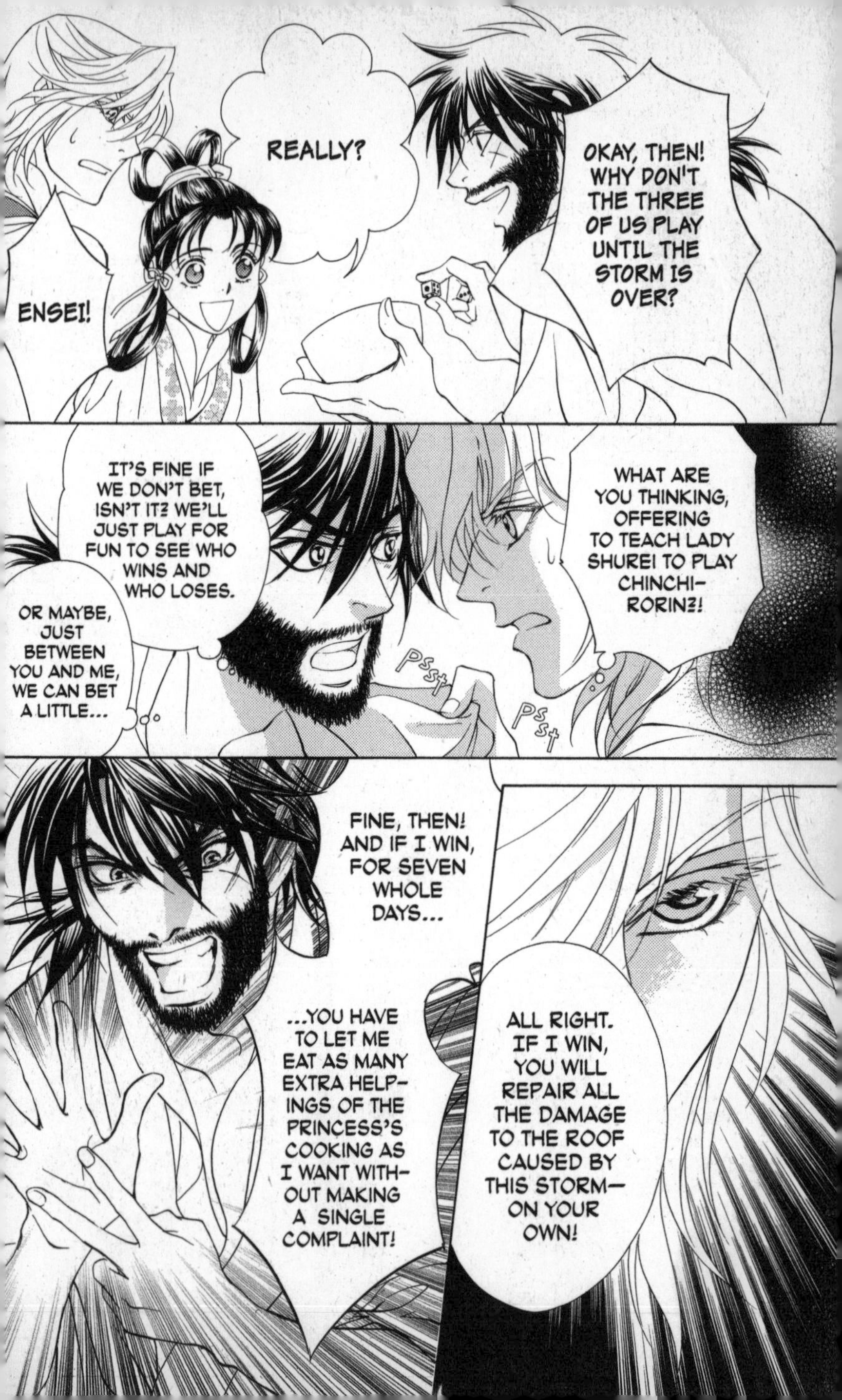
OKAY, THEN! WHY DON'T THE THREE OF US PLAY UNTIL THE STORM IS OVER?
REALLY?
ENSEI!
WHAT ARE YOU THINKING, OFFERING TO TEACH LADY SHUREI TO PLAY CHINCHI-RORIN?!
IT'S FINE IF WE DON'T BET, ISN'T IT? WE'LL JUST PLAY FOR FUN TO SEE WHO WINS AND WHO LOSES.
OR MAYBE, JUST BETWEEN YOU AND ME, WE CAN BET A LITTLE...
PSST
PSST
FINE, THEN! AND IF I WIN, FOR SEVEN WHOLE DAYS...
...YOU HAVE TO LET ME EAT AS MANY EXTRA HELP-INGS OF THE PRINCESS'S COOKING AS I WANT WITH-OUT MAKING A SINGLE COMPLAINT!
ALL RIGHT. IF I WIN, YOU WILL REPAIR ALL THE DAMAGE TO THE ROOF CAUSED BY THIS STORM—ON YOUR OWN!

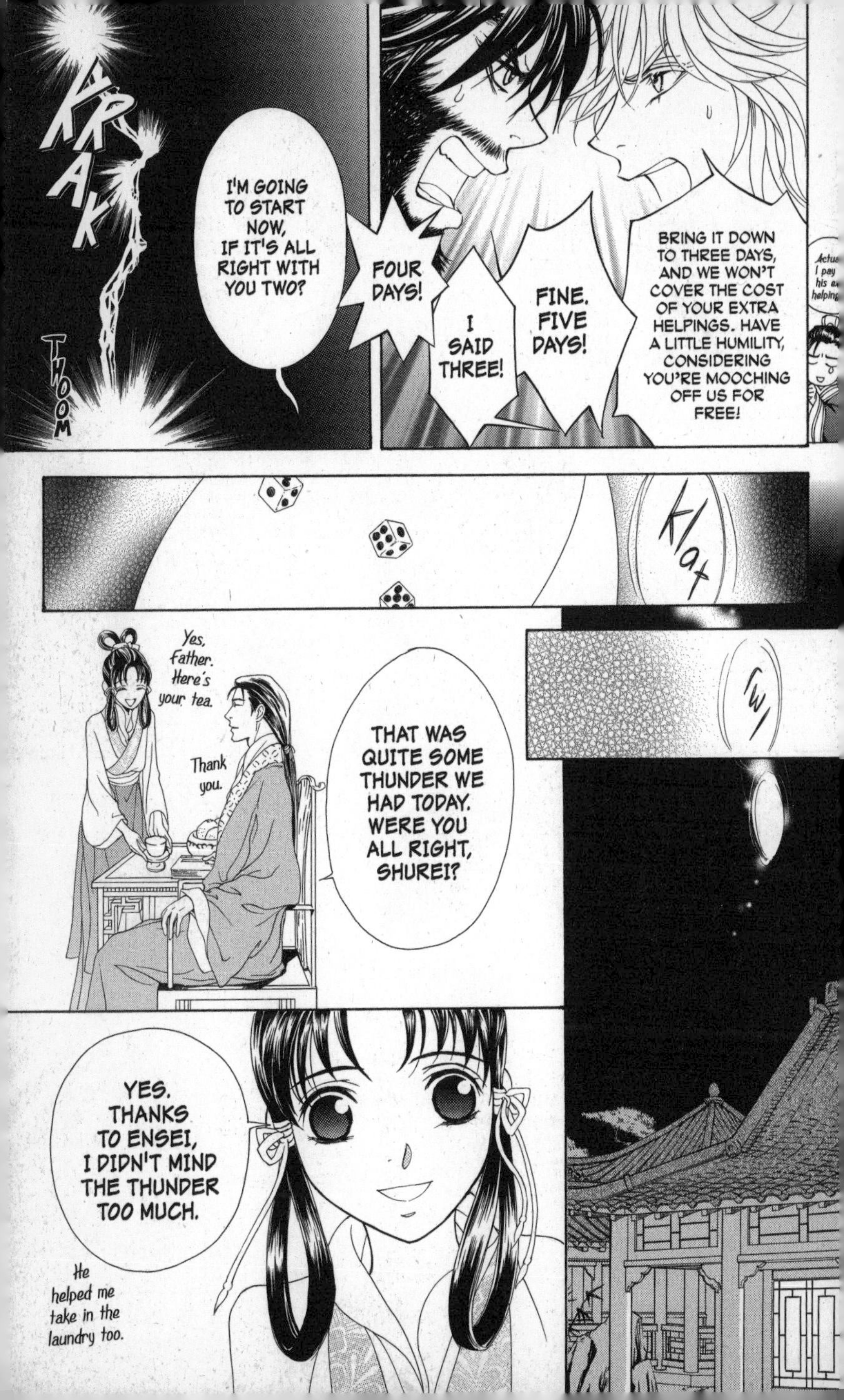
BRING IT DOWN TO THREE DAYS, AND WE WON'T COVER THE COST OF YOUR EXTRA HELPINGS. HAVE A LITTLE HUMILITY, CONSIDERING YOU'RE MOOCHING OFF US FOR FREE!
FINE. FIVE DAYS!
I SAID THREE!
FOUR DAYS!
I'M GOING TO START NOW, IF IT'S ALL RIGHT WITH YOU TWO?
KRAK
THOOOM
Klat
THAT WAS QUITE SOME THUNDER WE HAD TODAY. WERE YOU ALL RIGHT, SHUREI?
Yes, Father. Here's your tea.
Thank you.
YES. THANKS TO ENSEI, I DIDN'T MIND THE THUNDER TOO MUCH.
He helped me take in the laundry too.

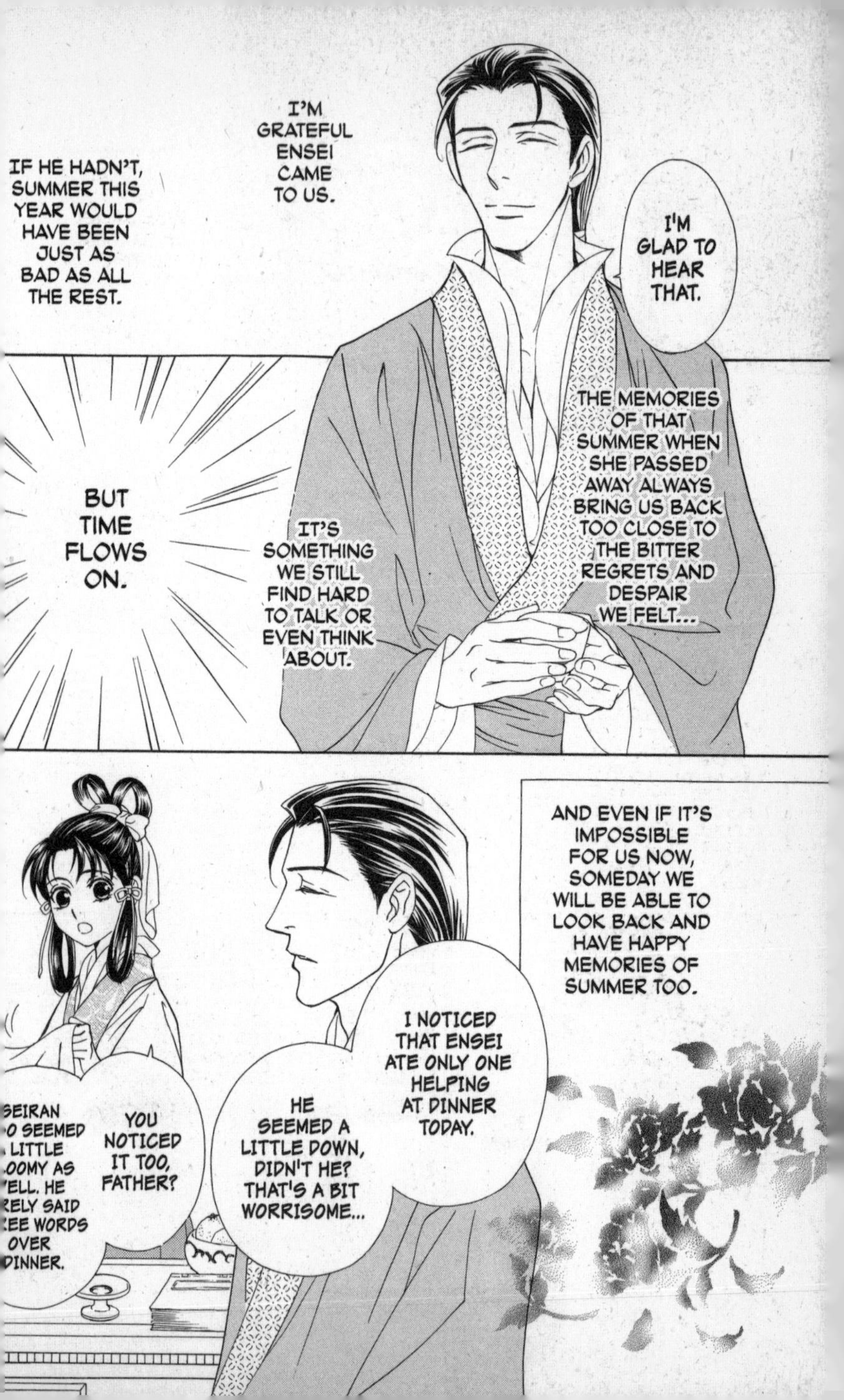
I'M GRATEFUL ENSEI CAME TO US.
IF HE HADN'T, SUMMER THIS YEAR WOULD HAVE BEEN JUST AS BAD AS ALL THE REST.
I'M GLAD TO HEAR THAT.
THE MEMORIES OF THAT SUMMER WHEN SHE PASSED AWAY ALWAYS BRING US BACK TOO CLOSE TO THE BITTER REGRETS AND DESPAIR WE FELT...
IT'S SOMETHING WE STILL FIND HARD TO TALK OR EVEN THINK ABOUT.
BUT TIME FLOWS ON.
AND EVEN IF IT'S IMPOSSIBLE FOR US NOW, SOMEDAY WE WILL BE ABLE TO LOOK BACK AND HAVE HAPPY MEMORIES OF SUMMER TOO.
I NOTICED THAT ENSEI ATE ONLY ONE HELPING AT DINNER TODAY.
HE SEEMED A LITTLE DOWN, DIDN'T HE? THAT'S A BIT WORRISOME...
YOU NOTICED IT TOO, FATHER?
SEIRAN O SEEMED LITTLE OOMY AS ELL. HE RELY SAID EE WORDS OVER DINNER.

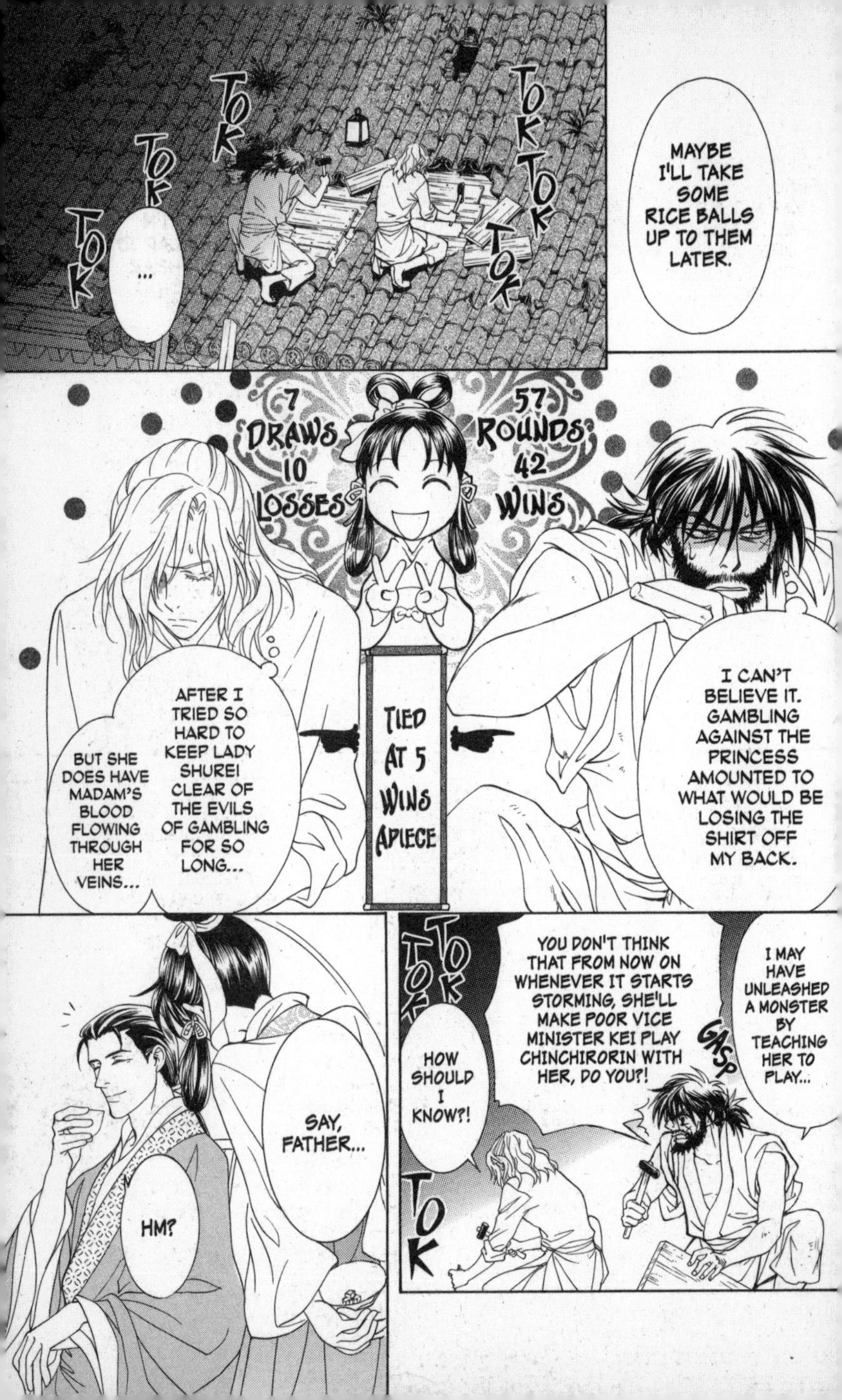
MAYBE I'LL TAKE SOME RICE BALLS UP TO THEM LATER.
TOK TOK
TOK
TOK
TOK
TOK
TOK
...
57 ROUNDS 42 WINS
7 DRAWS 10 LOSSES
TIED AT 5 WINS APIECE
I CAN'T BELIEVE IT. GAMBLING AGAINST THE PRINCESS AMOUNTED TO WHAT WOULD BE LOSING THE SHIRT OFF MY BACK.
AFTER I TRIED SO HARD TO KEEP LADY SHUREI CLEAR OF THE EVILS OF GAMBLING FOR SO LONG...
BUT SHE DOES HAVE MADAM'S BLOOD FLOWING THROUGH HER VEINS...
I MAY HAVE UNLEASHED A MONSTER BY TEACHING HER TO PLAY...
GASP
YOU DON'T THINK THAT FROM NOW ON WHENEVER IT STARTS STORMING, SHE'LL MAKE POOR VICE MINISTER KEI PLAY CHINCHIRORIN WITH HER, DO YOU?!
TOK TOK
HOW SHOULD I KNOW?!
TOK
SAY, FATHER...
HM?

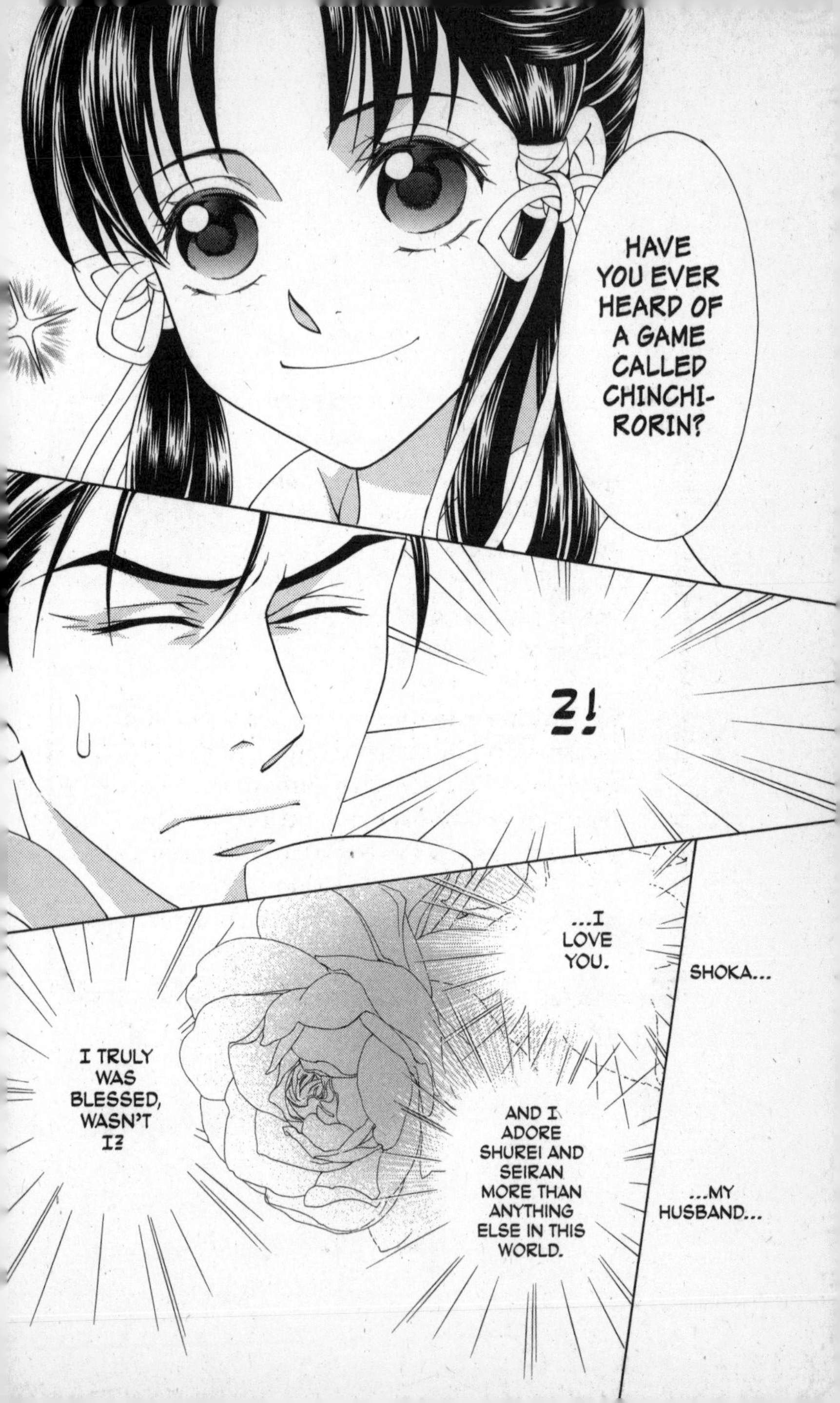
HAVE YOU EVER HEARD OF A GAME CALLED CHINCHI-RORIN?
?!
...I LOVE YOU.
SHOKA...
...MY HUSBAND...
AND I ADORE SHUREI AND SEIRAN MORE THAN ANYTHING ELSE IN THIS WORLD.
I TRULY WAS BLESSED, WASN'T I?

Kairi Yura was born on January 16. She is the illustrator of both the manga and the YA novels for *The Story of Saiunkoku*. She is also the creator of the *Angelique* series. Yura's hobby is going to the theater.

Sai Yukino was born on January 26. She is author of both the manga and the YA novels for *The Story of Saiunkoku*. She received an honorable mention and the Readers' Award for Kadokawa's Beans Novel Taisho Awards. When she's not busy writing, Yukino enjoys massages.

THE STORY OF SAIUNKOKU
Volume 3
Shojo Beat Edition

ART
KAIRI YURA
STORY
SAI YUKINO

Translation & English Adaptation/Su Mon Han
Touch-up Art & Lettering/Sabrina Heep
Design/Yukiko Whitley
Editor/Nancy Thistlethwaite

Saiunkoku Monogatari Volume 3
© Kairi YURA 2008
© Sai YUKINO 2008
First published in Japan in 2008 by KADOKAWA SHOTEN Co., Ltd., Tokyo.
English translation rights arranged with KADOKAWA SHOTEN Co., Ltd., Tokyo.

The stories, characters and incidents mentioned in this publication are
entirely fictional.

Printed in Canada

Published by VIZ Media, LLC
P.O. Box 77010
San Francisco, CA 94107

10 9 8 7 6 5 4 3 2 1
First printing, May 2011

PARENTAL ADVISORY
THE STORY OF SAIUNKOKU is rated T for
Teen and is recommended for ages 13 and
up. This volume contains suggestive themes.
ratings.viz.com

www.viz.com

www.shojobeat.com

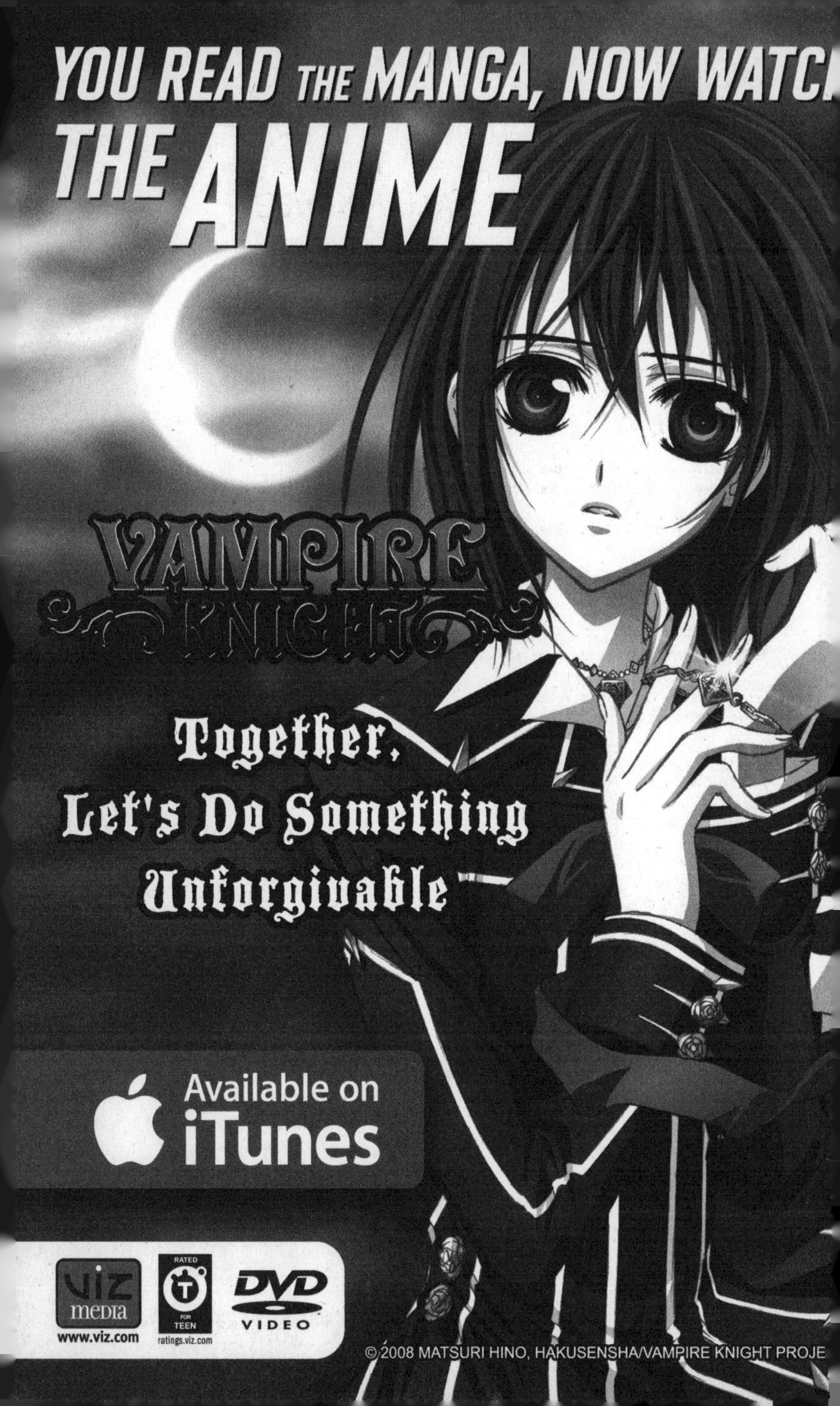
YOU READ THE MANGA, NOW WATC
THE ANIME
VAMPIRE KNIGHT
Together, Let's Do Something Unforgivable
Available on iTunes
viz media
www.viz.com
RATED T FOR TEEN
ratings.viz.com
DVD VIDEO
© 2008 MATSURI HINO, HAKUSENSHA/VAMPIRE KNIGHT PROJE

Art book featuring
216 pages of beautiful
color images personally
selected by Tanemura

Read where Mitsuki's
pop dreams began
in the manga—all 7
volumes now available

Complete your
collection with the
anime, now on DVD

ratings.viz.com

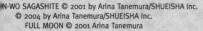

www.viz.com